THE
GREAT
NOWITZKI

THE
GREAT
NOWITZKI

Basketball and the Meaning of Life

THOMAS PLETZINGER

translated by Shane Anderson

with photographs by Tobias Zielony

W. W. NORTON & COMPANY
Independent Publishers Since 1923

Author's Note: The events depicted in these pages are based on my own experiences and those of others as told to me. Certain conversations have been reconstructed to the best of my ability based on third-party accounts, and certain names have been changed.

For information about permission to reproduce selections from this book,
write to Permissions, W. W. Norton & Company, Inc., 500 Fifth Avenue,
New York, NY 10110

For information about special discounts for bulk purchases, please contact
W. W. Norton Special Sales at specialsales@wwnorton.com or 800-233-4830

Manufacturing by Lakeside Book Company
Book design by Ellen Cipriano
Production manager: Anna Oler

ISBN 978-1-324-00305-2

W. W. Norton & Company, Inc., 500 Fifth Avenue, New York, N.Y. 10110
www.wwnorton.com

W. W. Norton & Company Ltd., 15 Carlisle Street, London W1D 3BS

1 2 3 4 5 6 7 8 9 0

For my team:
Martha, Fritzi, Anna, and Bine

Singin' they don't make 'em like this anymore.

—DAVID BAZAN,
"The Ballad of Pedro y Blanco"

CONTENTS

THE FINISH LINE (Prologue)   1

1. DIRK NOWITZKI   11

2. THE PATH   103

3. FADEAWAY   221

4. THE GOAL   257

5. IT'S A CIRCUS   295

6. OLD MAN GAME   323

THE FINISH LINE (Epilogue)   397

Author's Note   409

Acknowledgments   411

Bibliography   413

Index   417

THE
GREAT
NOWITZKI

The Finish Line

(PROLOGUE)

ALWAYS KNEW THIS DAY would come. I've followed Dirk Nowitz-ki's career for half of my life—first as a player, then as a remote enthusiast, later as a sportswriter, and finally as the author of this book. It's April 9, 2019, and almost seven years have passed since I first wrote about Dirk Nowitzki, seven years that I've been watching him work.

Nowitzki and I have sat in countless hotel rooms and cars, on locker room benches, terraces, film sets, and in a pasture in the Slove-nian Alps. We've also sat in doctor's offices, his daughter's bedroom in Preston Hollow, and arenas and dusty gyms. We've been in San Fran-cisco, Los Angeles, Kranjska Gora, Warsaw, Randersacker, and Shang-hai. We've talked about basketball and about everything else—our parents, the children, books, and our aging bones. We even worked out together once. I've witnessed a number of his milestones with my own eyes, and I've had the other ones described to me. I've watched when the bright lights were switched off and Dirk Nowitzki continued to do what he does: play basketball.

When he scored his 30,000th career point, I was sitting in the stands next to Holger Geschwindner—Dirk's mentor, coach, and friend—and I was deeply moved. By his achievements and accomplishments, by the love Dirk has attracted. I was moved because I sat there and sensed what it must have cost Dirk to get to where he was. I sat there, knowing I would write about this moment. But I also knew my words would always be a step behind Dirk Nowitzki's presence of mind, his absolute mastery of craft. Just like his helpless defenders, my sentences would always be a tenth of a second too late.

Nowitzki's world is a black box, a closed system with its own language and way of thinking. His inner circle is reserved and discreet, but once you get to know his people, they stay with you for good. Dirk's calendar was always packed, every year booked down to the last minute. Whenever he was unavailable, I talked to the people he cares about and to the countless others who care about him. I've tried to understand what makes him different from other basketball players, from every other athlete. What makes him unique.

I've never asked for an autograph, and we've never taken a selfie. But I've sat with Dirk at restaurant tables and ordered wine while he stuck with water. Together, we've been on planes, in cars, on walks. Once, in Oklahoma City, I even ended up in a fistfight because of Dirk. To understand the Nowitzki system, I've given up my journalistic independence. My daughters were born while I was researching this book, and whenever someone asks them what their father does for a living, their answer is: "Dirk Nowitzki."

For years, I had imagined driving with Dirk to his final home game. I had sketched out the details of this scene over and over. We had often talked in cars. Whenever I pictured the day of this last game, I pictured Dirk Nowitzki and Holger Geschwindner sitting together in the front. I'd be in the back seat, in the blind spot, notebook on my knees. But on April 9, 2019, the two of them are driving alone. This moment isn't meant to be observed. I'm taking a regular taxi to the arena.

The southbound traffic flows slowly, past all the familiar buildings and billboards, including one of Nowitzki. There's the skyline of downtown Dallas in the distance, the snow-white arches over the Trinity

River. The Reunion Tower. At some point, the car gets off the highway. I note the artificial waterfall above the street, the ad for Coors Light.

Approaching the American Airlines Center, I realize that this hope to go unobserved is exactly what has made Dirk Nowitzki so successful: he and Geschwindner never set out to fulfill the desires and aspirations of others—and today is no different.

The taxi passes under the battered bridge at the dip at North Houston Street, along Harry Hines Boulevard, then turns onto Olive Street. The American Airlines Center. The house that Dirk built. "Everything is exactly how it should be," I note. "Sometimes doors have to stay closed, sometimes the back seat has to be empty."

As I get out of the taxi, melancholy and ceremony hang in the spring air. The Dallas Mavericks' season has been over for weeks—or for months, if we're honest. Today, they're playing their final home game, against the Phoenix Suns, the worst team in the league. There's nothing at stake for either of these teams tonight, but three hours before tip-off, there are fans gathered on the plaza in front of the arena.

Dirk Nowitzki hasn't officially announced his retirement, but everything down to the finest details has been prepared for it. There are flags hanging from streetlamps, flags that have his face on them, flags displaying his life's work in numbers and pictures: 2011 world champion, sixth on the career scoring list, 14-time All-Star, and so on and so forth. The first player in league history to play for the same team for 21 years. His Dallas Mavericks. A huge, multi-story banner of Nowitzki is hanging on the front of the building, bearing today's slogan at the bottom: "41.21.1."

Dirk Nowitzki: Number 41 on his jersey.

21 years under his belt.

1 team.

Fans have come a long way to be here—from Germany and China and Argentina. They're carrying hand-painted signs and wearing costumes. Some are here for their first and perhaps last time. Many in Dallas only know their city with Dirk in it, many have grown up with him, and only the older people remember what it was like before: Clinton was the president. There were no smartphones. Aerosmith's "I Don't Want to Miss a Thing" topped the charts. This arena didn't even exist.

I survey the plaza in front of the arena. Fans line the streets waiting for Dirk's arrival, but they don't know what car he is in or which route he is taking—Victory Avenue? Olive Street? Almost everyone is wearing Dirk jerseys, Dirk T-shirts, both recent and vintage. They've painted signs of gratitude and respect; a few are bearing flowers. When his car finally turns the corner, people recognize him immediately and start to sing his song, a melancholic cheer, a jumble of emotions.

Dirk doesn't stop. I watch the Range Rover roll slowly into the belly of the arena. Silver garage. Everything will be the same as it always is: Dirk will follow regulations and turn off the engine, like always. A bomb-sniffing dog will check the car, the security guard will silently stick out his fist to Dirk, and the old lady at the gate will blow him a kiss. That's the way it's always been, for all these years. "Thanks, my boy," she'll say, as if Dirk were her beloved grandson. "Thank you for winning tonight!"

Everything is ready to go. There's a peculiar ceremonial air, at the press entrance, the security check, and the elevator to the catacombs. The lady operating the elevators is wearing a number 41 T-shirt. When Nowitzki and Geschwindner park the car, Mavericks communications guy Scott Tomlin and several hundred arena employees are waiting for Dirk. Security guards, food vendors, cleaners, technicians. Dirk has known many of these faces for years; their cheering touches him. Geschwindner remains in his seat and watches Dirk slowly work his way through the rows of people. High fives, fist bumps.

At the entrance to the loading dock, a blue carpet has been glued to the bare concrete floor so that Dirk can walk past the press and their cameras in befitting fashion. When he disappears into the locker room, it seems like he is in a good mood. What he doesn't know is that right now, in a VIP box four levels above him, his childhood idols Charles Barkley, Larry Bird, and Scottie Pippen are raising their glasses to him. Shawn Kemp is also there. As is Detlef Schrempf, the greatest German basketball player of all time—before Dirk.

A difficult season lies behind Dirk; it would be more apt to say a torturous one. The recovery from the ankle surgery last April went well at first, and there was hope that it would heal quickly. But it didn't. Instead, there were complications. An infection and a long and arduous recovery period. Dirk sat on the sidelines for the first 26 games of the season, watching the next generation take over, led by the über-talented Luka Dončić. He heard the cheers and watched Dončić follow in his footsteps. Dirk supported him. He worked obsessively on his body to be able to come back one more time. Dry needles were pierced into his damaged muscles every other day. Massages, hours and hours with his trainers and physios. It took an incredible effort to just get back on the court, but still, the foot didn't heal properly. It was good enough for 6.6 points per game and almost 15 minutes of playing time, though. Dirk tried to consciously appreciate every day. Every flight. Every hotel. Every arena. Every stupid joke in the locker room.

From our conversations, I know that Dirk always had a different image of his retirement—namely, quietly and unnoticed. One year ago, in his hotel room in San Francisco, he told me he didn't want a big production for his final game: "Just play and say, 'That's it,'" he had said. "'Thank you.' I'm done. My body's done. I've given everything I had to give. It was a blast. But at the end of the day, I don't want anyone to know about it beforehand."

But now the big production is here. Everything is covered in tinsel. Signs hang on the doors of the arena, warning, "Tonight's game will be using heavy amounts of pyro," and there are dozens of cases filled with various kinds of fireworks down in the arena's catacombs. There's a gilded commemorative card on every seat, as well as a cardboard cutout of Dirk's beaming face and a T-shirt with today's slogan, "41.21.1." For one last time, the merchandise stalls are almost exclusively selling Dirk-related memorabilia. Courtside seats for this game cost more than $10,000.

The Mavericks have had their hands full organizing these festivities, which include a laser show in addition to the pyrotechnics, and accommodating the unbelievably large media presence. Hordes of German journalists are here. This is their last trip to Dallas; editors won't be sending them over anymore. They all have their own personal stories about Dirk, and each wants a few private seconds with him. He's ours, we want to say our farewells. The same goes for the Americans, but the difference is that the Germans are more nostalgic and melancholic. "The German journalists are the most difficult," Scott Tomlin laughs outside the Mavericks locker room. He presumably means me, but doesn't want to say it.

As I step out of the tunnel and into the bright lights, I realize it's my last time in this arena. Everything has been prepared. The hardwood shines bright and some of the younger Mavericks are already warming up. The documentary *Der perfekte Wurf* (*The Perfect Shot*) is playing on the jumbotron, the movie features Dirk's father, mother, and sister. Donnie Nelson, the Mavericks' general manager. Don Nelson, who drafted him. Barack Obama. Everyone talks about what Dirk means to them. And to the game. Steve Nash. Yao Ming. Kobe Bryant.

The fans, journalists, ushers, and security guards are all staring at the cube. Thousands of people, thousands of versions of Dirk. Nowitzki means something different to all of them. To the bulky steward with the Tourette tic behind the basket. To the TV host Jeff "Skin" Wade on the sidelines. To the 12-year-old girl and her grandfather in section 107, wearing their green vintage jerseys. And to me. We all think we know who Dirk is.

But it isn't that simple.

For some people, Dirk is the nice boy next door; for others, he is the best European who ever touched a basketball. An innovator with a very unique way of thinking, a meticulous technician. The creation of a nutty professor. A free spirit. The reinvention of the power forward position and one of the main reasons for there being a major change in the way basketball is played. The kid from Bavaria. The superstar. To some, he is a financial asset; to others, he is their livelihood. A role model and a bitter rival. A shooter with a soft touch or a fierce competitor. A German workhorse and a Texan maverick.

7 p.m. The arena is popping when the players come out of the tunnel, as if it's an NBA Finals game. People are on their feet, filming every shot Dirk takes during warm-ups. When he dunks, the audience cheers in a way that is normally reserved for the end of a game. The arena wants to belong to him tonight. The house that Dirk built. His history is all around him: his childhood teammate Robert Garrett is sitting across from the Mavericks bench. Dirk looks for his father and sister, searches for Geschwindner, his coach and friend. His wife, Jessica. The red logo of his hometown club, DJK Würzburg, is stitched on the shoes that were custom made for today.

The game begins, and everything runs through Dirk. I take notes. I could count the makes and misses—but then it hits me that this has nothing to do with basketball. It doesn't matter that he scores the first ten points of the game or whether he does so with his fadeaway, his trailer three. It's not about winning. It's about Dirk Nowitzki and it's about us. It's personal.

Something catches him off guard in the second quarter. On the jumbotron, there's a video showing scenes from his visits to a children's hospital. Dirk has been making these visits for more than 15 years, but no journalist had ever accompanied him until last year. Dirk watches the video and can't hold his tears back, even though there are still a few minutes left before halftime. Perhaps it's the solemn tone, the narrator's heartwarming voice. Perhaps he's suddenly aware of how fortunate he has been over the years. Dirk Nowitzki is standing alone at center court, and when he's no longer able to control his emotions, he lowers his eyes, hands holding his knees. The arena is struggling with his tears.

At some point, he pulls himself together and finishes the game. When Luka Dončić makes a perfect pass to Dwight Powell out of a pick-and-roll and Powell passes to the cutting Dirk, who dunks, I ask myself whether we've just witnessed the final dunk of his career.

There's a last time for everything.

After the game, the Mavericks lay it on thick. Team owner Mark Cuban has announced that it will be a special evening whether Dirk likes it or not. Coach Rick Carlisle says a couple of moving words, and then images of Dirk's childhood idols flash on the screens. Dirk is watching from the bench, confused at first. Scottie Pippen? Charles Barkley? Larry Bird? Schrempf? Kemp? Why are they showing these superstars? What do these legends have to do with him?

A special task force has been assigned to this top-secret surprise for months. Dirk wasn't allowed to know anything about it, and he's apparently totally oblivious. Dirk had no idea they were coming. But when Barkley, Pippen, and Bird slowly walk onto the court one after another, it dawns on him. His teammate Devin Harris is sitting next to him and can barely contain his excitement. Dirk bites into his towel to hold back the tears. The legends are standing in spotlights, and time makes a loop: 15-year-old Dirk Nowitzki in his kid's room in the small German city of Würzburg-Heidingsfeld, a poster of Pippen above his bed and one of Barkley on his closet door. And Dirk Nowitzki, 40 years old, now one of them.

Dirk stands up and throws his towel to the side as if he's being called back into the game. He awkwardly hugs the legends, smiles, and stands beside them, listening to their farewell speeches.

"Man," Pippen says. "You have been an inspiration to me."

Then Dirk is all alone in the spotlight. We're all watching him.

The arena is dark; only the dim emergency lights sparkle. Dirk stands at center court. Someone hands him a microphone. And then Dirk Nowitzki says what everyone in the stadium knows he's going to say but didn't want to believe.

I take a look at all the pensive faces around me. A lot of them are crying, and whoever isn't crying will start crying soon enough. They all have their Nowitzki stories, their Dirk moments, fans and foes alike. We have watched him fail—we've failed so often ourselves. Everyone here knows exactly where they were when he won the world championship in 2011. Dirk Nowitzki's victory still feels like our victory. To those of us in the stands, those sitting in front of their computer screens in Europe, and those leaning on bars in America, Dirk has been a faithful companion, an emotional constant. I have watched him play basketball for the last 25 years. We've grown up with him— he's what's left of our youth.

To this day, I cannot say whether I've understood Dirk Nowitzki. But when he stands at center court in his arena, in front of his people, his city, and picks up the microphone at the end of a long, brilliant career, I'm raising my beer. The arena is full of friends, relatives, companions. His sister, his father, his wife. The arena below us is dark blue; only Dirk has lights on him. We catch our breath.

"As you guys might expect," Dirk Nowitzki says. "This was my last home game."

★   ★   ★

The book in your hands is not the standard sports book. It's not a training manual. It's not an inspirational hagiography or a motivational lecture. This book is the improbable story of Dirk Nowitzki, a scrawny kid from Würzburg-Heidingsfeld, Germany, who became a superstar in Dallas, Texas. Who became a citizen of the world, an ambassador for a truly global game. Who played for the same team for 21 years and became a legend in his sport. *The Great Nowitzki*. A player who shaped and changed the game he loves. Who achieved this with an almost inexplicable level of dignity, and without ever betraying himself, his love for the game, or his respect for people.

It's also my story. The story of someone who failed at basketball but never stopped loving it—loving what the game means. There are many like me. Everyone who watched Dirk Nowitzki for all these years, watching him as if he were an old teammate who went a step farther than them. Those who still ask themselves how someone can be so good at what they do, at the highest level, with unbelievable stamina and focus. And those who ask why we couldn't.

I've observed Dirk Nowitzki and the people around him—my observations are totally subjective, with all the blind spots of the participant observer; I've become enmeshed and fragmented. This book is my quest to find the significance of Dirk Nowitzki, his singularity, his precision, his accuracy. His meaning to the world, to the game, and to me. This book is not a biography. This book is my attempt to make sense of Dirk Nowitzki.

1

DIRK NOWITZKI

"You're meeting Dirk?
Are you fucking joking?"

A League of His Own

MAY 3, 2012

M Y YEARS WITH DIRK NOWITZKI started on a plane over the Atlantic. Berlin–Frankfurt–Dallas. I had just written a book about the world of international pro basketball and spent a season with the famous German club team Alba Berlin. On the lookout for a new project, I randomly inquired whether the German weekly *ZEITmagazin* would be interested in a long-form feature on Dirk Nowitzki. As a basketball fan from Germany, I had naturally followed Nowitzki's entire career. He had always fascinated me, and it had meant a lot to me when the Mavericks won the world championship the previous year.

My suggestion was simple and, admittedly, not entirely unselfish: I'd watch a couple of exciting playoff games, eat Texan barbecue, meet Nowitzki personally, and then write a portrait about his importance to his city, his sport, and me. Nothing more, nothing less. I figured two weeks would be enough to understand Nowitzki. Much to my surprise, the editor agreed, and now I was actually on my way to Dallas. On Thursday, May 3, 2012, I had no way of knowing that my journey with Dirk Nowitzki would take years.

Sleep was out of the question in the cheap seats, so I tried to read: an F. Scott Fitzgerald novel I had hastily fished out of the bookshelves as well as two photocopied essays about tennis by David Foster Wallace ("Roger Federer as Religious Experience" and "String Theory"). Two Nowitzki biographies. I wanted to be prepared. This was my first visit to Dallas, and tonight I would be setting foot in the Mavericks' arena for the very first time. I was delighted.

Sitting next to me was a heavyset engineer named Charles. He was from a small town in Oklahoma. Charles saw my Nowitzki books, nodded, and ordered a whiskey for me without asking. In front of him was the sports section of *USA Today*, and we started talking about basketball. That night, Charles's team, the Oklahoma City Thunder, were playing the Mavericks in the first round of the playoffs. Oklahoma City had won the first game by a single point, 99–98, and the second was also close, 102–99. Nowitzki had scored 25 points in the first game and 31 in the second, making him his team's high scorer. The Mavericks could have won both games; the losses came down to minute details. In Game 2, Nowitzki had the win in his hands but missed a wide-open three with a minute remaining.

The two teams had also faced off the year before. Dallas won that series, 4–1, on their way to becoming world champions, and Nowitzki probably played the best basketball of his career. The Thunder's three young stars—Kevin Durant, Russell Westbrook, and James Harden— were the future of the game, three future MVPs on a single team. In 2011, the Mavericks had been able to hold them off. Now a year older, the Thunder were more mature, and the team had a 2–0 lead. "Both games could have ended differently," I said. A made three, a solid defensive sequence. "But they didn't," Charles said, then ordered two more whiskeys. "We're ahead."

Then we talked about the absolute superiority of the American game (his take) and the greater tactical demands of the European version (my theory). Charles worked in construction equipment sales, had business in Europe, and was now flying to Dallas, after which he would drive up to Oklahoma. He was interested in the economic and statistical aspects of the sport in a way that only American sports fans are. Numbers matter more in baseball and basketball than in soccer. He praised Dirk Nowitzki for his free-throw percentage as well as for his economic clout in the region. That was all he had to say about him. He wasn't a big fan, he said. Nowitzki? Too soft, too European. He pronounced the word *European* like a disease. "He missed a crucial three last night," he said again. "And we won." I nodded and Charles patronizingly raised his plastic cup, then downed his whiskey.

"Sweep!" he said. "OKC wins, 4–0."

"Never," I said.

"Wanna bet?"

"I don't gamble."

"A hundred dollars," he said, fishing in his pocket. "What? You don't have any faith in your guys? You also think Oklahoma will win, huh?"

"Thanks," I said. "Let's just wait and see."

Even if the engineer wasn't willing to admit it, Dirk Nowitzki was one of the best players in American sports. He had proven himself in a world that had never reckoned with a "white bread from Würzburg" (these are the words of Dirk's coach Holger Geschwindner, not mine). Home crowds loved Nowitzki; opposing fans feared him. They understood basketball, and they understood that he was something special. In America, you could talk basketball at a barbecue in Grinnell, Iowa, or while drinking old-fashioneds in a bar in Brooklyn Heights, New York. Or with construction engineers aboard a Lufthansa plane.

Nowitzki's game stood up to America's immense knowledge about sports—statistically, strategically, and historically. He was probably the greatest European to ever play basketball, and he had fundamentally changed the American game; he had revolutionized it. He had unbelievable range for a seven-footer; he could run the floor and handle the ball. He had even invented his own signature shot. Basketball became a different sport with Nowitzki; now it's more agile and variable, less predictable, more refined and clever. The game has become more international and cosmopolitan. Yet, Americans could appreciate his influence even if they didn't particularly like him because of it. He had commandeered something that didn't belong to him.

In Germany, things were different. Over there, Dirk Nowitzki was more famous than the game he played. He did commercials for Nike as well as for a bank, ING-DiBa. He was a regular guest on German shows like *Wetten, dass..?* and *Sportstudio*; Angela Merkel received him in the chancellor's office and Barack Obama invited him to the White House. He was the German flag bearer at the Olympic Games, a perennial All-Star selection, an NBA champion. An ambassador for Germany in the world. Nevertheless, he remained for most Germans the nice, tall guy from the DiBa commercials. *Diba-diba-duuu.* Only we basketball nerds woke up in the middle of the night to actually watch the games. Germany had no idea just how magnificently Nowitzki actually played. They had no idea what he actually did. In Germany, he was famous for being famous.

From the perspective of a journalist, there was nothing new that I had to report about Dirk Nowitzki. His stats could be googled, as could the chronology of events, his victories and defeats. There were hundreds of interviews and portraits, including the biographies sitting next to me. There were countless game reports. Nowitzki was in *Gala*, *Der Spiegel*, *Westfalenpost*, *USA Today*, *The New Yorker*, and the *Pittsburgh Post-Gazette*. The story was always the same: a boy from Würzburg becomes one of the greatest basketball players in the world. He takes an unconventional course with the help of his eccentric mentor Holger Geschwindner, and he practices in the seclusion of a school gym in Upper Franconia until he reaches the NBA and ultimately becomes a world champion. Nowitzki had fame, respect, and seemingly limitless marketing value. I liked the story of the friendly hero, and I respected his struggles and defeats. His triumphs made me happy, his failures seemed excusable. Somehow, his victories were my own.

Like many others, I had dreamed of becoming a professional athlete as a child. I grew up in Hagen, in the Ruhr Valley, and basketball was pretty much the only sport in town. In the summer of 1984, I was nine, maybe ten, when my coach, Martin Grof, explained how to do a layup in the tiny Vincke school gym: right, left, up. Martin acted as though the game were music and our steps the rhythm: *tam-tam-tak.* And again: *tam-tam-tak.* Over and over.

I played in my first under-12 game the following autumn. I wore the number 14. The higher numbers were reserved for the bigger players. We got a serious thrashing.

On the weekends, my father and I went to watch our favorite club, TSV Hagen 1860, in the packed Ischelandhalle. There were 1,950 seats for 3,000 people; people stood everywhere, on stairs and entryways, a blind eye turned to fire safety. I collected the ticket stubs and newspaper clippings and screamed like crazy. With my pocket money, I subscribed to the magazine *Basketball,* which delivered the scores, points, and standings with a couple days' delay every Tuesday. I can still feel the rough paper it was printed on.

There were two first-division teams in our city, two Bundesliga teams engaged in a bitter local rivalry. The gym trembled during these duels. People drank and smoked in the arena's foyer the way they did in soccer stadiums; the smoke wafted upward. I can still name every player from back then: the enormous Sly Kincheon, the leaper Keith Gray, and the Lithuanians Rimas Kurtinaitis and Sergej Jovaiša, who played for our rivals, SSV. They were the first players from the Eastern Bloc to make it to the West. I remember being at my schoolmate Guido's house one Christmas afternoon. His father came from East Prussia and spoke Lithuanian, and when I stepped into the living room, I saw three giant men sitting around the Christmas tree, drinking vodka from water glasses: Jovaiša, Kurtinaitis, and the legendary center Arvydas Sabonis, who was visiting from Spain and would later play for the Portland Trail Blazers. Basketball was all over the place.

The two local clubs later joined forces against the rest of the league and called themselves Brandt Hagen; the local rusk factory sponsored the team. I remember the 1994 team that won the trophy: Coach Peter Krüsmann, the sharpshooters Arnd Neuhaus and Adam Fiedler, and Keith Gatlin, the talented point guard from the University of Maryland who only landed in Hagen because his teammate Len Bias died of a cocaine overdose shortly after being drafted into the NBA. Bias's whole team had been tainted by association. But now, Gatlin played for us, for Hagen—and how!

I remember my excitement as a child. Basketball was the game of our city, the game of the wider world. I remember the smell of the gym in Friedenstrasse, the soft floor mats, the wall bars, the games on Sunday morning. I also remember the malt beers afterward. The long days in the gym, the outdoor courts in the summer. Basketball players were different from soccer players; there was always a good vibe and smart jokes. In Europe, soccer was the sport of macho men and tough guys. Basketball was clever, basketball was smart. I remember bodies slashing, people flying, and I remember the rhythm, the tact. First I was a fan, and then I became a player.

For years, my goal was to become a professional basketball player; school and books didn't interest me. All my friends played basketball; my first girlfriend, Marta, was a point guard, in a league of her own and on the national team. The guys and I wore Chicago Bulls T-shirts; we had Scottie Pippen posters on our walls. On special days, we had our parents drive us to the Europe League games of Bayer Leverkusen, where we watched Henning Harnisch fly through the Dopatka Arena, and we had headbands and long hair like him. We watched Mike Koch hustle and Toni Kukoč of Benetton Treviso make his incredible passes. We soaked up everything that had to do with basketball. We ordered Air Jordans from mail-order catalogues, repeatedly watched imported VHS tapes of NBA games, and swapped Topps and Upper Deck trading cards. We knew all the names and all the legends, but we weren't totally sure how basketball was played in America. The NBA wasn't something that was real to us; it wasn't factual or even imaginable. The highest achievable goal was the linoleum at Ischelandhalle. At center court, "H A G E N" was written in red on white; it was the center of our world. This is how every fan in every gym in the nation thought. Braunschweig. Berlin. Leverkusen. Bamberg. It would take Dirk Nowitzki to change all of this.

The way the professional system for young players on German basketball clubs worked in the '90s was very simple: we were given tracksuits and bus tickets, and we came to practice every day. The best players were handed some cash under the table, and at some point they received professional contracts that would finance their studies. No one got rich. And for this fiscal situation, we willingly ran through the forest, sprinted up stadium stairs, lifted weights at a gym near the arena for what coaches told us was proper strength training, and helped ourselves to the case of Andreas Pils beer that was provided in the locker room or on the bus for team spirit. We won more than we lost. We weren't terrible; we thought we were the greatest.

I was around 15 when I hit a three-pointer from the left wing in a game—Brandt Hagen versus UBC Münster, if I remember correctly. The clock was winding down and afterward my coach put me on the bench and lectured me: I was a big, and my job was to stay under the basket; it was maybe okay for me to shoot from the top of the key, but three balls were reserved for our point guard, Marko, the son of the European coaching legend Svetislav Pešić. "Ball doesn't lie," I mumbled, but I sat down on the bench, docile. I knew I had done something wrong.

The basketball we knew was a regimented game that had clear roles for each player as well as clearly defined positions and functions within the team's structure. Basketball was bristling with choleric coaches and catchphrases like "offense wins games, but defense wins championships." The routes were already set; discipline was mandatory, as was devotion to the team. Our coaches swore by physical defense and offensive plays that were clearly articulated. Scores were low. As for us players, we just did what we were told. We played fantastic and enthusiastic basketball in Hagen, the game meant something in my city, but we didn't play so that we would have one more point than our opponents in the end; we played so that they would have one point less. Strategies were employed that had been known for ages. Deemed "the right way," we played an antiquated game, calling it "old school."

Maybe I would have become a solid three-point shooter if I had been allowed to shoot. Maybe I would have jumped higher if I had followed a different training regimen. Maybe I could have been a different basketball player. The truth is probably a lot simpler: I was too short and I didn't handle pressure very well. My movements lacked presence; I was constantly afraid of failure and didn't play with intuitive confidence. I simply wasn't made to play the sport at its highest level, mentally or physically. I stopped believing in my dream in the summer of 1994—but I've kept every single one of my jerseys from those years. They're at the back of my closet. At 18, I did the community service that used to be compulsory in Germany, then moved away for my studies. My basketball career ended before it even started. There are many others like me.

This took place around the time Dirk Nowitzki came onto the scene. Rumors spread in 1994 about a kid from Würzburg, born in 1978, nearly six foot five, very quick, with an excellent shot. In the gyms across the nation, it was rumored that he had the stuff to be the best player in Germany—even in Europe. He was better than Harnisch, maybe even better than Dejan Bodiroga, perhaps even as good as Toni Kukoč, the Spider from Split.

In Hagen, the game was also slowly starting to be played differently. We had two large and mobile players, Bernd Kruel and Matthias Grothe, who were allowed to play in the modern way without a fixed position. Grothe was the same age as Nowitzki; a forward with a strong physique, he had finesse and a nasty three. Kruel could shoot, too; he was the same height as Dirk and just as nimble. But what mattered most was that neither of them was scared. They understood the game. They weren't afraid of losing.

As for me, I traded in my basketball shoes for running shoes, met my future wife—a tennis player—and moved to Hamburg with her. I had spent my youth playing this fantastic game, but we had drifted apart. At some point, I found something that meant as much to me as the game: literature. My feelings for basketball—or let's just come out and say it: my love of the game—had cooled, but my body could still remember it, a kind of muscle memory, a strange phantom pain. I could still feel the exact rhythm of a layup—*tam-tam-tak*, right, left, up—as well as the game's intensity, the arcs of suspense, the drama. I kept counting down 3–2–1 whenever I threw a crumpled manuscript page into the trash can to beat the buzzer. *Swish.*

Everything stayed like this until September 13, 1998.

On that day, I was visiting my parents in Hagen. My father had arranged to get us tickets to the Ischelandhalle—section E, behind the basket, like always. We drank a beer in the arena's foyer before the game. We talked shop and teased one another. Everyone was talking about this Nowitzki kid—or whatever his name was. Was he Polish? And was it true that he was really that good? We drank our beers faster than usual and walked into the arena. Then we all gawked at the warm-up routine of the young team from Würzburg: Demond Greene, Robert Garrett, Marvin Willoughby. And, of course, Dirk Nowitzki.

The word on their team was they were wild. But "wild" was short-hand for everything that wasn't yet imaginable in German basketball: speed, mathematics, psychology, tact, tactics, joy, improvisation. The modern game. Officially, Klaus Perneker stood on the sidelines, but behind him was Holger Geschwindner, acting as a kind of shadow coach; he didn't have a coaching license, but he possessed a vision for the future. Nowitzki warmed up, and we wondered whether he was really all that special. People from Hagen tend to be critical. The game wasn't sold out. That's something I remember.

Then, we actually watched Dirk Nowitzki play for the first time.

He was now six foot ten and had already broken out of German basketball's prescribed roles for bigs. Because it was already clear that Nowitzki would soon be leaving for America and the NBA, our team gave him everything we had on this Sunday in September. And I say "we" because I hoped Hagen would win. We identified with the underdog.

Grothe, Kruel, and Nowitzki had known one another ever since they played on the youth national team. They had also played together just a few weeks ago at the Under-22 European Cup in Trapani, Italy. Some months before that, they were also on the starting five at a Nike exhibition game in Dortmund, where a select few talented Germans played against their childhood idols, Nike-sponsored athletes like Scottie Pippen, Charles Barkley, Vin Baker, Reggie Miller, Gary Payton, and Dirk's future point guard Jason Kidd. The Americans had come to Germany via Paris; they got bored in their hotel rooms, drove Porsches on the autobahn, and then bought rottweilers and small airplanes. To be honest, the American players in our league were second-rate, while Barkley and Pippen were the best in the world. At that game, the journalist Frank Buschmann, who came from my hometown, had stood knee-deep in dry-ice fog to introduce the stars to the Germans. Early in the game, Dirk Nowitzki dunked on Barkley off a fast break. Barkley would repeat this story for years afterward, and Dirk got better with each telling.

The sportswriter Marc Stein, a Mavericks beat writer for the *Dallas Morning News* at the time and later a good friend of the Nowitzkis, had decided to take a detour and visit Würzburg on his own dime after completing his yearly tour of English soccer stadiums, covering the games. The NBA players were locked out for the time being, and Stein was intrigued. He liked Europe and European players. He wanted to see where the mysterious player the Mavericks had just drafted grew up. He wanted to see whether he was actually good enough.

Two days before coming to Hagen, Stein had watched the Würzburg X-Rays play against Bamberg in the Würzburg arena. Nowitzki had scored 12 points, missed all his threes, and corralled only a few rebounds. He battled with Jens-Uwe Gordon, a German American on the Bamberg team. The game wasn't anything special, but Würzburg won, 79–66. Stein later told me it was only Nowitzki's third game in the first division of the Bundesliga, but it was clear he was talented. "I had never seen a seven-footer shoot the ball like he could. *No one* had ever looked so smooth from deep at Dirk's size. No seven-footer was a true three-point threat to that point." Most of all, Stein was captivated by the atmosphere at the game. As at soccer games, the fans sang and shouted, and they sat right on the edge of the court. The game meant the world to them. "I loved it."

Stein had met Holger Geschwindner before, in Dallas, and he rang him up again in Würzburg. Geschwindner picked him up at the Hotel Walfisch, by the Main. And, so the story goes, they had a noteworthy drive along the Autobahn. From Würzburg to Hagen. Had I ever been in a car with Holger Geschwindner? They drove to the Ruhr Valley, to another tiny gym without any frills, just basketball. Stein also sat courtside at Hagen's Ischelandhalle on September 13, 1998, and watched the game. Brandt Hagen versus DJK Würzburg. We must have seen one another. Later, Stein would recall that Dirk's blood sugar was really low and that Geschwindner had to nurse him with Coca-Cola and cookies. That said, Stein could immediately see why the Mavericks wanted to bring Nowitzki to Dallas.

The game was far from pretty. I remember the bright ZWACK lettering on the Hagen jerseys, advertising chocolate Zwieback, and I remember Nowitzki's headband. He was tall, skinny, and didn't move like the other players. He was flexible and fast and didn't get involved in the exhausting pushing and shoving under the basket. Hagen's big men, Grothe and Kruel, took turns guarding Nowitzki. Shortly before halftime, Nowitzki received a screen from the huge center Burkhard Steinbach, followed by a perfect pass on the right wing. Grothe fought around the block Steinbach had set and ran out to the three-point line. Nowitzki, who had seen Grothe coming, faked his shot, let him fly by, and bent his knees deeper, lowering his center of gravity slightly more than any basketball player I knew. He focused.

Kruel saw Grothe fly by and left the player he was guarding, James Gatewood, to help. With two or three long strides toward Nowitzki, he had his arms raised high, his mouth open wide, eyes on the ball. Nowitzki saw the approaching Kruel, quickly showed him the ball, just a tiny gesture, and then Kruel jumped, too, as he guessed Nowitzki would take the shot that every other player in the world would have taken. But Nowitzki knew what he wanted to do. He surveyed the scene: Kruel had sailed by, and the laws of nature and physics said he wouldn't be coming back any time soon, and Grothe was still consumed with gravity and himself. Gatewood was open at the free throw line and Steinbach's 265 pounds were hanging around under the basket. The play was out of balance. In that short little tenth of a second, Nowitzki could do whatever he wanted. He could decide.

And he decided on a move we would see hundreds, if not thousands, of times over the subsequent 20 years. At the time, it seemed unusual to me, that's all. Nowitzki brought the ball he had faked down from the air and bounced it hard on the ground. He took two small steps as an adjustment away from his defender, then bent his knees again. Then he and the ball moved upward, perfectly in sync. The ball bounced up from the floor into his left hand, Nowitzki and his shooting hand came under the ball in the exact tenth of a second, and he turned the ball's momentum into his own, *tak tadamm*, a perfect dactyl, the ball having no weight at all now, or almost none. It was doing the work for Nowitzki, who only had to fine-tune its direction. Nowitzki went up, high into the air, high above everyone, his fingers spread wide apart. The ball left his hands as if on rails, last touched by his index and ring finger, the arc high and precise. *Swish.*

That evening, Dirk Nowitzki only made one of his six three-point attempts—that's what the stats say. But you could tell he could have made them all. He had 18 points and eight rebounds in the end. He was tall, fast, and clever, he could hit baskets from all over the floor, he could dribble and find his teammates that were open—he could control every aspect of the game. One time, he ran a typical Würzburg fast break, made a cut past Bernd Kruel toward the basket and dunked on the head of his defender. The cameras clicked. Kruel still has a picture of it in a box on the cabinet in his living room. It was the fourth time Nowitzki played in the Bundesliga; he had just turned 20 and was still too slight, too skinny, but he was already the centerpiece in Würzburg.

My old team beat Würzburg, but we had just seen the future of the game without knowing it. "Not bad," my dad said. "They didn't call that one travel," Bernd Kruel smiled. "There's no other way to explain him getting by me like that." Kruel and Grothe would become very good basketball players. Kruel played in the Bundesliga for 20 years and Grothe became a legend in our city (he died much too young in 2017, and when Dirk heard about Matze's death, he was very quiet and visibly upset). When Stein returned to Dallas, the report he delivered was that there was no need to worry; Dirk had gifts you couldn't teach. It seemed like Nowitzki could read the game better than all the others; he seemed to think differently. It wasn't clear to me then just how fundamental this difference was. Dirk Nowitzki would later become everything we weren't even capable of imagining.

I've followed Nowitzki's career ever since. I watched his big games and crushing defeats in the middle of the night, first from the unreliable stop-and-go live tickers, then on illegal streams and later through the official channels. And then I studied the statistics in the morning. Even during the years I was no longer obsessed with basketball or set foot in a gym. I've always turned on the TV for his games with the national team.

I wasn't the only one. Every basketball player or fan has their own Nowitzki moments. Moments of gaping, waiting, marveling, exploding in celebration. In psychology, these phenomena are called "flashbulb memories": emotional and rich memories of special events that are recalled often—whether you want to or not. Memories that become more real the more you talk about them, stories that become more concrete and elaborate with each new telling. In those moments, David Foster Wallace writes in his essay on Roger Federer, "the jaw drops and eyes protrude and sounds are made that bring spouses in from other rooms to see if you're O.K. The Moments are more intense if you've played enough tennis to understand the impossibility of what you just saw him do. We've all got our examples."

For us Germans, it's the shot over Jorge Garbajosa in the European Cup semifinals against Spain, the 2002 World Cup in Indianapolis, the standing ovation in Belgrade in 2005, the 2008 Olympic qualifier against Puerto Rico, the 2008 Olympic Games. But once he became a star in America, the base of Dirk aficionados widened. First Dallas, then America, then China, then the world. We've all watched how the game has changed and we've seen how Nowitzki and his coach were at the center of those changes. We've witnessed the bumps in his career, too, the low points. Geschwindner's tax issue. The Miami series in 2006. The Crystal Taylor story in the tabloids. We all watched the Mavericks win the 2011 world championship—in bars, clubhouses, and living rooms—and we've wiped the tears from our eyes when no one was looking. We all remember June 2011. We remember Dirk's stutter step against Chris Bosh, the left-handed shot, the injured left middle finger, the banked shot, the soft touch, the kiss off the glass, the championship diamond. When Dirk Nowitzki finally made it, we did, too. That's how it felt. It was like we were the ones who won the championship. We've all watched and suffered together.

Our plane was now above the Great Lakes, the Midwest was on the seat-back screen in front of me; next came the plateaus of Kentucky,

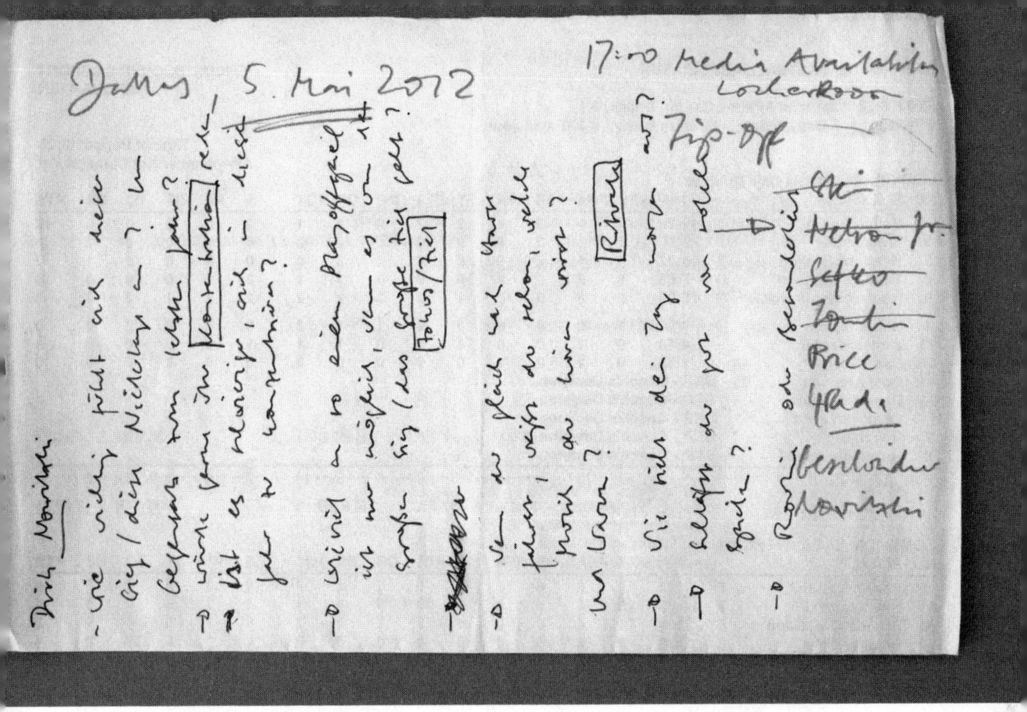

Dallas, 5. Mai 2012

17:00 Media Availability
Lockerroom

Tip-Off

[handwritten notebook notes, largely illegible]

Dirk Nowitzki

Rivers

Price

---

flyover country; and then, finally, there was Texas, with its oil pumps, warehouses, and fields for miles. We were getting close.

The front page of the *Dallas Morning News*, which my seatmate handed to me, trumpeted the headline "Gotta Have It." The Mavericks had to win tonight; otherwise, they'd be down three games to none, an impossible scenario. The Mavericks' PR people promised me Dirk Nowitzki would have time for a short conversation after the game, and I scribbled down questions in my notebook. I decided it would be best not to stick to sports.

My years with Nowitzki began where they would end—at the Dallas Fort Worth airport. As I stepped out of arrivals, I was clobbered by the heat. My clothes were way too warm for spring in Texas. There wasn't a single cloud in the sky; the concrete surfaces and glass facades were bathed in a burning blue light. I put my jacket in my bag, rolled up my sleeves, and hailed a taxi. I was here. I was ready to go.

Saint Dirk

S OMETIMES FATE GIVES YOU an answer before you even get the chance to ask a question. Haile, the Eritrean cabdriver who was going to take me downtown from the airport, was in his mid-forties. He believed in God, generosity, and Dirk Nowitzki. Haile was wearing a blue T-shirt with Nowitzki's number 41 on the back. His taxi reeked of licorice; there was a rosary of plastic beads dangling from his rearview mirror in Mavericks blue and white. On the dashboard was a prayer card of St. Christopher, the patron saint of drivers. Right next to it, an autographed trading card of long-haired, headband-wearing Dirk Nowitzki, framed in gold.

When the cabdriver smiled and said, "Saint Dirk, savior of Dallas basketball," there was no way for him to know that Nowitzki was the reason why I had come to Dallas. Traffic was bad on the highway; the sun beat down on the asphalt, the taxi's AC wailed. Haile honked, cursed, offered me some licorice. He asked why I was in Dallas. I'm here to meet Dirk Nowitzki, I said, nodding at his dashboard and the blue and white rosary. It's the playoffs after all. Driving at full speed, Haile turned around and stared at me in silence.

"You're meeting Dirk? Are you fucking joking?"

We raced toward Dallas and Haile answered my questions with enthusiasm. He got off the jammed highway and took shortcuts to the American Airlines Center. The cab weaved through residential neighborhoods, industrial wastelands, cacti here, dry riverbeds there, fast food chains to the left and right, birds sitting on bare powerlines, looking like vultures. Could that be? Parking lots, skyscrapers, parking lots. The American flag flapped in the wind. Dallas wasn't all that pretty on the surface.

Haile knew everything about Dirk. We waxed poetic on his big career moments: he talked about Indianapolis in 2002, Germany's bronze at the World Cup, and Nowitzki's MVP in the tournament. Back then, Haile was living in a suburb of Indianapolis and went to the games. Tickets were almost free, and it was the first time he ever paid attention to Dirk Nowitzki. He liked Germany. His brother had lived in Düsseldorf for a while—"You know Düsseldorf?"

I talked about the 2005 European Cup championship game, about the entire Belgrade audience giving Nowitzki a standing ovation for a number of minutes after he was taken out of the game shortly before Germany lost to the Greeks. Even the Greek fans stood up. I talked about Dirk losing the 2006 Finals—how he disappeared into the catacombs, hands over his head, as if he had been punched in the gut, as if he were struggling for air.

"Here we are," Haile said when he parked on Victory Lane. He was certain Dirk would win tonight. He banked on it, laughed his faithful laugh: "Welcome to the Church of Nowitzki."

I paid, Haile opened the door for me, and there I was, standing in front of the entrance. A giant banner, hung above the side entrance, featured a roaring Dirk and the Mavericks' battle cry for the playoffs: "Dallas Is All In." I was familiar with the arena from the countless telecasts I had watched; I had seen the red brick front hundreds of times. Now I felt like I was stepping onto a movie set. It suddenly dawned on me that I hadn't flown to Dallas only to conduct an interview—I was here because I wanted to witness something heroic. Today was the day Nowitzki would bring the Mavericks back onto a winning course. That's what I imagined. Haile set my suitcase on the sidewalk and gave me his number. "A friend of Dirk is a friend of mine," he said. "Call me."

I was late; the game was starting in a couple of minutes. Tired from the long flight, I hurried through the catacombs and was suddenly struck by enthusiasm when I entered the American Airlines Center's interior, directly across from the Mavericks bench: Dirk and more Dirk; everything was blue and white and 41. I hadn't expected such intensity; the air was filled with the scent of popcorn and melted butter, and with hope and confidence that the Mavericks would win. I listened to the national anthem and watched the fireworks. The arena exploded when the team came out on the court—but then this perfect production was immediately spoiled in the first quarter.

Things weren't going well for the Mavericks or for Nowitzki. I was too exhausted to understand the complex strategic textures of this game, but I could see that the Mavericks were stumbling. Nowitzki was subbed out. I spent the second half watching the game on a television in the janitor's corner beneath the stands and on the screens way up in the press box on the sixth floor, right below the arena's ceiling. I saw the victory move out of reach on flickering screens. The Mavericks couldn't find a way to crack the game open; they couldn't gain control. I heard the American journalists typing frenetically around me, I noted the scores and the janitor's cursing, but then the game was over and lost, 95–79. No heroics today.

After the game, I sat in the press room and waited for Nowitzki, who was obliged to make an appearance for the journalists after every important game. I leafed through my notes and questions: questions about his rituals, about boredom in the life of a professional athlete. The role his skin color played in his fame, the role of race in sports today. Whether he ever had financial difficulties (the difficulty of knowing what to do with roughly $20 million a year). How one maintains such an incredibly high level of concentration at work for so many years. Whether basketball was still fun. Whether he sympathized with other celebrities (or whether they only suffered alike). When the paparazzi showed up at his door for the first time. What he thought about when the tabloids printed photos of his ex-girlfriend or reported on his coach's tax issues. Whether he thought he was as down-to-earth as everyone said. What hurt him the most. Whom he could trust. What was real, what was fake.

The Mavericks' PR director, Sarah Melton, arrived after a few minutes and said there'd be no interviews today. Not after a loss like that. The press conference would have to suffice. But I would get 25, maybe 30 seconds to introduce myself after the press conference. "Dirk likes to know who's here," she said. Nowitzki entered the room, squeezed himself behind the podium, and answered the questions with strained politeness. After five minutes, Melton broke off this sobering performance. While a frustrated Nowitzki left the press room, I ran after him and, without introducing myself, asked a question too stupid to print here. Nowitzki looked at me with astonishment and immediately gathered himself. He signed the basketball of a little boy. "Goodnight, buddy," he said. Then he was gone.

★   ★   ★

There were two days until the game that would decide everything, and I wandered around Dallas without meeting Nowitzki. It was unclear when he would have time—if at all. The Mavericks were the reigning champions, expectations were high, the agitation in the press was intense. They were down 3–0; nerves were running thin. I was under pressure—I had flown over 5,000 miles and I owed the magazine a story about our meeting. I had hoped one thing would lead to the next when I arrived in Dallas. I pestered the press office. They reluctantly mentioned the possibility of a conversation.

When?

We'll see.

I called Haile and drove around the city with him in his taxi. I talked to barkeeps, librarians, drunken fans. Haile explained the city: Love Field. The Latinos of Oak Cliff. The Mansions of Preston Hollow. University Park. Oil and business. Mexicans and Colombians. Metallic reflective windows downtown. I collected impressions and talked *about* Dirk instead of with him. It was always the same: Dirk, Dirk, Dirk, mayor of our hearts, Dirk is unbelievable, Dirk is friendly, Dirk is one of us (everyone called him Dirk—pronouncing it like the Americans do: "Durk," with a U). At the arena, security greeted me in German. Sometimes people started suddenly singing "We Are the Champions." Just like Nowitzki did on the balcony of the AAC after the championship parade.

I went for runs around the golf course at Stevens Park, along the Trinity River, past the giant prison and the bail bonds businesses. It was hot, and sometimes the sidewalk ended abruptly—Dallas was built for cars. There were feudal mansion districts, poor shacks, highways and bridges and bridges galore. I didn't talk to a single person who didn't know about Dirk, who didn't have a personal story to tell. Nor did I meet someone critical of Dirk, a Dirk hater (I would only meet one seven years later—on the day of his final home game). It seemed like the championship had silenced all his critics.

On the second morning, I got into a conversation with a parking attendant named Shane Shelley in the hotel's driveway. Shelley was a lean man who moved like an ex-basketball player. He had three jobs, three children, and a 60-hour work week. He had diabetes but had grown used to it ages ago. As tall as me, six foot four, he had been a shooting guard at Cedar Hill High School. These days, he only played very rarely. The red polo shirt of his company—MetroParking—fluttered on his body. He looked tired, but enthusiasm kept him going. He was, he said, almost the exact same age as Dirk Nowitzki—born on October 3, 1978, in Dallas, Texas.

Shane was on the morning shift this week. I was still on German time, so we stood around, watching the shimmering Dallas skyline at dawn. Sirens howled and we drank black coffee from paper cups. Shane talked about the championship, because everyone here talked about the championship with eyes that glistened. They talked about *their* championship. About *their* Dirk. But unlike the other people I talked to, Shelley could describe individual sequences to such a level of detail that it felt like he had played in the game himself.

"I watched the playoffs in my living room," he said. "The Mavs lost the first game, and when Miami was up by 15 in Game 2 after Dwyane Wade's made three, I went to the fridge." His wife was out of the house; he sat alone in front of the TV, afraid that these Finals would go down the drain the way they had in 2006. "I was so depressed," he said, "that I put a six-pack on the table." Coors Light, the diabetic's beer of choice. Someone had to do something. And the Mavs made a comeback as soon as he started drinking.

"I started drinking," Shane said, "and the Mavericks turned the game around."

He dribbled an imaginary basketball around his parking attendant stand, faked a shot, and turned—a make-believe reverse at dawn. He knew that his story sounded unlikely, but he liked to tell it because it had worked. Because his story was the truth. "My daughter was asleep, I drank Coors Light, and the Mavericks won." Final score: 95–93. In Miami. Magical drinking.

The week after had been amazing. The Mavs lost Game 3 because Shane had to watch it in a bar with his friends, but then he sat on his sofa with a six-pack for the rest. The final seconds of Game 6 were very emotional. "On the verge of tears," Shane said, then threw his coffee cup into the garbage can with a perfect one-legged fadeaway. "Have a nice morning," he said. "Say hi to Dirk."

But Nowitzki couldn't be reached. Not even at the daily morning practices, where journalists weren't allowed to watch the team prepare. We could hear instructions, shoes squeaking and balls bouncing on the court, but a black curtain was blocking our view. We stood under the stands and waited for the team to finish (90 percent of the job is waiting: waiting for the locker room doors to open, waiting for flights to take off, for games to be decided and for press conferences to begin). When we were finally allowed into the arena, Dirk was already long gone. I then watched the press pounce on his fellow players Jason Kidd and Jason Terry. On Coach Carlisle. On Vince Carter and on the bench players Brian Cardinal and Ian Mahinmi.

The Oklahoma City Thunder players crept slowly through the catacombs of the arena in slides and crumpled T-shirts. Their hair was messy, they hadn't shaved. Their whole shtick was a pose. The young athletes limped like retirees; their gait was sluggish. "We just woke up, but we could easily beat you in flip-flops." But when they stepped on the court, they were wide awake. They were focused during their rituals, their shooting drills, their handshakes and signs of respect. Coach Scott Brooks and his assistants had meticulously prepared their young team for the older Mavericks. Durant, Harden, and Westbrook were all brimming with confidence; Father Time was on their side. They fooled around after practice, placed bets for ridiculous sums on half-court shots, and treated the Oklahoma journalists like old pals, ignoring the rest. Durant had his jersey wrapped around his neck like a scarf. The Thunder were confident that they would win.

The Mavericks, by contrast, had their backs to the wall—if they lost the game tomorrow, they were gone. Jason Kidd acted calm, but the stress could be felt. This wasn't just about a playoff series, it was about defending the championship—and about a ton of money. Jason Terry hammered out rote phrases, but the tone wasn't the same as the year before. The aura was missing. The *Dallas Morning News* called for the Mavs to rely on Dirk even more. While the other Mavericks talked to the press, Nowitzki kept practicing in a secluded gym. The team's press staff strung me along the way they strung all the other journalists along. "Dirk wants to focus," they said. He needed to concentrate. "He doesn't talk," Tomlin said. "He's shooting."

Cathedral of Possibility

MAY 5, 2012

I WAS WAY TOO EARLY the morning of the next game. No one was standing guard at the delivery entrance, so I pressed against the heavy metal door. It was unlocked. Nothing beeped, no alarm went off. No one was in the stairwell, nobody in the catacombs. Somewhere in the distance, empty bottles clattered; the air smelled of cold popcorn. The lacquered concrete glistened as if it had been freshly mopped for this big night. I slowly walked beneath the retractable bleachers, shoved the black curtain aside, and entered the arena.

It was dark inside; only the emergency lights were on. The air conditioning hummed softly; it was cool, almost cold. Beneath the hardwood was the ice rink for the Dallas Stars' hockey games. I walked to the edge of the court and was surprised by my glee. The huge arena felt very different in the semi-darkness than a few nights before, when the Mavs lost the game: six whole tiers up to the ceiling, rows and rows of seats right to the edge of the court. The huge jumbotron hung above the court, dark and gloomy; countless speakers dangled from the ceiling on thin chains and wires. Way up above, in the rafters, were banners bearing the retired numbers of Rolando Blackman and Brad Davis, as well as the conference championships, the division titles, and, above all else, the Mavericks' championship banner:

2011 NBA Champions.

I was alone; only a couple of luxury boxes across the way had their lights on. I looked around, then cautiously stepped onto the court, my shoes squeaking and cracking on the painted wood. I made my way across the court slowly—*Betreten mit Straßenschuhen verboten*—no street shoes. It was quiet, but you could sense the volume, the intensity. Tonight, the place would shine and sparkle and thunder. I stopped at center court. If I had a ball, I would have taken a shot—I would have made it; my dream from long ago would have come true.

I climbed the stairs of the stands, step by step, higher and higher. I pulled out my notebook in the darkness of the back rows. The Mavericks' court lay quiet beneath me. Empty stadiums are sentimental places for basketball players. We know what it feels like: the practice, the panting, the burning muscles. The sound of squeaking shoes is in our ears, the sound of the ball going through the net.

Swish. Swish. Swish.

Empty gyms are cathedrals of possibility. We imagine what could be: decisive shots, big wins, the now gray and empty rows of seats packed with people. I sat in the dark and peered at my memories, at all the gyms, all the pain, the games that were lost. The happiness. I wrote down how it could have been; I peered into another life. All the dreams. If I would have been a different player, bigger, faster, more flexible. Smarter, more levelheaded. Freer in my thinking, more present in the moment, less caught up in the rote narratives: what kind of player I was, what basketball meant, and how the game was supposed to be played. About before and after and the moment in between. The hardwood of the American Airlines Center shimmered.

Suddenly, the lights went on. *Clack, clack, clack.* Spotlights bathed half of the court in cold blue. A skinny boy in a Mavericks uniform pushed a ball rack across the court. He stopped in front of the scorer's table and carefully adjusted the rack. There were seven balls on it. The boy took each one into his hands, threw it in the air, rotated it, checked its pressure. The temperature of the lamps slowly rose; the light got warmer. I stayed where I was sitting. I wasn't even there.

Then two figures emerged from the tunnel, one in rolled-up training pants and a Mavericks uniform, the other in jeans and a checkered shirt. Dirk Nowitzki and Holger Geschwindner. The coach took off his jacket and hung it on a chair in the second row. Nowitzki put down a water bottle on the sideline. He went to the scorer's table, took a ball, spun it on his hand, and decided on another. Then they began.

He made almost every shot. Nowitzki shot with his right, with his left, from the key, from midrange, threes from the left, the right, the corner, out of pivots and spins, he wrapped the ball around his body, *tak, tak, tak,* adjusted his footwork, *tak tadamm,* reacted to imaginary defenders, faked—they were flying by like ghosts from the past. Grothe. Kruel. The ghosts from the future. Ibaka, Collison. In between: free throws. Free throws and more free throws.

Geschwindner fished the ball out of the net, over and over, and only occasionally indicated what Nowitzki should do differently. He gestured in an almost overly exaggerated manner: how he should roll off his feet and spread his fingers, how his body should move under the ball. From where I was sitting, I couldn't hear a word they were saying, or if they were even saying anything at all, but their concentration could be felt all the way up here in the dark. The transcendence of the moment. It was about the game tonight, the outcome of this playoff series; it was about defending the championship. It was about the past and the present and the years that would come after. It was about the minuscule details—the body, the angle, the placement of his fingers. Everything depended on this moment, everything was at stake, and no one was watching. Just me, hidden in the dark, notebook on my knees, watching Dirk Nowitzki and Holger Geschwindner get ready.

3036 Mockingbird Lane

GOT OUT OF HAILE'S TAXI on Mockingbird Lane at noon. I had waited a few moments after Geschwindner and Nowitzki finished training, but then my phone rang when I snuck out of the arena shortly after. It was Geschwindner. He had received my message. He could meet me at a Starbucks near Southern Methodist University at noon.

"Meet me there," he said. "Then we'll talk."

Our rendezvous was in a typical American strip mall: parking spots, a nail salon, a pizza place, a mobile phone store, and more parking. The light towers from SMU's football stadium towered over the rooftops. Highway 75 hummed close by. I recognized him as soon as I walked into the café: an older man amid students with their textbooks and MacBooks. Geschwindner was wearing the same shirt as this morning in the arena. Gray hair, an angular face, 67 years old and not an ounce of fat on his ribs. Notes and papers were splayed out in front of him, as well as two or three coffee cups. He was scribbling something into a small notebook; he seemed like a professor of German literature, a MacGyver, a specialist in ancient history, a visionary. Geschwindner saw me, nodded, and motioned for me to take a seat. Then he kept writing. I waited; his phone rang. *"Hier bei der Arbeit,"* he said—"At work"—before listening for a couple of seconds, nodding, and hanging up without saying anything else. At some point, I started getting embarrassed and took out my own notebook, jotting down the name that had been written on the coffee cups in front of him with a Sharpie: "Willie."

Holger Geschwindner and I had met once before when I was writing my book about Alba Berlin and the world of professional athletes. For years, Mithat Demirel, the club's sports director, had been Nowitzki's teammate and roommate on the national team, and he was, more importantly, a street-smart strategist. He and Geschwindner always got along, and Demirel thought we should get to know one another.

His plan didn't work. At an Alba away game in Bamberg, Mithat had arranged for us to be seated next to each other. Geschwindner was living a few miles away, in the countryside outside Bamberg. He was wearing a colorful felt hat that somehow looked like it came from the Far East (I would later learn it was from Mongolia). He wore his jacket for the entire evening, looking like he would rather be somewhere else. The game was awful, one-sided, uninspired, without any rhythm— essentially, not even a game of basketball. The coaches called all the plays; the players executed them against their intuition and without success. Geschwindner and I hardly spoke as we sat next to each other. I thought he was some sort of jester who saw the truth and was permitted to speak it. At first, I tried to say something meaningful, but Geschwindner just grumbled. What could you say about a game like this? It was the exact opposite of what Geschwindner understood basketball to be. Berlin was down by 20 at halftime, 51–31, and before we knew it, the catastrophe was over: 103–52. Geschwindner stood up, crushed my hand, and vanished.

There was no way of getting around Geschwindner if you were interested in Dirk Nowitzki. He was considered to be the person who'd discovered Dirk, his sponsor and creator (if there is such a thing). But it didn't seem like he enjoyed talking about himself; he remained out of the public eye. Everything known about him was a mosaic of headlines and keywords like *mentor, discoverer, madman* and *tax issues.*

He was ahead of his time.

I knew he had played professionally—600-plus Bundesliga games—but that he couldn't be found in the immortal basketball records because in Germany, statistics only started to be kept in the 1980s. Basketball wasn't big enough in the country during Geschwindner's heyday. The professional infrastructure was only created after him.

But Geschwindner was a baller. His last Bundesliga game was in 1987, but he kept playing in the Southwestern Regional League until he was almost 50. Holger and Dirk first crossed paths in 1993 at an away game of his TV Eggolsheim in Schweinfurt. I didn't know what he had been doing professionally in the meantime. Business consulting, I had heard, troubleshooting for companies in dire need. He's a problem solver, it was said, a man of action. And after meeting Dirk, he developed a multistep plan to make the kid into the man he is today. It was rumored that his method incorporated mathematics, psychology, education, discipline, and plenty of nonsense. Never one to make public statements, he was described for the sake of simplicity as an old eccentric, a Dr. Frankenstein, a mad professor, a megalomaniac, a troublemaker. I wanted to talk to him about all this, but it seemed he would rather stick to jotting down his notes in silence.

In the Starbucks on Mockingbird Lane, he didn't seem to remember our meeting the previous winter. Or, at least, he ignored all niceties and kept writing unapologetically. The young baristas called out one name after the other.

"Jesse."

"Laura."

"Tall caramel macchiato for Marc!"

"Peter."

A crazy preacher came into the café and announced the end of the world—"Doom is upon us, folks!"—and Geschwindner put his notebook into the inside pocket of his jacket, stood up, and looked at me.

"Coffee?" he asked.

"Great," I said.

When he came back with two grande lattes, the name on the cups was "Willy"—this time with a *y*. "They can't spell 'Holger,'" he laughed, and he seemed like another person while laughing. The lines in his face weren't from worrying; they came from cracking jokes. "And besides, no one can deal with 'Geschwindner.'"

When you talked to Holger Geschwindner, you got a sense of how Nowitzki could stay at the highest possible level for such a long time. Geschwindner seemed communicative and aloof all at once; he told stories, but they were never very personal. He didn't seem nervous about the playoff game against Oklahoma tonight; it almost seemed like he didn't care. He was only here to fix Dirk's shot if it was necessary. And he was also here to be sitting at his spot if Dirk needed him. "It's about the finest nuances," he said.

I tried to explain what it was that interested me about Dirk Nowitzki, but it felt like Geschwindner had heard all my ideas already, had answered all the questions and read all the stories ages ago. He seemed to think faster than he spoke. He simply left out certain sentences that were obvious to him. He jumped between topics and ideas, synapses sizzled, the links quickly shifted. We flew through Geschwindner's universe, from Rilke to physics to Nietzsche to Heisenberg's uncertainty principle. Whenever I went in a wrong direction, he said, "Easy," and turned around. If we stalled, he said, "Doesn't matter," and changed the subject to something that seemed equally important to him. Every now and then, Geschwindner paused mid-sentence, stared into the void above our heads, and jotted a thought down in his notebook.

He opened his laptop from time to time. A stick figure with Dirk Nowitzki's exact body proportions moved on the screen. The angles and calculations of curves demonstrated what an ideal shot looked like. The goal was to find the exact angle at which Nowitzki would have to shoot the ball for him to make the shot despite making mistakes. Geschwindner fished a piece of paper out of his pocket and stole my pen: he wrote down formulas, sketched shapes, drafted theories and theses, flung literary references on paper. He briefly spoke about basketball, then returned to geometry, drew an ellipse and explained that two points could always be connected via this shape regardless of what's standing in their way. And this might actually be the best way to describe his relationship to Nowitzki: "Close enough," he said, "but never too close." He grinned at my confusion. "How far away is close enough?"

He wasn't certain whether anyone could find the right words to write adequately about Nowitzki. Or whether the words that could describe what the kid—"*der Bub*," he said, "the boy"—had been doing for years existed at all. You would have to create a new language. Dirk Nowitzki is like an extreme mountain climber, he explained. Conventional sentences just didn't fit the extreme physical and mental demands. They couldn't do them justice. "If you've ever been above 20,000 feet," he said, "you know what kind of madness goes on in your brain." I had come with questions about basketball and kitchen sink psychology, with the interests of a biographer, but he spoke in allegories, the sport taking a back seat to his words. And the words dissolved into associations and stories.

Geschwindner reported being on top of Mera Peak in the Himalayas a couple of weeks ago with his friends Georg Kendl and Dieter Reder. They had taken a plane to Lukla, the most dangerous airport in the world, then traveled higher and higher every day, from lodge to lodge and camp to camp. And what happens to the head on the way to the 21,247-foot-high summit is treacherous. "It's difficult to describe." It's metaphysical. Or religious. However you want to describe it. When you're up on a summit, you get a glimpse of this, but Dirk lives it.

Metaphorically speaking, players like Dirk were living at around

26,000 feet. But this could also be taken literally: the physical and mental strain are exceptional. "Words are the first to go during an extreme experience," Geschwindner said. "They're not adequate." Reinhold Messner probably only wrote down what people thought he had experienced. "Call it 'God,'" Geschwindner said, "call it a 'spiritual experience.'" But this was only an unsatisfactory translation of a real and deeply subjective experience into language. Geschwindner looked at me. "Words without experience are insufficient," he said and pointed at my notebook. "And those who have the words don't have the experience."

"But . . . ," I said.

"Easy," Geschwindner said. He raised his hand and shook his head. In the 1970s, the philosopher Thomas Nagel had written "What Is It Like to Be a Bat?"—an essay that suggested you could never know what it was like to be a bat, even though you could know everything there is to know about them. Or Friedrich Nietzsche: "As a human being 'communicates himself,' he gets rid of himself, and when one 'has confessed,' one forgets." Geschwindner called Nietzsche "FN." Dirk Nowitzki couldn't express his innermost self, he said, because this stable core would be lost if he did. Or, at the very least, it would become less clear. And the ability to focus on what really matters would be lost as a consequence. I tried to counter with David Foster Wallace's texts about Roger Federer and Michael Joyce, with "Roger Federer as Religious Experience" and "String Theory."

"String theory?" Geschwindner asked. "Do you even know what that means?"

Holger Geschwindner gave me the feeling of being constantly tested. I pulled my scribbled-on photocopies of Foster Wallace's essays out of my bag and set them next to our coffee cups. I wasn't interested in elucidating Dirk's person and explaining him in psychological terms, I said; I would rather orbit around him. I would rather describe the phenomenon of someone like Dirk playing basketball. How he played. And what it would take to play the sport at his level for so long.

"I'm not trying to discourage you," he said.

"You're not?"

For almost two hours, we argued back and forth. Geschwindner seemed to love challenges and battles. At some point, Geschwindner looked at his watch, gathered his papers, and stood up. He had to meet a mathematician at SMU before he drove "up to Strait Lane" and took "the boy" to the arena. That was their ritual. The conversation was exhausting, but I cautiously asked whether I could join them. I had to give it a go at least. "It would be interesting."

"I'm sure it would be," Geschwindner said. "But no."

"That's OK," I said. "Good luck."

"We'll give everything we've never been able to do." Geschwindner gave me his business card, a double-sided photocopy. I'd had the impression during our conversation that I was a burden, but now he laughed and shook my hand. "See you later tonight," he said and left. I watched him walk across the parking lot. There were a couple of SUVs and a Porsche, but Geschwindner got into a Cadillac Escalade and slowly drove off. I had misread him. One of the baristas came to our table. "Sorry," he said, as he gathered the cups and scribbled-on napkins.

"Can I ask you something?"

"Sure."

"That guy," the barista said, beaming. "Was that Holger?"

I looked at the business card in my hand. A picture of Albert Einstein was printed on the left side, the famous photo of him sticking his tongue out. The barista had pronounced Holger's name with an American accent, but it was still pretty good. He seemed to know who he was. On the right side of the business card, it said, "Institute for Applied Nonsense—Holger Geschwindner." Address, telephone number, email. I sensed that the story of Dirk Nowitzki and Holger Geschwindner would be more than a simple timeline of an athlete's career with a beginning, middle, and end, defeat and triumph. I sensed that their variety of basketball had nothing to do with what I had always thought the game was.

"Yes," I said. "That was Holger."

Game Day

MAY 5, 2012

Back at the arena. In the midday heat, Nowitzki's face on the front of the building seemed more determined than it had two days ago. It seemed more rested. The plaza in front of the American Airlines Center was empty, only a few delivery trucks waited, and the sun hammered down like the Texas sun always hammers down. There were still a couple of hours until tip-off. A bouncy castle was being inflated, and images from last year's championship flickered above the arena entrance in a loop: there was Dirk with the trophy, Dirk on the parade through his city, Dirk singing "We Are the Champions" on the arena's balcony.

The vendors waited in the arena's air-conditioned fan shop for customers. All of them wore blue T-shirts printed with the playoff slogan. A friendly old lady with blue hair showed me the complete Nowitzki assortment: there were Nowitzki jerseys, shorts, shirts, headbands, backpacks, slippers, pajamas, cups, key rings, baseball hats, wool hats, cowboy hats, and panama hats. There were even Dirk Nowitzki cereal bowls.

Highlights from the 2011 world championship were playing on dozens of monitors here, too. Dirk took a shot, made it, shot, and made it again. The Mavericks eliminated the Portland Trail Blazers, then

Kobe Bryant's Los Angeles Lakers, then tonight's opponent, the Oklahoma City Thunder, and, ultimately, the Miami Heat. Dirk wore out
rows of defenders. He shot over smaller opponents and used his quickness against bigger ones; he was unstoppable. He handled the pressure,
matured with it. Nothing could get in the way of his dominance. "Out
of this world!" "Ridirkulous!" You could watch the flamingo fadeaway,
his one-legged shot that no defender in the world could stop, over and
over. Nowitzki played with a fever and a torn tendon in his finger. He
could be seen carrying the Larry O'Brien trophy and the Bill Russell
Finals MVP Award. "That was last year," the lady explained when she
saw me staring. "How do you like this year's jersey? The playoff edition
is only $99!"

Three hours before tip-off, I talked to Donnie Nelson instead of
Dirk. Nelson was the Mavericks' general manager and had been largely
responsible for bringing Dirk to Dallas almost 15 years before.

Nelson was a heavyset man in a dress shirt, jeans, and sneakers that
resembled rubber dinghies. A friendly face, always up for a good laugh.
He was sitting in his tiny office among stacks of paper, trophies, and
shoeboxes, and he got right down to business. "What do you want to
know?" he asked, but then started explaining where he had first heard
of Nowitzki: in the Phoenix Suns' locker room. When he was a young
assistant coach, he worked in Phoenix. A few players were talking about
German basketball—they had traveled through Germany playing on
a Nike promotional tour. When was that? And where? Was it called
Hoop Heroes? "I can't remember," Nelson said. "My brain doesn't work
backwards," he said. "I think ahead."

Thinking ahead was Nelson's talent and occupation. When his
father, Don, became the head coach and general manager of the Mavericks in 1997, Donnie followed him to Dallas and became his assistant
and international scout. In the late '80s and early '90s, Donnie traveled around the world of basketball, cracked the Eastern Bloc open—a
David Hasselhoff in gym shoes—and was the manager of the legendary

Lithuanian team that included Arvydas Sabonis, Šarūnas Marčiulionis and Rimas Kurtinaitis, "The Other Dream Team," in their Grateful Dead–style tie-dyed shirts. Nelson brought Marčiulionis, the NBA's
first Soviet player, into the league. Nelson had seen it all. He was someone who kept names and remembered faces. His brain did work backward perfectly; he was a player, a gambler.

Nelson told me about the difficulties of Dirk's first year in Dallas. "He arrived from Würzburg," he said, "and no one had even ever
heard of Würzburg here before." The fans' skepticism, the newspapers'
doubts, and the league-wide quips about the management exchanged
behind closed doors. The Mavericks had selected Dirk Nowitzki over
Paul Pierce, who was a much better player at the time.

Founded in 1980, the Dallas Mavericks' first decade was marked
by a few playoff appearances, a division title, All-Star players, and
universal optimism. These teams boasted the likes of Rolando Blackman, Brad Davis, Mark Aguirre, and Derek Harper. But the '90s were
a disaster; the Mavericks only narrowly avoided setting an NBA record
for losses in two separate seasons. The whole thing should have gone
more smoothly: they played in the pristine Reunion Arena, received
high draft picks, featured Jason Kidd, Jamal Mashburn, and Jim Jackson, "The Three Js," but then countless injuries, a lack of discipline, and
unfortunate coach selections stood in the way of success. The arena was
rarely sold out; the Mavericks got used to being the butt of jokes.

Then Don Nelson, nicknamed Nellie, became the manager and
rebuilt the team. He replaced one player after another, built the roster
around the wing Michael Finley, and fired the coach in the middle of
the season and took over the coaching duties himself. He developed a
fast-paced and unconventional style of play, "Nellie Ball," and his son
Donnie joined him. Donnie was the one who reported hearing about an
unconventional player from Germany. Everyone in the Phoenix Suns'
locker room had been talking about some German kid, a Kaminski or
Rumanski, a kid Charles Barkley said he'd played against in Germany.

At the 1998 draft, the two decided to select Dirk Nowitzki and then committed to trading for Steve Nash, the Suns' point guard.

Donnie Nelson told me that he and his father kept expecting to be fired and chased out of town—that's how awkwardly the team played at first. His father had boasted that Nowitzki would be the Rookie of the Year. "If we're honest, it was a high bar Dirk could never achieve." And still, they believed in him—or rather, they believed in time. When things didn't immediately pan out as they had hoped, they naturally had to ask themselves whether the risk had merit. Was the kid worth it? "We knew we'd have to be patient," Nelson said, leaning back, "but we didn't know whether we would get the time to be patient." He looked me right in the eyes.

"It took some time for Nash and Finley and Dirk to come together," he said. "But look at this now."

Nelson pointed at the framed *Sports Illustrated* covers on the wall, the trophies, team photos, and framed jerseys. "On the Mark: The Next International Star." Next to this was a giant whiteboard with the names of every relevant NBA player, including their salaries and the length of their contracts. If Nelson wanted to make a trade, he only had to turn his head to see which player would make sense for what team—primarily for the Mavericks. Trades can only happen in the NBA if the traded contract packages roughly match up, big contracts for big contracts, role players for role players. Next to Dirk's name was "$20 million," but I had read that he was only one of three players in the league with a no-trade clause in his contract. This meant Dirk would have a say in whether he could be traded and where he would be traded to. Dirk was an absolute exception.

Suddenly, Nelson threw a shiny object in my direction. I was lucky that I caught it. Nelson's laughter was louder than expected: I was holding the Mavericks' championship ring in my hands, gold and diamonds, 50 grand apiece. "That was a test," Nelson said. "Good hands."

Nelson was a jovial guy who appeared to make a joke out of

everything. But it could also have been that he was nervous. Millions of dollars were on the line tonight, as was the immediate future of the business he was running. The Mavericks were down three-oh, but the series would return to Oklahoma City if they won tonight. And you could never say what might happen. An injury here, a stomach bug there, an inexplicable loss of form by the Thunder—and then the Mavericks would be right back in it. Every game had been close so far. Admittedly, a comeback wasn't likely, but it was still possible.

Nelson was a good storyteller. He led me through Dirk's early years, the difficult times, the valleys, then through the good years and finally to the world championship. Through the window, you could see the players drift into the practice facility below us. Loud hip-hop was blaring in the gym. No one used the basket at the far end. "That one belongs to Dirk and Holger," Nelson said. At some point, he stood up and pushed me out of his office. "Let's go."

The arena was buzzing and booming now. Everything was all lit up, everything was ready. Nelson ushered me through the hall. He shook hands and kissed cheeks the whole way—"There he is!" and "Look at you!" An army of guides and stewards were now standing at their stations, waiting for the audience. The countdown to tip-off ticked on the clocks above the baskets. Another two hours and 21 minutes.

The Mavericks' offices were underground. Bare brick walls, ventilation ducts, daylight lamps, and neon lights. Very '90s. The giant logo was all over the place—in acrylic in the lobby, on the carpet, and on the employees' shirts. Nelson dragged me through the arena's back rooms. Here was the giant weight room; over there, the offices. There were treatment tables, physio-couches, the physiotherapist. "What's up, buddy?"

Nelson was a master of irony; he joked and smirked his way through the surroundings. He was a prankster. He offered me a coffee in the kitchenette, but the milk was sour and started flaking. Nelson grinned because he knew I'd have to inconspicuously get rid of the coffee. He showed me the extra-high custom-made toilets and the shower heads that were seven and a half feet off the ground. He acted like he was going to push me into the relaxation bath and grabbed me by the collar before I fell. The players' buffet was ready, as was the glass fridge filled with water, Gatorade, and drinks mixed specifically for each individual player. It smelled like coffee. Nelson told me to hold out my right hand, and then he bandaged my wrist with the blue tape that would stabilize Dirk Nowitzki's ankle tonight.

When we finally entered the Mavericks' locker room, he told me to take a seat at Dirk's locker, in his massive leather chair, right between his socks and shoes. Everything was prepared for tonight. Nowitzki's number 41 jersey on a hanger; it was either brand new or freshly ironed. A photocopied picture of the Larry O'Brien trophy was taped to the back of the wall. This was the center of it all, the heart, filled with the hopes of an entire city. Nelson took the jersey off the hanger, then handed it to me with a grandiose gesture as if I had been drafted. It was the jersey Dirk Nowitzki would wear in the first half: snow white, heavy, and handsewn. Looking down at us from the top of Dirk's locker was a tiny Lego figurine in the Mavericks' colors.

Back in his office, Nelson bade his farewells. "Any more questions?" Nowitzki and Geschwindner were now getting ready at the other end of the gym, their movements were the same as this morning. Nelson didn't wait for my answer, he kneeled on the floor and rummaged through some boxes. He didn't find what he was looking for, so he crawled under his desk.

"No," I said. "Then again . . ."

Behind glass, I saw Nowitzki putting up shots at the other end of the practice gym. It didn't seem like anything could distract him. It was unlikely that I would be able to interview him. If the Mavericks won tonight, the entourage would leave for Oklahoma City immediately. It would only bring bad luck to think about them losing. Plus, if they did lose, the mood would be terrible, and it probably wasn't going to get better before I left town—and there'd still be no interview. I needed some sort of conclusion, some closing remarks for my story about Nowitzki without Nowitzki. What does Dirk really mean to Dallas? I asked. On his knees under his desk, Nelson didn't hesitate for a second. "Dirk changed Dallas, economically and culturally—he changed the city's mentality," he said, coming up from under the table. "He deserves a statue—it's that easy." Donnie Nelson groaned as he got up from the floor. He was holding a shoebox. All of a sudden, he seemed very serious. "More," he said, putting the shoebox in my hands. He nodded and opened the door for me. "Dirk deserves more than one statue."

Thirty-four minutes to tip-off. The box contained two basketball shoes, size 16, much too big for my feet (I kept the box nevertheless). Now the setting was impressive and unreal. Camera crews were on the court, all six levels as well as the press and celebrity boxes were sold out, there were made-up décolletés, cowboy hats, "The Star-Spangled Banner," and then the Coca-Cola Two-Minute Warning. Dallas was all in. I wasn't sitting in the janitor's closet tonight; I snuck out on the court, armed with my credentials and my camera. The concentration was tangible.

I was standing only a few feet away from Dirk Nowitzki during the national anthem and I acted like I belonged there. Troy Aikman, the legendary Dallas Cowboys quarterback, sat in the first row, and I could make out Geschwindner in his seat behind the bench in Row J. He remained seated while everyone else stood in anticipation. The music was loud and swarms of towel boys, rich fans, coaches and physio, and beer and ice cream vendors surrounded us. There were cable pullers, security, mascots—a perfectly organized chaos, an anthill, a beehive, humming and buzzing. I could feel the heat from the fireworks. Nowitzki looked past all of it; he looked through it. He looked at what was coming.

Everything ran through Dirk. The arena was dressed in blue, waving blue towels. It oohed whenever Nowitzki had the ball, it howled whenever he was fouled. The Mavs put him in isolation and gave him the ball and he lived up to the responsibility and extra attention from his defenders. The *Dallas Morning News* had insisted that the Mavs shouldn't rely on Nowitzki alone—"Mavs need more from reserves"— but then, he was the most reliable option. He had the ability to ignore the world watching him. He was having a good game.

The Mavericks played the first half like the team that had won the world championship: Jason Kidd and Jason Terry made their threes, Shawn Marion defended. The rest of the team profited from the attention Dirk was receiving. They were now performing their given roles, the game plan was working, the game was wide open.

Early in the second quarter, Nowitzki posted up defender Serge Ibaka, dribbled twice and made contact in the high post. He could feel that Ibaka was trying to stop him from going toward the basket with all his might and he adjusted. He absorbed Ibaka's strength, backed away, and then there was his fadeaway. It was the shot that couldn't be defended, the shot he had developed in 2009 with Holger Geschwindner, the shot that had significantly contributed to the Mavericks winning the championship last year. Ibaka hated this shot. The arena loved it. Nowitzki buried it. The Mavericks started looking for this situation over and over. Shortly before the end of the quarter, Dirk received the ball in the low post on the left, again against Ibaka, but this time the Spaniard bodied him up. He was more physical and defended Nowitzki even closer. As their bodies collided and Dirk noticed how overzealous Ibaka was, he simply absorbed the momentum and strength of his defender and let himself be pushed out, flying out of reach of Ibaka's outstretched arms. The ball left Nowitzki's hands as if it were on rails and went through the net, 47–45. The score was even at halftime.

The first time I ever watched Dirk Nowitzki bend his knees and let his defender fly by before making a high-arc three was in my hometown, Hagen, on September 23, 1998, exactly 4,983 days ago, and now I'm watching him make the same movements on the exact same spot on the court in the third quarter: the bent knees, the rolling off the heels, the gliding of the body under the rock, the perfect economy of man and ball. But where his opponents had previously been my old friends, today there are two superstars in the making: Kevin Durant and Russell Westbrook. Dirk still made the shot today, just as he did back then, and the way he did in the empty arena this morning. The arena exploded. Nowitzki's three started a 14–5 run, and the Mavericks were ahead by 13 points at the start of the fourth quarter, 81–68.

It looked as though the Mavericks might actually avoid the sweep and postpone their inevitable demise. I took a look around me. The whole arena was standing and screaming; no one was paying attention to the cheerleaders or T-shirt cannons. The arena was a single entity. And although we knew it would be difficult to win this series, we believed it could happen. We believed Dirk Nowitzki would make it happen. We were caught up in the moment. It was as if the game had found itself.

And then the dams broke. Oklahoma regained point after point. Beefy and bearded James Harden kept driving toward the basket, unstoppable; he made everything from everywhere. The Mavericks went cold and couldn't hit a thing. Nowitzki had good looks, but many of them bounced out now. Nowitzki being the focus of the whole operation started working against the Mavericks. Where he had previously created openings for others, now he stood alone in a forest of defenders' arms and legs. Shortly before the game was over, the Thunder pulled ahead. The arena was shocked. When Dirk made his 33rd and 34th points at the free throw line with a minute and a half remaining and the public address announcer yelled, "Diiiiiiirrkk!" one more time and the clock incessantly ticked toward the end of the season, everything got quiet, then silent. It wasn't enough. Dallas lost, 103–97.

Afterward, Dirk's posture reflected the painful defeat: the slow gait while making his way to the locker room, the untucked jersey, arms on his head as if he were recovering from gut punches. The press trailed behind the players into the locker room; a shocked silence hung above them. No photos, no autographs. The players left the showers one by one, and the throng of press surrounded them, asking their dejected questions. The players were wearing towels with elastic bands around their waists and their jersey numbers on their hips. The swarm moved from player to player. The pack then descended on Nowitzki when the battered hero came out of the shower. Every camera and microphone was pointed at Dirk; you couldn't see him, but his towel flew by and landed perfectly in the dirty-laundry basket in the middle of the room.

Dirk had to make an appearance on the podium to explain the failure in front of the cameras and voice recorders. He was dressed in black. The season had been long, and now it was over. Last year's historic season wasn't going to be repeated. Nothing lasts forever. And what everyone had been afraid of turned out to be the irreversible reality: the Dallas Mavericks wouldn't defend their championship. After this game, Jason Kidd would only play one sad season in New York before becoming a coach, and Jason Terry would also leave Dallas after eight seasons. This had been the last game of Brian Cardinal's career. Dirk Nowitzki answered our questions, then got up and slowly walked down the corridor toward the loading dock. He just wanted to go home.

The Sudden Summer

DEFEATS ARE DIFFICULT TO fathom. The exit interviews were scheduled for the next morning, the last conversations before summer break. It was the end of the season; grades were to be handed out, the merciless verdict of the media. The coaches, managers, and players appeared in front of the press for one last time; melancholy hung in the air. In this business, everyone deals with defeat differently, but this morning all the suits that were worn yesterday in anticipation of something great were hung up in the closet. The big test was over. Now that the summer opened up in front of them, most of them wore T-shirts and sneakers. Some reporter or other had had too much to drink the night before; the room smelled like toothpaste and booze and Old Spice.

The Mavericks had lost, but everyone was still there: those reporters who had been following the team for years; the ones who identified with the Mavericks and said "we" when they posed a question—"What'd we do wrong, Coach?" "What can we expect, Jason?" There were also the critical reporters, those who constantly looked for faults in the system and wanted to find the person responsible for them: "How could this happen?" "Is the team too old?" "What's the plan now?" They were the ones who created their stories from the failures of others.

"Do you think it was because nobody could handle Harden?" ESPN, the *Dallas Morning News*, the *Fort Worth Star-Telegram*. The realists were also there—the ones who wanted to talk about tactics and who knew everything already. The enthusiasts, the assholes, the newbies, the old hands. Jeff "Skin" Wade, Marc Stein, Eddie Sefko. The Canadians, the Chinese—and me.

The players limped down the stairs of the practice court one after another and were asked questions. Nowitzki answered politely. A couple of journalists were somewhat forceful, as if he could have stopped the Mavericks from failing all by himself. This was presumptuous; they were acting like everything was his fault. They all expected him to turn back time. After all, he was Dirk Nowitzki.

"Can you keep playing?"

"Was it the knee?"

"Was this your last season?"

It was difficult for the reporters to imagine that the Mavericks could no longer be called world champions. For a year, the championship had made their lives easy; they'd adopted the title as their identity. Suddenly, everything was as it had been before: this year, the winner would either be San Antonio, as it had been so often in the past, or maybe it would be Oklahoma City, perhaps even Miami. Oh, how they hated Miami!

"Any more questions?" the media guy, Scott Tomlin, asked. "No?" "Thanks, Dirk."

"Have a nice summer, everybody," Dirk said, then labored his way up the stairs, a sad savior in a T-shirt and flip-flops. Tomlin followed him, and they disappeared through an emergency exit. The journalists gazed after them. "There goes another year of Dirk," one of them said. *There goes my story*, I thought, packing my recorder away. I would just have to write about Dallas, about the city's love of him, and about their hopes and expectations. About Haile and Shane Shelley, about Nelson and Geschwindner. About what I had seen, what impressed me—it would be enough for a magazine feature. I would write about his significance (his significance for me). My thesis would be that all this noise couldn't reach him. I was about to leave when Tomlin returned to the gym.

"Come with me," he said. "He has time for you now."

Up close, the difference between relief and exhaustion couldn't be discerned on Dirk Nowitzki's face. His eyes were wide and deep, his cheeks sunken. He hadn't shaved, he looked like someone who had been stuck on the sofa with the flu for a couple of days. His T-shirt was wrinkled. He seemed very tired and very relieved at once. The night before, he had played world-class basketball, and now he was sitting in the Mavericks' kitchenette. His schedule was suddenly clear. Suddenly, summer. The abrupt emptiness wasn't something he'd planned for.

Tomlin offered us coffee, but the machine didn't work and the milk was still off. Nowitzki got up and came back with some bottles of water. He set them down between us, sighed, and arranged his legs under the tiny table.

"Thanks," I said.

"Sure," he said. "What do you want to know?"

Over the last few days, I had continuously expanded my catalog of questions, but now it felt strange to work off that list. I didn't take my questions out of my bag. The fact was, in the four games of the series, he had tallied 107 points and 25 rebounds, and these were solid numbers. He made 44 percent of his shots against the Thunder's tough defense, as well as 90 percent of his free throws. It hadn't been enough.

Nowitzki analyzed last night's loss the way a linguist does a text. He could recapitulate and analyze sentence for sentence, paragraph for paragraph, chapter for chapter. He was familiar with the story's content, but above all, he understood its structure; he could even list and interpret individual words and sounds.

When I replayed last night's game in my head, there were the spectacular sequences and the moments when the momentum shifted, when the game changed. I remembered the spectacular dunks and three-pointers; I had watched Harden's powerful drives to the basket and noticed that the game was eventually out of reach for the Mavericks. When the game split open, when the win was out of the question, when Nowitzki was the only one who kept scoring. I had jotted his last nine points of the season down as if they mattered.

Nowitzki, by contrast, seemed to read the textures and structure of the game as a whole. It was shocking how rational and unemotional he was. The game took its course. His memory was impeccable. While I tried to grasp the dramaturgy of the game as well as causal and psychological correlations—while I searched for a story—he rationally observed the game, its sequences, details, mechanisms. A missed free throw at the end of the first quarter was just as important as the baseline jumper a minute before the final buzzer.

The journalists' questions about his knee, his age, and last night's defeat were still resounding. As were the questions about the end of his career. The cries of naysayers, the pessimistic forecasts. "I've been doing this for long enough," he said. "A couple of these guys need to be toned down. I don't give them any material."

We switched to German. Nobody was listening. I asked what he did after the game. "I pounded some fast food," he said. He grinned. I knew he never ate red meat or drank alcohol during the season, sticking to fish and chicken. "Normally, the whole team would have gone out after a loss like that. But last night happened so fast, it was so abrupt, I wasn't in the mood to see anyone. So, I had a burger, fries, and a shake. Then I watched the other game."

"You watched basketball after all that?"

"San Antonio versus Utah."

Dirk Nowitzki paused a lot; his answers seemed less automated or cautious than what he had offered the journalists before. Maybe it was the language. He spoke English whenever he talked about basketball and his role in it, whenever he talked about himself as an athlete, a superstar. That's the way it had been for years. German was the language of his childhood. In contact with journalists, he was always aware of what he had to say and what little comment could be turned into a headline in whatever medium. But in German, he used words like *reingedonnert* (pounded) and said, "Interviews and photo shoots and commercials aren't exactly my favorite," and "I still think it's embarrassing when I go into a restaurant and everyone applauds." The way he formulated his sentences became slowly more imbued with the Franconian dialect of his childhood, the conversation turned away from yesterday's game, and we talked about mutual friends, the past year, and the summer coming up. As always, he would stay in Dallas for a couple of weeks and then fly to Europe with his girlfriend when it got too hot over here.

We talked about differences, about Texas and Germany, his new world and his old one, where much was the same as before: "There's still the old supermarket and the tanning salon." It was actually true: he did stay at his parents' house in Würzburg when he was preparing for the following season. The bathroom had only been remodeled after last year's championship season—now he wouldn't have to bend over while brushing his teeth. We talked and we talked, and Tomlin eventually came in to remind him about his next appointment. "Push it back," he said and grinned. You could hear his teammates making a commotion in the background. Bottles clanked somewhere in the background; farewell beers were being raised.

Lepenies vs. Gumbrecht

AUGUST 20, 2012

THE SUMMER PASSED AND I sat in Berlin, grappling with my story. Dirk Nowitzki was just too complicated for ten magazine pages—the way he went about his work was too intricate, his environment too unusual. I wanted to get him right, as a person and as a phenomenon, and I also wanted to understand my own fascination with him. I held on to the idea of watching Nowitzki and Geschwindner work together during one of their summer training sessions, which I had heard a lot about but had never beheld. I wanted to know more, I wanted to be able to better appreciate him.

After the championship, I had read an article by the esteemed sociologist and historian Wolf Lepenies. There weren't many intellectuals in Germany who took basketball seriously. Running and tennis were covered sometimes, and soccer was a constant topic of debate. Everyone had something to say about soccer in Germany—all those people who could hold a pencil and kick a ball, everyone who was sentimental about sports—but Lepenies had followed the entire playoffs online at night, with clammy hands and a sense of urgency that surprised even him.

Berlin was only half as warm as Dallas in the early autumn, but the windows of the Institute for Advanced Study in Berlin's Grunewald district stood wide open. This was where Lepenies, dressed in a white shirt and linen pants, did his research and writing; a basketball hoop was visible in the yard behind the villa. Born in 1941, Lepenies had played for Rot-Weiss Koblenz as a young man—at a time when basically the only people who played basketball in Germany were university students. His career high was 48 points. Now it was his grandchildren who played the game. Lepenies had learned how to properly read and understand basketball while watching the Princeton Tigers play with the famous anthropologist Clifford Geertz. Lepenies was a young professor in New Jersey and Geertz was the star academic at the Institute for Advanced Study at Princeton, a model for the IAS in Berlin.

I was very excited when I heard about Geertz's passion for basketball. He was one of the most important proponents of participant observation, and it was my aim to write about sports subjectively while following my intuition, with all the risks and blind spots of a participant observer. In Madison Square Garden, Lepenies and Geertz had cherished the legendary forward Bill Bradley as well as his 1973 New York Knicks world championship team, which featured Willis Reed, Earl Monroe, and Walt Frazier. For me, Bradley's *Life on the Run* was the summit of basketball literature. The book told of the Knicks and of the world of sports, of racism in that era, as well as the radically different conditions that professional athletes worked in. With Geertz, Lepenies had ridden in cabs through midtown Manhattan to watch the Knicks play in the early '70s, and now we were sitting in a think tank in Grunewald, talking about Dirk Nowitzki. Everything seemed to be coming together.

Wolf Lepenies was an aficionado, and we started talking shop from the get-go. Lepenies recounted how he once observed Nowitzki and Geschwindner practice: 75 minutes of shooting without a single interruption—impressive, perfectly planned! "Geschwindner is crazy in the best kind of way. I was really impressed by the way he thought about peaks," he said. "Whereas the rest of us think about averages, the two of them are merciless. For them, seven out of ten baskets are three misses. They want ten buckets."

Last summer, Lepenies had woken up his wife right before the buzzer to watch the final seconds of the last Mavericks game in Miami— it was something she had to witness. He didn't go to bed afterward, he was too wound up, too touched. He remained at his desk and wrote about Nowitzki: "Nowitzki's triumph is a victory for justice."

For Lepenies, Nowitzki was much more than a star. "He exhibits greatness," he said, and that was something fundamentally different. Lepenies made reference to the French sociologist Pierre Bourdieu, then talked about Nowitzki's remarkable cultural and social capital. Nowitzki had genuine respect for his opponents—something that was rare. Lepenies considered him to be one of the few true legends of German sports. Like the 1950s soccer legend Fritz Walter, Dirk shaped how the world looked at Germany and Germans. In the minds of Germans, he had conquered America the way the boxer Max Schmeling had, and he was as dignified as the tennis player Steffi Graf. (For Americans, of course, Schmeling was first associated with the German foe in World War II and later served as the foil for a triumphant Black champion, Joe Louis.) "We grieve these athletes' defeats and we perceive their victories as just." These were weighty words, but Lepenies was convinced.

Lepenies had conducted an open correspondence about Dirk with Hans Ulrich Gumbrecht, the German-American literary scholar at Stanford University. Gumbrecht inquired as to why Dirk Nowitzki is perceived differently in America and Germany. It is an indisputable fact amongst basketball experts all over the world that Dirk Nowitzki revolutionized the game. And while his victories and his world championship connected him to legends like Max Schmeling and Fritz Walter in Germany, it was mostly only Mavs fans who really identified with him in America. The rest of the country looked on with mere respect.

Gumbrecht had an almost unconditional admiration of Nowitzki, but called him a "hero without aura." His theory was that Dirk wasn't a superstar in the mold of Kobe Bryant or LeBron James because the American public only saw him during the games; the normal viewer only watched what he did on the court. He didn't regularly appear in commercials, he never held up watches, shoes, or burgers in front of a camera. He had mastered the game with the media, Gumbrecht wrote, but he never wanted to be written about. He balked at the profit-maximization ethic of American professional sports. Dirk Nowitzki's face was not one for advertising in America. He did not invite the press over for a visit to make human-interest stories. Outside of Dallas, Dirk was merely a basketball player.

There was one other thing that Dirk's style of play accomplished, something Gumbrecht called "not what the casual American fan wants." Gumbrecht was right: Dirk Nowitzki came from a different era. When he entered the league in 1998, basketball was only broadcast on TV. In the phase of his career when Nowitzki's play was fast and athletic and spectacular, a basketball game was still mostly consumed as a whole unit. You watched the entire game, and later there were highlights and analysis. You knew which player was good, but you were mostly interested in the teams.

Then the game shifted to the internet and the relationship flipped: the way the game was perceived was changing while Nowitzki became less athletic but more mature and cleverer. Increasingly, the league was being viewed on digital devices through individual streaming. It became a rarity to watch a full basketball game from beginning to end. After the year 2000, basketball signified short clips and highlight reels. The complex structure of a 48-minute encounter was now condensed into two-minute summaries, the team's play broken down to the most spectacular individual actions, to dunks and blocks and game-winning threes (nowadays, you even see clips that feature the movements of individual players instead of the entire court or the whole play). You could say these developments passed each other by: the perception of the sport became one-dimensional, and Nowitzki's game became more complex.

Gumbrecht also alluded to Dirk's skin color. Basketball's racial history is complicated and often tragic, with Black players often subject to on-court quotas, abuse, and segregation. The overall conversation about the game frequently reflected society's racist assumptions about Black and white players, about their supposed athleticism and relative levels of intellect. Often, Black players were considered naturally more athletic and spectacular, while white players were thought to be smarter or more strategic—but ultimately less skilled. As far back as 1992, films like *White Men Can't Jump* were addressing such biases. But the stereotypes of white and Black players had hardly dissipated by the time Dirk arrived to the NBA in 1998. According to Gumbrecht, observers of Dirk's career had the tendency to stumble into traps of prejudice and assumptions.

Gumbrecht delineated this phenomenon and, of course, deemed it "politically problematic." Was Nowitzki perceived as an anomaly because he was white? Was he "not Black enough" for the game he played? Was Nowitzki an exception to the cliché assumption about Blacks being better basketball players while whites couldn't properly play the game? Is this why Nowitzki didn't figure into the eternal barroom discussions about the greatest basketball players of all time—among the likes of Michael Jordan, LeBron James, Kobe Bryant, Wilt Chamberlain, or Bill Russell? Were we Germans, who perceived his victories as "just," simply victims of our own prejudices? Our own systemic racism?

In German bars, people talked about soccer, and Nowitzki was the only basketball player they were familiar with. But this vague, and vaguely good feeling about him transcended all hard facts. The warmth toward him covered up for the lack of knowledge about his field goal percentage or usage rate. Almost no one in Germany could factually say how good he was. People just vaguely said that they thought Nowitzki was "good." As in "a good man," not as in "as good a passer out of double teams as LeBron."

Lepenies and I briefly considered putting up a few shots on the hoop outside, but we couldn't find a ball. His grandchildren must have taken it with them. So we sat down again, the curtains were blowing, and Lepenies's observations turned from Nowitzki's historical greatness to that of him being down-to-earth and then to concepts like "honesty," "performance," and "authenticity"—and suddenly we were analyzing Nowitzki's wedding photo as if it were a Renaissance painting. The tabloids published the photo a few days after the fact; somehow, the Nowitzkis and their guests had succeeded in keeping the press at bay. Before the wedding, Holger Geschwindner had flown halfway around the world and back, creating false trails and traps, and the newspapers repeatedly wrote about the wrong places. The Nowitzkis celebrated their wedding three times over: first, in Kenya, with his wife's family, then at the courthouse in Dallas, then with friends and family in the Caribbean. Who was there and what was on the menu was only leaked gradually, with the wedding photo appearing days later: Dirk and Jessica Nowitzki in traditional Kenyan garb, and then on the beach in the Caribbean.

In the background of the official wedding photo was an intimation of the ocean's blueness. Like two crazy art historians, Lepenies and I analyzed the cut of Nowitzki's suit as well as the bride's modest jewelry. "This may sound a little over the top," Lepenies said and laughed, "but this photo isn't that of a star. It's not style and surface. You can sense a core that you can't really get to. What I'm saying is vague, but there's something here that's 'right.' Sincere." Lepenies glanced out at the basketball hoop in the academy's back courtyard. Now he seemed to be very serious. "Sincerity is really rare." He smiled and returned to our conversation. "Dirk Nowitzki," Wolf Lepenies said, "is one of the greatest sports stories we've ever had."

Unterer Katzenbergweg

S UPERSTARS EXIST OUTSIDE THE realm of time; they are frozen in their iconic moments. George Clooney always looked like
George Clooney; Audrey Hepburn will forever be standing in front of
Tiffany's. In my mind, Michael Jordan will stay the Michael Jordan of
his sixth world championship forever, even though he's now a heavyset
man in his mid-50s. It's almost like superstars, larger than life, are not
bound to the passing of time. Their hit movies, their most famous videos, and their greatest games will always define them—and I can't help
but be surprised when they grow old.

This idea works in the other direction as well. Whenever I see a
childhood picture of someone famous, I think: Oh, right, they were
born like the rest of us. They had a childhood. They used to be like us.
This thought may not be spectacular, but it is intriguing, and I believe
we are interested in these childhoods because we want to understand
when they diverged from "our" paths. And why. What characteristics,
relationships, and wounds made them the people we know today. We
want to construct a plausible story from the hypercomplex causal con-
nections in a person's biography.

Even though Dirk Nowitzki was actually 19 years old when I saw him play for the first time in 1998, he'll forever be 33 in my mind, the perfect age for an athlete—still in shape, but experienced and battle-tested, the same age he was when he won the world championship—and it's hard to imagine that he'll ever age beyond that.

I've often tried to picture where he grew up in order to make him resemble a living person: Würzburg-Heidingsfeld, a residential neighborhood in the hills southeast of the city. A house that can be found in a few pictures on the internet, that you can track down in Google Maps, unpixelated, including the backyard and the garage. It's situated alongside other single-family homes and duplexes, and there are hills and meadows in the distance, a few fields, a bus stop, a gas station, and a supermarket. The only unusual thing about the house Dirk Nowitzki's parents live in is the name of the street: Unterer Katzenbergweg—*Lower Cat Hill Drive*. Otherwise, everything else is very normal. The highway hums in the distance.

It isn't difficult to imagine growing up on this street. How you'd run down to the bus stop on a late-summer morning and up to the sledding hill in January. Dirk Nowitzki grew up in this house with his sister, Silke, and his cousins Bettina and Holger Grabow. In kids' rooms with pine beds, Sony stereos, tennis trophies, and posters of Scottie Pippen and Michael Jordan on his wall.

★ ★ ★

When Dirk Nowitzki is born in 1978, his parents, Helga and Jörg-Werner have been living in the house for a couple of years already. The Nowitzkis live on the first floor and the Grabows live in the apartment below. Dirk's father runs a painting business that he took over from his father, and the mother is in charge of the organization—the classical West German family model. The man makes his business deals at the local pub, the woman is the heart and soul of the family. Father and mother, the company's spokesperson and its almighty office manager.

Both parents are passionate athletes. His mother plays basketball,

his father team handball, and both occasionally play tennis. Their social
life revolves around sports, the city's gyms and fields. The clubhouse.
A middle-class family—not rich, but well-off and firmly rooted in the
social fabric of Würzburg.

Dirk is the youngest child; Silke is four years older. There's a cousin
in between. Dirk always tries to play with them. No matter what the
game is. Jumping rope, hide-and-go-seek, racing. Their parents take
them to their mother's basketball games and their father's handball
matches. Dirk sleeps in a baby carrier behind the bench when he is only
a couple of months old.

Later, the kids climb on the wall bars and cheer their father
on—"TGW! TGW!" They wait for halftime to start so they can put up
some shots for five magnificent minutes on the court. Whole weekends
are spent in the TGW gym situated on the bank of the river, or out on
tennis courts and running tracks, or even in the small forest nearby,
right behind the employment center. They eat french fries with mayon-
naise and drink lemonade in the clubhouse. Their parents laugh out on
the terrace, glasses clinking, mosquitoes swarming around the floodlights on summer evenings.

"Saturdays were my favorite," Dirk will tell me years later on his
patio in Dallas. "I was nine, ten, eleven, twelve. The junior games were
in the afternoon, and then my dad played—he was still on the third
team. Then came the second team, and then he played on the first team
between 7 o'clock and 7:30. We didn't leave the gym from 12 noon until
11 o'clock at night. We'd have ice cream, fries, and soda in between. We
played hide-and-seek with ten, fifteen kids in this big old equipment
room full of nooks and crannies. We laid these blue mats out on the
ground, then jumped from like ten feet up." While he tells this story,
his own children are climbing all over him, time does a somersault, the
memory glows. "Saturdays in the gym on Schiesshausstrasse," he says.
"Those were my favorite days. I'll never forget them."

The Nowitzki children decide to test the waters, and their parents let them. For the Nowitzkis, sports mean fun. Sports are everywhere, but sports aren't everything. Sports have nothing to do with money or career aspirations for them. Helga and Jörg don't project their own ambitions onto their children, but that doesn't mean the Nowitzkis don't want to win. Sports are played because it's fun to be as good as possible at something. The Nowitzkis are people who belong to team sports and clubs.

The children start to entertain their own ambitions. Silke gets into track and field at first, hurdles and long jump, but changes to basketball because she grows quickly and likes the game her mother plays. Dirk's first sport is handball, under-8, which is followed by tennis. Boris Becker wins his first Wimbledon championship in 1985 and Dirk, age seven, makes his mother cut his hair just like Boris: a layered bowl cut down to the nape of his neck, the part in the middle. He wears awful pastel-colored sweatshirts and tapered jeans. He sits in front of the TV on Sunday afternoons with his father and watches the big games of the handball team TUSEM Essen. Dirk loves Jochen Fraatz and the great backcourt player Alexander Tutschkin.

Dirk is always the tallest. He thinks he looks ridiculous: an eighth grader who can spit on his teachers' heads. His T-shirts flutter around his wiry frame, his body makes him uncomfortable. He can never find clothes to wear and he doesn't like those he does find. He never feels like he fits in. "It's incredible how thin I was back then," he will later tell me. Some of the boys in the same grade call him "Skeletor," referring to the villain from *Masters of the Universe*. Dirk doesn't think it's funny; he fakes his laughter. He isn't quick-witted enough to stick up for himself yet. "Maybe I had some complexes," he'll say, looking back. "Not consciously, but somewhere below the surface."

It is around this time that his mother takes him to the doctor to have his carpals X-rayed. The screening is fashionable at the time; many children are given vague prognoses of certain body dimensions. The pediatricians have a serious talk with his parents about hormone treatments in order to stop his growing. Arguments for it: clothes and shoes will be difficult to find; normal beds are too short as well. Dirk is predicted to grow as tall as six foot eight, which is tall, but not worth making an intervention, his parents think. "I must have been 13 or 14," he'll remember. "Six foot eight seemed huge to me."

It's clear that Dirk has a special feel for balls that fly and bounce. His service in tennis is very powerful, and it isn't due to his size alone. He instinctively anticipates the place where his opponent will return the ball. He runs to that place where the ball and waits for the ball to come. He isn't remarkably fast or flexible, but he masters the mechanics of the game. He moves at unusual angles, his routes are different from his opponents, more unconventional, more intuitive. "My parents drove me all the time, and they always supported my decisions." He'll always remain aware of his parents' role through it all. "They were my first role models," he will tell the *Athletic* in 2019. "They obviously gave me the touch and I'll always be thankful."

In handball, his size isn't a disadvantage, either. He pretends to be Tutschkin and hammers the ball over the heads of the smaller boys, but the other kids laugh about the beanpole when he plays away from home in tennis. One time, the father of an opponent insists that Dirk has a forged player card. "That boy's two years older," the father insists. "Just look how big he is." If Dirk wins, his height is an unfair advantage, but if he plays poorly, everyone just giggles about his lankiness. Or at least that's what Dirk believes. Out on the tennis court, he's all alone and the other parents all have high expectations of their kids. Tennis is the boom sport in Germany in the '80s; it's a status symbol, a projection screen for hopes of prosperity and fame. Everyone wants to be the next Boris, the next Steffi, and countless parents invest in the tennis futures of their children, paying for private lessons and expensive equipment.

Dirk wins more than he loses, but he's not happy playing tennis. He loves the game, but everything that goes with it, the ambition and intrigue, is starting to get on his nerves. The waiting between matches is exhausting, and sometimes he and his father are gone for the whole weekend. Car rides and downtime. You play, but then you stand around waiting most of the day and watch others play. All the prima donnas annoy Dirk; he's irritated by the parents' posturing, the talk, the whispers, the backbiting.

Nowitzki's father and uncle set up a basketball hoop behind the house. By now, Dirk's cousin Holger is playing for a club and Silke is on the CVJM Würzburg team. Dirk still goes to handball practice, and his father has become his coach in the meantime. Dirk likes being around the others on the team all the time; he likes that you win and lose together. A lot of joking around takes place in the locker room; it's cutting, and sometimes harsh, but always said to your face. Handball players don't whisper.

When his cousin Grabow plays basketball in the backyard with his friends, Dirk stands on the sidelines and watches. He catches the important names: Magic and Bird, Jordan and Pippen. If someone doesn't show up to play, he gets to join in and the others don't notice that he's younger than them. This is where he learns to talk trash. Dirk is 12 when Jürgen Meng, his sports teacher at the Röntgen-Gymnasium, asks him whether he'd like to join the basketball team. He's 12 and a half when he practices with DJK Würzburg for the first time. At 13, his coach, Pit Stahl, lets him play the smaller positions despite his height. Dirk is 14 when the US Dream Team wins the Olympic gold medal in Barcelona. He watches the German team, featuring Henning Harnisch and Detlef Schrempf, lose to the Americans, 111–68. He puts a Scottie Pippen poster up on his wall and imagines what it would be like to play against him. He imagines what it would be like to be Scottie Pippen.

In 1992, Dirk and the Röntgen-Gymnasium school team make it to the final round of Youth Training for Olympia, the national scholastic championships, in Berlin. He gets a running start during warm-ups and dribbles from the left side of the free throw line, leans into it, and jumps. He got used to jumping off a single leg while playing handball;

his left leg is his jumping leg. Dirk rises and flies through the air. The first dunk is a moment of initiation for every basketball player. "That was my highlight," he'll later say. "Hammering one in before the game."

At the age of 15, he's a little over six foot five. Dirk stays at home when the other teenagers go to the pool in the summer. He doesn't like taking his T-shirt off; he's ashamed of his boniness, his visible ribs, his body that is long and out of proportion. There's a new giant slide at the Dallenberg pool, the largest inner tube slide in all of Europe. "That was a real sensation, of course," he'll remember. "You had to wait in line for hours to get an inner tube and then you were shot down the slide, it was fantastic. But I never dared to go to the pool." During the summer, the other boys go every day; it's 85 degrees in the shade, but Dirk stays at home and shoots on the hoop in the yard alone.

You coming to Dalle?

Nah, I'm gonna stay here.

Are you nuts? You're coming with us.

No.

What are you going to do?

Stay here and shoot.

Dude!

He knows how to pass the time; he doesn't need much, just himself and the ball. Out in the backyard, his height isn't a problem, and it's suddenly an advantage in practice. He starts making his shots more often, and everyone else starts noticing. Suddenly, he's the best player on the school team. The sun beats down on the asphalt, the dandelions grow through the cracks at the edge of the court, and Dirk takes shot after shot after shot, shooting for hours and hours. For days, his friends say, the whole long summer. That's probably how it was.

In September 2012, I stood in front of his parents' house, waiting for Dirk Nowitzki. This was where it all started. In this very yard, the

groundwork was laid for his precision and rigor, for his concentration and ability to not get distracted. Not by Popsicles, the ten-meter
dive, the giant slide, or the next showing of *Beverly Hills Cop* featuring
Eddie Murphy at the Corso movie theater. Not by the first cigarettes
the others smoked behind the transformer station on the embank-
ment. And not by 10,000 people on the biggest basketball stages later,
by the millions of viewers in front of their screens, the expectations
and demands. "Dirk could always focus way better than anyone else,"
his teammate Marvin Willoughby will later tell me. "Better than all
the rest of us."

The noise in Texas had been immense, then there was the blinding
spotlight and fame—but what I really wanted to do was describe how
Nowitzki worked when he wasn't on the biggest stage. Geschwindner
and I had stayed in contact, and I knew they'd be doing their summer training in Rattelsdorf and Würzburg, taking their turns driving.
When I cautiously asked whether I could come, I didn't actually expect
to get an answer, but then Nowitzki texted the time and address. Be
there! We would be driving to Rattelsdorf, 45 miles to the northeast,
workout at 10:30 a.m. We'd have time to talk on the way.

I was early, so I sat on the curb, looking at the front of the house.
It seemed too easy to make the link between the larger-than-life image
of Dirk hanging from the front of the American Airlines Center and
the boy who grew up in the duplex in front of me. The story seemed
unlikely, but it interested me all the same. I walked up and down the
block. Ringing the bell was out of the question, I didn't want to intrude
on the Nowitzkis, so I waited in the morning sun. Sat down on the curb,
got up again. A neighbor rolled a trash can onto the street and made a
friendly greeting; a couple of kids were headed to school. And just as
I was getting ready to text him, the door opened and Dirk Nowitzki
came out with a sports bag over his shoulder.

"Oh, it's you," he said when he saw me. He opened the garage door.
"Let's go."

6/19/1978

Here's a story about Holger Geschwindner: on the day Dirk Nowitzki was born, it was 104 degrees in Afghanistan's Upper Panjshir Valley. It was late in the afternoon of June 19, 1978, and a narrow dirt road wound along the bare flanks of the hills, a hundred different shades of brown and red and dirt and violet. There were almost no trees to be seen, no flowers, only some scrub clinging to the rocks. On the other side of the river, the afternoon light still rested on the crest of the hills, but it was hot even in the shade of the gorge. The river was clear and blue, the rushing of the rapids the only sound.

A battered VW bus slowly bounced along the gorge. White roof, a turquoise body, and a luggage rack with a leather suitcase and spare tires on top. Munich license plate number M-VS 610, both taillights shattered. A Land Rover was holding up the rear. Dust drifted over the chasm. The bus belonged to Georg Kendl, born in 1939, an English and physical education teacher at the Amani Secondary School in Kabul. Reclining in the back seat, Geschwindner was reading aloud from Lane Fox's *Alexander the Great*, a book about Alexander's travels. The canister of drinking water gurgled; it reeked of onions and gasoline.

The travelers had been on the road for four weeks. Their route had taken them over the Bosporus and the Dardanelles, along the Biga Çayi (called the Granicus in Alexander's time), toward Issus and Gaugamela, past the Black and Caspian Seas, through Isfahan and Persepolis. Most of the time, they slept in the open air; wild dogs yapped and howled, the evening fire trembled. They ate goulash out of the can along with peppers they purchased at the village markets they drove past. They read to one another during the drive. Every evening, they unpacked a portable typewriter and hacked out the daily travel report.

The men could have hunted—they had heard rumors of wild boar, of rabbits and pheasants—but they didn't bring a gun with them this time around. The situation in Afghanistan had recently taken a turn for the worse, and because of political and religious turmoil, it wasn't totally safe; guns would have only endangered them even more. They took turns sleeping on the roof and in the bus, one up top, the other below. Sometimes they picked up other travelers, sometimes locals. Sometimes they rented horses for day trips or to recreate a couple of Alexander's battles, one-on-one. On the long stretches through the barren landscapes, they took turns behind the wheel, but Geschwindner drove most of the time. Parts of their journey were accompanied by a couple of other Germans in their Land Rover, and when its differential crapped out in the Hari River Valley, Geschwindner removed it with a screwdriver and a hammer. Then they pressed on with front-wheel drive only.

"Stop, Schorsch," Geschwindner suddenly screamed. "Stop!" Kendl hit the brakes; the bus came to a halt. The Land Rover only barely stopped in time; rocks sprayed, dust blew over the chasm. The travelers got out. Blue trickled through the rocks and cliffs below them. Was that a ford in the distance? According to the map, they'd be crossing the river today; the next village appeared to be on the other side, and the unpaved road should turn into a road of concrete slabs that would head toward Kabul after another 15 miles or so of gravel.

A wire stretched over the abyss; a rusty gondola dangled in the middle, a basket of sorts. On the other side of the ravine was a shack behind a couple of trees. Two goats ran through the bushes. Geschwindner looked at the gondola and imagined what it would be like to glide over the gorge. Ideas like that were something he liked. He enjoyed going off the beaten path. Maybe things were nicer on the other side, maybe he'd meet locals—their hospitality was renowned—maybe there'd be a good story over there. Maybe, maybe not. But he'd only know if he went.

"I'm heading over."

"You're nuts."

"They've got goats. And I'm hungry. We're nabbing that thing and we're going over."

"You're crazy. That thing's broken."

"And it's way too high. You're nuts."

"Easy," Geschwindner said and started to climb onto the rusty rack the wire was attached to, a kind of tripod bolted into the stone. He checked the wire and cogitated. Calculated. The gorge was maybe 100 feet across, 150 tops; the gondola hung maybe 30 feet above the water. The hemp rope that could have pulled it over blew lazily in the wind. He would have to climb hand over hand for 50 feet, the point of no return, and only then could he sit in the basket and pull himself to the other side. Geschwindner took off his shirt and hung it over the tripod, then took some rags and tore them into strips. He carefully wrapped the scraps around his hands, kneeled, and looked at Kendl and the others.

Georg Kendl was laconic. He wasn't one to panic; he always kept a clear head. On Mount Rinjani in Indonesia; in Afghanistan after the putsch. Decades later, he would call his friend Holger a "beast," tough as nails, flexible, buff. "It was nuts what he could physically do." But this stunt was too brave, too wild, too risky, even for Kendl. The rope whistled in the wind; the river splashed beneath them. Geschwindner didn't seem to notice. "We're not here just for fun," he said, grinned, and threw himself onto the rope with a single powerful jump.

Geschwindner was a wiry man with a checkered shirt and a kind of Afro in 1978. He was a bon vivant who had studied physics and was interested in feng shui and astrology. He was a physical specimen who loved philosophy. A cosmopolitan out of a small town near Frankfurt. He was a rebel and a teacher. He was also Germany's best basketball player. A star of a marginal sport in a country obsessed with soccer, an athlete at the peak of his career, a free spirit and infiltrator. A six-foot-three guard with springs in his legs. He was the captain of the national team at the 1972 Olympic Games in Munich, and he was the most modern and unconventional player in the Bundesliga by far.

He had a day job at the Max Planck Institute, lived in a commune, and zipped around 1970s Munich in a Porsche 911. Communes, bars, the banks of the Isar. They were wild years. The Pill had just been approved, and AIDS was as yet unknown. Geschwindner attended lectures by Carl Friedrich von Weizsäcker, read Mao, and watched Charlie Chaplin films. Lee Marvin in *Cat Ballou*. "You've got about 30,000 days to live," he will later tell me, "so why wait until you're 70 to drive a Porsche?"

It was on one of these wild and crazy nights in the bars of Munich that Georg Kendl approached him. Kendl also played basketball, but was nowhere near as successful. A mutual acquaintance had told him that Geschwindner wanted to travel in a VW bus across the Middle East, and he asked if he could join. "Sure," Geschwindner said, "we can go together." The two of them became travel companions, then friends. They could tell each other stories for hours, going off on tangents, but they could also be silent together. Neither was interested in opulence. What they had was enough.

And now Kendl was watching Geschwindner inch hand over hand toward the middle of the wire. To him, it seemed like the wire was too rusty and full of splinters, it bobbed too hard. The hot wind whistled through the gorge. One of the other travelers tested the tripod as if that would help. Geschwindner kept heading forward—20 feet, 30 feet. The chasm yawned beneath him. For Kendl's taste, there were too many rocks peeking out of the trickling current. Not enough water. You could see the rocky ground even from up here.

After 35 feet, Geschwindner noticed that the fine fibers of the rusty wire were piercing through his cloth bandages. His hands were on fire, and as he hung above the gorge with only his right arm for a second, he could see blood seeping through the white cloth on his left hand. The rope started swaying even more. He made two more pushes forward, and that's when he knew it was a bad idea to hang over the abyss. "Come back," Kendl yelled. "Come back, you idiot!"

Geschwindner was now dangling twenty-five, thirty feet above the ground, only air and water and stone beneath him. It was exhausting to hold on to the rope. His weight made it swing and the wind made it worse. The swinging couldn't be halted, the amplitude increased, the rope bit into his hands and ripped his arms and wanted to shake him off. Geschwindner made an estimation, he calculated, but the calculations he made didn't give him much of anything. The gondola was still ten feet away and the way back was farther—and now it was uphill. The rope was shaking so hard, it was totally unpredictable where he would land if he let go. By now, Geschwindner's palms were totally raw, his muscles burned, it took all his strength to just stay on the rope. He dangled and rocked and calculated, the brook rustled below, Kendl cursed, and the others held their collective breath. Geschwindner looked down, the sparse water sparkled, and his strength slowly left him.

Rattelsdorf

SEPTEMBER 11, 2012

T HE SESSION WITH GESCHWINDNER was scheduled for 10:30.
Dirk Nowitzki was so familiar with the roads from his parents'
house to the gym in Rattelsdorf that he could drive them in his sleep;
he'd been taking this route for more than half his life. "We've been
doing this for 18 years now," he said, and for the last 15, he's driven
himself. From Würzburg to Rattelsdorf, first the Autobahn 7, then the
A 70, in less than an hour if everything went well. Most of the time, a
brand new Audi with dark windows and all the frills was waiting for
him whenever he landed at the Frankfurt airport.

Nowitzki sorted through his summer. He used his knuckles to
count which month had how many days; he laughed—the memories of
the last months seemed to please him. A lot had happened since we met
in the kitchenette in Dallas. He stayed in Dallas for a while because his
girlfriend still had to work (she had been managing the Goss-Michael
Foundation's gallery for a couple of years now). "My wife," he corrected
himself and grinned; he'd have to get used to being married. He started
hitting the weight room just a week after losing to Oklahoma City. The
wedding celebration was at the beginning of July, and it was kept secret
from the tabloids. Then there was the legal ceremony in Dallas. Then

the party in the Caribbean. A commercial shoot for DiBa on Majorca. A new visa. "Watched a little Wimbledon," he says, and he doesn't mean turning on the TV. He and his wife spent a few days in London on their way to Würzburg. They visited friends and watched tennis. "The strawberries," he said. "Ridiculously expensive."

Kenya was amazing. He barely picked up his phone, which was why he only heard about the final breakup of his championship team by chance. Only when he had reception. Nowitzki paused. Sometimes bits of English slipped into his German, but he always tried to correct it: *"Empfang!"* When he had reception, he learned that his playmaker, Jason Kidd, his sidekick, Jason Terry, and his best friend, Brian Cardinal, wouldn't be back next season. He didn't seem to be all that upset about it. After 14 years in the league, he seemed to take these things in stride. When he talked about sports, Nowitzki sometimes sounded like a machine, his words like shots, practiced hundreds of times. But the summer had left its mark: Nowitzki had a tan and was rested. He drove calm and fast, the car smelled new, the route was old.

Outside the windows, fall was turning the corner. We rushed along between rows of poplars and fields of gladioli; a hint of gold lay over the hills. Dirk talked about the contemporary art at his wife's gallery, which he didn't always understand; he talked about flying, how it's like riding a bus, and about the summer's celebrations. We were silent for a while. Now would be a good time to ask my questions, I thought, but once again I let the opportunity slip away. Dirk drove and we looked ahead.

"We used to practice like the old Russians," Nowitzki said as we approached the tiny town of Rattelsdorf. Tough. Mechanical. This sentence was a standard from his repertoire for the press—I knew that, but I still wrote it down. The boy from Katzenbergweg was now a grown man, a superstar, and he had been the best basketball player in the world for a few bright moments in June 2011. This story was something they had imagined at the Nowitzkis' kitchen table years ago. All those years left traces on his face; his body had changed because that's what bodies do. Now the training was more carefully regulated, more routine, he said. Nowitzki learned his lesson after last year and he worked out the entire summer. He "ran a bit" to keep in shape. "Even when I take a break, I can't do absolutely nothing anymore." He could feel his age, he said. "It takes a toll."

Nowitzki turned right after the city-limit sign and parked the car in front of a gym that looked like every other gym in Germany. The parking lot was almost empty this morning, just a couple of bikes, a solitary car. A woman with a dog and a cigarette nodded at us with the customary courtesy of a villager. No cameras, no one. "I didn't have a ball in my hands for almost three months this summer," Nowitzki said, taking a threadbare leather basketball from the trunk. "This thing's 11 years old. Holger and I have been using it every summer since 2001."

Geschwindner was already there when we stepped on the court. Gray synthetic flooring, no hardwood. He was coaching a couple of 12- and 13-year-olds; two fathers were watching. The boys were doing the same pirouettes and sidesteps, whipping the ball around their bodies the way Nowitzki did in the empty arena in Dallas. It looked like stumbling from some of the boys; from others, it was a choreographed dance. "Wrap," Geschwindner cried, "inside pivot," all vocabulary from the language he and Nowitzki had been speaking for years. The boys were doing their best to ignore Nowitzki, who was tying his shoes. But the gym fell silent when he stepped on the court with his spindly gait and started shooting. The boys watched him, and you could see their minds racing. I wrote the word *reverent* down. We watched the rehearsed movements and gestures and understood their mutual story.

Nowitzki shot and shot and made his first 21 attempts. The gym counted along; we were witnesses. Geschwindner and Nowitzki had gone through these steps and drills so many times over the last years and decades that hardly any words were necessary. A racehorse and its trainer. Dirk shot, Holger passed, Holger nodded, Dirk understood. We were observing a ritual; the sound of the ancient basketball was a mantra—*swish, swish, swish,* over and over. Dirk became faster and faster, jumped higher, hit better. The concentration filled the gym, the boys, the fathers, the janitor and me.

Up close, you could tell just how broad Nowitzki's shoulders really were, how wiry and angular and fit his body. He was only three years younger than me, but what appeared to be lanky from a distance or on a screen was like a painting upon closer inspection. Every muscle and tendon was visible. I started to miss the game deep in my bones while I watched Nowitzki. The feeling of practiced movements, the speed, the curves, the angles, the shots, the noises. I decided to take up basketball again.

After a two-hour workout, Nowitzki got down on the ground and the two men did a few dozen push-ups on their fingertips. Then Geschwindner started stretching and adjusting Nowitzki. It was totally silent in the gym; the only thing you could hear was the sound of shoes squeaking on the linoleum and Nowitzki's rhythmic panting . . . *pfft, kchrr* . . . again and again, his leg above his head . . . *pffft, kchrr.* While Geschwindner mauled him, he observed the emptiness in his mind as well as the discomfort in his muscles. Geschwindner stretched and bent him. Nowitzki moaned and groaned.

Nowitzki turned onto his stomach and put his hands under his chin. Geschwindner adjusted Dirk's spine with his thumbs, working his way up, vertebra after vertebra. It popped loudly. Then Geschwindner took off his shoes and walked up and down Nowitzki's back in colorful, self-knitted socks. When Geschwindner got off, Nowitzki turned around. "Oh God," he said. "No wonder I'm a total wreck." He got up, picked his T-shirts and towels up from the ground, and rolled the ball toward me. "Write that," he said, leaving. "I'm a wreck."

After Geschwindner and Nowitzki hit the showers, and after the fathers and sons said farewell and the janitor opened the windows, I stood alone under the basket. I was holding Nowitzki's ancient ball in my hands. Empty gyms are cathedrals of possibility. The sun was shining at an angle on the linoleum, the dust was dancing in the air. I walked to the free throw line, dribbled three times, rotated the ball in my hands, and bent my knees. My 25-year-old ritual: the game was tied, there were only a few seconds left on the clock, I breathed out, I breathed in, I looked at the back of the rim. And shot.

Their Mutual Story

THE FIRST TIME GESCHWINDNER and Nowitzki meet is around
1993. In a multipurpose gym like any other in Germany: linoleum
and pinewood, sideline ads for regional sponsors—ready-mix concrete,
savings banks, beverage wholesalers. Dirk's been playing for a club for
a couple of months now. He played for his high school team first, and
soon joined DJK Würzburg's under-16 team. Sometimes, he practices
with the men's first team. He's also been selected to play for the state
of Bavaria. He's good because he's different. His coach, Pit Stahl, lets
him play on the wing because he's a walking mismatch. If a defender is
anywhere near as tall as him, Dirk can run laps around them. And he
shoots over the shorter and quicker players without any hesitation. He
is evidence of a rift in the philosophy of the game; Nowitzki is a paradigm shift. But it's not as if anyone is saying it at the time.

In those years, Holger Geschwindner only played basketball as a
hobby. After his stretch in Munich, he played professionally in Australia, Bamberg, Göttingen, and Cologne. But he had always kept a
day job—at the Max Planck Institute, the electronics chain Saturn,
or the cable car manufacturer Doppelmayr. For a couple of months,
he even ran a giant pecan farm in Mississippi (and, like many other

Geschwindner stories, this one includes wild details, including the illegal sale of machinery, fraudulent fertilizers, and hairy situations with handguns). His career in the Bundesliga just ended a few years ago. Now he is 49 years old, living in a rundown castle in Bavaria and playing for the DJK Eggolsheim regional team. He's a player/coach, and everyone else on the team is half his age.

Nowitzki is 16 when they meet. He has long since grown past the six-foot-eight mark he was projected to reach. But he doesn't stand out now that there are all these other tall boys. He's really enjoying himself with the other basketball players. And what's more, he starts forgetting about himself and starts thinking about the game. His inhibition has turned into focus. Where he used to have doubts about his body, he now regards it as a tool—a weapon, even. He's been playing with the Bavarian state team for a couple of months and he's the best shooter and rebounder on Würzburg's under-16 team. His defenders have never seen anything like him. Neither have their coaches.

One Sunday afternoon in April, Geschwindner is playing with his team against Schweinfurt. It's an away game. There's a youth match going on when he enters the gym. Geschwindner is as astonished as everyone else. A kid who is as thin as a rail isn't running around confused like all the other 15-year-olds. Unlike them, he doesn't focus on the ball the whole time. The game is like water for him, a break in the surf; the waves push him here and pull him there. Everyone else paddles and pants, but he lets the game flow by for a few seconds. It's like he's the only one with solid ground beneath his feet. The others scurry around, and then the kid is suddenly standing exactly where he should be. When he takes a shot, you can't tell where his favorite spot on the court is. The kid shoots from all over the place. And whenever he misses, Geschwindner can immediately see why.

He's got an eye for such things. If he looks at a bare mountain, the rugged cliffs, the ravines and slopes, he can see the cable car that will lead to the summit. If he glances at an electronics shop, he envisions an electronics chain. He thinks in hypotheses. In hypotheticals. Could be, should be, will be. He sees a solution where everyone else fears a dilemma. Whenever he looks at things, he sees what they will become.

Geschwindner grabs his leather bag and walks over to the bench where the kid is sitting, drinking soda. Maybe he remembers the day when he himself was discovered; maybe he imagines on this Sunday afternoon what it would take to make this lanky kid be the best basketball player in the world.

"Hey," he says. "Number 14."

Dirk looks up.

"What's your name?"

"Dirk," Dirk says. "Nowitzki."

Geschwindner sets his bag down behind the bench and sits next to the kid. He holds out his hand. Dirk looks at him. He doesn't totally understand. Who is this guy in sports clothes who's as old as his father? He's wiry and broad, but there's gray hair on his temples. Is he the coach? A player? It looks like he's in good shape. The guy fishes a ball out from under the bench and whips it over the court to the Eggolsheim players. It could very well be that House of Pain's "Jump Around" is blasting out of the gym's stereo—it's playing in all the other German gyms at the time. Years later, neither of them will remember what precisely happens next. The teams warm up. The guy gets up. "You know how to do things that can't be taught," he says. Dirk is confused by the guy's accent. "Who's your teacher?"

"My coaches," Dirk answers. He looks at the guy. Who else should be teaching him? Right now, he's practicing with three different teams: the under-16, the first men's team, and the school team. He pays close attention to what's happening on all of them, and he tries to implement new things in his game when he sees them. He feels like he's learning, like he's getting better.

"Do you have someone teaching you the tools of the trade?" the man asks. "Someone who's properly training you?"

Dirk shakes his head. "Think about it," Holger Geschwindner says. "You need to learn this."

He ties his shoes, stands up, and steps on the court—layup line!—gets the ball and lays it up high off the board and into the net, then walks to the half-court line, turns around, grabs a rebound, and passes. Dirk sits on the bench and watches the old dude: he moves like a young man; you can see that his body knows how the game is played straight away. The next time in the layup line, a soft floater falls. Next time, he pivots and shoots out of the spin. Next time—no joke—he dunks. Dirk is shocked. Who *is* this grandpa?

"I'll see you soon," Geschwindner says, running by Dirk again. "And then we can talk."

Dirk doesn't say all that much at home. He forgets the old guy's name, but mentions at breakfast the next morning that someone in Schweinfurt talked to him about becoming his trainer. "Private workouts," he says. He's aware that this isn't a standard practice in German basketball. Helga and Jörg don't give it much thought—it's hectic and Dirk needs to get to school—but they decide to go to the TGW gym next weekend to see Eggolsheim play. Later, he won't be able to recall this conversation, either. "It's 25 years ago," he'll say. "But I guess that's what happened."

When they arrive at the Feggrube gym a week later, the game has already started. The Nowitzki family sits in the stands. Eggolsheim is down, but then one player seizes control, takes over: the old guy from last week hits basket after basket against his much younger opponents, bringing his team within striking distance, and then finally rallies them into taking the lead. "That's him," Dirk says to his father and points at the old guy. He suddenly remembers his name: Holger.

Geschwindner rings a bell for Nowitzki's mother: they belong to the same generation of athletes. Helga Nowitzki is only two years older. She's stunned that Geschwindner is now a coach; she didn't have a clue. She's surprised by his interest in Dirk. "Dirk said you want to train with him?" she says.

When the game is over, Geschwindner explains his plan to Dirk's parents. He offers to drive to Würzburg twice a week—it's not all that far from Bamberg and he often passes through the city on his way to Frankfurt anyway. He wants to work with Dirk twice a week, no commitment, a trial of sorts. Dirk wants to give it a shot. Let's shake on it, Jörg Nowitzki says, we'll give it a go. Helga Nowitzki is pleased with the idea.

The next weeks establish the foundation for everything that will come later. It's a crash course in the game's philosophy, a systematic tabula rasa for training. The two of them work out during the day and Geschwindner sits at his desk at night in his castle, constructing a coherent teaching concept, a plan, from everything he's witnessed and experienced.

Geschwindner jots down everything he thinks he knows about basketball. About life. He knows that the kid has to have ambition, that it has to come from the kid alone and no one else. He makes the assumption that what was good for him will also be good for the boy. He has worked with a number of coaches and has often been left desiring something else, something more. He doesn't want to be didactic, not a disciplinarian or someone who insists on the rules. The only rules he adheres to are the laws of nature, physics, mathematical formulas, and the official rules of basketball. Everything else is up for grabs. Geschwindner aims for the highest level of accuracy and absolute freedom. He wants to pay attention to the smallest detail while also looking at the big picture. He doesn't want to reinvent the game, he wants to widen its scope. The horizon of possibilities.

He's never seen a player like Dirk Nowitzki. The kid has all the physical and mechanical tools to become one of the greatest of all time. He can hardly believe what he's seeing after the first few sessions. No matter what he throws at Dirk, the kid immediately integrates it into his game. Mechanical tips, methodical alterations. When Geschwindner talks about him, he starts saying "the boy" in dialect: "*der Bub.*" They start drawing up fictional game situations, and Dirk responds to the scenarios in real time. It's a form of improvisational theater. He can grasp the game in abstract terms as well as tangible ones.

"We're down by four, nine seconds left?"

"Quick three, foul immediately."

"We're up one, 17 seconds left?"

"Hide the ball, make the free throws."

"One hundred and fifteen seconds to go, up 12, we have the ball, how many possessions are left?"

Geschwindner writes page after page in those days, he formulates his plans and ideas, puts them in envelopes, and then seals them. He inscribes the dates on the front, as well as when they are to be opened. They're secret messages, time capsules, letters to his future self. He wants to examine what will become of his ideas and he doesn't want to fool himself. His ideas should remain incorruptible.

Geschwindner takes the boy's measurements, then sits down at his desk in the evening to calculate the ideal shot. The length of his arms, the size of his feet, thighs, lower legs, the point of release at full height, the angle of entry. How high can he jump? How should he square his elbow?

After three months he's convinced that Dirk is unique. "I could tell that he would become one of the absolute greatest ever," he'll later say when he opens one of his envelopes. "The talent was there; the physical conditions were special. The only open question was whether he would receive the proper education. Or whether conventions would eclipse us."

Geschwindner lets the Nowitzkis know that he absolutely needs to speak to them. He sits down in the kitchen on Katzenbergweg and asks how they picture Dirk's future. What do they both think? How good can he be? They've been told that Dirk could be one of the best players in the Bundesliga, but Geschwindner has already been thinking in other categories for a while.

"You have no idea what you've got on your hands," he says, "right?"

"We know Dirk will be a good player."

"Right," Geschwindner says. He puts his coffee cup down. "If Dirk wants to become the best player in Germany, we can stop training immediately." Geschwindner looks at the Nowitzkis. What he's about to say sounds like megalomania. "If he wants to mess with the best in the world, then we'll have to train every day."

To mess with the best in the world.

Dirk needs to make a decision, and he does. They start training three times a week, and then every day. Dirk's game develops rapidly. Geschwindner's methods are unconventional: he has Dirk walk on his hands in the gym, jump up and down from boxes, wear a lead vest while practicing shooting. They shoot and shoot and shoot, sometimes for two hours at a time. In the world of German basketball, individual components are usually developed separately: strength, stamina, speed, tactics. But Geschwindner and Nowitzki pack it all into a single go. It saves time, and every movement is specific to a game situation, every moment involves various aspects. Practicing shooting is practicing stamina is practicing strength is playing.

These two improbable companions talk about things that have nothing to do with practice. But they can also be silent when they drive together. They become friends even though they're from different generations. They read novels and ask themselves moral questions whenever problems arise. *Jamila* by Chinghiz Aitmatov. *Typhoon* by Joseph Conrad, and *Heart of Darkness*. What do you do when your ship approaches a storm? What do you do when the girl of your dreams is promised to someone else? How do you react when you're down by four and there are only seven seconds on the clock, but you've got the ball? They think up scenarios and practice reacting to them in these imaginary worlds. Dirk learns to calculate what you need to do to have the last shot in the game. The two of them are alone in the gym and they're acting out big, decisive moments many years before these moments actually happen.

Europcar

CAN'T REMEMBER WHAT WE talked about on the drive back. I remember the fields outside and the smell of the brand-new car. I remember Nowitzki stopping at a gas station just outside of Würzburg. He knew every corner here, something that seemed remarkable to me. A global superstar was supposed to get lost in the provinces. Or, if he didn't get lost, he'd have to make some speech about the importance of every park bench and every greasy spoon to the development of his career—here's my elementary school, here's where it all began! But Nowitzki didn't describe a single thing, didn't point anything out; he just got off the highway and stopped at the Aral gas station. A couple of cars were at the pumps; three construction workers were leaning on a high table, drinking coffee outside.

"When's your train?"

"At three," I said. "But I can take the next one, at five, too."

"Great," Nowitzki said. He fished two 50-euro notes out of his pocket. "Can you do it?"

"Fill it up?" I asked. "Super unleaded?"

"And pay." He looked for the gas tank button; it was his first time at the gas station with this car. "You'll never make it to the train station if I get out."

Nowitzki stayed in the car while I puttered around at the pump and paid. When I came back to the car, I saw the flip side of success. I could have gone over to the construction workers and we could have talked about the weather or soccer. Nowitzki had to take the time of day into consideration when he wanted to fill up his tank. Would the place be empty enough? I was free; Nowitzki had to strategize about these things and then wait behind darkened windows until the coast was clear.

We left, and I didn't take any notes. I'd seen enough. Nowitzki seemed candid. I remember him laughing about the newspaper reports that he didn't know how to use an ATM, a story that cropped up every summer in Germany. The rumor was that his mother still gave him pocket money. He was asked about this whenever he came to Germany, even by me. "Yeah, sure," he said every time. "My mom gives me pocket money."

We journalists took this to be part of his personality, but for him it was a running gag, a joke he kept to himself. Just like the thing with David Hasselhoff's song "Looking for Freedom," which he allegedly hummed while taking decisive free throws in front of 20,000 booing fans. A myth that started as a stupid joke in the 2006 playoffs against San Antonio took on a life of its own as a meme. Such stories floated around Nowitzki, obscuring what was really important to him and what he actually achieved. They provided the calm he needed to do what he did properly.

Nowitzki parked next to a car rental agency near the Würzburg train station. He stayed in the car so no one would recognize him. A woman working at the agency, dressed in bright green, inconspicuously looked through the windshield. Her look asked, "Is that who I think it is?" My list of questions was still in my pocket. I promised to send Dirk the text of my article when it was finished, and Nowitzki nodded. "It's fine," he said. My story would only be another distraction.

The woman in the Europcar agency talked on the phone without ever taking her eyes off us. She nodded. "They're coming," Nowitzki said. He nodded in her direction; I opened the door and got out. "*Hau nei*," he said. "Take it easy." I grabbed my bag out of the trunk; the basketball and a couple of water bottles rolled around.

Whenever people wrote or talked about Dirk Nowitzki, the term that was almost universally used was "down to earth." In its standard usage, it has a slight undertone that he's a simpleton, a big child lost in the wide world. But that was wrong, I thought outside the Würzburg train station. Nowitzki made a much more mature impression than I expected. Wise in a worldly way. Less naïve, more straightforward and focused. He seemed to be very aware of his superstardom. He knew he was different from everyone else—but he didn't let us in on it, he kept it to himself. Nowitzki was friendly and attentive, but he came off as cautious whenever he talked about himself. He retreated to formulaic sentences and stories, well-trodden realms of language.

The door made an expensive sound when it closed, the engine hummed softly, the car backed up. Nowitzki raised his hand, I raised mine; we'd probably never see each other again. I stood next to my bag on the street and was surprisingly touched. It smelled like pretzels and train-station pizza. The car with the basketball in the trunk drove off. There went the best basketball player I'd ever met and ever would.

The car rental woman stepped out of her office and watched the car drive away. She checked me out from head to toe. "That A8 over there," she said. "Was that this Nowitzki guy?"

Dirk Nowitzki had everything that lulls other players to sleep. To taking it easy, stagnating, quitting: money, fame, awards. Interviews, portraits, interviews. "I've never cared about that stuff," he had said on the drive. "I always wanted to be a basketball player, nothing more, nothing less." You believed him if you watched him practice. You'd believe in focus, the power of normality and humility. The simple truth about Dirk Nowitzki was in the trunk of his car: that ancient basketball, dribbled and shot millions of times, almost black from sweat and gym dust. If you held that ball in your hands, it became clear why Dirk Nowitzki was such an unbelievably good basketball player. The boys in the gym wanted to become like him, and he wanted to stay like them.

Puttin' on the Ritz

A FTER MY STORY ABOUT Dirk was published (the title: "A League of His Own"), I went back to the novel I had been working on, a book about an old man who reminisces about his life the night before his left lower leg is amputated. He reminisces about all the things he did with the leg, who he ran away from, who he kicked, who he danced with. The book would be the story of an alert mind in an aging body; it would be about the passage of time, the struggles with this reality, and the final acceptance of one's own fading. There'd only be one very brief scene in my book about basketball. It would take place in my hometown in 1974; the great Jimmy Wilkins would make an appearance, and maybe Holger Geschwindner would as well.

I never heard back from Nowitzki. I had put the magazine in an envelope and sent it to the Mavericks. Maybe it reached him, maybe it didn't. I knew he never actually read profiles about him, that he'd developed a thick skin against media reports. He never watched himself on TV, never googled himself, ignored headlines. There were dozens of game reports, analyses, interviews, and observations after every game. It was too much. The stories repeated all the time, and mine would be no exception. I had always wanted to write about Dirk Nowitzki, and now I had—and that was that.

I had portrayed Nowitzki as a man living in different worlds, a man who moved confidently in all of them. The way he changed from one to the other still kept me wondering. I described him as a public person who found a way to protect his private sphere, a way to stay centered and focused on his work, despite the fame, success, pressure, and expectations from others. He was aware that people cared about him, and he met this interest with respect and with well-chosen and rehearsed words.

He had seemed approachable, almost curious, and yet there was a part of him that couldn't be accessed. It was as if Nowitzki didn't want to betray himself, although he was constantly being asked to do so by people like yours truly. We were asking for explanations, revelations, confessions. I had noted his restraint, a form of well-trained prudence. "As a human being 'communicates himself,' he gets rid of himself," Geschwindner quoted Nietzsche again and again, "and when one has 'confessed,' one forgets," and I refrained from writing about it.

I had met someone who lived in a glass house for pragmatic and rational reasons; all could see, but were forbidden to touch. "What a zoo!" Nowitzki had said in the Mavericks' kitchenette, and this image seemed fitting. "What a circus!" This thought stuck with me: Dirk Nowitzki knew he was being observed, but he refused to yield to the demands and expectations of those who were observing him. He kept to himself.

★　　　★　　　★

September came and I still caught myself clipping out articles about Nowitzki and sticking them on my studio wall instead of doing research for my next novel.

"Is that going to turn into a book?" my wife asked and laughed. "*The Great Nowitzki?*"

"No way," I said, not really believing myself. My wife would have crumpled up the clippings had she known how much I would talk about basketball and Dirk in the coming years, how much time I would spend in Dallas and wherever else.

In October, I received an invitation to a gala evening in honor of Nowitzki. He was to be presented with the AmCham Transatlantic Partnership Award in Berlin, not for his athletic achievements but for his social engagement and his work as a transatlantic ambassador. It would take place the night before the Dallas Mavericks' exhibition game against Alba Berlin. I had planned to go to the game anyway, and maybe there'd be an opportunity to exchange a few words with Nowitzki beforehand. I accepted the invitation.

My wife laughed when I put on my suit. "*The Great Nowitzki?*"

When I arrived, the Ritz-Carlton on Potsdamer Platz looked like a drawing. Nineteen floors of faux art deco bling from the early 2000s, an entrance made for carriages, fur collars, and top hats. If ever they had traveled to Berlin, F. Scott Fitzgerald and his wife, Zelda, would have bathed in the fountain (had there been one). One would expect to find tuxedos and sequined dresses there, bobs and old-fashioneds, but not basketball players.

The ballroom had been prepared for around 100 carefully selected guests at round tables; an army of liveried waiters whirred around us and poured too much champagne too quickly. Thick carpets, smooth marble, a huge chandelier. Music played softly, heels clacked loudly. I had hardly met anyone in person, but many celebrities and politicians were present, along with musicians and actors, family and friends.

The game against Berlin was an important event—economically and culturally. The NBA sends a few of its teams on promotional tours around the world in the preseason. It was a question of prestige and of opening up new markets. The European teams they played against were already deep into their seasons and the Americans were just getting started. It made sense that the Mavericks had been sent to Germany a year after the championship—14,500 spectators would want to see the game tomorrow. But now we were waiting.

When Dirk Nowitzki finally entered the hotel in a bow tie and tuxedo with an entourage of serious-looking suits, all faces turned toward him like flowers to the sun. Flashes, cameramen, Dirk here—"Dirk, please!"—Dirk there. Nowitzki and his wife, Jessica, slowly worked their way through the lobby and up the stairs and sat down at their table for dinner.

The unavoidable happened between the appetizer and meat course. A man in a tuxedo cautiously approached the table, lingered, acted like he wasn't doing anything, and, when no one was stopping him, got over his hesitation and seized the opportunity. He leaned over Dirk, who was chewing. "I don't want to disturb you," the man said, "but my son would love . . ." Nowitzki looked up, put down his knife and fork, and signed. He nodded, then took another bite. But the dam was broken. The selfie line started wrapping around the table. Business leaders lined up with their sons, sports people, politicians, artists, waiters, waitresses, radio hosts. Everyone wanted a picture, a signature, a souvenir. Dirk Nowitzki couldn't even eat in peace in the company of invited guests.

I looked at everyone's faces: children sat rooted to their chairs, starstruck, enthralled. I saw Wolf Lepenies and a couple of the Mavericks players, coach Rick Carlisle, and Mark Cuban, the owner of the team. Dirk's sponsors. Dirk's friends. Dirk's family was there, his sister, Silke, and his parents, who were noticeably proud of him. Illustrious company. Nowitzki's wife, Jessica, was beaming; the room revolved around her and it seemed to me that the spotlight searched for her and not the other way around. I saw the journalists, the sports officials, the transatlanticists. The official representatives of the NBA.

Dirk Nowitzki represented something different to each and every one of them. He was their promotional figure, their friend, their brother, their life insurance, their role model, and their promise. He

was the face of the league at the time, its new hope. He was an ambassador for Germans as well as for Americans; he was a symbol of America's openness to foreigners. Others saw him as a business opportunity.
A way out. A glimmer of hope. For me, he was the realization of an old
dream, a kind of surrogate for a life that I and all the other basketball
players I knew were never able to live. When Dirk got up and hobbled
onstage to receive his award, I realized just how many different concep-
tions were projected on the man as if he were a screen.

His speech was touching, if a little awkward, but I understood why
the entire ballroom loved him. Still, he seemed to retain an untouch-
able and unattainable core. Something Lepenies had called "sincerity"
and others called "down to earth." Something basketball fans used to
heatedly discuss, something they tried to grasp in numbers and words.
Dirty. Wunderkind. GOAT.

As I watched Nowitzki leave the stage and struggle to get back to
his seat through the noise and hopes and expectations, I wondered
whether this core was something that could be described. If it would
be possible to get close enough to understand how the Nowitzki system functions. Whether I'd have to talk to all these satellites orbiting
around him. What was it like to be Dirk Nowitzki? What could be said
about someone who had realized their dreams, who seemed to really
love what they were doing? And who was damn good at it. You don't
often meet people who are so ardently and fundamentally devoted to
one thing. Who master their craft. Maybe that's what fascinated me
about Dirk Nowitzki. I looked around. All of these people had countless stories about Nowitzki; everyone in the ballroom had their own
memories and moments. Geschwindner had his, Lepenies had others.
The musicians, the cabdrivers, the teammates—they all had their own
subjective connection to Nowitzki, big stories and small anecdotes. I
had mine (and to me, it looked like a book).

The guest of honor disappeared as quickly as he had come. Tomorrow was game day. The ballroom stood up again and applauded while

the Nowitzkis left. Dirk briefly teetered by our table, briefly looked at me—or at least I think he did. I raised my hand, he gave me a thumbs-up. Then he was gone.

The game the next evening would be the anticipated spectacle. The arena would be sold out, the Mavericks would barely win. Dirk would limp across the court and only score nine points, but both camps would cheer him on. He would tweak his knee, but force himself to stay in the game because it was important to him to play in front of his friends and family. In the third quarter, he'd miss a wide-open layup, and everyone would smirk. The Mavericks would move on to Barcelona the day after, but Nowitzki wouldn't play anymore. His knee would become a serious problem, and this problem would cost him the first 27 games of the 2012/13 season. People would occasionally start talking about his age, the challenges of a long career, and his battered body. They would talk about Dirk Nowitzki with an undertone of everything already being over.

People would expect the end—but wouldn't say it.

2

THE PATH

"Basketball is free—like jazz.
You can't plan a solo, you have to play it."

—ERNEST BUTLER

Jetstream

SEPTEMBER 2014

K RENZ AND I ARE too early. The landing strip of the former Giebelstadt Army Airfield is stretched out in the late summer. An elderly gentleman is sweeping the parking lot in front of the small office building. There's a Cessna Citation Sovereign waiting on the tarmac, a jet for a dozen passengers, plus crew. The pilot's leaning on the gangway, smoking; the flight attendant is dumping sewage next to the runway.

We're here today to fly to Slovenia, to Ljubljana, a direct flight right over the Alps from Giebelstadt. Dirk Nowitzki's main sponsor has chartered the plane to cut down on costs and time—Nowitzki's contract specifies the number of days he must be available to work for them, and travel days are wasted days. Over the next three days, he will film four commercials and appear in photo shoots for their print and online campaigns, hence the jet from Giebelstadt rather than a commercial flight from Frankfurt.

Florian Krenz is in charge of organizing the day, and he's the one who booked the plane. He's been working in ING-DiBa's corporate communications department for a couple of years now. He's in his late twenties but looks like he's in his late thirties, a six-foot-seven, 265-pound giant who is extremely alert and mobile. He started as a student trainee, but then organized the massive championship cele-bration in Würzburg, 10,000 people losing their minds in the June heat. Ever since, he's been running the show when Dirk is in Ger-many. Krenz likes things like air travel, press conferences, and mass gatherings. He always has a water bottle in his hands—no one drinks as much water as Krenz.

Inside the barracks, they're finishing up the paperwork, the flight clearance and landing rights, and we're standing around on the empty tarmac, chatting. After the gala in Berlin, I ordered a drink at the bar and got into a conversation with Krenz and his boss, Uli Ott. We got along, and now I was here to watch the filming of the commercials. The work that went into producing Dirk's image.

Dirk Nowitzki has a very small inner circle. There's his family and Geschwindner, as well as a couple of old friends, teammates, and the people overseeing the organizational work around him—the press stuff and accounting, logistics and security, people who take care of the lawn and the children. Beyond this close circle, there are a couple dozen oth-ers whom he interacts with professionally: his charity coordinators, the same journalists over and over, and . . . his advertising partners. That I am allowed to fly with them today was a stroke of luck; a seat just hap-pened to be free.

After some minutes, a few cars roll into the parking lot. Father Nowitzki is delivering his son. Mind you, Dirk's the one driving, since he wants to drive his dad's car whenever he's in Germany; it's one of those father-son things. Holger Geschwindner parks right next to them, and a handful of staff from the bank's advertising department arrive in a taxi at the last minute. Before we leave, Nowitzki takes the time to shake hands with all the guys in the barracks. We walk across the runway, then comes another group photo with the pilot and stew-ardess before the Citation dashes over the Alps toward Ljubljana.

★   ★   ★

Nowitzki and Geschwindner, and Krenz and I, are sitting in cream-colored leather seats. There's Bavaria and then Austria below us, and Falco's "Jeannie" and David Hasselhoff's "Looking for Freedom" are quietly droning from the speakers—and I swear I'm not making this up. The flight attendant peels back a plastic wrap from a fish platter—salmon and trout or something. She pops open a bottle of Veuve Clicquot Rosé, the cork flying through the plane. Krenz and I take a glass—sure, why not?—and grin as we stare out the window. We're only used to flying coach (I usually take the train), but Nowitzki shakes his head and sticks with water and the vegetable garnish. It's September, and his preparations for the season have already started, including a strict diet. This year, Dirk's only eating what can be hunted and gathered: meat and berries, nuts and vegetables—the so-called Paleo diet. He doesn't touch processed foods—or rosé, for that matter—and while we're eating, Dirk reads the storyboards of the commercials that are going to be filmed so that he can see how much text he has. I make a note: "Dirk Nowitzki pays attention to his diet on private airplanes, too."

While Krenz and I raise our glasses in ignorant celebration, Nowitzki sits in the Cessna as if it's a commuter train, working through the shooting schedules for the next couple of days. He laughs at the scripted jokes and tries the different faces he will put on in the days to come. Having a chat is out of the question; we're sitting in rows in the narrow jet, and Nowitzki and Geschwindner have a table for four to themselves. I observe the faces they make, hear their conversation, watch them leaf through the pages and confabulate. Sometimes, Nowitzki glances out the window and stares down at the alpine peaks and valleys for a few minutes. As a child, he went skiing somewhere down there with his parents and his sister, but that was decades ago. The NBA forbids its players from skiing.

At the airport, a mirrored van transports us directly from the gangway to the location. Time is money. We're introduced to Aleš on the way; he'll be the chaperone taking care of Dirk in the coming days. There's always someone taking care of stars on such occasions, and that someone should be familiar with the place and be able to solve any imaginable problem. Aleš knows every restaurant and shortcut in the city, and he can get his hands on everything. All of the important numbers in Ljubljana are on his phone. He also has a head of monstrous curls, which Dirk starts making fun of instantly. "You look like a young Holger," he says, "Afro and all," but Aleš doesn't know Holger's story yet.

At the shooting location on a quiet side street in Ljubljana's center, a 60-person film crew awaits us. The spotlights are already glaring through the window of a toy store that, in the commercial, will look like a toy store in Berlin or Frankfurt or Munich. Nowitzki greets the director, the director's assistants, the ad men, the lighting technicians, makeup and sound crews. He shakes everyone's hand; he recognizes a couple of them from last time. Everyone calls him Dirk. He exchanges his T-shirt for another in the costume department, then gets powdered and combed—but that's it. He doesn't need anything else. He's playing himself.

The commercial is a sketch: A mother enters the toy store with her child. The boy desperately wants a bright red Big Bobby toy car, but it's too expensive for his mother. The car is on the highest shelf, and she acts like she can't reach it. The matter seems to be settled, but then Nowitzki comes around the corner when she's not paying attention. Happy to help, he takes the toy down from the highest shelf for the child. Easy for a guy his size. The mother is upset and berates a confused Nowitzki, the helpful goof, who is now holding a little toy pig. "Nice pig," she sneers, and Nowitzki makes an astonished face, just the way he practiced it on the plane. "If you want your dream car without hassle," a voice will later say, "then it's gotta be diba-diba-duuu." The advertised product is a car loan.

I'm standing to the side, watching Nowitzki take the toy car off the shelf repeatedly. The actress repeatedly berates him, and the team laugh their heads off at every take. "Look how he's holding that stuffed animal," one of the cable pullers says on the edge of the set. "Not like he's got kids."

"He does," one of the lightning technicians says. "A daughter."

"How old?"

"Not sure," the lighting technician says, then asks about her name and age during the next break. "Malaika," Dirk says. "A year old."

"Nice name," the light guy says, as if he's talking to an old friend. "Congratulations, my man!"

Nowitzki has been working with the bank for almost 15 years, which is a ridiculous amount of time in the advertising world. It's rare for a spokesperson and their company to grow up together. Apart from Nike, the sports equipment company Bauerfeind, and ING, Nowitzki has no other partners. There are no yogurt companies or energy drinks or cars or airlines. Not even watchmakers, although he once flirted with the idea. He likes watches, they're basically the only luxury item he cares about, but then he realized he'd always be stuck with the watches from "his brand" after signing an advertising contract. "Sense of freedom," he says. "It's important to maintain a sense of freedom."

When he filmed the first commercials in 2003, Nowitzki was known, but far from the level of superstardom he would reach after the world championship in 2011. Private use of the internet was still in its infancy and smartphones didn't exist yet. DiBa was a midsize online bank trying to compete in the market. So, they started with the analogy between great interest rates and athletic greatness. The commercials dynamically filmed an athlete in action with interest rates flying around them—"3.75%," "4.25%," and so on. That was 2003—a very long time ago.

Since then, Nowitzki has led the German national team to medals in the World Cup and European Cup and he has won the NBA championship with the Dallas Mavericks in 2011. According to the market research firm Nielsen, that success story made him the "most marketable man in the NBA." Ahead of Kobe Bryant, LeBron James, and

Dwyane Wade. Right now, in 2014, he's still the most famous German athlete in the world.

Dirk Nowitzki has a rather abstract relationship to money. It isn't likely that he has a bank account at DiBa. He made his first million in his first year in the NBA, and he steadily earned more—going up to around $22,721,381 for the 2013–14 season. At some point, he turned down a lot of money so that his team could stay below the salary cap and invest in other high-profile players, but he is said to have earned more than $250 million from his playing contracts alone (an estimate says that he chose to forgo another $194 million).

Nowitzki is sometimes amazed to be "getting so much money to pursue a hobby." But star players like him aren't actually paid for putting the ball in the hole. They're the faces of a system that grosses large sums. Arenas are filled, jerseys are sold, soft drinks are poured. Superstars support an entire fiscal system. They create jobs and careers. "We're all sitting at Dirk's table," the journalist Jeff "Skin" Wade once explained. "We're all eating from his plate."

Holger Geschwindner subscribes to a theory that you need around $70,000 a year to be happy in the Western world. If you have less money, then you're busy with what you're unable to afford. But if you have more money, you're busy with what you should do with it. With $70,000, you can do whatever you want as a private person. But a basketball star like Dirk Nowitzki obviously isn't merely a private person, he's also a midsize enterprise. Which means higher expenses, of course: home security, flights, administrative and organizational costs. Nevertheless, Dirk has only spent an estimated 10 percent of his income. He doesn't have an entourage sponging off of him and he doesn't own planes or villas situated on the ocean. If he wants to take a vacation on a beach, he rents a house instead of paying for one that sits unused year round. He doesn't own a yacht, and therefore doesn't pay a captain or harbor fees. He rents a paddle boat like the rest of us when he wants to go out on the water. It's this attitude that makes people believe that he's a normal person. And the commercials dramatize this disposition.

Whenever I observe the commercials and Dirk Nowitzki's public persona, it isn't always clear to me in which direction the semantic transfer is going—who's influencing whom in this system. Do people think Nowitzki is the polite and humorous boy next door because of these commercials? Or is it his disposition, which the ads only need to find an appropriate scenario for? Any way you look at it, he's a stroke of luck for marketing people. Dirk Nowitzki can convincingly be portrayed as a nice guy because there's a very real overlap between the man and his image. Whenever the ad people look back on their collaboration with Nowitzki, they talk about the transition from a "top-performance narrative" to "softer factors" like humor, personal appeal, and visual memorability. On the set in Slovenia, people talk to him as if he really were the character he's playing.

★   ★   ★

When the shoot is over, Dirk is driven to a boutique hotel with its own weight room and fruit bowls and white pebbles in the courtyard. There's still an hour of cardio to be done, as well as stretching. He cancels on the dinner with the team. The rest of us are staying in the Grand Hotel Union, and we naturally hang out at the bar all night, raising our glasses to Dirk.

The second day of shooting starts at dawn. The commercial's plot involves a taxi ride and engages with the rumor that Dirk isn't capable of withdrawing money from an ATM. Dirk once joked about his mother giving him a daily allowance, and people believed him. He kept telling this story year after year for laughs. And so, they've flipped the cliché: with a DiBa checking account, Dirk can withdraw money wherever he wants. No fees, no big deal.

Nowitzki is being carted around in a German film taxi for hours this morning. The car is on a flat trailer, almost like a float, and it's crammed full of cameras and lighting equipment. The cabdriver is a crank with a thick Bavarian accent who is annoyed that Dirk doesn't have any cash. The director is sitting on the trailer, facing backward, giving his commands.

Taxi driver: "Don't tell me you don't have any cash."

No answer. Dirk frantically looks for his wallet.

Taxi driver: "Great. Just great. And?"

Dirk keeps searching.

Taxi driver (annoyed): "What bank do you need?"

Dirk (laughing): "Doesn't matter."

Taxi driver: "What do you mean it doesn't matter?"

Slogan: "When every ATM is the right one, then it's . . ."

While Nowitzki's being incessantly driven around the historic part of the city in the stage taxi, the rest of the team is waiting in an empty industrial lot next to the train station. We watch everything on a monitor. My name somehow appeared on all the crew lists, and no one finds it strange that Dirk has a writer accompanying him the whole time (I'm guessing Krenz made this happen).

The stress level is high, the demands unique: Nowitzki needs to be friendly, he needs to act, and he has to hit the timing perfectly, since the scene can only be filmed on a specific stretch of the street that could pass as Munich (in the commercial's final cut, all of this will be unrecognizable). When the car finally comes back after a couple of hours, Nowitzki looks stressed out. He has to go to the bathroom, and he's had to listen to the crank's cursing dozens of times over and then laugh at just the right moment—it was cramped in the back seat. Aleš hands him his lunch, a club sandwich with home fries, which isn't what he ordered, but it no longer matters. "Doesn't matter," Dirk says, but he's not smiling anymore. "It doesn't matter." We hop in the van and drive off. His gym bag is in the back.

The contract stipulates that Dirk Nowitzki must be available for four days a year for shoots. The contract also stipulates that a decent basketball gym needs to be made available during breaks. He can't afford to take four days off before the season. The van slinks through the afternoon traffic, Aleš has the driver take shortcuts, and we lose our sense of orientation. Nowitzki is eating his sandwich in silence. Every once in a while, he looks at his phone. The rest of us stay quiet, too. I've never seen him this annoyed.

When the van arrives at the Tivoli arena, Nowitzki gets out without saying a word. Aleš has notified the janitor, and everything is ready—the man has even arranged for there to be a towel for Dirk. He requests a photo as a souvenir, but Dirk says no for the first time since I've met him. Or rather, he says: "Later. Okay, my man?"

Another empty gym, this time in the middle of Europe. We sit in the stands and wait for Holger and Dirk to leave the locker room. The famous Hala Tivoli, constructed entirely out of wood, has a couple of decades under its belt. The air is cold, the floor is hard, and the baskets are hanging from the ceiling the way they did in the old days. Slovenia is a basketball nation—Olimpia Ljubljana played big games in this arena; the great Yugoslavian teams, too. The European Championships were played here only a year ago. It's actually two gyms under one roof; there's a skating rink and a basketball arena. It's totally silent, but you can hear the crowd of 5,000 that would fit in here.

Dirk doesn't notice us when he steps on the court. He doesn't notice anything. Normally, he would warm up the room with a couple of jokes—by now, I've become accustomed to this. But not today. The next NBA season is starting in less than six weeks, his family is waiting at home, and he has to film another commercial—the next set is already being prepared, 60 people are waiting for him, and there's a photo shoot scheduled for this afternoon, plus a TV crew coming to film an interview afterward. It's a lot.

Nowitzki moans when he and Holger step on the court, but this time, he's really groaning, he's cursing in all seriousness—his bones are really bothering him at the moment. His knees. He moves awkwardly and cautiously, and his shots are not falling today. Sometimes he makes one, but his shots mostly hit very unusual and unusually wrong parts of the hoop, the ball bounces through the gym, and Geschwindner has to run and dive to snatch the rebounds. The gym is too cold, Nowitzki complains, putting on a long-sleeved T-shirt. The floor is too hard, the ball is flat. "What's with this bullshit? Come on! What's going on?"

It's the first time I've ever seen him like this. Aleš, Krenz, and I are trying to hide in the stands. I observe Geschwindner stoically rebounding the ball without saying a word. It seems like he's waiting for something. No banter, no jokes.

After a couple of minutes of struggling and cursing, of tirades and dozens of missed shots, fuck this, fuck that, what a bunch of bullshit, what a load of crap, Dirk stops talking. Suddenly, there's only the squeaking of his shoes on the old floor and the sound of the flat ball, the dull clunks of missed shots—*clunk, clunk*—that gradually become less frequent. He's not talking anymore. Krenz and Aleš have climbed way up in the stands; the janitor is hiding halfway behind a curtain, furtively watching.

After another five minutes, a door squeaks. Quiet music is suddenly wafting in from somewhere—piano, followed by strings. At first, the two men on the floor ignore the music; they stick to their regimen. The janitor comes out from behind the curtain and raises his hand as an apology. The noise is coming from the figure skating practice next door, but Geschwindner gives him a sign when the janitor is about to close the door.

"Leave it open," he says to the janitor, throwing the ball to Dirk. "What is that, Junge? Do you recognize it?"

Dirk catches the ball, pivots on an axis once, dribbles, shoots, and misses. He runs under the basket to the three-point line on the other side, receives the ball, pivots, shoots, misses. Runs. Receives the ball. Shoots. And makes it. "That's my boy Handel," he says.

"Oh God," Geschwindner says, as he laughs and passes the ball back to Dirk. "Way off."

"Modest Mussorgsky?" Dirk asks and shoots. "Haydn?" He misses, but he's also laughing now, even though the ball launches way off to the right side. He sprints out to the midcourt line. Geschwindner gathers the ball, Nowitzki pivots, sprints back, and receives the ball. He makes the three this time. He remains standing, his follow-through hand frozen as though he has just hit a perfect bucket in crunch time.

"Parzifal!" he yells, "Wagner!" And "Stockhausen!" And "Tchaikovsky!"

"Nailed it," Geschwindner says.

The figure skaters in the rink next door keep repeating the same piece of music. They're probably spinning loops in sync with the rapid piano passages and sweeping strings—and for a second, it's almost as if Nowitzki is gliding on skates; he sticks his arms out, he shoots and he shoots, and the clunks become snaps and flaps. The ball swishes through the net. Nowitzki is warmed up and the tension—a knot or a calcification—is no longer in the Tivoli Hall air. The looseness they usually train with can now be felt. He comes over to the sidelines, dripping, and hums along. He drinks some water, throws the bottle into the corner, and keeps going.

For the most part, everything seems like all the other workouts I've been able to observe: the sequence of shots and moves and pivots and sprints. The drink breaks. The mechanics and systematics are the same but something's slightly different today. Geschwindner has explained the technical aspects to me as well as their strategies and calculations, how the upper arm and lower arm need to be placed, a triangle with the elbow acting as a scope. How the ball should leave the hands off the index and middle fingers, two stable rods directly behind the ball's center of mass so that lateral deviations are avoided. He has explained that they always perform the same exercises to perceive where the hitch is, the smallest deviations, the most subtle flaws.

Dirk strides across the old gym with giant steps and shoots his threes in a full sprint as if he were the trailer receiving the ball in transition, as if a guard has kicked the ball out to him while driving to the basket. But today it doesn't seem like this has to do with the exercises themselves or with making fine adjustments to the movements. The two of them are cracking jokes now, they're talking about this and that, and I have the impression that it doesn't really matter what the conversation is about.

They change the subject. While passing the ball, Geschwindner is now asking about the way the Kyrgyzstani wheat fields move in Chinghiz Aitmatov's novel *Jamila*, and Dirk knows the answer. While shooting, he describes the wind in the blades of grass, the swaying and surges over the hills, the colors and forms and husks of wheat.

And suddenly I understand what's going on. I'm sitting on a wooden seat in the Hala Tivoli and it's the first time I comprehend the mental aspect of this training. That it's not only about technique and concentration, it's not only hard, disciplined work on the body. Or physics and calculations. Dirk Nowitzki was preoccupied with other things when we entered the arena: with the film shoot, the appointments piled on top of one another, the wrong lunch, and the busy phone line at home. The pressure was intense, as were the expectations to deliver in four days what will be shown for the next two years on every station, something that will also shape his public image in Germany. The constant realization that he's supposed to be someone important, someone whose food is delivered to him and whose hair is combed. The center of everything. The whole thing could have been inconsequential to him, but it wasn't. I used to think he must have grown used to all of these things a long time ago, but I was wrong.

The talking releases Nowitzki from the exhausting surroundings. He's worked his way past the difficulties—the noise coming from the other hall that should actually serve as a distraction has become part of his training, has helped to undo some mental knots. The two of them have talked about music hundreds of times, and the same is true of *Jamila*. It's not shop talk—it points them in a direction that's different

Previous page: Downtown Dallas

Mural on Taylor Street

Silver Garage, American Airlines Center

The Mavericks' practice gym

Kalkstein & Nowitzki

Sharpies

Dirk Nowitzki's garage

The Mavs' locker room

Dirk and Steve, downtown LA

Right: Old Man Game

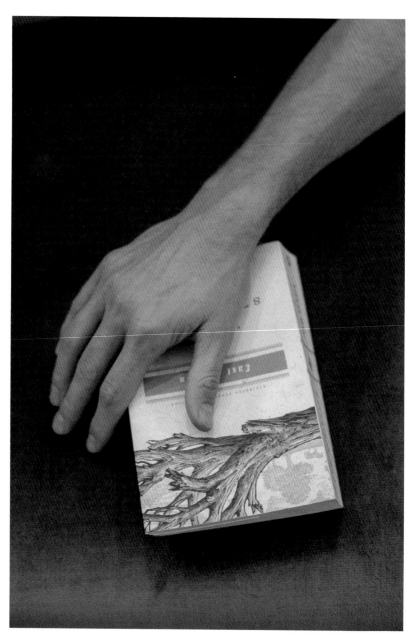

East of Eden

St. Regis Hotel, San Francisco

San Antonio Spurs vs. Phoenix Suns, 2018

Holger Geschwindner at the Thomas Mann House, Pacific Palisades

from what you'd expect to be the mindset of a professional athlete. It's about introducing something from another sphere of thinking. Something that grounds him and has nothing to do with private jets and hotel rooms. The words and the music clear the necessary space, and slowly the general mood of the game can come back, the calm in the middle of a storm. Dirk Nowitzki slowly recognizes himself as being the basketball player that he is.

In the meantime, Krenz and Aleš have come back to the sidelines and Krenz, full of excitement, gives me a hard elbow to the ribs. There's an almost meditative quality to the workout we're watching, the same quality I had observed last summer but didn't grasp. We're happy to be here because we understand why Nowitzki masters his craft. He's going up and down the gym, there are shots with his right and his left hand, and now they're falling—*swish, swish, swish*—for 90 straight minutes. Despite all the pressure, despite all the noise. He works on his ability to focus on what's essential.

When the workout is over and the two of them emerge from the wooden locker room freshly showered, the van and the driver are already waiting. We hop in; we have to get back to the set. The storyboard is on Dirk's seat with smoothies and cereal bars; some Slovenian hit plays on the radio. But when we're about to leave the parking lot, Dirk pipes up from the back seat.

"Aleš!" he yells. "Tell the driver to go back."

"Forgot something?" the chaperone asks.

"Yessir," Dirk says. The car turns around and stops. Dirk peels himself off the back seat, goes back to the arena, knocks, and waits, and when the janitor opens the door, he gets the souvenir picture Dirk promised him.

★   ★   ★

The days are full. The next morning, we're sitting in the van again, this time on our way to the mountains outside the city. By now, everyone has established their spot in the car: Geschwindner and Nowitzki in the back, Krenz and I in the middle. Aleš sits in the front and gives directions. We're a little hungover this morning since we celebrated—past midnight the night before—my birthday, German style. Cursing and cheering, we stayed at a Slovenian restaurant called Spasje very late, drinking red wine and schnapps. Nowitzki joined in the discussion without drinking and said goodnight before the conversation got out of hand. The rest of us told tall tales about basketball, then sang as we walked back to the hotel, across the city's bridges, but this morning I wish I would have left early as well. Dirk did the right thing. We're drinking water by the liter, the van leaves the city, and we drive with the windows down to air out.

As we head into the mountains, Geschwindner picks up where he left off in the restaurant: he tells his stories. About hunting wolves in the Carpathians and catching fleas. About memorizing poems while the other soldiers were on cigarette breaks in the military service (Rilke! Nietzsche! Hölderlin!). About driving a battered UPS truck across the States and taking a train along Lake Baikal. Anna Karenina! Tears of joy are streaming down his face and Nowitzki is laughing his head off, although he must have heard these stories hundreds of times. He's laughing about his friend's happiness.

The morning is spent on the edge of an alpine meadow; a stream babbles and we observe the filming of the next commercial. The sky is overcast; clouds hang on the top of the summit. It's not entirely clear to me what happens in the commercial: a married couple imagines what it'd be like to build a house here; they've taped a floor plan to the meadow and are running through the imaginary rooms. Dirk makes his way through some cows and manure and delivers his lines. It seems like he's in a better mood today.

The only deviation from this busy schedule is when we're rolling back down the mountain toward Hala Tivoli during lunch break.

Everyone thinks we're going back to the gym. But when the car is out of the film crew's sight, Dirk quickly decides against his midday workout. He could do it tonight, Aleš should try to organize it, but right now he wants to show us somewhere nice in the mountains, a good restaurant or a good view.

"The alpine slide?" the chaperone asks. "Kranjska Gora?"

"All right," Dirk says, "why not?"

The car turns and we drive northwest on the twisting, narrow roads. To the left is Triglav National Park, ahead are the borders with Italy and Austria. We all seem to be in better shape; the color has returned to our faces. It's story time again, this time from Dirk. He talks about the last time he was on a carousel, at Universal Studios during the 2012 All-Star break in Orlando. He had a gap in his schedule, so he and a couple of his guys went to the amusement park—Holger, Dirk's friend Nick Creme, and Ingo Sauer were also there. To avoid the crowds, they were brought to every attraction via service routes and back entrances. There were no waiting times; they used every second available to them: two whole hours of doing nothing but riding roller coasters until everyone got sick. Dirk laughs. He rarely has such breaks in his summer plans, almost never really allows himself to take time off. That's the difference, I think. Given the chance, Dirk has to ride roller coasters until he gets sick. Before someone recognizes him.

The mountains around us are getting steeper, the meadows greener. We turn past the giant ski jumps at Planica, and Geschwindner talks about trajectories and take-off velocities. We drink a lemonade mixed with cola, a Spezi, in an empty inn and the owner practically loses his shit when he sees Nowitzki. We drive by the World Cup slope, past haystacks, stacks of firewood, and farmhouses with hanging geraniums. Slovenia looks like a painting. Very different from the world Dirk Nowitzki usually sees—a series of gyms and shuttles and hotel rooms.

Very different from the world seen from airplane windows.

A late-summer rain is falling when we arrive at Kranjska Gora, and the alpine slide is closed. We stand under a lone patio umbrella at the base. Dirk seems disappointed. It would have been amazing to take the chairlift to the summit and then look over the mountains and hurtle down into the valley on one of those narrow sleds.

Yippie Yi Yo Kayah!

SEPTEMBER 2013

I'M STANDING IN FRONT of the jazz bar Mister B's in Munich, almost exactly one year after the evening in the Ritz. It's autumn now and the Munich Oktoberfest is roaring on Therese's Green. The streets are full of drunk people wearing lederhosen. You can't just enter Mister B's—you need to be buzzed in.

The joint is dark, all turquoise and wood; two couples are sitting in front of their drinks, a few aficionados are leaning on the bar. The barkeeper is quietly serving cosmopolitans and Bavarian beers, and there's an unusual trio standing on the small stage. The singer is a young woman, the guitarist is a nerdy white guy, and the sax player is an old man: the Naima Butler Trio.

I'm here to meet the elderly gentleman: Ernest Butler, the man who allegedly discovered Holger Geschwindner in the 1960s. When I enter, the band has already started its first set. Butler's playing while sitting, clad in a bright red sweatshirt, his hair snow white, and his daughter Naima is singing. Sometimes Ernie tells an anecdote and sometimes he starts singing along with Naima. Her voice is as soft as terry cloth and his is rough, like Louis Armstrong's. You can immediately see that Butler used to be an athlete as he plays the tenor saxophone; the instrument seems to be a part of him. Sometimes, he gets up from his barstool and plays a solo; Naima teeters and taps in rhythm. Sometimes, he closes his eyes while playing, moving with the notes as if he is a surfer and the music is his wave. That may sound strange, considering Butler's heft and bent posture. But you can see the strength and explosiveness he once had, you can sense his inner quickness. He doesn't treat his saxophone with reverence—he and his instrument know each other well.

Ernie and Naima lean on each other; he establishes the deep notes and she picks them up, she twists and turns them. He assists her, she complements him. Neither of them is a perfect player or singer, but when there's a mistake, they dance around the dissonances and sometimes play right through them. The next tone turns the mistake into an intermediary logical step. Jazz always points forward, but never forgets what happened before.

At the end of the first set, the trio falls into Bing Crosby's "I'm an Old Cowhand," a silly song, a funny game—*yippie yi yo kayah!* Naima sings, glasses clink. It's a regular weekday at Mister B's, the joint isn't full, the stage is small, but none of this seems to matter: Naima and Ernie play music because they like to play.

The daughter introduces us—she's the one who arranged this meeting. Ernie Butler's handshake is like Geschwindner's—*padapam!* We take a seat in the corridor that leads to the storeroom, where it's quieter—the clinking and laughter don't reach us. The next set is in half an hour; no worries. We're talking about Holger? Butler nods, then I rip. I barely have to ask any questions. Ernie apologizes: it's the adrenaline, the caffeine, "my drug of choice." He drank a few cups of coffee before the first set and the notes and stories come flooding out on their own accord with coffee, it gets him in the flow. That's his theme in general: flow. Flow is Ernie's true love, flow is the feeling of the second beer after the first one. Flow is music and playing, time and dance, forgetting oneself and concentrating.

Sometimes, there is structure and exactitude to Ernie's narration, and sometimes it's wild and wise and mystical. His voice alone would be enough to keep you on your seat. He snaps his rough fingers, pats me on the shoulder, smiles, laughs.

"Let's start from the beginning," he says. "Nineteen thirty-four."

★　　　★　　　★

Ernie Butler is born in 1934 in Connersville, Indiana, a no-man's-land on the way toward Ohio. He's the eldest of eight children, the son of a civil rights activist and preacher at the Mount Zion Church who then takes over the Second Baptist Church in Noblesville. He moves his family to Bloomington, a university town, in 1956. Indiana is the heartland of American basketball at the time—Larry Bird will grow up in French Lick, less than an hour's drive away. *Hoosiers*, probably the most famous basketball movie of all time, will be set in the fictitious small town of Hickory, Indiana. Mark Cuban, later the owner of the Dallas Mavericks, will run Motley's Pub in Bloomington while studying at Indiana University. The NBA's Pacers play in Indianapolis, but to this day, in many of the state's smaller cities and towns, basketball is played religiously. The field houses are even packed when headlined by high school teams. Basketball plays a central role in Ernie Butler's childhood.

All his teenage summers are spent on Bloomington's outdoor courts, and he plays at the local YMCA in the winter—soon semiprofessionally, three or four games a week, sometimes twice a day. He plays against legends like Oscar Robertson. Now and then, he tells his coach he can only play the first half before he has to zip across the city to his next game.

Butler comes to Germany at the beginning of the 1960s, working as a teacher at the American Junior High on the army base in Giessen—physical education, art, and history. He enjoys working with kids, but only rarely has the chance to play basketball. He plays alone in Miller Hall on the army base when he's done teaching, but as a civilian, he's barred from playing on the soldiers' team. He misses the game; he didn't think he would miss it so much. He's not happy during his first weeks in Giessen, depressed even, although the city is full of Americans. He's older than most of the soldiers, and he's alone and foreign. He doesn't know many people off the base, but he's fascinated by the Germans. Germany in the early 1960s isn't exactly welcoming to this dark and physically imposing African American, however.

One night, he stumbles into a strip club, the Casanova Bar, after a couple of beers. Years later, he remembers it being pretty chic. Ernie sits alone at a table and contemplates life. He's not really drunk, just incredibly tired, and he almost falls asleep. And just as he's about to leave, a couple of big guys enter the bar. They ask if they can sit at his table. "Sure," Butler says, half-asleep. "Of course." The men are looking to party—they're loud, they're laughing—and they pay no attention to the American. Ernie even falls asleep briefly over his beer, they'll later remember. Ernie doesn't totally understand what the guys are saying; they're speaking German with a slur. They've just got back from some trip, and they're drunk and noisy. At one point, one of them pats him hard on the back, he's startled, they laugh, and he gets up and goes home.

When he wakes up the next morning in the base's bachelor quarters, he vaguely remembers the encounter. He's hungover. Weren't those guys all about six foot four? Didn't he hear the words "away game"? Was it a basketball team, maybe? Why didn't he ask? He's not all that shy, usually. The next night, Ernie goes back to the Casanova Bar and waits. A bartender knows the guys. And Ernie's right: they're basketball players. The bartender knows when they practice, and in February 1962, Ernie Butler from Connersville, Indiana, 28 years old, practices for the first time with MTV Giessen's men's team. He makes all his shots, the guys slap him on the back once again, and he goes to the train station to take pictures for his player's pass the next morning. He's in the lineup for his first league game that very weekend. Giessen qualifies for the Southwestern First League at the end of his first season.

At MTV Giessen, everything changes for Butler. He's a basketball player again. At home, he was one of many; in Giessen, he's exotic: a Black man who knows and loves and lives the game. He looks a little lost out there with all the white sons of teachers in pulled-up shorts, all of whom have learned basketball as if it's a foreign language. Some have come from handball, others from track and field, but none of them have grown up with basketball like Ernie has, none of them play the game as naturally as him. But his teammates make the same crude jokes as the people from Bloomington's YMCA—only in German.

Butler is the first African American in the league, and he quickly becomes the leader of the team. MTV Giessen is suddenly one of the best teams in the country. In Ernie's first full year, the club competes in the German championship, losing to Alemannia Aachen in the final.

"And now comes Holger," Ernie says. He orders another coffee. There's still time before the second set.

Opinions differ about their first meeting, but one version goes like this: Ernie randomly arrives at Giessen's Pestalozzi School gym before practice, but he's too early; two high school teams are on the court. It's winter 1963. Butler gets himself ready, then enters the gym. He likes observing other players, their moves and abilities. It calms him to watch a game go back and forth—it reminds him of Indiana, where he spent thousands of hours, whole days, watching basketball whenever he wasn't the one playing. Butler leans on the doorframe and watches. The schoolkids recognize him; he's a bit of a celebrity in Giessen after last season. He waves when he notices a couple boys staring at him.

One guy on the court is better than the rest. He runs faster, jumps higher, and shoots better. He's physically superior, he's wiry but strong, and he has a primal physical force that the other players don't know how to handle. He can dunk—something seldom seen in the German game of the time. He literally hangs in the air when he shoots a midrange jumper; most of the others only shoot with their feet on the ground. The kid sometimes cuts into the key and then elevates; he flies and scores at will. He launches forbidden passes, but they reach their target. He sees holes before they happen. The other boys all scamper around him, but he's always standing in the right spot. He's courageous enough to take over the game completely: by halftime, he's already scored more than 40 points. "Forty-one," he'll say half a century later, grinning. Forty-one. The 17-year-old is Holger Geschwindner.

It's a twist of fate that the kid plays basketball in the first place. Or maybe it's providence. He's a child of the postwar era, born in the winter of 1945. His father is on the parish council and is self-employed in finance and construction; his mother keeps the business running. The boy goes to boarding school—Graf-Friedrich-Magnus-Alumnat in the tiny town of Laubach. His best friend there is Karl Clausen, whose father, Theo, is the headmaster.

Theo Clausen studied basketball in the 1930s with its inventor, James Naismith, in Springfield, Massachusetts. He was sent to America by the Nazis to learn the sport firsthand ahead of the 1936 Olympics in Berlin, in which the Germans were entitled to participate in every discipline. In the end, they rank 15th out of 21 countries. But Clausen remained a basketball enthusiast, one of the first in Germany. Two degrees of separation—there's a direct lineage from the inventor of the game to Holger Geschwindner. And hence to Dirk Nowitzki.

As an educator, Clausen is ahead of his time; the boys at the boarding school love him because he shows them respect. He speaks their language without trying to be buddy-buddy. He takes the kids seriously, but he can also be goofy and affectionate. He's one of the central figures in German basketball during the 1950s and 1960s, he's even the coach of the national team for a couple of years. In Laubach, he converts an old cinema into a gym and trains his students amidst the thick brocade curtains. There's something theatrical about basketball, it's a performance. Holger and Karl are his best players.

Ernie's teammate Bernd Röder has known about Holger Geschwindner for a long time; the kid is the reason why he has arrived so early this afternoon. Theo Clausen informed his acquaintances in

Giessen about Geschwindner a couple of months ago. "That one there with the ball bag and the hair," Clausen told them. "He's going to be a really good player." Geschwindner's hair is a kind of Afro. The Giessen team keeps an eye on the boy. Sometimes, they travel to Laubach, a half-hour drive from Giessen, and every time they come, Holger's a little bit better, a little faster and more developed as a basketball player.

Ernie Butler watches the kid. He notices that Geschwindner only uses his strength in small doses. He gets better when the level of play increases. He's there when it matters. He makes shots from all over the court; he runs and runs and unpacks one tool after another. Deep shots, drives to the basket, clean midrange jumpers. The kid isn't perfect, but he does a lot of things you can't teach. He can play.

In the end, Laubach wins the game, 196–20; the young Geschwindner beats Giessen practically on his own. He's 17, but has scored 100 points—or 98, or "more than 80, for sure." Fifty years later, opinions will differ about the total. The entire first-division Giessen team—Dschang Jungnickel, Röder, Butler, coach Pit Nennstiel—stands on the sidelines and discusses what it has seen. For Butler, it's not even a question: he wants to see this kid at practice. One hundred points in a game? Come on, man, it's not even a question!

In another version of the events, the game takes place in Laubach, and Butler drives out to see the kid his teammates have been talking about. Butler watches Holger score 100 points and can identify with him. At a team meeting at Kürbis (Pumpkin), their favorite bar, some of Butler's teammates voice their doubts: they think Geschwindner is an "independent thinker," pigheaded. Butler says anyone who scores 100 points in a game has to be stubborn. Some vote yes, others no. But Butler wants to see the kid practice; he stands up and slams his fist on the table. Guys! A hundred points! It's not even a question!

In the backroom of Mister B's, Butler now recalls how quickly everything went: Clausen and the guys from Giessen agree that three of the older players—Jungnickel, Röder, Butler—will take turns picking up the carless teenager in Laubach and drive him to Giessen and back. "We got along straight away," Ernie Butler says. "It probably sounds strange, but Holger was a quiet boy back then. Most of the time it was me talking, shooting shit, philosophizing." The car ride conversations are about basketball and music and life. Quickly, the two of them become friends despite the age difference. "It must have been on one of those car rides," Butler remembers, "that I talked about basketball and jazz."

After practice, they often hang around and play one-on-one because practice isn't demanding enough for them. At first, Butler beats the kid, but it's only a couple of weeks before it becomes more difficult. "Holger was a quick learner," he says. "He only needed to be shown something once, and then he could do it himself." The high school student is like a sponge. "He could soon do everything I could do, only better," Butler says. He laughs, and you can't really tell whether he's exaggerating or telling the truth. "Holger was a genius."

Naima Butler politely interrupts our conversation and asks her father to come back onstage. Ernie downs his espresso and they play the next set. Now Mister B's is jam-packed, the windows are steamed up, and Butler looks tired and happy when he sits down in front of me after a half hour of playing Fitzgerald and Coltrane and Rollins. He stretches. "The Casanova Bar was . . . ," he says, and picks up right where he left off—the mid-1960s, the stories about basketball, about Holger and himself.

B-Ball Is Jazz

BASKETBALL IS A NICHE sport in Germany in the 1960s. There's little money to be made from playing it. There are no nutritional guidelines, systematic training plans, or rules about doping, and you don't need to make appearances before the media. Basketball is a very different sport from what it will be during Dirk Nowitzki's era. Players receive payment in soup and schnitzel at the local restaurant, and a championship means free haircuts for a year. The basketball world is small; everyone knows one another. Beers are consumed after the games; Ernie Butler and his teammates hang out in the city's clubs—basketball players are legendary drinkers. At first, Holger Geschwindner has to be smuggled into the bars, but it's not long before he's old enough. He mostly drinks Spezi—lemonade mixed with cola. He never turns into a beer drinker.

Ernie Butler remains his mentor. Geschwindner can sense that there's more to the world than church and hometown gyms, more than school dormitories and the army base. Butler and Geschwindner come from different cultures and languages: whereas Geschwindner is an upright child from a Protestant home who attends a religious boarding school, Butler is a man about town and 11 years older. Geschwindner will later call Butler someone who "opened up worlds."

"And suddenly, there's this world," Geschwindner will say. "Suddenly, everything's new. As a 17-year-old, you can't understand what's happening at first. I mean, the Bahnhofstrasse in Giessen back then was different from everything I had experienced before. There was music and drinking and sex. If you want a Christian analogy, it was Sodom and Gomorrah. For a boy at that age, it's an important question: What's right and what's wrong? How can it be that both of these universes exist? Two extremes meet. And you get pretty worked up. What do you tell your parents when they ask you where you were? What you saw? You didn't see anything, of course. You have to figure it out on your own. And that keeps you pretty occupied."

Giessen has three large bases in the mid-'60s, home to 10,000 American soldiers. The Bahnhofstrasse is known as "Shanghai on the Lahn"; there are bars and brothels and movie theaters. There's Star Klub and Casanova Bar. Every joint has a record player; jazz is played all over: John Coltrane and Thelonious Monk, Sonny Rollins and Charlie Parker. Sometimes, there's even live jazz on the weekends—duos, trios, quartets, it depends. The quality isn't always that great, but that isn't what matters.

The basketball players like to mingle with the Americans and the other night crawlers; it gets late and rowdy and loud. Ernie has to drive the kid home after their late workouts, and sometimes he drags him out to carouse. Then they sit at the bar and talk. Sometimes, the kid has to wait for Ernie and his ladies, so he sits at the bar, listening to the music and drinking his Spezi (sometimes they even claim to have invented this drink). During these weeks, he makes a habit of taking notes to remain in control of his thoughts. To sort things out. Album titles, melodies, instruments, women, stories. He wants to experience everything and never forget any of it. The music does something to his mind and body that he had only ever experienced with sports.

Before now, music had mostly been a Sunday affair, a way of distinguishing oneself from brutal Nazi songs and harmless hit parades. "We sang hymns every Sunday," Geschwindner says. "I can still sing most of the Protestant hymns forward and backward."

People his age listen to pop music—the Beatles and the Rolling Stones. "(I Can't Get No) Satisfaction" is on the radio in the summer of 1965. A young Geschwindner and his classmates sit around a record player at the boarding school; pop music gives them a new sense of power. He's also interested in classical music—Liszt and Beethoven. He's fascinated by Franz Liszt's explosive life, his travels and wild affairs. He realizes that he can really hear music. Rationally. He can feel music and he can think it.

The young Geschwindner sits at the end of the bar, waiting for Butler. He's too young to be here and shouldn't draw attention to himself in the bars. He's a good listener, a fly on the wall. Jazz is impulsive, but it isn't kitschy; technical, but not mechanical. Jazz has rules, but it's also free. Jazz seems closer to life than anything Geschwindner has ever known before. The music doesn't come from here, it's not from Giessen or Laubach, but it suits him. The standards never stop playing in his head; he still teeters and taps in rhythm when he's back in Butler's car.

On their nightly drives between Giessen and Laubach, Butler explains his world to Geschwindner, and he does in actual fact talk about basketball being the same as music for him; he compares jazz with the game. Holger asks what he means, and Ernie tries to find words for his years of experience—with the ball and with the saxophone: b-ball is jazz.

Sports and music are alike, metaphorically and literally. First, there's the training: musicians practice like athletes; they need to grasp the mechanics of the movements then learn how to master them so that they don't have to constantly think about them while playing—about how to hold a saxophone, about which notes are on what keys, about how to bend your arm while shooting. Unconscious movements and freedom: the runner puts one leg in front of the other without ever thinking about it, the swimmer swims lap after lap of freestyle, the tennis player returns the ball faster than they can think. The basketball player makes a layup, *tam-tam-tak*, Sonny Rollins plays, *yippie yi yo*. Like athletes, musicians develop an arsenal of individual moves and standards, they create a toolbox and have to practice for a long time before mastering the tools.

Athletes and musicians require routines and rituals. They need maintenance: brass players clean their horns, pianos need to be tuned, musicians and athletes stretch their fingers and strengthen their backs. They practice on focusing, visualizing their music; they breathe and glide through pieces like a skier down a slope. Athletes string their racquets, wax their skis, and calibrate their weapons. They take care of their bodies.

Both groups work in highly regulated systems and both strive toward the highest level of freedom within these confines. It's a paradox: sports and music are a daily struggle with your body and craft as well as with the continual attempt to not be aware of your body all the time. It's about letting your skills and your body just do what they do. It's the joy of knowing: I'll make it if I shoot. It will sound good if I sing. What my fingers do is music. If you have this certainty, you can start working on the nuances, the intricacies, the details. You learn to play music by playing music. You learn to play basketball by playing it all the time. Certainty gives you the ability to improvise. A unique musical or athletic individuality will evolve.

Great athletes and musicians are able to let go. They can stop monitoring their own bodies, they can free themselves from the incessant rational considerations about what could or should come—what note, what movement. They're obedient to whatever *needs* to be done. They act and react. They play.

Musicians and athletes work toward reaching that rare and joyful unconscious state that the psychologist Mihály Csíkszentmihályi called "flow." The intoxication of succeeding. When you forget yourself and just act—when you have practiced and mastered the foundations, and now you're free for the intricate nuances that distinguish happiness from unhappiness, success from failure. The fine details that distinguish greatness from great mediocrity.

Flow can be provoked. You can work toward it; you can train and practice. Most musicians and athletes are familiar with it, even those who do it as a hobby. "You don't go to the well once but daily," the writer Walter Mosley says. "You don't skip a child's breakfast or forget to wake up in the morning. Sleep comes to you each day, and so does the muse." Rituals are shortcuts to flow. Every amateur runner knows this: you have to get past the pains of the initial stretch, and if you keep going and don't give up, you can be almost certain that you'll run into the flow. The awareness of gasping for breath, of an aching knee, of the worries and fears, all of these dissolve into movement and music for a while. Every cellist and clarinetist can tell you about how a successful piece feels, about a difficult sequence and an unexpected harmony. Everyone knows how different the world appears when there's music playing.

But there's one critical difference in all the similarities between sports and music: the opponent, the competition. In basketball, you go toe to toe with a defender who tries with all their might to stop you from succeeding. They step into the passing lane, they hold you and tug you and block you. They want to disrupt your rhythm and sour your harmony. They want to get under your skin and into your head.

You have to react to these attempts at sabotage and find solutions and ways around them, to offer your opponent new propositions. A dialogue takes place, formally and according to rules; hopefully, it's fair and sportsmanlike, but sometimes it's also aggressive and destructive. It's not only about dealing with the opposing team, but with everything around it. You want to make a stand against these adverse circumstances: against the screaming fans, the fatigue, and the weight of expectation. The bodies of the defenders, their skills, their capabilities. Your own body, its limits and weaknesses.

Action and reaction are also very important to jazz. The instruments talk to each other as well as over and past one another. Jazz isn't simply played; the musical communication between the musicians— their game of passing—is almost always part of the performance. There's a back-and-forth, a to-and-fro. There's also an element of competition, even if it's more playful and not as rough.

"B-ball is jazz," Ernie Butler explains on those drives through 1965, and Geschwindner is listening. "B-ball is jazz," he writes decades later in his book *Nowitzki*, a wild and confusing trip through his way of thinking. "A basketball team is a jazz band with five people," he says. "Everyone can do something different, everyone's waiting for their solo within the structure of the team. And it's crucial for the five to harmonize and attune to the same theme. In jazz, the basic structure of a piece of music is defined at the outset. Then come virtuosic impulses, counterpoints and the instrumentalists' voices. Then, the momentum of creative solos emerges from the piece's original form. Drums, piano and bass provide a steady and stable framework for the soloist."

In *Nowitzki*, Geschwindner jumps between all the theories and ideas that have shaped him. And jazz is the metaphor he always returns to. It explains Holger Geschwindner's understanding of basketball: creative and productive, with five individual players in a network. The five musicians and their instruments are his conception of the ideal game. His sports philosophy.

What really makes sense to him is how mistakes are dealt with. If a musician plays a wrong note, the piece doesn't pause; you don't stop and start all over. Nobody scolds a musician; nobody screams at them. Instead, the wrong note is taken as a challenge, it's integrated and played with, it's used as a jumping board for the unexpected. "Mistakes are the salt in the soup," Geschwindner will later write before quoting Miles Davis: "When you hit a wrong note, it's the next note that makes it good or bad." The next note decides whether it was a mistake or the beginning of something greater. "Mistakes are permitted, sometimes even desired, because something new and creative grows out of them. As a matter of fact, making mistakes is a part of jazz."

What would happen, Holger asks himself, if you could play basketball like that? If the coach wasn't pacing up and down the sidelines, screaming his head off when the players made a mistake? If practice wasn't interrupted all the time to correct the cuts and shot selections? If the players incorporated the deviations and mistakes into their game? If only basic plays and strategic guidelines were required and everything else emerged out of improvisation, flow, and freedom? If the group could facilitate solos and integrate them?

Geschwindner obviously isn't thinking like this yet. He's still a dog-tired teenager sitting at the counter in the Casanova Bar, the red light on his face, or later in the passenger seat of Ernie's bright green Opel Kadett, heading toward Laubach. He listens to the music and feels it; he slowly learns to read and understand it. In 1965, the parallels between music and basketball are still pre-linguistic; he can feel them, but it will take a few more decades before he can define and formulate them.

1994-1997

DIRK NOWITZKI'S LIFE CHANGES after meeting Holger Geschwindner. And the change is fundamental. He still attends high school, but they're in the gym together almost every day during the summer of 1994. They slowly develop a plan that's very different from the training techniques German basketball is accustomed to. Geschwindner has Nowitzki walk on his hands, makes him wear lead vests while shooting, has him stride across the tiny gym in giant steps. Nowitzki gets a little stronger every day. Geschwindner takes the kid's shooting motion apart, examines it on a drawing board, and then puts it back together in a new way. Nowitzki now shoots from a different and higher angle; his elbow and wrist aim at the basket like iron sights.

They improve the positioning of Nowitzki's fingers: the thumb supports the ball, the spread index and middle fingers guide it into the air. They also change his leg positioning: Nowitzki's legs are now spread wider, the knees bent slightly inward, he squats lower, unusually so, and pushes himself upward with more balance. Geschwindner calculates the ideal point of release based on Nowitzki's body measurements, the length of his upper and lower legs, the size of his feet, the length of his fingers, the structure of his torso, his average jumping strength and his eight-foot seven-inch reach. Ideally, the ball will leave his fingers at exactly ten feet, the same height as the basket, no defender can get there all that easily.

The progress can be quickly seen on the court, too. The 16-year-old starts dominating every aspect of the game when he plays against others his age. He plays on the under-20 team and with grown men in the regional league. The other boys his age don't have a chance against him, and the men only do because of their experience and body strength. He regularly practices with DJK Würzburg's men's team, which plays in the second German division. He is invited to the Bavarian select team and is soon noticed by the German Basketball Federation's youth program. He could always dominate the game—based on his height alone—but he gets in his own way from time to time. Nowitzki is still a cautious boy. He'd rather wait and read the game, and only then react. It's not good enough to merely dominate and win; he wants to do things perfectly. To do them the right way. "You can also make yourself bored to death with winning," Geschwindner says. He sometimes talks in aphorisms like this. "Only use as much force as necessary."

Dirk's coach on the club team is Pit Stahl. He's known the kid since under-13 and lets him play all five positions. He resists the impulse to use Dirk the way bigs are normally used, even with the adults. The kid moves too well, and his shot is too pure to let him rot at the five. In the late summer of 1994, Nowitzki and Geschwindner decide to make the jump into the second division. Dirk now goes up against experienced second-division players, some of whom are almost twice his age.

Holger Geschwindner makes his official return to basketball. He shares the coaching duties with Stahl, but they don't get along. Or at least, they have different ideas about the kind of game basketball is. As coaches, they resemble the players they were: Stahl was a solid second-division point guard, Geschwindner a body freak and free spirit. Stahl prefers clear, strategically wise, and patiently played setups. Defense is what matters to him. Geschwindner sees the future of the game in a flowing offense. To him, that is the design of the game. He wants the players to run; shooting is more important than patience. Dirk benefits from these ideas as an individual, but the rest of the team struggles with them.

In his first season with the pros, Nowitzki mostly just follows the others. The team is dominated by Robert Heinrich, a Hungarian national player, and Nicolas Wucherer, a young German law student and playmaker. Nowitzki watches and learns and gets used to the more rugged game. He's familiar with this situation: his cousin Holger Grabow also plays for the team; it's almost like being out in the backyard. He watches the older players go at it, but it isn't obvious that he's younger than everyone else when he's called into the game. And the others notice that Dirk's a special player, of course. None of them were as tall as he is at 16, none of them as good.

The center on the team is Burkhard Steinbach, a farmer from Moos, a village nearby. Dirk doesn't have a car yet, so someone has to drive him. Steinbach passes through Heidingsfeld every day on his way to Würzburg and picks Nowitzki up. It's just like it used to be with Holger and Ernie Butler: Nowitzki and Steinbach are friends to this day.

The tone in the locker room is rough and raw, just as it is with every other basketball team. There's a case of beer in the locker room after the games. Nowitzki occasionally drinks one, but never overdoes it. He's a shy kid, an observer. He analyzes the team, the leaders, the spokesmen, the jokers. Nowitzki becomes acquainted with adult humor and wants to become one of the jokers. It's only toward the final games of the season that he shows just how great he will become. The others have known it for a while; they've been watching him practice all season.

The Würzburg team ends Dirk's first season in the lower reaches of the standings—they even have to play in the relegation round. Nowitzki keeps improving, averaging twelve points and four boards in the final six games. In the second German division. That's remarkable for a player his age. During the games, Holger Geschwindner stands on the sidelines and gives him tips, sometimes directly contradicting Pit Stahl's instructions. In practice, he often pulls Dirk to the side and explains details to him, then sends him back out on the court. "Now give it a try!" Later, Dirk won't be able to remember these moments, nor will he be able to remember the game in Schweinfurt or Geschwindner's meeting with his parents at the kitchen table. "I know Holger always tells that story," he will say. "But I can only remember one thing in particular: Holger standing on the sideline and babbling nonstop."

His grades keep getting worse at school. A D in math, a D in physics, a D in German, a D in English. His midterm report card is miserable; his parents receive a warning letter. The principal is angry and acts like he's alarmed. The school isn't happy that Nowitzki's attendance is dwindling because he has games or has to go to the select team's practices. Dirk's not stupid, he just has other interests. He isn't lazy, either, but he's often tired—all the driving is getting to him, he can't do everything at once. What the teachers are unable to see is that he's working toward perfection. If it were up to Dirk to decide, he'd choose basketball over school.

His parents see things differently. Sports aren't a sure thing and an injury could derail the whole scheme. Geschwindner also tries to talk some sense into the boy and doesn't mince words. "There's no way you're not graduating," he says, and he can hear his own teacher Theo Clausen in these words. "The world is your oyster if you graduate." The fact that Holger never finished university is something he keeps quiet for the time being.

Dirk isn't convinced. What he wants is to play basketball. It's something he's really good at. And didn't Geschwindner always say that that's what's important in life? Geschwindner warns him and then outright forbids him to drop out of school: "We're not going to continue if your grades don't get better." Dirk gives in and promises to get back on the job. His parents hire tutors for every subject except physics and math; Geschwindner will take over these duties himself.

Also helping out is his teammate Klaus Perneker, a teacher-in-training at his high school.

In the summer of 1994, Nowitzki plays for the German national team in the qualifying round of the FIBA U18 European Championships and is named the MVP of the tournament. Suddenly, the basketball world knows who Dirk Nowitzki is. His father can still remember that the telephone started ringing more often. The first German division is calling.

Dirk Nowitzki is sick of standing on the sidelines and watching. The following season, he becomes one of Würzburg's most important players. Martti Kuisma of the Finnish national team dominates the game, but Nowitzki garners all the attention. In the 1990s, the Bayer Leverkusen team is the face of German basketball. Henning Harnisch, Michael Koch, and former University of Washington Huskie Christian Welp rule the league and compete internationally. Their coach, Dirk Bauermann, speaks English with his team and has them play a style that he brought back from his time as an assistant at Fresno State. Now he's watching Nowitzki play and calls him "the greatest talent Germany has produced in the last 15 years. Maybe even the last 20." The reigning German champions are interested in Dirk. Würzburg finishes the season strong, but missed out on being promoted to the first division. Dirk is only 17, but he needs to leave the second league.

The work with Geschwindner becomes more intense. They practice every day now, and Dirk is busy with Geschwindner's conceptual world even off the court. He starts reading the books Holger gives him: *As Far as My Feet Will Carry Me* by Josef Martin Bauer. And Conrad's *Typhoon* again. All these books are about dealing with particular situations: How do you behave when a storm hits with headwinds? You act like the captain in *Typhoon*. You don't try to go around the storm, you go straight through it. What do you do when the road seems like it will never end? You go step by step. Nowitzki learns to play the saxophone; he likes how, after a couple of weeks of practice, his fingers know what to do. It almost plays itself once you get going. It flows.

Nowitzki reads *The History of Nature* by Carl Friedrich von Weizsäcker, written in 1949, a book about the history of Earth, the temporal and spatial structure of the cosmos, the galaxies, life, and the soul. He would have never picked up a book like that in school, but now he's reading it in the gym and on car rides. He's learning to work through conceptual worlds. He reads about the inner history of humans: "Man does not know himself to be a being that can be observed without getting involved. There are constantly demands on him that he must obey or reject. Adversity, sorrow and hope, love and hate, customs and conscience, fellow humans and God make demands on him."

The next summer is jam-packed. First, weeks of individual training, then the FIBA U18 European Championships in France, and there still is the battle to get his grades up. Nowitzki often brings his tutors along. Geschwindner has assembled a team of Dirk enthusiasts who are ready to jump in whenever they're needed: Klaus Perneker, the physician Dr. Thomas Neundorfer, Georg Kendl. The national team has a splashy win in its first game against Greece, but everything goes downhill after that. The tournament is awful; the Germans lose every other game. Only Nowitzki is convincing.

Dirk's father drives to France in a VW bus with Geschwindner. He's let go of his initial skepticism; now he trusts Geschwindner, even if he doesn't always understand him. They sleep in the car on the way, but Dirk's father gets a toothache and a fever upon arrival. He has to recover in the hotel. As for Geschwindner, nothing gets the better of him. He watches the games and yells out advice to Nowitzki. The German national team coaches aren't amused; they ask Geschwindner to cut it out. The coaches care about authority and chains of command; Geschwindner wants his boys to succeed.

Much has been forgotten from this time and cannot be perfectly reconstructed. The stories are a quarter century old; the participants recorded hardly a word. The only one who keeps a diary is Geschwindner. Nowitzki still has only a few game sequences from the tournament in his head—a couple of defenders, some shots. The arenas, the hotel rooms. It's all new to him. What causes problems for his memory is the order of events, not the details. At the time, he's still only a boy playing basketball. His coaches do their job and he's devoted. They come with their professional training and he has the desire to do something great. Like every other boy, he has aspirations and posters hanging in his room. But one thing he does remember, aside from the defeats and the hubbub, is that working with Geschwindner was making him a better player.

A couple of days after the European Championships, Dirk joins a select group of Europeans born in 1978 to play in a tournament against the best US high school teams: the Peach Ball Classic in Augusta, Georgia. Nowitzki has been on Nike's radar for a while, but it wasn't until this past spring that their sports marketing manager, Frank Gaw, showed up at the playground in Zellerau where Dirk and his friends shoot hoops (Geschwindner had called Gaw, the ex–national team player, saying he should come by, he wanted to show him something). As Dirk stepped onto the court that day, the two men watched him warm up and talk trash with the other guys. That's something he was able to do now—he learned it in the locker rooms of the second division. A bucket was worth one point, a three counted for two. The two men watched him play five on five; at first, he was calm, letting the game come to him, and then he took over. Years later, Frank Gaw will still be able to remember how Dirk got the ball in the backcourt, dribbled past his defender at the half-court line, danced around the next one with a spin move, and sank a three, stone cold and without hesitation. He held up three fingers as he ran back. Game over. "That's what I wanted to show you," Geschwindner said.

Gaw takes his courtside observations from Würzburg to the Nike headquarters just outside Portland, Oregon. The boss, Phil Knight, and the legendary coach and mentor George Raveling like the story of a boy from the basketball diaspora becoming one of the greatest players in the world. That's how they picture it, and that's what Nike is looking for: stories. That's why they try to sign athletes at an early age.

Nike invites him to Georgia, they pay for everything, Dirk does a good job. There are agents and scouts in the stands. And none of them has ever seen anyone like Nowitzki, either. So quick, so accurate! From now on, the telephone line at J. Wolf's painting company in Würzburg never stops ringing. The Nowitzkis buy an answering machine. Geschwindner has to deal with the interest; he becomes a manager of sorts.

On the way back to Europe, the Peach Ball crew stops in Atlanta. The Summer Olympics are currently taking place. It's a hot summer in 1996; the peach trees are blossoming in front of the arena. Four years ago, in Barcelona, the Dream Team led by Jordan and Pippen sparked Dirk's passion for the game, and now the third Dream Team has Grant Hill, Shaquille O'Neal, and Penny Hardaway. Dirk sits high up in the Georgia Dome's bleachers for one of the games the Australians play and imagines what it would be like to be one of the players. The youngest aren't much older than him. Geschwindner has repeatedly told him about playing in Munich in 1972, and now Dirk is seeing what the Olympic Games could be like. A dream sets its anchor in him.

At the beginning of the next season, Perneker hangs up his sneakers and becomes Würzburg's head coach. Pit Stahl has left the club. Geschwindner agrees to be an assistant. Basketball is experiencing a shift in tides in Europe: the famous Bosman ruling is revolutionizing the structure of the European leagues, and now clubs are allowed to engage as many cheap foreign players as they want—Spaniards, Lithuanians, Serbs. The old limitations no longer exist. But Würzburg goes in the opposite direction: initially, they play without a single foreigner. Dirk gets a lot of playing time; no longer a sleeper, he's dominating the game. The secret is out. People in Germany are talking about the kid from Würzburg. But once again, it isn't enough to get the club promoted to the first division.

Nowitzki is invited to his first real international game in February

1997 and plays three short minutes against the Portuguese in Lisbon, a 73–66 victory. He doesn't score, but the team wins, and he's standing on the same court as Henning Harnisch and other German legends—all those players who had been on the EuroBasket title team in 1993. He's reached one of his small goals: he's a real German international. It's this stage that he wants to be on. He graduates with a GPA of 2.5. It's early in the summer of 1997, high school is behind him, and the world of basketball is at his fingertips.

Dirk tries out for FC Barcelona and Bologna—or, rather, they try out for him—he has a secret training session with Rick Pitino in Rome and sorts through some of the college offers that have been piling up on Geschwindner's desk in his Peulendorf castle ever since the tournament in Augusta. Dirk decides to stay in Würzburg for one more season since he loves his teammates and loves working with Geschwindner. All summer long, he obsessively works on his game with Robert Garrett and Demond Greene. Behind the scenes, Geschwindner keeps working on the big picture. The 1997–98 season is going to be a big one; it's going to be fast and wild. The team will be made up of young athletes who are able to play exactly the way he imagines the game.

Camp

Try to picture Munich RSV Bayern 1910, the rowing and yacht club beautifully situated on the shores of Lake Starnberg. The water is calm and flat, the early morning sun hangs on the hills on the other side of the lake. A two-story boathouse, a restaurant with a glass front and a café terrace. A couple of sailboats are tied to the wooden jetty, the rowboats are stored in the shed. A dog is barking somewhere, and you can hear the flopping footsteps of the first joggers along the Seestrasse. It's a beautiful Saturday morning in the spring of 1997, and the town of Starnberg is just starting to open its shutters.

Now imagine a middle-aged man dressed in light blue track pants and a faded T-shirt unlocking the restaurant. He's schlepping a sack full of bread rolls, 60 at least, fresh from the bakery up the hill. He unlocks the doors and starts setting the tables: he sets out giant jars of Nutella and strawberry jam. A box with cutlery, 20 plates, 20 cups. The morning dew still sleeps on the meadow in front of the boathouse; there's the smell of coffee. The middle-aged man pauses for a second and looks at the boats and the water and the mountains. He takes a deep breath. His name is Georg Kendl, he's 57 years old, a physical education and English teacher at the Starnberg Gymnasium. Basketball player, rower, world traveler. The clock in the restaurant strikes seven. Somewhere, an alarm clock goes off.

The dormitory on the first floor of the boathouse awakens. Fifteen sleepy boys, between 15 and 17 years old, crawl out of their sleeping bags, yawning and cursing, morning wood and bad breath. They roll up their sleeping bags.

"Dude, it's too early!"

"Way too early!"

"Come on! Dessssssmond!"

"Leave me alone, you Polack!"

"Moron!"

The horde of teenage boys slowly creeps downstairs. One by one, they step out of the boathouse, rubbing their eyes, rubbing their arms, squinting in the sun. It's still chilly, but it's going to get warm. You can now see that the boys are huge; some are clearly taller than six foot five, their shoulders wide, their bodies sinewy and flexible. The boys stumble over the meadow in socks and arrange themselves in a circle, complaining. There's a swan feeding on the bottom of the flat water and one of the boys spits at the bird but misses. The other boys make fun of him. We can hear a toilet flushing.

Now imagine the boathouse door opening and another man in a tracksuit stepping outside with a CD player in one hand and an extension cord in the other: Tom Thallmair, a morning fitness enthusiast and rowing coach at the club. He plugs in the CD player.

"Howdy."

"Morning, Tom."

"Morning."

"You guys ready?"

"You betcha, Tom. I was born ready."

Out on the lake, an early foursome with coxswain passes by. The cox looks at the shore and raises his hand; Thallmair returns the greeting. The coxed four is now privy to a strange scene without sound: 15 teenagers in shorts or pajamas are standing on the field and moving to an inaudible rhythm; their long arms flap about, they bend and they stretch, they spin in pirouettes and reach toward the sky like they're picking apples, one hand after the other. Something must be prompting this strange ballet; it looks absurd from a distance, but the boys seem to be taking it seriously. Sitting on the clubhouse terrace is Director Geschwindner, taking notes in the morning sun. It's their first shot.

The training group has breakfast on the porch; a couple of the guys are still in their hot-cocoa years, while others are already drinking coffee. Now they're awake. They've been at camp for a couple of days, and they will be staying a couple more. It's not a training camp in the traditional sense: the boys all play for different teams. Dirk Nowitzki and Robert Garrett come from Würzburg, as do Burkhard Steinbach and Demond Greene, but Branko Klepac is from Bonn. There are younger guys here as well. Most of them are on the national team. Geschwindner had asked around and offered a "training camp on the lake," but didn't say much more.

Geschwindner makes his observations. Now joining him at his table on the terrace are Ernie Butler, Kendl, and Thomas Neundorfer, the "Doc." He's actually a family physician in Rattelsdorf, just under three hours away, but this week he's sleeping on an air mattress next to the restaurant's kitchen. A couple of weeks ago, Geschwindner had convinced him in a bar in Bamberg to be the camp doctor. The men joke around as much as the boys; they talk their talk and tell their stories. The training camp is an experiment for all of them, the first of many.

All functioning basketball teams are alike, no matter what age or league. A team's language takes on a life of its own, and an outsider wouldn't be able to understand a thing—and that's only after a single week on the lakeshore. There's cursing and dissing, irony and figurative speech, politically incorrect and careless words like *moron* and *dumbass* and *knucklehead*. Every team develops its own code, its own

language and pecking order, a vocabulary that's more precise and particular than anything that's said otherwise. Things receive the meaning the group ascribes to them. Nowitzki insults Garrett and Garrett
laughs; Garrett makes a joke about Greene and Greene fires back. Their
language is another playground on which the boys can compete. Insults
turn into declarations of love. Their trust is so fundamental that words
cannot shake it. They have a sharp sense of humor that's on point; it's
raw and passionate. Some things never change. Everyone here is full of
youth's invincibility and strength; they're all infallible and innocent.
They sound like bad boys, but they mean well.

The middle-aged men are sitting at their table, watching the boys.
Holger, Doc, Schorsch. Their language is more old-fashioned than
Dirk's. Geschwindner carefully listens and makes notes. He's read
about things the boys have never heard of. He has been places the boys
don't even know exist. "All of a sudden, I met these guys who never
learned Latin," he'll tell me later. "They couldn't get into mathematics. Or any of the other things that I was busy with—architecture and
art and God knows what. At first, I asked myself whether I could even
speak to them. 'What do they understand?' I never thought they were
stupid; it was more a question of intersubjectivity. How do they think
today? What can you say to them? What are you *allowed* to say? How
far and how fast can you go?"

Geschwindner knows what he doesn't want: to be a teacher in the
old mold. Coming from the ancient Greek *paidagogos*, pedagogy literally means "to lead the child." He doesn't want that. He remembers his
own teenage years, the all-nighters, the wild ideas he used to come up
with. And he also remembers the hard-ass coaches, the disciplinary
measures and practices as punishment. He knows all too well that the
traditional education methods of a number of teachers and coaches
only made him stubborn. "I've wrung out all these concepts by myself,"
he remembers. Geschwindner muses: Where do you point the boys?
What direction are you pulling them toward? The men drink their cof-

fee and discuss. "We didn't follow just one single idea in the beginning. We weren't trying to educate them, we wanted to let them grow. We wanted to see what plants needed more water to grow. It wasn't my idea for Dirk to go to the NBA. He wanted to go. So, we had to water here a little bit and pull some weeds over there. And then we egged one another on with our aspirations."

After breakfast, the boys pull the boats out of the shed, an eight-man scull and a four, all hands needed to turn the boats over and put them in the water. Kendl gives the orders, but the seating arrangements are established. The boys fold their big bodies into the rocking boats— they're actually too big and too awkward for the narrow things. Greene stumbles and almost falls, but Klepac holds onto him. When Burkhard Steinbach balances his 265 pounds in the boat, the boys *ooh* and *ahh* as the water splashes. Nowitzki's sitting in the front; he's the tallest and has a few more inches of space in the stroke seat. Geschwindner and Kendl are the last to get in; they're wearing heavy track pants and baseball caps to fend off the summer sun. Then they're off.

The boats pull out onto the lake. Geschwindner steers the four, Kendl the eight. The helmsmen keep a slow tempo at first—the bodies need to get used to the pace, the boats are still rocking and rolling a little, sometimes an oar hits another, wood on wood, and then all the oars have to be pulled out of the water, everyone has to wait and breathe and set the tempo again, everything from the top.

"Ready, all!"

"Paddles up! And row!"

It isn't very easy to find a common rhythm. Some guys are bursting with power and others get into the groove through sheer technique. None of them has ever been in a rowboat before; their bodies feel too big and too heavy for these shaky, narrow boats. It's hard for them to turn the paddles properly, to avoid putting them flat on the water. Sometimes one of them fools around and sometimes one of them relies too much on his strength, and then they're out of rhythm and have to start from the top again. There are many things to consider if you want to get ahead.

More than 20 years later, I'll visit the camp at Lake Starnberg and sit in a boat myself—a two with helmsman. Doc will determine the direction and set the tempo, Uli Ott and I are on the sculls. At first, I'll row with might and conviction to bring the boat forward—after all, Uli is older than me—but then I'm the one who keeps slipping out of rhythm because I want too much too fast. I'm the one who needs to understand how a team works. Pulling ahead on the horizon is an eight-man scull with a new generation of basketball players. Geschwindner's still sitting at the control cables, and the lake will always look the way it did when Dirk and the boys rowed along the shore.

To the right are Starnberg's boat sheds and mansions, the British-looking teahouses and Bavarian balconies, the architecture of new money. Bathers are at the swimming bays and jetties. The boys row past the daughters of respectable families who are in polo shirts and bikinis with boom boxes and picnic baskets. The only thing between the boys and this world is water. They could jump in and swim over; they could drop their oars and whistle and jeer like teenagers.

One or two of them is thinking about it—Robert Garrett, for instance. He's easily distracted by stuff like this; he loves the water and the beach, and he likes lying in the sun and staring into the sky, but then there's Dirk's broad frame in front of him, the back of his head, the muscles in his neck, the places where muscles are supposed to be, the dripping wet T-shirt. He sees Dirk establish the pace, and he sees Holger, who's looking at him with a smile since he knows exactly what Robse is thinking. He's smiling because he doesn't hold it against him for almost whistling and jeering, for being only a hair away from jumping in and swimming through the clear water and the boys' yelling toward the laughing girls on the shore. Holger knows all of this, and Robse knows that Holger knows. But above all, he knows he's allowed to do whatever he wants.

"Ready all!"

"Paddles up!"

"And row!"

And Robse keeps rowing because Dirk doesn't allow himself to get distracted while maintaining the pace and because the rhythm of the boat continues. He's all in, and now he's feeling ambitious, he's rowing and concentrating on the next stroke, the turn of the handle, the clean dip, the pull, the constant out-turn-in-pull, out-turn-in-pull. The boat glides and moves faster and farther with every stroke, faster and faster and farther and farther; there's a little more pull with every stroke. You can hardly see the other boat anymore—eight people are faster than four—they row and they row and they turn around at the Island of Roses. They drift in the water, they pant, and they smile.

When they land back at the club, two cars are waiting for them. Their arms are like rubber, their hands are rubbed smooth or blistered over from the wooden handles. Totally exhausted, they're vaguely happy from the sun and the summer. The boys shout and jump in the water, cannonballs from the dock, then lie out to dry in the sun. A short break, a quick lunch—souvlaki with rice, Mezzo Mix from beer steins, iced tea from cartons—then the horde piles into the vans, sneakers in their hands. It stinks in the bus the way it stinks when 15 teenage boys are busy rowing for a week and no mothers are there to do the washing. It smells like freedom. The two cars drive on the Seestrasse toward Starnberg's town center and stop at a big multipurpose gym.

Now they've got the ball in their hands. They dribble and play shooting games; it gets louder and louder and wild and silly. The boys are like cows let out onto the meadow in spring—they buck and they holler and can only stand still for a couple of seconds as Geschwindner announces the next exercise, giving brief instructions that are more like suggestions.

Then they play. That's why they're here. In the mornings and afternoons, the boys reconnect with themselves in the gym, the music and jokes, the exercise and dribbling. The slapping of the sculls fades to the backs of their heads; only their bodies remember the labor. The boys run, their bodies fly, they cut at an angle, they crash into one another—the speed alone is madness. Everything here has flow and pace; the level of play is incredible. The best of the best are going at it. Nowitzki and Garrett. There's no ref—the offense calls fouls, but the offense almost never calls a foul, the players are too good and too fast. Willoughby, Greene. It's the joy found in one's own abilities that keeps the boys going, farther and farther, the happiness in what their bodies are capable of doing, how high they can jump, how well they can shoot, how fast they can run. The boys could run and keep playing forever. It's not that they think they can win. They know it.

This—or something like it—is what it must have been like.

Robert's a Free Man

A BEACH ON THE BALTIC SEA near Zingst: a village on the water—red bricks, reed roofs—packed in summer, empty in winter. The tourists' cars are parked bumper to bumper on the street behind the dyke. Zingst isn't a dream destination; it's the reality of vacationing in Germany. But what's more, Zingst isn't a basketball town. Still, I'm here to meet Dirk Nowitzki's old teammate Robert Garrett. This is where he spends his summers.

"Robert's a free man," Dirk once told me, so I drove to Zingst to talk about the old days, but when I arrive at the kite surfing school at Dune Crossing 6, he's nowhere to be found. There are bikinis and coolers, sun hats and the scent of SPF 50. Summer people. I ask around, everyone knows who he is but not where he is. At the surf shack, they're grilling, sausage and Red Bull, patio umbrellas and deck chairs, reggae pop trickling in from somewhere. The flags are raised. It's early afternoon, but everyone looks like they've finished a hard day of work long ago.

I find him down on the beach. Robert is standing in the flat water of the Baltic Sea, gathering his equipment. He only taught today; there wasn't enough wind for him to head out. Robert is standing amongst the screaming children and waves when he sees me. He trudges toward me through the sand—he's a big guy, the spitting image of a surf instructor—as beach balls fly around him. He's gotten rid of the cautiousness of many professional athletes; he's living a different life now. He looks right at me and thumps me so hard with his left hand that my shoulder cracks. "Follow me," he says, and walks ahead, through the laughter and screaming, the summer peoples' high fives and fist bumps.

In my memory, Robert Garrett was a forceful player with a powder keg torso—explosive and raw, but under control. He could overpower his defenders, but also slip by them—he was a bull with finesse, Charles Barkley–like or Zion Williamson–esque, even though he played two positions smaller. His drives to the basket and the quickness of his shot: I remember just how special this combination had been in the German league at the time. Now he's standing barefoot in the water, dressed in board shorts and a T-shirt, tan and fit, even if he's gained some weight since his playing days.

Garrett talks to everyone at the same time. He grabs two soft drinks and a sausage, introduces me to his boss and colleagues, and everyone here looks exactly the way you'd imagine them to look: blond hair, broad shoulders, freckles. Everyone's on a first-name basis. The music coming out of the speakers isn't commercial crap; I remember the Shins. Life on the coast just seems to be easier. Trash is talked on the beach just as much as in the gyms of Robert's past, but it's more friendly and sophisticated. It's not only a man's world; women are also present. People talk about the fantastic weather; they talk about the wind, which is supposed to pick up tomorrow. Everything is going to be better tomorrow. On the surface, none of this has anything to do with basketball, but if you look deeper, you can see that it does. Wind hangs in the poplars, seagulls scream.

Robert Garrett has known Dirk Nowitzki since forever. The two started playing against one another as under-13s—Dirk for Würzburg, Robert for the tiny town of Ochsenfurt. Garrett's mother is German, his father an American stationed in Franconia. A younger brother,

Benjamin. A very normal family from a south German city. There's an army base nearby. But problems surface quite early: the father struggles with gambling, the marriage falls apart. "Let's just say," Garrett will later curtly wrap everything up, "I come from modest beginnings."

The boy throws himself into sports headfirst. He masters everything he picks up immediately. Tennis. Basketball. He does somersaults from the three-meter springboard while the others are still hopping off the starting blocks with pinched noses. At this age, he's the exact opposite of Dirk: carefree, T-shirt off, cannonballs from the high dive. Hey you, watch how I can fly!

He and Dirk occasionally play against each other and later become teammates on the under-14 select team. After working with Holger for a couple of weeks, Dirk asks Robert if he would like to join. The story is pretty much the same: Garrett watches Holger Geschwindner play, Eggolsheim against whoever else, and when the old man beats his opponents practically by himself, Garrett figures he could learn a thing or two from him. Holger doesn't need to make any big declarations; he gains the youth's respect immediately.

Robert, Dirk, and the former track athlete Demond Greene train together in Würzburg and Rattelsdorf. Greene is an incredible athlete, Dirk a crazy combination of height and talent, Garrett of power and perseverance. They go about things systematically. Geschwindner stands on the sidelines during team practices and calls his boys over to a side basket one after another. He works with them for a few minutes, then throws them back in the game so that they can put what they've learned into practice—do it now! The exercises seem strange to the more experienced players, but soon the boys overwhelm them. They fit together perfectly and they keep getting better. At the time, nobody else is doing individual training tailored to the requirements and needs of each individual player.

Geschwindner's pedagogical ideas receive some pushback—or at least they're viewed with skepticism. At the time, the development of young athletes is primarily concerned with technical and physical aspects. You shoot, you lift weights, you run. The only goal is to be successful as a team. To win games. You do whatever the coach tells you.

But this doesn't fly with Geschwindner's boys. And it doesn't have to. Geschwindner doesn't even desire to be taken seriously. At least not out of respect for one's elders or authority. He relishes the role of the lateral thinker and court jester. He prints business cards with the company name Institute for Applied Nonsense, which he will continue to use throughout Dirk's entire career. People with the club teams and in the federations aren't totally sure how to deal with this humor, seeing as Geschwindner is dead serious about his pedagogical approach. Sometimes it leads to bickering about responsibilities, sometimes the situation escalates. Geschwindner wants his boys to want to play and win on their own accord. They should go to practice because they want to go to practice. Because they understand what needs to be done. Geschwindner views the usual rules and hierarchies as being counterproductive. Disciplinary measures are foreign to him; everything needs to make sense in a playful manner. Geschwindner wants a "system that's there for the kids," not the other way around. He doesn't want to put the boys through the wringer. Even though it looks laissez-faire on the surface, he takes all of it very seriously.

The Würzburg club team accepts him and his boys because the results can be immediately discerned. Things are more complicated with the national team, though. Geschwindner often clashed with the officials and coaches when he was a player himself. He ended his career with the national team at 30—or, rather, it was ended on his behalf. Officially, he was too old; unofficially, he was too unruly, too obstinate. Today, you would say he was ahead of his time. He repeatedly pulls his boys out of the training camps and doesn't care what the officials think or threaten. He doesn't care because he has the upper hand. Greene, Garrett, Willoughby, and Nowitzki are indispensable.

Geschwindner listens to his boys when they find themselves in a jam. He doesn't want to explain the world to them, he leaves that to books and films. He renounces educational traditions and pedagogical doohickeys; he only gives "tips" and "assistance" (his words, not mine). This pleases Robert, who essentially grew up without a father. He remembers that Geschwindner had an answer for every question and situation in life—he never focused on basketball alone. An example: once, his girlfriend at the time was studying in Austin, Texas, and he was lovesick ("and I mean seriously lovesick," he says). And although there was an important game against Frankfurt coming up, Holger sent him to Austin. "You're flying over there this very minute," he said. "It's more important." Garrett laughs. "'If the smock is on fire,'" he says, sounding a little bit like Geschwindner, the mentor's quirky turns of phrase imbuing his boys' sentences. "When the smock is on fire, you need to go." When Robert's brother, Benny, overtired from night shifts at two jobs, died in a car accident, Holger saved Robert. He has his brother's name tattooed on the inside of his arm. Nothing's changed, he says. Holger Geschwindner is always there when it counts. And the same goes for the others.

If you drive with Holger Geschwindner, there's always a point when his phone rings and one of his boys is on the line. "*Bei der Arbeit*," Geschwindner says, and he's always at work. Greene or Willoughby, Garrett or Nowitzki. When Boniface N'Dong needs help with one of his camps in Senegal: Holger. When Burkhard Steinbach needs advice about his farm: Holger. Life poses questions, and sometimes Holger has an answer. Or an idea. Even if it's a crazy one.

Geschwindner lets his boys do whatever they want. If they want to go to parties, he lets them. Curfews? "We don't get involved in that circus." But you still have to show up at practice. He doesn't want anything to be off-limits; he wants them to experience everything and make their own decisions. Lovesick? Go! Looking to party? He'll drive you to the club in Munich personally. Hungover? Pull through! They call it "alcohol evaporation training." He doesn't want to protect them from anything. In his mind, they should follow the right path because they've discovered it on their own. They shouldn't chicken out. There are no excuses. There's no giving up. Geschwindner and his boys are committed to living the way they play basketball. They're always ready, no matter what other people and their conventions dictate. The path of least resistance leads nowhere.

Geschwindner tries to deal with all the different characters according to their needs. When Greene lets his apprenticeship slide, he scolds him; when Garrett misses his girlfriend, he's an understanding friend. When Dirk has doubts, he sweeps them out of the way. Soon, they know each other so well that he's aware of the situation in advance, and he steers straight through it in complete control.

The coach doesn't want his guys to have tunnel vision, so he gives them books and shows them the world outside the arena. He doesn't allow them to drop out of school or not take it seriously. "Graduate," he says. Even though Garrett doesn't come from a middle-class household, he also starts reading. "Cheating's out of the question," the coach says.

The Würzburg kids are a motley crew. At first glance, they don't seem to fit together. Garrett, from Ochsenfurt, has the unique experience of the Afro-German army kid; Greene is a long jumper and hurdler from Aschaffenburg with a similar experience. Neither of them comes from an affluent household or intellectual environment. Both are "bursting with power," as Geschwindner remembers it. Marvin Willoughby comes later; he's tall and skinny, but also blessed with special athletic abilities. He's from Wilhelmsburg, a rough part of the northern German city of Hamburg. Back then, all of them have something to prove, all of them are burning with ambition, and they're instructed by a roughshod intellectual. But in the end, it's the middle-class Dirk Nowitzki who stands out.

Greene and Garrett work on their game like mad, but Nowitzki works even harder. He's even more focused. The guys take turns driving, 45 miles on the A70, 45 miles back. Every single day. Sometimes, one of them can't make it because life gets in the way. But Dirk doesn't relax, never makes exceptions. Now Robert is sitting behind the dyke in one of the surfing school's deck chairs, remembering his younger self— a "sloppy genius," as he calls himself. Sometimes, he let things slide.

"Whenever I went to the pool," he says, looking around and observing the eternal pool day his life has become, "Dirk went by himself to Rattelsdorf. Mornings there, practice for two or three hours, then back to Würzburg for team practice in the evening."

"Robse was not always about putting in his full effort," Dirk once told me about Garrett. "He was extremely talented. At everything. An incredible tennis player. He'd destroy me even now. Great volleyball player, great swimmer. An all-around talent. He could have done whatever he wanted."

These months feature a lot of laughter; strengths are put to the test, games are won. The development of their basketball game is incredible. Times are good.

It's 1997. Summer is quickly approaching; the boys are 18 and the future is theirs. But then there's the question about the military service that is mandatory for all 18-year-old men in Germany. A full year! Surely something could be done, at least for Dirk, who's seven feet tall— there's got to be a way to get out of this! The beds and the boots and the uniforms would all be way too small for him; the rifle would look like a pistol in his hands. But Geschwindner remembers what it was like to be a soldier. He encourages the boys. The military can be seen as a symbol, a structure that can be transferred to team sports and their structures almost one to one—that is, if you look at things practically and aren't romantic about sports. You have to learn to deal with boredom and hierarchies, constraints and rules, physical challenges and strict procedures coming from others. You have to be able to deal with irrationality and stupidity. "You can't chicken out," he says. "Go to the Bundeswehr." Geschwindner isn't a militarist by any means. For him, it's about something else (even if it sounds absurd): it's about freedom.

The results are in front of my eyes on the beach in Zingst: Robert Garrett doesn't have a home or a steady job or a family or responsibilities. There's a row of mobile homes and buses parked behind the surf shop; one of them is his. The bus he lives in generates its own power, has enough potable water for a week, and is prepared for every contingency. Everything is sorted; there's a cubby or drawer for everything. Garrett designed the bus on his own, everything just the way he wanted it. He spends his summer months on the Baltic Sea, autumns on Maui, winters on the ski slopes of Colorado, and then surfs in the Caribbean in spring. Then everything starts over again. The only things Robert Garrett has to obey are the seasons and the weather. There are a couple of books on the dashboard, and his tattoo on the inside of his upper arm reminds him of his priorities in life.

"Robse always said that one day he'd just go and leave," Dirk told me. "He always had this nonconformist mentality that's totally foreign to me."

Robert drives to Franconia once a year and gets a checkup from Doc Neundorfer in Rattelsdorf, visits his mother in Ochsenfurt, and plays a couple hands of cards with his old teammates. Only a few still play basketball. When he needs advice, he talks to Geschwindner on the phone, and he passes through Dallas once a year to visit Dirk, but he stays in a hotel nowadays. Not because they wouldn't get along, but because of his sense of freedom. Life changes and he doesn't want to be a burden for anyone. At the end of the year, he's spent exactly as much as he has earned. "Robert's a free man," Dirk says.

On a Sunday afternoon at the end of the summer in 1997, Garrett and Nowitzki are sitting in Geschwindner's car again. They're driving through the countryside, over the hills on their way up north, past the wheat fields and the vibrant green. The massive gray sky. Dirk is looking out the window; they're not talking all that much, but when they do, they crack jokes. Military service starts tomorrow in the Volkach barracks, and neither of them knows what's in store for them. They're nervous—Dirk will later say "anxious." They had one last practice that morning, then they packed their things and drove off. They are scared when they get out of the car in front of the barracks gates. They pass through the gate, and when they turn around one last time, Geschwindner is standing on the other side of the fence. "Now you'll see what freedom means," he says before getting in the car and driving back to Peulendorf. They have to stay here, and they don't know what's waiting for them—and they wouldn't be able to change it if they did. Now they know what freedom is.

Robert and Dirk are not allowed to leave the barracks for two whole weeks, and basketball is out of the question. For two whole weeks, they don't practice for a single minute; the military doesn't make exceptions for talented basketball players. For two whole weeks, they take their guns apart and put them back together and sleep in tents and march in a circle with their packs on their backs. The beds are too small for Dirk, the shoes have to be specially ordered, the pants are highwaters, the bivouacs are exhausting. Robert and Dirk are in the maintenance department, but they're in different platoons. Robse's room in the barracks is downstairs, Dirk sleeps upstairs. They only see each other occasionally; they don't march a single time together.

Dirk misses what it feels like to shoot the ball. He misses the speed and his guys and their yelling and the gym. He misses the game of basketball. Daily life on the barracks is regimented and totally joyless. Dirk isn't a beer drinker, but everyone else is. He wants to win whenever he plays Uno or poker, and he's so tired at night that he can't even read. He looks out his window at the world on the other side of the chain-link fence. The payphones are almost always occupied. He wonders whether the weeks in the barracks will mess with his career goals. He's a German international who has been told that he will be Germany's best. He's been working his butt off for three years now. He has high ambitions, but he wonders whether he'll have to start from the beginning when he gets out. Why is he taking guns apart when he could be refining his shot?

After a couple of weeks, they're allowed to leave on the weekend. They take turns driving; one time they ride in Dirk's Golf II, the next time in Robert's Corsa. When service is over on Friday, they race straight to the gym, play on Saturdays, and drive back as late as possible on Sunday. They leave at 9:30 p.m.—they have to be there at ten. They arrive at the last minute, and Dirk feels like he's sitting in a jail cell for days, even weeks. He thinks about his game while he marches in the hard shoes or screws something or other together or lies on his cot. *Tak tadamm. Swish.*

Dirk has very solid games on the weekends, even though he doesn't really practice. Once, he scores 41 points against Langen, followed by 39 against Breitengüssbach. He's relieved whenever he has the opportunity to play basketball. He doesn't belong in the barracks. A burden falls from his shoulders as soon as he enters the gym. The 18-year-old dominates the league despite not being properly prepared. Garrett and Greene think Dirk's performance is uncanny, but Dirk doesn't talk about the attention all that much. He hits almost every shot. Dirk turns to Geschwindner on the drive back to Volkach after a game in Heidelberg.

"How is this possible, Holger?" he asks.

"That's what freedom is," Holger says. "This is what a free person can do."

Years later, Nowitzki will be able to remember this conversation. Every single word. "Sense of freedom," Hodge always said. "Always try to maintain your sense of freedom." ("You know how he talks," Dirk will say to me in his hotel room in San Francisco before imitating Geschwindner. "Sense of freedom!")

Behind the scenes, Geschwindner is ramping up the contact with Nike and George Raveling. Nowitzki and the boys are traveling with the national team, and Geschwindner sits in the stands, giving his

tips. Dirk injures his ankle in a tournament in Holland, but he and
Geschwindner still drive to Paris afterward to meet Raveling.

Dirk is a thin, blank slate and Raveling is a legendary American
scout. Born in 1937, he's from the same generation as Geschwindner
and was a college coach for a long time. Now he's responsible for dis-
covering and developing international talent for Nike. Raveling sees
basketball as an international game, and he's on the hunt for good
stories. He finds the advertising faces of the future. Raveling is someone who knows what it means to be at the right place at the right time
(he worked as stage security at the Lincoln Memorial in Washington
during Martin Luther King Jr.'s famous "I Have a Dream" speech in
1963, and he had the courage to ask King for the manuscript at just
the right moment as King left the stage afterward. King gave him the
papers, Raveling has kept them, and the highest bid—according to
Wikipedia—is now higher than $3 million).

In Paris, Raveling is pleased to see Nowitzki and Geschwindner in
person even though Dirk is injured, and he will remember the young
German when he sends out the invitations to the Hoop Summit in San
Antonio a couple of weeks later.

One Saturday in September, Geschwindner is standing in front
of the gates to the base. He tells the boys to get in his car. They have
received special permission from Senior Staff Sergeant Herrmann. They
race toward Dortmund. Nike has invited the boys to compete in an
exhibition game against a team of superstars, including Charles Barkley. Dirk has just completed a pack march, he has blistered feet, but he's
still got enough in him to dunk on Barkley. Barkley will later say that
Dirk scored more than 20 points in the first half. Thirty. Fifty. Barkley
is a storyteller, and he'll even tell this exact story at Dirk's retirement
more than 22 years later. After the game, the players still have a little
time to celebrate with the Americans. "Where are you going to play,
son?" Barkley is said to have asked Dirk when he is getting ready to
leave. He has to go back to Volkach, the barracks.

"I'm in the military," Dirk is said to have answered.

"There aren't any seven-footers in the military," Barkley replies. "If you want to make something of yourself, go to Auburn University, son!" Auburn is Barkley's alma mater; he's recruiting Dirk. And in fact, in the days after the exhibition game, colleges start calling Dirk and his parents. Berkeley. Kentucky. Duke. North Carolina. Geschwindner will later sort through the recruitment letters and set them to the side. When Dirk gets back to the barracks well after midnight, he's happy. He's just played against Scottie Pippen and Barkley. Does it get any better?

After basic training, Robse and Dirk become soldiers in the Bundeswehr's sports corps. On the weekends, they dominate the second division. On the court, you can tell that they are best friends. Their game is intuitive, they trust each other. Each knows how the other moves. They make space for Demond Greene when he has the ball. Würzburg has the beast, Steinbach, for the rough stuff, and the law student Nico Wucherer to bring the ball up the court and direct the traffic. Dirk plays out on the wing, Steinbach heaves the big defenders to the side, Garrett gets in position and receives the ball right on his shooting hand, just the way he likes it. He shoots faster than everyone else, he never hesitates.

The rest of the league is playing almost exclusively with cheap import players from America and the Eastern Bloc. Würzburg is unusual for being led exclusively by young Germans. Klaus Perneker and Holger Geschwindner play an unconventional game. Their guys shoot the ball from all over the court and without hesitation. Their game is similar to the way the Phoenix Suns will later play with Steve Nash, Amar'e Stoudemire, and coach Mike D'Antoni—or the Golden State Warriors' approach under Steve Kerr 20 years later. Perneker stands on the sidelines and Geschwindner is right behind him. Perneker takes care of the rules and Geschwindner bends them. The boys don't feel bad when they miss a shot, they don't lament their mistakes, they just quickly iron them out. This style is considered risky, but it is undeniable that the Würzburg way is a lot of fun. For the players and for the audience.

At the beginning of the season, the young Dirk has to battle with experienced and powerful men who don't believe the hype surrounding him. They do what people in the second division of the Bundesliga are good at: play physically and with full effort. Dirk can shoot from all over the court, but he gets pushed around under the basket—he doesn't even weigh 200 pounds yet. He only gradually learns that he won't survive if he pushes back and fights for position. He learns to use the force and mass that are mobilized against him to his advantage. Like a dancer or a judoka, he absorbs the defender's strength and lets himself be pushed off. The ball leaves his hand at an unusually high angle for the second division and he's more accurate. You can already tell he'll go far.

Würzburg has just barely missed out on advancing to the first division in each of the past two seasons. If they don't qualify for the first division this year, they won't be able to keep Dirk. He's being pulled in every direction—toward Spain, Italy, California. Berlin and Leverkusen, the two leading first division teams, are positioning themselves in the race for Nowitzki.

Würzburg only loses two games the entire season. Dirk scores at will and averages 28.1 points per game—incredible for the tough, defensive-minded, and shorter European game. The familial structures of the club become more professional; everyone knows that this is crucial. Actually, the team is way too good for the second division; Garrett is also about to play for the national team, and the Croatian player who joined the team later, Ivo Nakić, has already won EuroLeague titles. The others teams' coaches heap praise on Nowitzki in order to spur their own players on; the defense gets intense and rough on him, but now he can handle it. He knows how to draw attention to himself and then pass the ball. He's the best player, but he knows what his team needs.

In those days, Robert Garrett plays in Dirk Nowitzki's shadow to some degree, but he learns to live with it. He shoots whenever he wants. He's part of a functioning ensemble, his body will never be as fast and flexible and strong as right now. He's doing what he loves and the team wins. Würzburg marches through the advancement rounds. The city is going crazy. Just one more win and they'll be in the first division, just one more win and their dream will finally come true. Just one more win!

"And then, all of a sudden, Dirk was gone," Garrett says in his bus behind the dyke. The door is open, the poplars and the sea are rustling, the sun is sinking. Dirk and Holger are said to have driven to Frankfurt before the critical game and gotten on a plane at dawn. To Dallas. San Antonio. The Hoop Summit. Garrett rattles off the buzzwords without any sense of melancholy. "A couple insiders knew what was going on, of course," he says. The indignation was considerable; the city was up in arms for a couple of days. What about decency? Moral maturity? But the team wasn't all that worked up. "If we're honest," Garrett says, "we already knew back then that Dirk would eventually have to leave."

Down to Earth

SUMMER 2015

A HOUSE IN THE HILLS above Würzburg—nothing fancy, just a respectable residential neighborhood. There are no old villas or massive trees here, just freshly planted fruit and birch trees. Families with children, no old money. The house is big and spacious, glass and granite; the sun beats down on the hills and the city is stewing in the valley below. There's no car in the driveway and not a soul in sight.

Dirk drops me off in the driveway to the house that was originally built in case he ever decided to return to Würzburg. But he has never owned it. He's been gone for more than half his life, he's put down roots in Dallas, his wife and kids feel at home in Texas. He will probably never come back. His sister, Silke, lives here now, with her husband and children, but they're currently on vacation. Dirk's father is here to take care of the house today and to clean the pool. "At least that's what he claims," Dirk says. "But he really just wants to have a swim in peace."

Nowitzki has just been practicing in Randersacker, I did the rebounding, even though it was way too hot in the gym without air conditioning. He was planning to join me while I interviewed his father, but Jessica and the kids have plans this afternoon and his mother made lunch. So, he drops me off and honks, but no one answers.

I slink around the house and onto the terrace. There's a plastic basketball hoop that's too low and too crooked to practice on. Soccer balls, volleyballs, inflatable rubber animals. "Hello?" I call. "Excuse me?" Nothing. I feel like a burglar for a second; I consider going back or at least ringing the doorbell.

I've written a few profiles of Dirk over the past couple of years. I kept watching his games, hung out in media dining rooms, and waited for press conferences. Over the course of three years, I interviewed players and coaches and friends, watched Dirk and Holger practice, and spent countless hours in coffee shops with Geschwindner. Someone told me I had been vetted and was now approved to sit at the dinner table, too. And by swimming pools. A ceremonial book is being planned for Geschwindner's 70th birthday, conversations with old companions and friends, and I'm in charge of the book. *Applied Nonsense* will be its title. Dirk's father and Holger have lived through a bunch of crazy things together, and to me it seems their roles in Dirk's life are similar. Father and coach, coach and father.

Then Dirk's father is suddenly standing in front of me, in swimming trunks and a T-shirt. "Howdy," he says and shakes my hand, grinning. "Jörg." The Americans call him J-Dub, as in J. W., for Jörg-Werner. And so does his family.

Jörg-Werner Nowitzki is a friendly man. He's an old-fashioned tradesman who was born in Altmittweida in 1943 but grew up in Würzburg. He's a jester and wisecracker, a jovial shoulder slapper—someone with people skills, as you'd say today. He's a professional painting contractor. His business relations start at the local bar, contracts are signed with a handshake. The Nowitzkis have worked a ton in their lives, and they've earned a decent amount of money, enough for their own house with a backyard. Now J-Dub is retired, but sometimes he still goes into the office, just to see how things are going. It would never occur to him to just kick back and relax on the dime of his successful son.

J-Dub and I have only ever had casual encounters: once at the gala in

Berlin, another time at a charity soccer game in the Würzburger Kickers'
stadium, and again when he wrote me an email to thank me for a profile
I wrote about his son. He knows who I am and can remember faces (Dirk
probably got that from him). But that's the extent of our interactions.

Dirk's father waves me over to the pool, which is currently in
the house's shadow. He inspects the edge of the pool with a net and
fishes a few leaves out of the water. When I ask him if he would mind
if I recorded the conversation, he suddenly interrupts me. "It's too hot,
man. We can also talk in the water."

"Sure," I say, "but I don't have a towel with me. I guess I could—"

But Nowitzki has already taken his shirt off, jumped into the water,
and dunked under.

Jörg Nowitzki used to be a good handball player and is still a large,
strong man with a lot of oomph in his throwing arm. He's over 70 now.
His health could be better—it's the heart—and his voice is hoarse. You
can sense a certain sportsmanship in the first few seconds of our meeting.
The handshake. The jokes meant as a challenge. The come-on-already-
and-take-your-shirt-off-and-hop-into-the-water-dude!-imperative.
Father Nowitzki floats in the pool and looks at me from below.

"You scared?" he asks. "Water too cold?"

I put my recorder down on the edge of the pool, fold my T-shirt,
and climb into the water in my Alba Berlin shorts. My plan had been
to start talking about Geschwindner and the first, turbulent years,
when it wasn't clear whether Dirk would make it. Before the championship, before the NBA, before he ever became a professional basketball
player. I want to talk about the overlap between the roles of fathers and
coaches, something Father Nowitzki experienced firsthand—after all,
he was Dirk's handball coach long ago and accompanied him to tennis
tournaments for years.

I don't have to ask all that much. Jörg Nowitzki simply cuts loose.
He's an anecdote machine, he talks without worrying about the
consequences—good stories are good stories—he's a man without a

filter. Better said: he's a man who wears his heart on his tongue. The first autumn leaves are drifting around us, as we bob like buoys around the microphone at the edge of the pool. Father Nowitzki unpacks one story after another, leaking tidbits of information, toying with hearsay, things I could never write down. Whenever it gets too hot for him, he plunges underwater time and again. When I listen to the tape later, it will be difficult to understand what we're saying due to all the spluttering and gurgling. He says "Geschwindner," the emphasis on the first syllable and not the second as is common in German.

I ask about beginnings. Was it difficult for him as a father when Holger's role in Dirk's life kept growing? A "father figure," he says; he can see where I'm going. "Holger's protégé." He goes below the surface and stays there, and you can sense just how strange it must have felt— it'd be hard to imagine it not being strange. I've been worried about this question. I'm a father, too; my daughters are still young, but I can imagine it would be difficult to completely hand over your child to a coach and the sport.

Dirk's father comes up for air and briefly thinks, but then continues without giving a clear answer. He delivers a veritable storm of anecdotes and untold stories; I'm familiar with some of them. Like the trip in the battered VW van to the FIBA European Championships in southern France, the time Holger confronted the German basketball official, and how Jörg was suffering from a toothache, the drive back on painkillers. Or the story about the bet: after a national team tournament, a group of family and friends were having a luxurious meal in a restaurant that was a veritable Versailles, and everyone was dressed accordingly. "Everyone but Hodge." Geschwindner showed up in his lumberjack shirt and jeans, and when somebody noticed his attire, they proposed a bet: the most expensive bottle of whiskey in the place, if he could come back in finer threads within ten minutes. Everyone knew Holger only ever traveled with a tiny suitcase. Deal, sure thing, you've got yourself a bet! Holger, thanks to his special technique of folding suits, appeared in a dignified tailcoat less than five minutes later. He could fit literally everything in his tiny red suitcase. "And not a single wrinkle!" Afterward, they shared the whiskey like brothers.

I tell him about my visit with Robert Garrett on the beach in Zingst, where we talked about their early years and about Dirk's military service in Volkach as well as his early years in the second division. Father Nowitzki can also remember the day when Geschwindner arrived early in the morning at their front door to take 18-year-old Dirk to the Nike Hoop Summit in San Antonio rather than playing in the advancement game for Würzburg. He remembers the bitterness of the press and the Würzburg basketball scene. "Dirk and Holger were gone," he says, and it seems like he doesn't have fond memories of these events, even though they happened long ago and aren't really important anymore. "But we were still here."

Clouds appear and Father Nowitzki gets out of the water. "We need to cover the pool," he says. That's why we're here, after all. I climb out after him. We share a towel and fish the remaining leaves out of the pool. We pull a tarp over it and try to make coffee in the kitchen, but can't find any beans. No coffeepot, either. Everything in this house is slightly higher than in normal houses—everything here has been made for Dirk, so the fridge is higher, the kitchen counter goes up to your chest. We decide to have tea.

The clouds pass over the valley, the chance is passing, and our conversation ends when Dirk's mother knocks on the patio door. Her greeting is polite but reserved. She was worried, she said, because her husband didn't pick up the phone, which is why she decided to pass by. J-Dub laughs and says things like "charger" and "battery," and I take a look around. She nods when I properly introduce myself. Yes. She remembers.

Helga Nowitzki is a closed book, a mystery. In all these years during Dirk's career, she's never given an interview, there have been no articles, and she's mostly in the background in the photos. For decades, she ran the family business and she has also managed Dirk's finances.

Born in 1943, she's a basketball player who made it to the national team. She reportedly has a good grasp of the game, but she doesn't talk about it. People always say that she manages what is probably the largest Dirk Nowitzki archive in the world and that she has watched every single game—not live at night in Germany, but on recordings in the morning. But she doesn't talk about that, either. The only time she let herself be pulled in front of the camera was for Dirk's movie, *Der perfekte Wurf*, in which she appeared in the redecorated kitchen of Geschwindner's Peulendorf mill—after Dirk and Holger used all their powers of persuasion. It is quite clear that she would rather not be sitting in front of the camera. Dirk is the one who invented her nickname, Helgus, and to this day all of them say this nickname like it's a title of honor.

I briefly consider taking a chance and asking Dirk's mother for an interview, but she closes the doors and windows with precision, then casually waters the flowers and puts the teacups in the dishwasher. All of this takes less than five minutes. And when I finally ask—maybe we could talk sometime soon?—she declines politely but definitively. She's never spoken to the journalists, she says, her smile friendly and crystal clear. And things always went well when she didn't.

Dirk Nowitzki's parents take me with them, down to the city center, then they'll return to the house on Unterer Katzenbergweg where Dirk grew up. They're spending the afternoon with their grandchildren, a summer evening with Dirk and his family. This time, when I get out of the car at Würzburg Central Station, I think I understand how the Nowitzki family ticks: the maternal resilience, her insistence on staying in the background; the paternal self-assertiveness and his practical wit. The changing standard of living and their resolution to remain with what's proven and known. What's also known as being "down to earth."

NOWITZSKI

A GAIN, THERE ARE DIFFERENT versions of the story.
As Dirk's father remembers it, Geschwindner knocked on
their door at six in the morning to pick Dirk up. Dirk remembers his
remorse. His doubts. His Würzburg team had been working toward
that critical game for months; they all shared the common dream of
advancing to the Bundesliga. It was also a financial necessity—the club
had invested a lot of money, labor, and enthusiasm to achieve it. Everyone was counting on Dirk to lift his team into the first division.

Geschwindner, by contrast, remembers telling Helgus only a couple of days before they left. She had wanted to know whether the trip
was really essential. In these months, Dirk was on the road all the time,
but this trip meant her son might go to America, and soon. That Dirk
would at some point leave Würzburg was obvious to everyone who
knew anything about basketball. But only a few people thought it possible that he would change continents. Most thought the idea was nuts.
It wasn't easy to convince Dirk's mother, Geschwindner says, but she
was the key—as always.

"Yes," he answered. "This is our only chance."

In the early morning of March 24, 1998, Dirk and Holger drive an hour and a half to Frankfurt Airport. They barely speak. When they do, they talk about the game, the annual matchup of the best American prospects against the rest of the world, but they do not talk about the potential consequences for Dirk's career. Geschwindner calls Würzburg once more from the airport and gets the final approval from Dirk's mother. Then they get on the plane.

Everyone's on edge in Würzburg, J-Dub says. The city is thinking about the advancement game and not about what comes next. They're thinking about the task at hand and not the future. The local newspaper, the *Main Post*, second-guesses Dirk's style and calls his "character traits" into question. Geschwindner is called the "mastermind of a secret USA mission." A distraction, a conflict of interest, an alternate idea about the future. The *Main Post* wants to get into the first division and Dirk and Holger want to play with the world's greatest.

Dirk's father is torn. He understands the importance of the advancement game for Würzburg; it's important to him as well. But it's a question of athletics and not of character. But then, maybe it is? At the time, he isn't sure, but looking back—bobbing up and down and fishing late-summer leaves out of the pool—he can smile about these wavering days in the spring of 1998.

On the day Dirk disappeared, it was impossible to know that the team would be good enough to win the game with just Garrett, Greene, and Nakić. That it never was an either-or situation. No one could foresee the advancement to the first division and the advancement of Dirk's career in America. This one missed game is only a pale memory; in most of the books and newspaper reports, the opponent is nameless and the score is never mentioned (for the record: SSV Weissenfels, 113–83).

While Würzburg stews in anger, Dirk Nowitzki and Holger Geschwindner are sitting on a plane over Greenland. No one is waiting to greet them when they arrive in Dallas. They take the highway into the city, totally fatigued. Flags are waving, billboards are advertising the Cowboys. It's warmer than in Würzburg. Two decades later, when

I ask them about it, they're no longer sure what they talked about as they approached the city. And they don't know whether they were in a taxi or driving a rental. Maybe they get off the highway on Commerce Street and drive by the white cross where John F. Kennedy was assassinated. Maybe they turn onto South Houston Street. The mirrored skyline actually looks like it does in the opening credits of the TV series, the one that the Nowitzki household and all of Germany watched in the '80s (Dirk remembers the yellow capital letters and can still hum the theme song). They drive past the redbrick buildings, the faded lettering and company names in downtown Dallas. Down Main Street. For the first time, Dirk sets foot in the city that will one day be his.

They stay at the Hyatt Regency, right next to the Reunion Arena where the Mavericks play. The arena is old, and basketball isn't all that important in the city—at the time, the team is one of the worst in the league. Dallas is a football town, the home of "America's Team," the most valuable sports team in the world, the Cowboys.

That evening, the world select team will have its first get-together with the Italian coach Sandro Gamba, high up in the revolving restaurant in the Reunion Tower, the so-called spaceball. For the next three days in Dallas, they'll be preparing for the game in San Antonio. The players are all the same age, but they come from all over the world. English is the lingua franca, but none of them speak it fluently. Most of them came without their coaches. Luis Scola from Argentina, Darius Songaila from Lithuania. When Dirk and Holger step into the restaurant, they're told that only Dirk can come. *Players only.*

While Dirk eats dinner with the team at the top of the tower, Geschwindner hangs out in the lobby. Suddenly, Donnie Nelson leaves the elevator. He's 36, average height and weight. Nelson works as a scout and assistant coach; he has great contacts in the Old World and will be managing the training camp of the world select team in the coming days. He has seen how Holger was sent away and decides to buy him dinner. He's a jovial man who understands hospitality. "That's just what you do," he'll explain to me in his office many years later. "Everyone with blood in his veins would have done the same thing." It isn't an entirely selfless gesture, of course. Nelson is also a strategist who recognizes an opportunity when it presents itself. He has a sonar detector for situations like this; he immediately senses that the guy in the lumberjack shirt must be someone important to young Nowitzki. He has heard about Dirk before, but he's surprised by his actual size when he sees him for the first time in the Hyatt. He is well aware that if Dirk Nowitzki is even half as quick as everyone says he is, he could be an interesting player.

Nelson and Geschwindner philosophize about the state of global basketball. They compare their visions and understand one another right off the bat. This encounter is more important to Dirk's future than any team meeting at the top of the tower.

Over the next few days in Dallas, the world select team prepares for the game against their American colleagues. They practice in the Mavericks' training facility in the Baylor Tom Landry Center. Gamba is the coach, Donnie Nelson one of his assistants. The Mavericks' general manager, Donnie's father, Nellie, sits in his office in the training facility and peers through the blinds. What's he supposed to do? He's in the right place at the right time. He's been in the business for ages, and the greatest talent he's ever seen is practicing right under his nose. At least that's what he'll say later.

Everything comes together, both fortunate coincidences and previous arrangements: if the team preparation hadn't taken place in Dallas, in a training facility right in front of Don Nelson's window; and if Nelson father and son hadn't been so open and innovative, and if Dirk's mother hadn't granted her approval and ignored the doubts of Dirk's father, and if Geschwindner hadn't taken the risk with this trip, and if Donnie and Holger hadn't gone out to dinner, and if they didn't have similar ideas about modern basketball—everything could have turned out completely different.

But on March 19, 1998, Dirk Nowitzki steps onto the court of San Antonio's Alamo Stadium Gymnasium to represent the world select team. The stands are full, mostly with scouts and university coaches. George Raveling and the Nike people are there, too. The cameras are rolling. The American players give their opponents American flags as a gesture of welcome. The best high school players are on the American side; they're used to being wooed and courted. There's Al Harrington and Rashard Lewis; later, they'll have solid NBA careers. Standing in front of the cameras and being written about is nothing new to them. Most of them have already committed to prestigious universities. They're used to winning and talking about their victories in sound bites suitable for television broadcasts. They know that their talent will earn them a lot of money. They've never heard of the players on the other team, which is literally called the "Rest of the World."

Such callousness is foreign to Dirk. He's nervous when the team walks through the huge parking lot of the football stadium and enters the small auxiliary gym. These are the moments that define why he plays basketball: observing his opponents warm up, checking out their size and disposition, then going out and showing who he is. Geschwindner has reminded him to be aware of what he can do at all times, and Dirk knows it. There's TV footage from this day where you can see Geschwindner staring at the court, totally frozen, highly focused. You can see that he has exchanged his lumberjack shirt for a knit sweater; it's almost as though he's dressed up for the occasion. Raveling has made sure that Holger can sit directly behind the bench. During the international team's time-outs, he barks his comments in German. Sometimes Coach Gamba looks over at him with irritation. He doesn't know who these comments are coming from and what this guy is doing behind his bench with his arms crossed.

The Americans go on the attack at the start of the game. Soon, the score is 10–4. They play a full-court press and steal the ball from the Rest of the World. Repeatedly. Nowitzki is in the starting five; he's the tallest player on his team. His opponents guess he must be a big, but they don't show him any respect—he's too skinny. But then Dirk gets the ball on the right wing. He's being defended by Jason Capel. Dirk has the ball in his favorite position; he probes the situation. When he sees that Capel is counting on him passing, Dirk puts the ball on the floor without fear or hesitation and blows past his defender with one, two steps over the free throw line. Geschwindner has drummed it into him that he shouldn't make a weak cut, so Dirk moves toward the basket with all his might and is fouled on his vehement two-handed dunk attempt by both Capel and JaRon Rush at the same time. There are many things they have been expecting, but a thin German kid trying to stuff the ball in their face isn't one of them. Dirk makes both of his free throws, and this is another thing that he and Geschwindner have discussed: get fouled, stand up, and make your free throws—two points are two points.

The game is close. The Americans are the better athletes and dominate the first half, but the world select team reacts and relentlessly attacks in the second half. Dirk goes to the line 23 times; he wears his defenders down and gets them to foul out one after another. His defenders are surprised; their coaches are stumped. If they get up in his feet, he blows by them, and if they give him space, he shoots from behind the three-point line so that they get up on him again on the next possession. When the Americans press in the backcourt and the Rest of the World guards have trouble getting the ball across the half-court line, Dirk goes back and brings it up himself. He's not shy about taking contact; he's more physical than he looks. He lets the Americans' prejudices work to his advantage. The game in San Antonio is quintessential Dirk: everything he will become is basically already there. And there's even more that is possible.

The scouts and coaches in the stands scribble in their notepads. They will later report that they realized they were seeing a new kind of player: a seven-footer who could move. Who could shoot the ball. Who could concentrate and not be distracted or intimidated; who—in what might have been the most significant game in his life—was mentally capable of doing what he set out to do.

If you watch tape from the game today, one thing that stands out is that Dirk's name is constantly misspelled. N O W I T Z S K I. In the opening minutes, the television commentators are still totally convinced by their own guys, by Harrington and Lewis, but then their skepticism gives way to surprise and finally to enthusiasm. Dirk is asked to deliver the postgame interview, something that's reserved for the best player on the winning team. In his shy schoolboy English, he states that he wanted to show that Europeans can also play basketball. And they can. At the end, the field reporter calls Geschwindner "Coach Holger"—it's like he's known him for years.

The Nelsons watch the game with the rest of the NBA managers and college coaches but decide to not talk about Dirk and silently use the minuscule advantage they have. Not only have they seen him play, but they've also watched him practice. And not just once. For three whole days. "I had no idea what to expect," Nelson says. "We scouts have a saying: looks can be deceiving. You see a seven-footer who moves fluid on the first day of training. 'Not bad,' you think. But on the second or third day, it became clear to me that he wasn't a fata morgana." The Nelsons think his combination of physical capabilities and creativity, of conventions and innovations, is the "real deal." They think he can turn into a player. A real player. And, on top of that, they have spoken with Geschwindner—even dined with him. As such, they know the particulars and they want to keep their knowledge to themselves as much as possible.

★   ★   ★

Steve Nash watches the game on TV, then forgets Dirk's name shortly after. Michael Finley reads about it in the papers. Scott Tomlin is working for the University of Kentucky's athletic department, which will invite Dirk to visit the campus less than two weeks later. Larry Bird will check the tape and reminisce about his youth. Rick Pitino watches the game and decides to try and bring Dirk to the Boston Celtics. Svetislav Pešić from Berlin and Dirk Bauermann from Leverkusen leave messages on the Nowitzkis' answering machine. In Würzburg, Robert Garrett hears about the results and is relieved to hear that his friend played well. At the airport, Geschwindner buys a newspaper as proof of the trip's success: "International Team Blitzes US" is the headline. The trip has been worth it, he says. "It was his only chance."

When Dirk returns to Würzburg, the seas have calmed. The team beat Weissenfels without him. But to this day, Holger Geschwindner still talks about the intense emotions directed at the two of them. "They murdered us," he says. "They were really pissed. I was someone who ruined the youth. They really killed us." He is accused of pushing individual interests over the interests of the team. Which is true, of course, but the ensuing decades will prove that it was the right decision. The end will justify the means, his vision will be certified by the events that transpire. Geschwindner will gradually become Dirk's manager, their complex relationship developing further: the various titles, the unclear roles, the deep friendship.

The team wins a meaningless final game of the season against Freiburg, 95–88, this time with Dirk. The arena is packed. He scores 26 points, and then his teammates carry him through the gym (the same goes for Garrett and Greene, I'm told; they take turns).

The college recruitment letters are piling up on the Nowitzkis' kitchen table and the answering machine is blinking every time they come home. Geschwindner writes friendly but firm letters requesting patience.

The two of them travel again to the US in May to get to know the country and to calmly consider Dirk's next step: Will he become a professional in Europe? Will he go to an American university? Which college programs would let him continue to play such an unconventional style? Or does he stay at home and play for Würzburg in the Bundesliga?

They visit Geschwindner's favorite universities, Berkeley and Stanford, hike in the Grand Canyon (down and back up in a single day, a kind of psychological endurance test for Dirk), and walk around Las Vegas. The University of Kentucky invites Dirk in order to sell him on its program and campus. Then Geschwindner declares Dirk for the NBA draft. Dirk's a top ten prospect after the Hoop Summit. It's looking good; the door is wide open: Dirk could become a pro in the National Basketball Association if he wants to. His childhood dream could become real.

Later, Dirk won't be able to remember when they took the college option off the table or when they scratched Europe from their plans. Presumably, the Nelsons and the Mavericks are concrete and passionate enough about their interest, their vision for Dirk so clear that everything else is put in its shadow. It's likely that the Nelsons and Geschwindner talk on the sly, and they probably speak the same language. The situation would be perfect for a player like Dirk: a coach who likes taking risks, a smart assistant, a team that loses more than it wins but will get better in the long run. They could give Dirk a lot of playing time. Plenty of space to develop.

Don and Donnie develop a plan to make Dirk a Maverick. They have the sixth pick in the 1998 draft, but Don Nelson wants more than Dirk alone. He wants to turn the Mavericks into a team that can win the championship. As soon as Dirk declares for the draft, Nelson starts looking for possible trade partners. The Mavericks contact the Milwaukee Bucks, who have the ninth pick.

The Bucks desperately need a big and powerful player for their team, a power forward. They've been eyeing Robert Traylor from the University of Michigan for months; his nickname is the Tractor, and he plays like one. He's the polar opposite of Dirk, even though he plays the same position: big, heavy, vehement. Milwaukee's afraid that Traylor won't be available at the ninth pick, so Dallas should take him with the sixth pick. They'll make a trade afterward and Dallas will receive another draft pick as a sweetener. It's risky, but taking risks is Nelson's hobby. Both teams announce the trade in advance, and everything goes as planned on draft day, June 24, 1998: the Mavericks receive Nowitzki, select Pat Garrity with the 19th pick, and trade him to the Phoenix Suns in a package with Bubba Wells and Martin Müürsepp for Steve Nash. Everyone is happy.

Donnie Nelson knows Nash from his time in Phoenix and thinks highly of him. He watched him practice in Phoenix and knows that the Suns aren't using him enough. And when they do, they don't do it properly, he thinks. Nash doesn't shoot enough in Phoenix, and his passing prowess isn't exploited, either. They think he could be a lot better. He seems like a perfect fit for the Mavericks' game as the Nelsons envision it.

In Würzburg, Dirk works out with his accustomed precision and stamina. Friends see an abstract idea becoming concrete reality. It's clear that he could go to Dallas if he wanted to, but the next day, they are back in the tiny Rattelsdorf gym for practice.

The Nelsons and team owner Ross Perot Jr. land in Würzburg the following day to pitch the move to Dirk. For an evening, they sit in Holger Geschwindner's backyard and drink beer and eat sausage, and the next night they have dinner with Dirk's family in the historic restaurant Backöfele in Würzburg. They get drunk and talk in broken English and German, then eventually pledge eternal friendship (for J-Dub, business always starts at the bar—the same is true for Texans). The Mavericks delegation invites Dirk to visit Dallas again; four days after the draft, Dirk and Holger are on another airplane.

This time, all stops are pulled out when he's picked up at the Dallas Fort Worth airport. The Mavericks lean into it: there are Dirk posters, cheers, a shuttle service, a better hotel. It's a perfect production. Dirk will only find out later that the people he took to be fans were actually employees of the team. The Mavericks desperately want to see Dirk in Dallas, they own the NBA rights to him, but the rights do not guarantee he will sign. If Nowitzki wants to stay in Europe, Dallas has no contractual access to him.

Dirk and Holger work out in the Mavericks' training facility, which is obviously more beautiful and luxurious than German gyms. A couple of other players are also there. They let Dirk play one-on-one against power forward Samaki Walker. Walker is in his second year in the NBA, and technically, Dirk's still only playing for an obscure German second division team—but he does well.

"Four weeks," Dirk says to Holger, panting, "and then I've got this."

"My thoughts exactly," Holger says.

At a men's apparel store, Dirk and Holger are outfitted with typical 1990s suits. Then Don Nelson introduces Nash and Nowitzki at a hastily convened press conference. He makes a couple of well-intended jokes that Dirk only vaguely understands because he's too nervous to think about jokes. You can sense his discomfort in the TV footage. They are images that will later epitomize his first years in Dallas: the Backstreet Boys haircut, the earring in his left ear, the boxy American suit, the insecure smile.

On their last evening in Dallas, the Mavericks invite Dirk and Holger to Don Nelson's house for a Texan barbecue. Everyone who will play an important role in Dirk's new life is there: Nelson father and son; Michael Finley, the Mavericks' star player, who will become Dirk's mentor and friend; Lisa Tyner, the Mavericks' accountant and fairy godmother in the office; the newly acquired Steve Nash, with his frosted tips. Everyone assures Dirk how happy they'll be. That the next years are going to be good. That they're going to achieve many things together. If—yes, if—he decides to come to Dallas. Dirk shakes their hands, clinks their glasses with his soft drink, listens, and broods.

When all the other guests are gone, only Dirk and Holger remain at Nelson's pool, the stars and constellations above them. They go back and forth through all the arguments for and against as cicadas chirp in the background. It's their last night in Dallas; they're flying back tomorrow. Holger's plan was actually to come to Dallas to check out the situation. He had planned on just showing the boy America and its possibilities. And he also wanted to present Dirk Nowitzki to America. He wanted to show them that almost anything was possible. After the trip, he had wanted to plead for two more years in Europe to get Dirk ready for this opportunity. Maybe in Barcelona or Milan. But everything is happening so fast now; everything has gone better than expected: the Hoop Summit, the dinner with Donnie, the Mavericks' draft tactics. Everything fit. And now it's time for a decision.

Money isn't an issue during the night by the pool; they're more concerned with athletic questions. Dirk could go anywhere. A big European club? One of the two relevant German teams—Leverkusen or Berlin? What matters are friendship and family, self-confidence and visions. Will he be up to the pressure here? The hustle and bustle? Can he meet these expectations? Is this system ready for someone like him? What will his parents say? His guys back home? Is this the chance of a lifetime?

"Let's do it," Dirk says when he's too tired to keep thinking. "Let's do it. But you have to help me."

★   ★   ★

Back in Germany, this night at the pool will soon feel like a distant, unreal memory. While Würzburg prepares for its first season in the Bundesliga, the NBA engages in a bitter labor dispute about the distribution of revenue between team owners and players. As long as the negotiations are being held, practicing and playing are prohibited. The players are locked out. It's even forbidden for team officials to speak to the players. Dirk has made his decision and will one day become an NBA player, but for now, this step is being postponed. His dream is on ice until the players association and the owners reach an agreement.

Dirk keeps track of the negotiations in the mornings and practices with his guys as usual. Marvin Willoughby from Hamburg has joined the team in the interim. The friends have developed into a team with a lot of potential, the kind you rarely ever see in German basketball. Everyone is a year older now, and they're stronger and smarter. Dirk Nowitzki, Greene, Garrett, and Willoughby play their first Bundesliga game on September 4, 1998, against Alba Berlin, a club loaded with national team players. They are blown out, 108–70, but Dirk scores 17 points. He's now a first division player.

All eyes are on him in these weeks. Würzburg plays against Braunschweig, Bamberg, and Bonn. Detlef Schrempf is a beacon of German basketball, the only German to ever really make it in America. Many have doubts about Dirk becoming his successor; there is a certain relentless scrutiny, there's jealousy and schadenfreude. German basketball is still rough and raw.

One night, Nowitzki sits on the gym floor next to his friend Burkhard Steinbach after losing an away game. Among sports bags and cases of water, they talk about the frustration of the defeat. A young fan plants himself in front of Dirk. "I didn't play all that great," Dirk will later say. "I scored maybe ten, twelve points. It was my first year in the league. I was 18, maybe 19. And then this teenager came up to me." The teenager is a few years younger than Dirk. He can no longer remember what the kid looked like or what he was wearing, but he remembers exactly what the kid said.

"Hey," he says. "I thought you were a lot better. You'll never make it in the NBA. Never."

Dirk plays a total of 18 games in the Bundesliga, averaging 22.5 points per game and 8.1 rebounds. Then, one morning, he turns on the TV and sees the teletext about the players' union and team owners reaching an agreement. "Season is saved," reads the headline. Dirk practices with his guys once or twice more, and then receives the official fax from the Mavericks: "Report to Dallas." Dirk packs his bags and moves out.

Byron and Drexel

'VE KEPT THE NUMBER of Haile the taxi driver in my phone ever since my first visit to Dallas. On a Sunday without games or appointments, I decide to drive around and look up all the places where Nowitzki's career has played out, to see how long he's been here and how connected he is to the city. I dial Haile's number to see if he will take me on this tour, but his number is not in service anymore. Maybe he's driving for Uber or Lyft now.

A lot of time has passed since Dirk arrived in 1998; a lot has changed. There are wastelands and parking lots where the old Reunion Arena used to be. There's a giant convention center, highway bridges, and railroad tracks. The arena where Dirk played his first difficult season no longer exists, the arena where the crowds initially booed him and Steve Nash, the arena where Dirk sometimes sat on the bench for entire games.

Reunion Arena had a small weight room, 16 feet by 16. Dirk has described it to me. He can still remember riding the stationary bike sometimes after games so that he at least got in some exercise. Whenever Coach Nellie went to his press conferences, he'd walk past Dirk, struggling on the machine, and pat him on the back. "Sitting on the bike," Dirk remembers. "Lonely. Probably still wearing my jersey. Frustrated and disappointed. That was my year in Reunion."

I park my rental in the lot of a giant Rite Aid—right where Dirk's favorite bar from those early years, The Loon, must have stood. It's gone. Dirk and Nash and Finley often ate in this bar—an approachable, accessible troupe. This was where the championship celebration took place, too, shortly before it was demolished.

His apartment in those years was in a complex on Cole Avenue, a little farther north. Despite it being Sunday, the streets are crowded. Right across the street is a bustling pedestrian mall with cafés and restaurants. The complex is still standing; clad in beige plaster, it's nothing spectacular. There's a communal pool in the courtyard to the buildings. At first, his teammate Steve Nash was his neighbor, and then they became friends, spending almost all of their free time together— either late at night in the training facility or watching TV on the sofa. Until his mother and Holger set up a halfway decent bed, Dirk slept on a mattress on the floor for the first few days on Cole Avenue.

Dirk never cooked; the guys always ate out or ordered in. Sometimes, their neighbor, the Chinese forward Wang Zhizhi, invited them over. For years, after morning practice, young Dirk drove to Eatzi's, an Italian delicatessen on Oak Lawn Avenue off Rawlins Street, to get pasta and salad. Every day. The place still exists; an opera singer wearing an apron and an Eatzi's uniform still sings arias on the hour on the weekends. Holger Geschwindner still likes to come here to sit on the bench in front of the store and have lunch with the pigeons. The staff still talk about Dirk with enthusiasm—he came in every day for years and only stopped when he had to sign autographs for 15 minutes before every meal. "We always cooked for the kid," the women at the sandwich counter say. "Every single day."

I head south—the highway is empty this Sunday afternoon. The

Reunion Tower is straight ahead, the spaceball, where Dirk had dinner with the Rest of the World. To the right is the Mavericks' new state-of-the-art practice facility; the arena the Mavericks built for Dirk's third season is on my left. The highway bends east, and I drive through the deserted inner city toward Deep Ellum where the famous murals of Dirk adorn the walls, places of pilgrimage for fans from all over the world. The championship mural of Dirk with outstretched fingers—Nowitzki for three. The mural on Taylor Street, the one with Dirk's outstretched arms, Jordan style, is probably the most photographed artwork in Dallas. I drive by a flat warehouse building right around the corner that was the Mavericks' headquarters for decades: 2909 Taylor Street. This is where Nowitzki used to stop in a few times a week to sign autographs. Here is where Lisa Tyner taught him how to navigate a new country and a new world. The dreary warehouse facade is now painted in a screaming bright blue. The accounting, ticketing, and management people used to work here; now, it's the headquarters of the Mavericks' e-sports team.

This is where I met Lisa Tyner for the first time. She's watched it all unfold. She's been the Mavericks' accountant forever, and will later work for Dirk's foundation. She picked Dirk up from the airport on his first day and helped him get his paperwork straight. "He's tall, he's thin, and his hair is too long," was what she thought when she first saw him. She has children the same age as Dirk and has always provided him with a sense of security and regularity.

Lisa tells a story about noticing at some point that Dirk wasn't depositing his checks and that he was getting his fan mail and finances mixed up. That's when she adopted the boy. She's the one who established Dirk's ritual of coming to her office once a week to sit in her cubicle and sign autographs for a few hours. She taught him what commitment means to the game, to the fans. She told him to take people seriously. To be approachable. Respectful. Down to earth. She gave him his first Sharpies. To this day, Tyner is his friend and confidante;

there are photos of Dirk and his family hanging over her desk. I wonder whether Dirk Nowitzki could have ever become Dallas's favorite son had Lisa Tyner not taken on her role in his life.

"When Dirk's in America," she had laughed at our first meeting in Taylor Street, "I have custody."

From Deep Ellum, I drive north on I-35, the afternoon sun peeking through the downtown skyscrapers. The Dallas of the Hoop Summit in 1998 has turned into a different city; it's more open and friendly. Dirk, too, has moved to the nicer parts of Dallas. After he established himself as a player—and after the first long-term contract was signed and his buddy Nash left Dallas to return to Phoenix—Dirk Nowitzki started looking for a decent house. He owned a decent car by then and often had visitors. In 2004, he was 26 years old. He needed a garage and more space. That house is my last stop today.

I drive by the Southern Methodist University campus and along Mockingbird Lane, the houses slowly become bigger and nicer. Dirk's first purchased home is in a neighborhood straight out of a picture book: University Park. It's a midsize house of whitewashed brick amidst oaks, maples, huge plane trees, and American flags. Squirrels scamper up and down the trees. There's a basketball hoop in every other driveway. Dirk's house is at the corner of Byron Avenue and Drexel Drive, number 5311. There's a high school next door. Turtle Creek runs behind the house, and Dirk can remember how kids eventually started knocking on his kitchen window all the time, yelling "Nowitzki!" and "Dirk!" on their way home. A considerable part of his career transpired while he lived on Byron Avenue; he always came back here after big games and tough practices and devastating losses. I walk around, I ask around. It's easy to imagine Dirk becoming an adult in this house, and the city starting to see him as one of its own. Wherever you go in the city, people share anecdotes about personal encounters, mutual acquaintances, and big moments. Two degrees of separation.

Dirk no longer lives in the house in University Park; he's moved a few miles to the north. It's a new house with new stories. But people still talk about him here, about Dirk, the famous basketball player, the nice neighbor down on Turtle Creek, on the corner of Byron and Drexel.

Filthy Dirty Nasty

FEBRUARY 4, 2018

I T'S SUPER BOWL SUNDAY, and I have an appointment with the man who interests me more than the other 200 or so teammates who have played with Nowitzki: Steve Nash. It's not only his unlikely career and his advancement of the game of basketball, and it isn't his MVP awards or his field goal percentages or his wild and precise bounce passes through holes in the defense that no one saw but him. All those things are fascinating, but they don't account for my sense of excitement. Nash is one of the protagonists in Jack McCallum's *Seven Seconds or Less*, a fantastic book about a single season with the Phoenix Suns. A story that reveals Nash's obsession with details, his meticulous preparation, and his seemingly anarchic play on the floor. I have almost as many memories of Nash as I do of Nowitzki; much of my understanding of the game has to do with him. Basketball was both physical work and an intellectual exercise for Nash. He played against improbabilities in physics and physiques, against clichés and prejudices. He seemed to be thinking and playing the game at another level. When Steve Nash retired, there went the last great player who was older than me.

But it's the things Nash did—and still does—off the court that I find convincing. Nash is a political person who eloquently expresses his

opinion; a vocal leftist, he's candid and committed, hilarious and sometimes rightfully angry. He's an exception to the hesitant wariness of
professional sports. I remember how he protested against the Gulf War
at the 2003 All-Star Game in Atlanta: he warmed up in a T-shirt reading "No War. Shoot for Peace," and I remember how sports reporters,
politicians, and even opposing players wanted to muzzle him ("Shut up
and play," the exasperating commentator Skip Bayless said). Nash no
longer plays, but it appears that he has made the transition from superstar to social actor. He makes documentary films with his production
company, manages his foundation, and uses his voice and means to
fight for freedom and equality, for minorities and the underprivileged.
And for 20 years, he's been one of Dirk Nowitzki's best friends.

Dirk and Steve spent six seasons together in Dallas, but nowadays
they only see each other sporadically. Both have children—Dirk three,
Nash four. Dirk is still playing, and Nash is working on millions of
projects. The Mavericks are playing tomorrow, today's a rare off day, so
the two old friends decided to hang out in the team hotel.

We meet in the lobby of the giant Ritz-Carlton in downtown Los
Angeles, right next to the Staples Center, where the Lakers and Clippers
play, with its statues of sporting legends Jerry West, Wayne Gretzky,
Kareem Abdul-Jabbar, Magic Johnson, and Shaquille O'Neal out front.
Nash walks across the lobby, wiry and tanned, wearing Vans and a
cashmere sweatshirt, a grown-up boy in his mid-forties, maybe a surfer
or skater. He walks with good posture and composure, much different
than I had expected (I figured he would have a slight limp—after all,
he had to end his career because of back problems). Nash looks like
someone who does yoga at dawn while overlooking the Pacific. Like
someone who eats raw food and goes grocery shopping on a longboard.
(He probably does do these things.) He's been living with his family
in Manhattan Beach ever since he joined the Lakers in 2010, and he
drove downtown to meet Dirk today. Whenever they see each other,
it's mostly in the team hotels in Los Angeles or San Francisco, some-

times in New York (where Nash has an apartment), sometimes in Dallas. They seize the opportunity whenever it presents itself.

The first thing Nash does when he arrives is order two beers: one for him, one for me. I look at him in surprise. There are many stories about ex-athletes becoming drunks when the applause and adrenaline have fizzled, but this doesn't seem to be the case with Nash. He grins. It's Super Bowl Sunday. These beers are an exception. "Let's start from the beginning," he says as the waitress sets the glasses down.

It's likely that Nash has told his stories about Dirk hundreds of times, but he seems to enjoy sitting here and talking about his friend. He's here today because he wants to record an episode of his new podcast with Dirk—the topic is excellence. Nash has questions, too.

He first saw Dirk at the Hoop Summit in San Antonio in 1998. Dirk had played well, especially when it came to making his free throws, but Nash didn't think he was spectacular—just another talented high school player like so many others. After the game, he turned the TV off and forgot about Dirk Nowitzki until he met him in person a few months later. The Mavericks acquired Dirk through the draft day trade with Milwaukee and brought him over from Phoenix. "We were introduced at the same press conference in Dallas," he remembers. "Dirk with his buckteeth and this unbelievable bowl cut and earring. I had dyed my hair platinum and half of the color had already grown out." Nash remembers sitting on the podium and constantly thinking that he probably should have gone to the barber before. "We looked like a boy band," Nash says. "NSYNC or something." (Dirk uses the exact same phrasing when he and I talk about this moment.) The pictures of them awkwardly sitting in terrible suits will hound them for the rest of their careers.

Dirk was a shy boy, Nash says. "He still had to get used to what it means to be seven feet in this world," he remembers. "He didn't feel comfortable in his body. He was self-conscious. A giant teenager far away from home. Who couldn't hide. He didn't deal with the attention very well."

"They used to call him 'Skeletor' at school," I note.

"Like the blue guy in *Masters of the Universe*?"

"It's because you could see his bones."

"I'm going to call him that today." Nash grins and raises his glass. "To Skeletor!"

Nash can still remember just how complicated the first months were. First, there was the lockout, then the sudden announcement that the season would begin in a few days. Everything happened so fast: Dirk wasn't familiar with America, the customs and manners and language, and he wasn't strong enough physically. He missed training camp because of the lockout, and he was practically torn out of a German gym one day and transplanted into an NBA arena the next. The expectations were very high, which made the disappointment all the greater. "Nellie had announced that Dirk would be Rookie of the Year," he says, "and then Dirk sometimes only sat on the bench."

Things weren't easy for Nash in the beginning, either. The fans saw a lanky point guard who didn't shoot often enough to turn the lousy Mavericks into a good team. "You need to have patience with international players," Marc Stein wrote in the *Dallas Morning News* in March 1999. In a game against Houston, Nash missed nine shots in a row and the fans booed louder and louder with every miss. The Mavericks' experiment seemed to be failing. But then Nash dribbled into the frontcourt, through the boos and the screaming, and took a running three. Fuck it! He made that 10th shot. Dirk later remembers how much he admired Nash for having the courage to do it. "That guy's got balls," he thought, and planned to emulate Nash.

He was probably a sort of big brother for Dirk in those early years, Nash says in the Ritz-Carlton's lobby, or at least during the first half year. He had played college basketball at Santa Clara and had two seasons as a professional under his belt. He could deal with American culture. "I'm very open," Nash says, "and I liked Dirk right away." Both were new to the city, both had weird haircuts and a strange sense of humor, and both understood that they could help one another pretty quickly. Both of them always had time for another workout. They spent their evenings in the training facility, playing H-O-R-S-E, shooting rep after rep, working on their pick-and-roll game and playing one-on-one. Nash was way too fast for Dirk and Dirk was way too tall for Nash, but each moved into the other's domain and learned from it. Michael Finley, the Mavericks' best player at the time, saw what was happening and started practicing with them. He was the rare star who didn't find it difficult to bring the others into the limelight. When Geschwindner was in the city—and he was often in Dallas—the three of them started working together, even though the exercises were totally unlike anything Finley and Nash had encountered in college. Afterward, they would go for a drink around the corner and joke around.

Dirk slowly adjusted: to Cole Avenue, the Mavericks, and America. In spite of all the difficulties, he has fond memories of these first months. "I owe a lot to Nashy and Fin," he later tells me. "Steve had friends in every city we passed through, and he always took me along—'Come on, we're going to get some food,' he said. 'We're going to the movies' and 'Come on, we're going to do another workout.' He made sure that I didn't just sit around at the hotel, getting homesick."

Nash takes a sip. Dwight Powell, the Mavericks' giant and angular Canadian center, walks through the lobby. Powell can jump like a bouncy ball and think like a professor. He comes over when he recognizes Nash. Handshakes and hugs, a nod to the reporter. The two make small talk for a few minutes, since one of the many jobs Nash now has is managing the Canadian national team, and Powell is one of its players. It's noticeable how open Nash and Powell are as they speak—an unexpected candor. It gives an indication of how Nash must have influenced

Dirk back then, and it explains why Powell is one of Dirk Nowitzki's favorite teammates. Coaching seems to be in Nash's future.

When Powell says goodbye, Nash picks up where he left off: 1999. He immediately realized that Dirk could become a very good player. "He had an amazing physique for a shooter," he says. "He wasn't strong, but he was physically dominant. He wasn't the fastest, but he was coordinated. He was tall, he could dribble, he could move his feet and always get to his favorite spots. I knew he could go far if he would fight. And then when I saw how he worked on himself, I just knew it: he's going to be a major problem for our opponents. I knew he was going to be really great." He raises his glass as if he's toasting the young Dirk, as if the Ritz-Carlton IPA were a can of beer in The Loon in 1999.

At first, Dirk's prospects were overshadowed by his modest and shy nature. By the pressure and expectations, by all the eyes focused on him. By being a foreigner. By being alone. The laundry that needed to be folded; the furniture that needed to be assembled. The mail, the bills, the checks. But toward the end of the season, he started to respond to the demands physically and mentally. There was no particular moment, Nash says, not one game or play—or at least, not any he could remember. Dirk Nowitzki just stopped letting himself be pushed around the court.

When the shortened season was almost over and it became clear the Mavericks would miss the playoffs again, Coach Nellie pulled Dirk aside. Dirk played three minutes in an away game in Miami, four against Golden State, and then Nelson threw him into the starting five and told him to go out there and play with joy. "The pressure is gone," he said. "So, just play." Three days later, he was on the court for 32 minutes against San Antonio. He played 44 minutes against Phoenix and scored 29 points. "I'll never forget that game," Dirk will later say. "Those 29 points were huge for my self-confidence." He played against Charles Barkley again, who was now with the Houston Rockets, and it was different from the way it had been two years before in Dortmund— this time, it's a serious competition—and he scored 22 very real and convincing points. "The last few weeks were super important," he says. "I realized this could actually work."

"He trained his mental muscle back then," Nash says. Dirk transformed his desire to train into a competitive desire. "All of a sudden, it was clear to him: I belong here. *I'm good.* From then on, he stopped worrying about everyone else; he wanted to go up against them and he started believing in himself." The Dirk Nowitzki we know today—the player—was born during these days. "Because of his height and mobility, he always got open looks, and he was an incredibly good shooter. He turned a corner and became a competitor."

When Steve Nash talks about Dirk Nowitzki, his words have rhythm and flow; it almost sounds like he's reciting a poem: "He moves so well, he moves his legs, he always found his spot, always got the shot off, he always put the ball behind his head before anyone could get to it, he could dribble, and no matter what happened, he could always get a shot off." Nash picks up my recorder, which is sitting on the table between us, and speaks directly into it: "I knew then he was gonna be a great player."

Nash pauses for a second. Now would be a good time to talk about the good years they shared, but Holger Geschwindner slips into Nash's field of vision. Holger is wearing a leather jacket and his standard checkered shirt; he's thinner in the face than he was a couple of months ago. In this world of standardized design ideas and industrial marble, of lounge areas and atriums, he seems foreign but also invisible. He fits in everywhere and nowhere at once. Nash raises his hand; Geschwindner sees us and comes over. He's got his grubby grin on his face, a casual nod. The two toss out a few fragments of memory and names, this and that, it's not easy to understand what they mean exactly.

*　　　*　　　*

The shared years of Nash and Nowitzki can be quickly related: Dirk doesn't take a break in the summer after his first NBA season. He hastily leaves Dallas when the season is over, then plays with the German national team in the European Championships in France and barely misses qualifying for the Sydney Olympics. The defeat crushes him; he thinks it's "brutal." When he comes back to America, he plays for the Mavericks in the summer leagues in California and Utah. The nonstop training pays off; he can now meet the physical demands; he's a different, more dominant player.

It is clear that Dirk is physically farther along at the start of their second season together. Nash is, too. Dirk has gained experience at the highest European level and now knows enough people in Dallas to not feel so lonesome. He has worked out with Holger all summer. He is in shape. The team has its own training facility to prepare for games, and when Gary Trent, Dirk's main competition for the power forward position, tears a muscle in his thigh, Dirk is the best player available at the four. "I was really lucky," he will say. He replaces the player who badgered him with rookie rites of initiation the year before, making him pick up balls, carry duffel bags, or buy doughnuts. There's no getting past Dirk now; he's the first option. His playing time increases, his rebound and point averages double.

"Then it was clear," he remembers. "It's working."

In the middle of the 2000–01 season, the Mavericks change ownership. Ross Perot Jr. sells the team to Mark Cuban, a fan and internet billionaire. All the players and coaches worry about their jobs at first, but it quickly becomes clear that Cuban wants to be around the team and get involved. He sits right on the bench during the games, he hypes them up and curses at the referees, he cheers. Most importantly, he changes the infrastructure and perception of the Mavericks. People start talking about the team with enthusiasm in Dallas. The Mavericks are suddenly flying in a private airplane, they build a new arena, and get luxurious locker rooms and the best medical care. Cuban gives interviews before the games while sweating and panting on a Stairmaster. Sometimes, he's already going through his shooting routines when

Dirk and Nash step into the arena. Cuban is serious about basketball, and he cares about his guys. Sometimes, they go out drinking together. But the biggest change of all: the Mavericks start winning.

Working with Finley and Nash takes Dirk's game to another level. The three of them are insanely ambitious, but they're not pretentious. They're willing to put in the work; they're competitive, but they aren't stubborn or inflexible. Nash directs the game with a level of audacious courage and control that neither Dirk nor Finley has ever seen. They perfect the pick-and-roll, whose theory they have worked on in the empty training facility at night (Nowitzki opens some space, Nash pokes in; Nash penetrates and draws the attention to himself, but the defenders can't leave Nowitzki to help: both can shoot whenever and from wherever, bringing their defenders out of balance both physically and intellectually; pick-and-roll, pick your poison). If you watch the highlight reels from Nash's career, you see a music conductor at work. One thing that sticks out is the way he licks his fingertips before free throws, the way he whips the ball to his open teammates when he's trapped, the way he wriggles out of every hopeless situation. Steve Nash is a paradox: he finds solutions where no solutions seem possible.

The Mavericks of these early years have fun playing. It's a style and a setup like the one in Würzburg, and maybe that's exactly what Dirk Nowitzki needs in those years: three guys who become real friends off the court and who, as a consequence, want to spend more time together in the arena. They're the most talented and interesting team of the early 2000s; their enthusiasm is contagious and awakens a whole city from basketball fatalism. Maybe the Mavericks' big three are so good because they trust one another. Nash describes the mood of those years as totally atypical for a professional team. "We were a college team," he says. He briefly thinks and laughs. "We were a high school team." Maybe that's why the early Mavericks don't win a championship together: maybe they aren't hard-nosed, calculating, or professional enough. Maybe the trio simply met too early.

The team reaches the playoffs for the first time in Dirk's third season. After a hard fight, they erase a 2–0 deficit against the Utah Jazz in the first round. Dirk accidentally unleashes the rancor of Jazz fans when he calls "Utah" a "bad city." From then on, he will be booed loudly, but the Mavericks win the series, 3–2. "We grew up against Utah," says Michael Finley, "especially Dirk."

They collapse in the second round against the San Antonio Spurs, who have the Twin Towers, Tim Duncan and David Robinson. The Mavericks lose the first two games by 14 and 16 points. Dirk pukes his guts out before the third game (food poisoning—bad fish) and catches an elbow from Terry Porter in the fourth game, but keeps playing with a bloody gap in his teeth and a crazed smile. The Mavericks don't stand a chance in the fifth and final game of the series—they lose, 105–87— but Dirk has 42 points and 18 rebounds (I can remember down to the finest detail how I read this stat line at a so-called "internet terminal" in the Hamburg State Library. "Crazy," I said to my friend. "Did you see that, Tobi? Nowitzki! Crazy!").

The successful years of the big three start in the 2002 playoffs, the wonder years of the "dirty three": Michael "Filthy" Finley, Steve "Nasty" Nash, and Dirk "Dirty" Nowitzki. Years later—decades, even— basketball fans will still speculate about what might have happened if Finley, Nash, and Nowitzki had stayed together. If they had grown and matured together. If Nash hadn't left in 2004 and Finley in 2005, both for financial reasons. What could have happened if the Dallas Mavericks had never become Dirk's team.

★   ★   ★

Geschwindner says goodbye and Nash still has more stories to tell. Players with takeout bags walk through the lobby in flip-flops, the beat writers come over, the coaches, radio broadcaster Chuck Cooperstein, and Al Whitley, Nash's old high school buddy. Steve Nash is still part of the team he left years ago. Every once in a while, he looks at his phone, waiting for Dirk's call, but Nowitzki is still at the physiotherapist.

"Mental muscle?" I ask.

Nash is a good storyteller; he doesn't lose his thread, but picks up where we were interrupted. "At some point, Dirk was so good," he says, "that he could just show up when it counted. Time and time again. It was amazing to see that Dirk was in complete physical and mental control over what he was doing."

"How much of that is talent?" I ask. "And how much is will?"

"What do you have inside you? And what can you learn? That's exactly what I want to ask him for the podcast today. The old debate: nature vs. nurture. Dirk definitely has the will to assert himself and keep going, he doesn't let himself get distracted, he doesn't give up. He never hesitates or lets himself be intimidated. Most of that will be innate. And if you can cope with the difficulties and overcome the hurdles, then you gain a sense of power, a very particular belief in your own abilities. Dirk can decide for himself what's going to happen in the big moments. He can dictate how the game will be played. It's complicated to describe without using basketball terminology. Dirk dictates what will happen, when it will happen, and how. He reads his defender and knows who is coming to help, and he knows what . . ."

Steve Nash has talked himself in a flow. Maybe it's out of enthusiasm, maybe because it's a Sunday afternoon, and maybe it's because he is already setting things up for the conversation he will have with Dirk. He tries to find words for Dirk's singularity; I try to write it all down. The clock keeps ticking; the half hour has long since turned into a full one. We're both anticipating the call from Dirk.

The empty glasses are standing in front of us, and I ask about the end of his time in Dallas. Nash smiles. "Right," he says. He knows exactly where he was when the Filthy/Dirty/ Nasty era ended: in his car, heading toward the Dallas airport. Mark Cuban had made him a good offer: $45 million for four years. Then the Phoenix Suns flew in just for him and made him a fantastic offer that he couldn't really refuse. He was told to make a decision immediately; he shouldn't gamble or haggle or tell Mark Cuban about the amount that was offered and then wait for a new counteroffer. But as he drove, he called Cuban and told him. He outlined the scenario and explained to Cuban once more that he'd really like to stay with the Mavericks. Seriously. The Suns were offering $65 million for six years—$20 million more, and two more years. The owner hesitated and then decided he couldn't take the risk. Years later, when Nash has been inducted into the Hall of Fame and Dirk has played his last game, Cuban will speak of "probably the worst move he made since he bought the Mavericks." "He was probably afraid that my body would give out at some point," Nash says. "I was a 30-year-old point guard with a lot of playing time in my bones who played with a lot of energy, up and down the court, over and over, and . . ." Nash looks at me. "And of course, that's a very plausible evaluation."

"As an older NBA player without a no-trade clause, you can't turn down a contract that runs much longer and earns you significantly more money," he explains. "If you take less money out of loyalty to the team, you can still get traded two months later. And then what?" It isn't only about loyalty in the league, he says, it's also about money. Nash knows that this assessment isn't always met with approval, especially from fans and sports romantics. "But if you were traded, you'd keep asking yourself why the hell you stayed."

He remembers how he called Dirk from the car. "That's tough," Dirk said. Nash remembers these exact words, which, years later, sound much more sober than they must have felt back then. "That's tough," he said, "but you have to go. You can't turn that down."

It was a short conversation because Nash was arriving at the airport. But Dirk texted him later and found the words to express how much their time together had meant to him. He doesn't often ask himself what could have been, Nash says, if he had stayed. There's no point to such speculation, he says. "The idea of what we could have achieved together, if . . ." Nash's hands paint an explosion in the air, a bursting or popping. *Poof!* He's a realist and doesn't seem to regret the team's breakup—it's an attitude that I've also noticed in Dirk. Nash stayed in Phoenix for seven years, became a two-time MVP of the league, and Dirk remained in Dallas. The Mavericks were now officially his team. "I knew back then that the change wouldn't affect our friendship," Nash says.

Nash is interrupted by his phone. He picks it up from the table, looks at the display, and shows it to me.

"*Schwachkopf*," it reads. Dickhead.

"It's him," Nash says.

I stare at the display. I knew that NBA players use code names when they save one another's phone numbers—the worry is that the phone could go missing, the contact list would be mined, and then the phone would suddenly ring and there are complete strangers on the other end. I know these stories from Dirk. For a while, he had to keep changing his number to retain his privacy. The Crystal Taylor saga started with a call just like that. There are nicknames, noms de guerre, initials, and figures of speech. "Mamba" for Kobe Bryant, a Chinese character for Yao Ming, "Coach" for Rick Carlisle.

When a call from Dirk Nowitzki appears on my display, it reads, "The Great Gatsby."

Nicknames are nicknames. When Dirk was a young player in Würzburg in the German gyms of the 1990s, and when Nash and Nowitzki met in the American arenas at the turn of the century, the names you came up with for someone were seldom PC: *idiot, dingleberry, guido.* And then, also, *dickhead.* The name on Nash's smartphone screen has become disassociated from its meaning, and *Schwachkopf* is only a remnant from the thoughtless years when you think you're invulnerable and infallible. Today, they would give each other different names. Nash stands up.

"Dirk's done," he says. "He's going to pick us up."

Sometimes the Pressure Wins, and Sometimes You Win

HERE'S THIS ONE PICTURE by the photographer Tilo Wieden- sohler where you can see the kind of pressure weighing on Dirk Nowitzki. It was taken in a locker room in the OAKA Arena in Athens on July 20, 2008. A couple minutes earlier, the German national team had beaten Puerto Rico, 96–82, in front of stands that were practically empty. Both teams have parted ways in an orderly and sportsmanlike manner, but then the Germans' euphoria explodes: the national basket- ball team has qualified for the Olympics for the first time since the 1992 Games in Barcelona, which was also the first time pros were allowed to play. That was 16 years ago, the year of the first Dream Team—with Jordan, Pippen, Barkley, and Bird. The best team that ever existed, a global inspiration for the sport. Back then, Dirk's generation of Ger- man national players were children sitting in front of the TV, and most of them made the pledge to become Olympians.

The Puerto Ricans sneak off the court in Athens, and the Germans scream and hug at the center circle—Sven Schultze and Patrick Femer- ling, Steffen Hamann and Konrad Wysocki, Jan Jagla and Coach Bau- ermann, they jump and shout and pump their fists. Nowitzki hugs Sven Schultze, but Schultze is staring at him with confusion: "What's the matter?" Later, Nowitzki will only be able to remember that he didn't understand what Schultze meant at first. Then, however, he realizes that something is bursting out of him. Something overwhelming. Something that had been buried for a long time. "It never hit me so hard," he says. "It was tough." Nowitzki throws his towel over his head. He hides his face from the world and vanishes from the arena with the losers.

But seeing as the game is taking place in Europe, where the locker rooms always remain locked during games, Dirk has to sit on the ground in front of the door for five minutes. "Not a soul passed by," he explains. "They were all still out there celebrating, and I sat in front of the locker room, crying. I went straight into the physio room when somebody finally came."

Wiedensohler's photo shows Nowitzki lying on the treatment table, completely exhausted and powerless. You can't recognize his face because therapist Jens Joppich is bending over him. He's wiping away the tears with a towel, perhaps offering some soothing words, but you can't see that, either—he has his back to Wiedensohler's camera. The room is dreary and functional, there's yellow chipboard walls and the same gray tiles you can find in every other change room in Europe. A team doctor can be seen with a tape cutter; there's a mop leaning on the wall in the background. It's a strange place for such great liberation.

The game against Puerto Rico was closer than the score suggests. Everything had been on the line for both teams: qualifying for the Games in Beijing and the realization of a major dream. On the other team was J. J. Barea, Dirk's teammate in Dallas who had fought countless battles with him in the NBA. Only one of them could survive, and it was Dirk.

Nowitzki has played on the German teams since he was a teenager, and at the time of this game, he's been the best player on the German team for about ten years—he has basically been carrying them on his shoulders for a decade. He led them to the bronze medal at the 2002 World Championships in Indianapolis, dominated the 2005 European

Championship in Serbia, only collapsing with his team in the final against Greece. When Dirk was subbed out shortly before the end of that game, the entire Belgrade arena gave him a standing ovation for his performance—the Greeks, Serbians, and Germans could all finally agree on something. He was the top scorer in the 2006 World Championship in Japan, and whenever people have talked about German basketball over the past ten years, they talk about Dirk Nowitzki and his teams.

Amidst all the celebrating, Joppich has realized that this sense of relief is likely to floor Nowitzki. He's known him for years, his body and his thoughts, he knows the people around him, and he knows what this moment means to him. What's going on in his head. Joppich knows that a 14-year-old Dirk watched the Germans lose to the Americans in Barcelona. He knows how much Dirk adored Pippen and Barkley, Bird and Jordan. He knows Holger Geschwindner, too, and he's heard the stories about Munich in 1972, about the famous wrestler Wilfried Dietrich, the "Crane of Schifferstadt," of track star Heide Rosendahl and the spirit of the Olympic Village. He knows that Dirk has assimilated Holger's enthusiasm for Olympic sports. Joppich also knows that Dirk was somehow able to get tickets for an Australia game featuring Andrew Gaze at the Georgia Dome in Atlanta in 1996, way up in the cheap seats—and he knows how Dirk had imagined being down on the court one day as well. He knows that Dirk and the Germans missed qualifying for the 2000 Games in Sydney, as well as the qualifiers for the 2004 Athens Games.

Dirk doesn't forget things like this. "Norrköping, Sweden, 2003. We lose to Italy and then fly home. And of course, we have to drive by the arena where the final qualifying round is going to be played on our way to the airport. I'm sitting on the side of the bus facing the arena. I still remember driving by the place the others were playing in. That I thought, *There go the Olympic Games again.*"

Dirk has watched the Games from a distance ever since he was ten or eleven years old, and his team has never managed to be there.

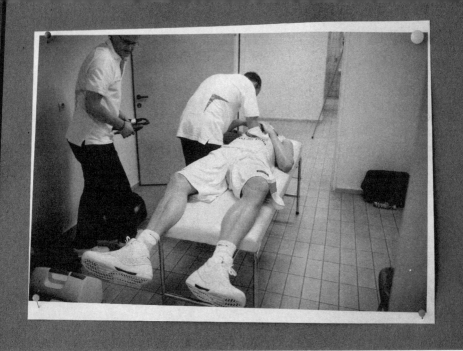

Tilo Wiedensohler's photo shows Dirk in the exact moment when it becomes clear to him that he's finally achieved something he always failed to do before. "I always had two dreams," Dirk will later tell me. "The Olympic Games and the NBA championship." Normally, he thinks from game to game, from practice to practice, from shot to shot—but these two goals were always present in the background. They'd hovered above everything else.

Lying on the table between the yellow dividing walls of the dressing room in Athens is someone who has just achieved something he has been working toward for more than 20 years. Longer even than he has been able to fully understand what the word *work* means. Dirk looks like he's been relieved of a burden. An enormous amount of pressure. He's lying there like a deflated rubber toy.

★   ★   ★

Pressure is a complex phenomenon in the life of an athlete. Pressure is a driving force, but also a burden; it comes from the outside and from within, makes many things possible while also preventing others. Pressure arises from one's own expectations of oneself as well as from the expectations of others, from loyalty and love, from fears and desires. Diamonds are created under pressure, the saying goes, but pressure shatters dreams more often than not.

It's surprising that Dirk collapses in these seconds in Athens, but it's not astonishing. His teammates know him as a jokester, a team leader, and a player who always delivers in crucial situations. He scored 32 points and won the game against Puerto Rico today. He dominated every aspect of the game—as a rebounder, passer, three-point shooter, and under the basket. He could celebrate, but instead he's lying on a daybed, crying.

When I look at Wiedensohler's picture, I wonder what was pressing on Dirk in those seconds. It can't be the crowd—almost no one had been there. Only a few hundred people had stumbled into the arena, a couple of fans and some aficionados; the game was practically played behind closed doors.

Is it the responsibility? The German national team from the "Nowe years" is a tight crew; most of them have known each other since their youth teams. It's probably the best German team ever assembled. Everyone describes Dirk as being personable, but more than anything else, they know he never shies away from important games and situations; they know that they can depend on him. That he enjoys the intensity. They're only here because they can count on him.

They also know that whenever Dirk fails, he is able to see the failure as part of the process. He briefly hangs his head and grieves, but then goes back to the gym and just keeps working. He hasn't worked enough. He can do better.

He can handle pressure from outside, he can handle the possibility of failure. But there's more to it than that: he has considerable responsibility for an entire organization in Dallas, both in terms of finances and identity; hundreds of employees depend on his success, on his shooting hand. This pressure is abstract and invisible in Athens today; a whole basketball nation profits from his performance. But that can't be it, either—he's been doing this for years and continually fulfills the expectation of others. The pressure definitely isn't coming from outside.

When Dirk and Holger Geschwindner met, they started simulating and integrating scenarios of being under pressure almost from the beginning. They've enacted these fictional situations for years in practice; they have their strategies to get in the right mindset before the games. Dirk ends every practice with a simulated game winner—decisive shots in critical game situations. They have always worked on his confidence, which is created through constant repetition, the freedom of improvisation, and trust in one's own body—all of these are tools to deal with tight game situations, with resistance and unruly defenders. There's the awareness that winning is possible. That the mind and body are prepared.

Dirk Nowitzki's career is the story of steadily increasing inner pressure. The expectations that Nowitzki has for himself go beyond individual games, particular victories and defeats. His expectations keep growing. This is the case with most athletes: they begin with hopes and distant dreams, then work toward these goals before the window of actually reaching them slowly closes.

When Nowitzki joins the national team in 1997, he knows that he has a long career ahead of him. He has worked on this confidence and self-awareness. During the first practice, Henning Harnisch and Henrik Rödl take turns guarding him. At the time, they're the national team's best players. Dirk is often compared to Harnisch—talent and discipline and upside—and they've already heard of Nowitzki, of course. They want to show him who the top dogs are. Neither of them can remember the year or the location, but they both know how well Dirk Nowitzki played. "We tried to guard him hard," Rödl explains. "We wanted to see how he would react."

"You practice with him," Harnisch remembers, "and then you notice: he has a lot more potential. He's going to be really good, but he's not there yet. As an older player, you've got all your tricks." He and Rödl give Nowitzki everything they have on defense, they want to challenge Dirk and test him, and they probably receive the same calls from the refs that every legend gets—but Dirk doesn't let himself be intimidated.

"I know what you're doing," he tells Harnisch and Rödl, who can remember his words and facial expressions perfectly. "My time will come."

Dirk hardly takes a break between 1999 and 2002, playing non-stop: in the summers, he trains in Germany, then plays in summer league and for the national team, and then he's in America, with the Mavericks, in fall, winter, and spring. In those three years, the rookie turns into a star who will carry his team in the 2002 World Championships. "It only took three years to go from a newcomer to a global star," Rödl says. "He had the height, athleticism, and talent—but those are all essential things you need to get to this level. Above everything else, it's his attitude and his ability to concentrate that differentiate him from others. This 'I'll keep working on myself and then do it again and again' mentality. Learning things and being able to implement them—that in itself is a huge talent. I've worked with a lot of people, but only Detlef Schrempf and Dirk had that skill at this level."

Dirk is the high scorer and MVP at the World Championships in Indianapolis; he plays the best tournament a German basketball player has ever played on such a stage: 24 points per game, 8.2 rebounds, and almost three assists. Everyone knows they're indebted to him, and Dirk knows what he gets from his team.

In the US, Nowitzki's old companion Steve Nash leaves Dallas for Phoenix in 2004, and Michael Finley heads to San Antonio a year later. From then on, Dirk bears the responsibility for the Mavericks on his own, and he embraces it. He wants to win the championship for his city.

Dirk's first summer of crisis comes in 2005. The European Championships in Belgrade are approaching; Dirk and the national team will probably be the best side Germany has ever seen. They will have a chance at winning this thing. Nowitzki flies to Europe right after the

NBA season ends. He wants to work with Geschwindner and be as prepared as possible—but then, one early-summer morning, tax investigators knock on Geschwindner's door and take him with them. They also
wake up Nowitzki and take files and folders. The charge: tax evasion.
Geschwindner spends a number of weeks in custody. No one is allowed
to visit him, not even his partner or Dirk. It's a matter of millions. Risk
of obfuscation! Risk of absconding! Apparently, they signed a contract
when they started working together, back when Dirk was a kid, but
they never activated this contract. Apparently, Geschwindner has been
sloppy with his paperwork. Apparently, the prosecutor can't imagine
that someone would work with a superstar and not make money off
him. The investigators search through everything: Geschwindner's
office and their sponsors' headquarters in the US and Europe.

Dirk asks to be allowed to train with Geschwindner in prison, but
that's out of the question. So, he works out alone. Sometimes, his pregnant sister rebounds for him, his cousin; sometimes old friends pass
him the ball. At the same time, he tries to pull together the implausibly
high bail sum for Geschwindner—in the millions—and when he finally
scrapes it together, his mentor is let out of jail right in time for the start
of the tournament.

Despite the hardships of the summer, Dirk is once again the gold
standard for international basketball. Germany beats the powerhouses
from Spain, Russia, and Slovenia and advances to the title game. They
lose to Greece, getting the silver medal, but what remains is the image
of Dirk being subbed out shortly before the end and the entire arena
saying goodbye to him with a minute-long standing ovation.

After the game, the tournament MVP title, and the outpouring of
respect, he sits in his hotel room with his roommate, Mithat Demirel,
and a couple of the other guys when there's suddenly a knock at the
door. The lobby of the Interconti Hotel is full of people screaming and
cheering, it's full of autograph collectors. Dirk figures the door knocker
is someone who snuck through. He goes to the door, but when he opens

it, there's his teammate Marko Pešić with a middle-aged woman standing next to him. "May I introduce," Marko says, "the mother of Dražen Petrović." Dirk immediately stands at attention, shakes the woman's hand, and almost bows.

Petrović is an absolute legend in the sport, and people would compare him and Dirk a lot more often if he hadn't died in a car accident in 1993—at the premature age of 28. In those days Belgrade, there's a nonstop debate over who is the greatest European of all time, and Petrović at 28 and current-day Nowitzki are the only names you keep hearing.

"I want to congratulate you, my boy," Dražen Petrović's mother says to Dirk Nowitzki in the team hotel in Belgrade. She holds his hand while Marko translates. "Since my son died, I have not seen a player be so loved. You remind me of my son. You play the game the right way."

The other guys wipe a few tears from the corners of their eyes. Femerling, Stephen Arigbabu, Demirel, and Pešić are standing next to Dirk when he receives what may be the biggest compliment in European basketball, a kind of knighthood, a great legacy. No cameras or audience members are there, and Pešić will remember this moment many years later. "This encounter," he will say, "shows exactly who Dirk is and what he means to us."

Not only has Dirk Nowitzki carried his team and his country, but he also carries an entire continent. This privilege—this burden—will remain. Europe's a heavy continent. "That was the greatest compliment I ever received," Dirk will remember and smile. "From Dražen Petrović's mother."

In 2006, Nowitzki leads the Mavericks to the NBA Finals for the first time. He dominates every statistical category and his defenders are no longer able to figure out his game. He can do everything. The Mavericks beat the Memphis Grizzlies in the first round of the playoffs, then win the second series in overtime of Game 7 against their archrivals, the San

Antonio Spurs, featuring Tim Duncan, Tony Parker, and Michael Finley. Then they beat the Phoenix Suns and Dirk's best friend, Steve Nash.

The Miami Heat are waiting in the Finals. They're a completely different team than Dallas: loud, attention-seeking. Dallas wins the first two games and is leading by a large margin in the third. Everyone is counting on the Mavericks winning the championship; the title is within reach. The parade route is printed in the paper, and Mark Cuban announces that he'll be wearing swim trunks at the trophy ceremony. But all of a sudden, things stop working properly. Nowitzki misses a decisive free throw right before the end of the third game, the victory that seemed so secure slips out of their fingers, and the Heat gain the upper hand. The Mavericks fall apart; their coach gets nervous and moves the team to a cheap hotel in Fort Lauderdale to cut down on distractions. The Mavericks crack and crumble, lose four games in a row, and Miami are the champions.

The pictures of Dirk—a beaten boxer sneaking into the locker room—are burned into the memories of the basketball world. There will never be such a unique opportunity again, this we are sure of.

Nowitzki takes responsibility for the defeat. Sure, the team had been too confident, the victory parade had been planned too early, but it was he who let his concentration slip—there were too many guests at his house, there was too much talking, he lost his focus.

He makes a promise to himself to bring the title to his city. Someday.

The summer after the Miami series, he's the best player in the World Championships in Japan, but his team only reaches seventh place. Nowitzki returns to Dallas and decides to change his diet and train even more intensely. His aspirations infiltrate every aspect of his life; his concentration and his desire are the parents of all his thoughts.

In 2006–07, Dirk plays what might be the best regular season of his life, but the Mavericks sensationally lose to the Golden State Warriors in the first round of the playoffs. Dirk is named the league's most valuable player two weeks after the end of the season, but he can't even look at the trophy, he can't rejoice, let alone put the thing in his trophy room. "Sometimes the pressure wins," he says.

★   ★   ★

Dirk will later tell me that his father came into the locker room in Athens, after he had calmed down a little. He was just about to get up and go back into the arena to celebrate with the others and give interviews. But when he saw his father, everything welled up again and he couldn't contain himself. Dirk sat next to his father in the locker room the way he did as a kid in front of the TV during the 1984 Olympic Games in Los Angeles, Seoul in '88, Barcelona in '92.

As an athlete, he had always harbored two wishes in his life, and it's clear that one of them will now be fulfilled. Hence, his tears.

As for the Olympic Games themselves, they're practically a bonus. Dirk experiences what Geschwindner had always talked about: the Olympic Village, the other athletes. Things don't revolve around him for a couple of weeks, they revolve around one and all. He has the honor of bearing the German flag into the Bird's Nest in Beijing; in the photos, you can see the happiness in his eyes. It's too hot, and the German team has been standing in an adjacent stadium for hours and again in the overheated catacombs, everyone is sweating their heads off, but they all start singing "*Wir wollen die Fahne sehen*" ("Show us the flag") at some point, and Dirk stands in the catacombs and lets the flag fly.

Dirk meets the German table tennis player Timo Boll and they talk about the parallels between their sports and about focus and concentration. Dirk watches Roger Federer play. He watches handball games, his old sport, and the German pivot player Christian Schwarzer wears number 41 in honor of Dirk. People recognize who he is, of course, but they let him be. And he makes friendships that will last a lifetime.

When he returns to Dallas from Beijing, Dirk Nowitzki is a different athlete: he's more knowledgeable and confident.

And he still has unfinished business.

★   ★   ★

Another kind of pressure: what other people say, what they think, and how to retain control over your own story. Over the years, Dirk Nowitzki has maintained a healthy distance from the commentaries and criticisms that he receives after every game and every public appearance. He also keeps praise and cheers at a distance. But that's also something he would have to learn the hard way.

On May 5, 2009, Dirk's personal life suddenly becomes public. This is because a woman whose real name is unknown at first—Crystal Taylor, Cristal Ann Taylor, Christian Julie Wellington, etc. (the *Dallas Morning News* later lists 24 aliases)—is arrested at his house. The Mavericks are playing a playoff game in Denver, so Dirk isn't home when the police pull up and try to talk to the woman who allegedly lives there. The police have received a tip. They have questions, but the woman reportedly doesn't want to answer them. Does she have any form of identification? Is she the same person they have been looking for? With outstanding warrants in two different states? Is she who she claims to be? Does Dirk know?

The woman asks to be allowed to change and then come to the station with the officers—at least, that is how the papers will summarize the events of that particular operation. The police have good reason to believe that she is a wanted fraudster, and when she tries to escape through the bathroom window, they have already called for backup. And as these things go, somebody has been listening in on the backup call—legally or illegally, who knows—and even before the backup arrives, the cameras and floodlights are there. A helicopter, too.

The two of them met years earlier, via a random phone call—sorry, wrong number, if you can believe it—but they didn't become a couple until some years later. But at some point, there was skepticism in Dirk's inner circle; something didn't totally seem right. She would not travel to Europe—there were always excuses and unspecified commitments, there was always something.

The standard vetting performed in the circles around NBA players didn't come up with anything. There was nothing suspicious to be found under the names she used. But a lingering sense of doubt led to further investigations, which unearthed something that seems totally absurd in Dirk's world, a system strongly based on authenticity, trust and intimacy: the woman apparently had a number of identities and was being sought by the police. At first, Nowitzki couldn't believe what he was hearing. Which seems sensible. It would probably be more precise if I said it's totally devastating for him. It shakes Dirk to the core. He mulls and broods and worries for a couple of days, and then the Mavericks play in the second round of the 2009 playoffs in Denver.

Dirk has led a relationship with this woman over the last months and years. There are many variations and speculations about her names and her past. It may be the most public and speculative phase in Dirk Nowitzki's career: What was their relationship like? How long did it last? How "serious" was it? How important? "Dirk mired in off-court drama," the *Dallas Morning News* writes. "Fake love," writes the German weekly *Der Spiegel*. What is clear is that this relationship fell apart in a loud manner and under unique circumstances.

The stories you can find today consist mainly of speculation and tabloid material, a lot of it made up. Basically, everything that has been shown on TV and printed in newspaper reports or magazines or tabloids takes place while Dirk and the Mavericks are sitting in a plane on their way back to Dallas. He can't be reached while his house is being filmed from a helicopter and snapshots are taken from the bushes.

Dirk turns his phone off when he boards the plane in Denver, and he already has a new telephone number when he lands in Dallas a couple hours later. A new email address. He doesn't go back to his house, which was just assailed and filmed and photographed. He moves straight into Mark Cuban's garden house. No one but those in his closest circle knows where he is. He's completely hidden from view.

The only public appearances he makes are in the arena. His team is down 2–0 against the Nuggets, and Dirk is playing an unbelievable playoff series against the Nuggets. He's been the top scorer in both games. But he breaks off a press availability for the first time ever because he sees news crews and society reporters standing in a line at the shootaround. He answers questions about the Nuggets, the playoffs, and his opponent Kenyon Martin for five minutes, but then the journalists get impatient. "It's pretty obvious that I'm going through a difficult time in my private life," he says. "There's not much more to say." He has to repeat "no comment" twice, three times, and then Sarah Melton and Scott Tomlin break off the round of questions.

During these days, he only has a couple hours of peace whenever he steps onto the court. "The arena was freedom," Dirk remembers. "I could do what I've always done. There were no questions." In the middle of this drama, he scores 35 points in Game 2, and then gets 33 and 16 rebounds in the next one. Despite everything, the crowd in Dallas cheers him on. Forty-four in Game 4 against the extremely tough and physical Denver defense.

Dirk turns on the radio sometimes while driving back and forth to the arena and hears his private life, which he never thought was very interesting for others, being taken apart and put back together by the media. Dirk sits in the car and learns what is said to have happened.

In spite of all these difficulties, Dirk plays, statistically speaking, the best playoff series of his life. Just like in Volkach ten years earlier, he doesn't have control over his story, who they think he is. Back then, he had just been an anonymous underling in the military, but now he can read about his thoughts and feelings in the newspaper. But none of that matters when he enters the arena. He's still Dirk Nowitzki, the player who wears number 41 on his jersey. The rules are still the same on the court. "Basketball had always been a form of freedom," he says when he thinks back on this time.

When the Denver series is over and lost, he leaves the city and the country and goes on vacation with his family for a few weeks in Crete. He sits in the sun and jumps in the water; he exits the news cycle and waits until the story has fizzled out, until it's just one story of countless others that people vaguely remember without being able to say exactly what happened and when. The woman receives reporters in prison and claims she's pregnant. She isn't. Then the tabloids run out of material and people to quote. Mockery becomes compassion; people feel for Dirk. "A story like that can happen to the best of us," they say. It's been an interesting story, vague and juicy. It will stick, but interestingly enough, it will become proof that Dirk is human. That he is one of us.

The Mavericks hire experienced security personnel and develop a cohesive security system. Derek Earls, from London, has been protecting heads of state and vulnerable celebrities for Scotland Yard his whole life, and Dwayne Bishop is a seasoned bodyguard from Dallas. The two of them become good friends with Dirk; they'll still be around ten years later. When Dirk returns to Germany, he gives a press conference and briefly explains what happened, short and to the point. For the record. For everyone listening. Ask, he says, and they ask. He gives his answers. That's it. Dirk Nowitzki once again takes control over his own story.

If you address this issue with Dirk today, it no longer throws him for a loop. What is certain is that it is a story of betrayal and deception, but it's hard to judge from the outside just how shocking something like it really is. For Dirk, it's a story from the past, a love story with an unhappy ending, the sort many others have experienced (but usually without police helicopters and television trucks and reporters hiding in the hedges). "The thing with the woman," he calls it now. Dirk has found a way to deal with it. But the story must have created a ton of pressure in 2009; it must have been a breaking point, a moment that could make a human crack.

★   ★   ★

In Wiedensohler's photo from the locker room in Athens, it's easy to see just how demanding and challenging it is for an athlete at the highest level to deal with pressure and expectations—the public's, his own. It has a magnitude that is always present and multifarious. This phenomenon has always played a complex role in Dirk Nowitzki's career: there's athletic pressure, economic responsibility, and moral demands. Dirk's inner drive, his wishes, his dreams, what he's working toward. What's expected of him. For many, Dirk is larger than life, a screen on which many others project their dreams and wishes. You could crack from this pressure that has so many faces—but you can also accept it and try to overcome it.

"Sometimes the pressure wins," Dirk Nowitzki will say in 2019 after everything has been over for some weeks and months. By then, he'll know what he achieved.

"And sometimes *you* win," he will laugh.

3

FADEAWAY

"In this city, you can park anywhere, son."

Fadeaway

DIRK'S LAST GERMAN SUMMER begins in Frankfurt. Two days in early summer, two days that Dirk calls "zoo days." Bleachers have been set up in front of his sponsor's corporate headquarters in Frankfurt, and a few hundred fans are sitting in the blazing sun. As he does every summer, Dirk Nowitzki makes one big appearance to bring the German fans and press up to speed. The coach of the national team, Chris Fleming, is also there. This year, the European Championships are being played in Berlin, and everyone here shares the secret hope that this year might be as successful as 1993, when Germany became European champions on home soil. That was ages ago.

When Nowitzki enters the stage, Jadakiss's "The Champ Is Here" is blazing from giant speakers. Screams, high fives, then Nowitzki chats with host Frank Buschmann about the previous NBA season, about what it's like to become a father for the second time, about his bones and joints. The audience is sweating and waiting, the crucial question hanging heavy in the air. It's unclear this morning whether Dirk Nowitzki will even play for the German national team again, but he will let them know in a few seconds. Will he suit up one last time?

Jam-packed with interviews and mandatory appointments, days

like these aren't really his thing, but at some point Nowitzki understood that they are necessary, so he packs the calendar in order to get as much done as quickly as possible. He's good on stage, engaging and polite and funny, but you always know that he knows all of this is essentially absurdist theater. The dramaturgy of an afternoon that revolves only around his person and his decision is suspicious to him. It's a paradox: he sits on stage and explains to journalists that the most important thing for him is the rare time he has with his family and friends, his free time, days without questions, days without the same old stories. Sometimes, he looks a little incredulously at his audience. On zoo days, it is never quite clear who is the observer and who is the observed. Holger Geschwindner stands on the sidelines and quotes Nietzsche again. "For as a human being 'communicates himself' he gets rid of himself," he says. "And when one 'has confessed' one forgets."

The German national team and Dirk Nowitzki have a special relationship. For most professional basketball players, international games are the pinnacles of their careers, but for Dirk, the situation is more complicated. Since he joined the team, he has carried them, and whenever he has played, public interest has focused almost exclusively on him. Demirel and Pešić, Garrett and Willoughby, Femerling and Johannes Herber and all his other companions remember the gigantic lines of people in front of the team hotels, the standing ovations; the functionaries remember the incredible insurance sums that had to be paid at Lloyd's of London for Dirk's left ankle. Athens and Beijing in 2008, Belgrade in 2005, and Indianapolis in 2002: Dirk Nowitzki has always been the main man. He is the team's best scorer, he's the greatest and most famous basketball player to ever suit up for Germany. Since 1993, German basketball has arguably remained relevant only thanks to Nowitzki. That's a quarter of a century.

When Nowitzki finally announces that he wants to play this summer, the good news instantly gets tweeted and broadcast. He has always enjoyed playing for the national team, he says, but for German basketball, his participation means much more than that: This afternoon, the anticipation is suddenly tangible, sports journalists and sports directors hug one another, hope turns into enthusiasm. Fans in Frankfurt hold out their pens to Nowitzki. He signs. It is the last chance of his era; he is the last remaining player of the bronze and silver generation. He has prepared the ground for what will come after him.

Berlin is next. Nowitzki lands, opens a new sneaker store in West, shows up late at night to a basketball tournament in the East, briefly takes a nap, then puts in another early and long morning of tightly timed interviews for newspapers, radio, and television. Nowitzki sits in a loft-like conference room at the hip 25hours hotel and answers prying and chummy questions; he listens to the personal stories of the press. You get a sense of how much he means to them. Just sitting there makes you dizzy, and the sense of place and meaning gradually fades. Where are we? Who is he talking to? Didn't I just hear that? Was I just thinking it? Zoo days are a kaleidoscope of hectic activity, a mosaic of faces, flights, hotel lobbies and elevators, microphones, and randomly posed questions.

At lunchtime, Nowitzki disappears into the gym at the Waldorf Astoria across the street and hammers through his cardio and strength program. Even on days like this, he can't let things slide, otherwise it would take him weeks to get back into shape. These hours are sacred to him, even on media days, when he runs and lifts weights to find a haven of calm in all the hustle and bustle. Nowitzki is now 37, and as of yesterday, everyone knows what he will do this summer.

When he has checked off the entire list of appointments, we sit down on the hotel terrace high above the Berlin Zoological Garden, hidden in the last corner behind a palm tree. Tonight, the final match of the soccer Champions League will be played in the Olympic Stadium, FC Barcelona versus Juventus Turin, Messi versus Pirlo. Nike has invited everyone, and all the superstars of sports have come. You can hear the cackling of the peacocks, the screaming of the monkeys from below; up here, glasses and dishes clink. We order the drink of the day, something with cucumbers and Madagascar citrus. Summer is just getting started, Dirk's PR work is finished for the day, and although the fun should start now, he has a hard time switching off his autopilot. He looks tired; we're all on the ropes. I ask questions in order to say anything at all, but everything I say sounds like an interview.

"When Germany decided to host the championship in Berlin, I knew that I wouldn't be able to get out of this thing," says Dirk. "I didn't ask Holger, because he always wants me to play. And so do my parents and my sister." I ask whether there have been complicated negotiations with the Mavericks again about playing for the national team. It's been clear to coach Rick Carlisle for a long time, Nowitzki says, and owner Mark Cuban had no objections this year, either. "'Yeah sure, go,' he said, 'you earned that.' In the end, I only discussed it with my wife, but Jessica knows how important a European Championship is for an athlete if it's in their home country. Berlin is a basketball city; the arena is amazing. It's going to be a big thing."

A nervous waiter interrupts us, a huge, faux-leather guest book in his hand. He asks if Dirk wants to write something in it—he'd be the first. "Sure," Nowitzki says, "give me that! What do you want? A poem?"

I ask him why he would do that to himself again. What role does loyalty play in this? "The key is that I really want to do this. I can't pull something like this off if I'm not fully committed to it." He looks around at all the famous athletes and celebrities. "Fans, family, coaches, and full arenas are motivating, but ultimately, I'm the one that has to be up for it." Nowitzki leafs through the empty guest book, grabs the pen, thinks for a moment, and then puts it back on the table.

And patriotism? "I've always enjoyed representing my country. From the juniors on. The places we played! France, Poland, Italy—that was crazy for a 14-year-old. It was always clear to me that I would always play for the national team if my body was still up to it."

Nowitzki looks contemplative for a second. The sun is low over

Tiergarten, you can hear a predator scrambling, somewhat hoarse or throaty or pseudo-croupy. Dirk lives in Dallas, his parents live in Würzburg, his wife is a Swede with Kenyan roots, his passport looks like a Boy Scout stamp book. It is unclear whether they will live in America, Sweden or Germany after his career. A sense of home, a citizen of the world.

"Carrying the flag in Beijing was awesome," Nowitzki says suddenly, interrupting his own thought. "The biggest tingle I've ever had." He has to smile at this touching moment; the pen in his hand clicks and clicks. "A European Championship would be a good way to end my international career, don't you think?"

Little by little, a couple of Nowitzki's friends trickle in. A few famous soccer players briefly say hello—Mario Gomez, Miro Klose, everyone is in town. The conversations drift off, finally the interview tone fades. There are more important things than sports. It gets silly, it gets honest. We discuss what to write in the guest book. A song? A famous quote? A poem? "Shit, who knows a poem?"

A little later, someone blows the whistle, the VIPs are driven to the stadium, and the rest of us have to watch the game on TV. The guest book remains on the table; on page one, Nowitzki has scribbled a variation of Rainer Maria Rilke's famous tired-panther-in-a-cage poem, signed: "Im Zoologischen Garten, Berlin, von Rainer Maria Nowitzki, #41."

After the game, the crowd moves on to Avenue, the club in the basement of the former Café Moscow, a hip venue with a tough door policy and long lines, but we slip past all the people waiting. FC Barcelona is celebrating its victory here; the players are spraying bottles of champagne into the crowd on the other side of the velvet rope, the music explodes in our ears, Gerard Piqué fires up the crowd, the place escalates. On the table in front of us is a baby bathtub of ice and bizarrely overpriced booze bottles; the drinks are mixed before our eyes by a scantily clad bartender. It feels like we're in a boat, floating through a vibrating, twitching thunderstorm, parade-like, carnival-like—"We

Are the Champions," sha la la. I'm stuck between Klose and Nowitzki. The Spanish soccer players rip off their shirts and a lady from their entourage dances skillfully on the table between us, accidentally kicking over some glasses and laughing about it. The waiters immediately wipe and mix new ones, the dancer smiles and says something and raises her hands apologetically, we nod, but we don't understand a word, and I get a vague idea of how Champions League winners celebrate their victories. It's all exactly as I thought it would be. When we leave the club a few minutes or hours later and stand on Karl-Marx-Allee in the Berlin dawn, Krenz explains that the dancing woman was Shakira. We laugh, we cheer—we didn't recognize Shakira!—and then the shuttle comes and takes Dirk and his people straight to the Tegel Airport. The zoo days are over; now it's back to the gym. In 91 days, the tournament begins, just behind the houses over there, right where the sun rises, less than two miles from here.

★   ★   ★

A little less than a year ago, Dirk's physical therapist, Jens Joppich, and Holger Geschwindner made it painstakingly clear to me at a dinner at the Hillstone on Preston Road in North Dallas that I was too heavy for my age. We were having the famous slow-cooked, fall-off-the-bone-tender ribs and Heineken. "Here," they said, pinching my arms and stomach. "Here," and "here." My body fat percentage was just barely acceptable, they laughed. Just barely! Geschwindner grimaced. Joppich explained that there were players in the league who only had 5 percent body fat. Dirk was still average for the league despite his age, but in his late thirties, even he had to invest more and more work and tenacity into the fundamentals in order to physically keep up. "He's in better shape than he thinks he is," Joppich had said. "But it's really remarkable that he's even still here."

Geschwindner cracked jokes, but at the heart of these jokes was an undeniable truth: body fat percentage increases with age, cardiac performance declines, as does the stability of the tendons, muscle tone, and bone elasticity. We break and tear more easily, we become stiffer and softer at once. Exercise by itself is no longer sufficient to maintain one's physical condition. "At some point, you need to widen the scope of how you work," Joppich says. "The effort it takes grows exponentially."

After talking to Geschwindner and Joppich, I went to my hotel room and stood on the scale, resolving to see for myself what it would take to remain an athlete at 40. Dirk Nowitzki had to keep his body in a condition that would allow him to compete against opponents who were half his age. He did this despite all the distractions and commitments, despite the children. I wanted to see what would happen if I started training seriously. What it would mean physically, what it would mean for my daily routine. I wanted to be able to appraise the amount of effort that Nowitzki made.

So, a self-experiment: I started running more rigorously and regularly, I lifted weights, did yoga. I swore off alcohol for months and repeatedly experimented with strict nutritional programs: Paleo diet. Interval fasting. Just like Dirk. I got the keys to a gym nearby and, for a few weeks in summer, rode my bike there every morning before my family woke up, then went through the training program that I had watched Geschwindner and Nowitzki perform so often (empty gyms are cathedrals of possibility). In the evenings, I would shoot on an outdoor court until the sun went down.

The development was rapid: my midrange jumper became pretty consistent after a couple of weeks (there were no defenders), I was lighter and in better shape, I ran a half marathon in a pretty decent time, and even signed up for a full one. I systematically and rigorously prepared myself for it, and I would have run the race had I not caught a nasty cold three days before. Woulda, coulda, shoulda. I ran through the winter, forcing myself onto the running track or into the gym (occasionally, at least), and I even stuck with mineral water on New Year's Eve. I made the resolution to make up for the run in the coming year. I turned 40, and I still considered myself to be in good shape.

★   ★   ★

A few weeks after the night out in Berlin, things start to get serious. The German national team has already started training camp for the European Championships, but Nowitzki is still working out on his own. We're supposed to meet in Randersacker, not far from Würzburg, because I want to see how he's getting prepared for what will very likely be his last major international tournament. Normally, he wouldn't be doing what he's doing right now for another month. And while I'm out running along the banks of the river Main, I get a text from Dirk:

"Bring your gym shoes, I need you to rebound."

A couple of hours later, we're standing in SG Randersacker's weight room, the powerlifting section. Certificates hang on the bare walls, there are trophies above the counter as well as pictures of the hometown bruisers. Nowitzki's lifting weights, skipping rope, tearing through interval runs on the treadmill; sometimes, he sprints up the hill behind the gym or goes out on the running track. I do my stabilizing yoga exercises, the half pigeon and downward-facing dog, and think that I'm faster than him on the track; after all, I've been doing my interval sprints in the stadium for weeks and months now. We talk about how much he hates running, but for me, there's nothing better than my 10-to-12-kilometer runs. While everything he does has to be basketball-specific, I try to get specifics out of my system and train as simply as possible—one foot after another, step by step. Dirk's a specialist, I'm a universal dilettante.

Dirk's athletic trainer Jeremy Holsopple has sent him the training schedule from Dallas. Exercises, precise repetitions, and instructions for performing them. Dirk's phone is lying next to him, playing music the entire time; he looks at the program every now and again, a cheat sheet in top-notch workout theory, but he actually knows everything by heart. Holsopple will be coming to check on him next week, and the dirty work has to be done by then. Dirk has been playing at a professional level for more than two decades, and it's the same thing every year: he's familiar with the pains at the beginning of every new season. It doesn't get easier with time.

As we head onto the court, we stumble on a women's team playing bubble soccer, a game played in transparent inflatable suits, which appears to be a lot of fun. We have to wait, so we watch the women waddle around, laughing enthusiastically. No one takes notice of us. "I need to be with the national team in two weeks," Nowitzki says, "and the gym's closed because of bubble gum ball."

When the women are done, Nowitzki sets up a few cones and markers for the indoor training session, then sprints through the course, forward, sideways, backward. I keep the time and bark orders. "Ten more!" I yell, feeling somewhat ridiculous as Dirk Nowitzki's drill sergeant. "Five more!" I yell. "Four, three, two, one . . ." He gasps and looks at me with mild annoyance. He doesn't need these encouraging orders; he's been doing this voluntarily for years.

While I watch Dirk Nowitzki train in Randersacker, while I keep his time and pass him the ball, I witness once more what I've understood for a while now: how thorough and rigid his discipline is, how insanely strict and rigorous. That his body has only been able to keep up for so long because he works without compromise and because he has the perfect infrastructure to do it: optimal childcare for a good night's sleep, an accomplished chef who prepares the proper meals for him, coaches and physiotherapists who are always at his disposal. His sports psychologist, Don Kalkstein. As well as the ability to turn down tempting offers. To stay at home when everyone else goes out. To really sleep as much as necessary, not just as much as circumstances allow. To persistently turn the phone off. To cancel everything that isn't important. To stick with water when everyone else is drinking red wine. The ability to stop the passage of time.

I've known why I never became a great athlete for a while now. And while I work out with Dirk, it becomes even clearer to me. Autumn is approaching, the days will get shorter, and on some rainy day in November, it'll be too hard for me to muster the energy to go running in the dark. I'll manage to do it three or four times, then I'll allow myself to make an exception. Then the exception will become the rule. Someone or other will be calling me all the time, wanting to go out for lunch to discuss an important project. There'll always be something to celebrate—book publications, birthdays, theater openings. My kids will have a fever, the babysitter will be sick, and I will have to stay at home. My kids will want to eat pasta with butter and cheese for dinner every night, and I don't have the time to bake a special loaf of nut bread just for myself. Something always has sugar in it, comes with special glaze and extra cream on top. My kids want to have ice cream; there's red wine on the table after every reading. The pain in my knee and the colds throw me off track, my physiotherapist is on vacation and can't fix my shoulder problems when they pop up. I slouch at my desk for too long so that I can meet the deadlines for my articles. I'll let it slide for now and will start again in the spring. I'll realize what I've known all along: I'm a middle-aged man with a family and a job. I realize I'll never be 23 again and I'll never be able to run a half marathon in 1:23:22 again (Staten Island Half, 2003). I'll never be able to dunk with two hands again, but that probably isn't what matters anyway. Despite all that, I always start again from the beginning. I keep going.

Two weeks later, Nowitzki is still training in Bavaria, now with Geschwindner. His athletic coach has arrived and left; he was pleased. "I could barely walk in the end," Nowitzki says. "That's how hard I worked." He speaks less, seems more focused; trim, in better shape than he was two weeks ago. The European Cup is less than three weeks away. Dirk doesn't want to talk, he wants to act. He sinks shot after shot, with the right, the left, three-pointer, free throw. Geschwindner passes, Nowitzki shoots. Geschwindner passes, Nowitzki shoots. No one says a word. *Swish. Swish. Swish.* And maybe that's what's so special about Dirk Nowitzki: he, too, knows what's coming. Eventually. But until then, he'll keep going.

★   ★   ★

In one week, the 2015 European Championships will open in Berlin, the first major international tournament in Germany in more than 20 years. The national team is a transitional one at best, even if the players are making it seem like the best possible team of the present. Nowitzki and Dennis Schröder of the Atlanta Hawks are the big names, but they couldn't be more different: Nowitzki is a child of the German sports club, Schröder started as a skater. One is at the end of his career and the other at the beginning. They were born in 1978 and 1993—15 years apart. The two are fundamentally different in almost everything—playing style, size, sociocultural circle, skin color—and everyone hopes they will complement each other in the best possible way. And everyone knows it won't be easy.

Actually, the tournament was supposed to be played in Ukraine, not in Germany, but then it was moved here because of the war. Many players are missing, and the coach is said to be on his way to an assistant job in the NBA. The tournament would come too late for Nowitzki, they say, and too early for Schröder. Nevertheless, hopes in the German basketball landscape are irrationally high.

Dirk makes sarcastic jokes the way he always does when the situation could be better, but he still has hope. Before a friendly match in Strasbourg, his German jersey had to be altered because it was too short. They added 20 centimeters of fabric, which seemed symbolic to him. His teammates are half his age and half as experienced, and they didn't stand a chance against Tony Parker's French team. But Nowitzki wants to experience it all again. He has now slaved for almost three months for this big tournament in front of a German audience.

Geschwindner expects something terrible, but Dirk brushes the bad mood aside with jokes.

He just wants to play again.

Before the opening game, an irrational euphoria can be felt in the arena. Hopes have risen even higher. I remember the 1993 European Championships, when the German national team, with Henning Harnisch, Mike Jackel, Hansi Gnad, Stephan Baeck, and coach Svetislav Pešić, won the title in Munich. That was a long time ago. I remember how the whole family sat in front of the TV, licorice and malt beer, uncle, aunt, and cousin Andreas. How we jumped up when German point guard Kai Nürnberger drew two Russian defenders and passed to Christian Welp, who then dunked on two Russians and sank the ensuing free throw: 71–70. Dirk was 15 at the time and he, too, was watching the game on TV with his family.

A decade later, "Generation Nowitzki" won the bronze medal at the World Championships in Indianapolis, the European Championship silver medal in Belgrade in 2005, and went to the Beijing Olympics in 2008—but they never got to play a major championship tournament in Germany. Players and fans have hoped for this day, and most had given up hope.

September 5, 2015. When the tournament begins, everything is different than Dirk had hoped for three months ago on the stage in Frankfurt. The opening game against Iceland is won, but it is much closer than expected, 71–65. Tomorrow, against Serbia, things will get serious.

September 6, 2015. The match against the Serbs is up for grabs until the end. With 0.9 seconds to play, Germany is trailing by two, 68–66. The referee hands the ball to Dennis Schröder. The decisive moments, the noise deafening, the last chance, the Germans run their play, set their screens, and Schröder is looking for Nowitzki: "Where's Dirk?" Nowitzki has shaken his defender—pass, pass!—he has taken the last shot in this situation so very often, gotten them the necessary two, but Schröder decides to go for the game winner and passes the ball to the small guard Heiko Schaffartzik, who gets it in the left corner, has an open look, but can't get rid of the ball between the Serbian trees, and Serbia wins. Nowitzki watches, stunned.

September 8, 2015. Nowitzki doesn't talk much. In a tournament like this, there's no room for error. There are only a few days, a few hours, even a few seconds that separate success from defeat, and as those decisive moments approach, Dirk keeps the distractions to a minimum. He has warned me. "I don't talk then," he's said. "Only when I have to."

From the first second, the game against the Turks is a barely comprehensible mess, a mass of indecision, pure chaos. The atmosphere in the arena is as grotesque as the game itself. Everything becomes a metaphor for disaster. Everything is head-shaking, guesswork, insanity. The score is 9–0 . . . 16–4 . . . 31–11. Nowitzki sets pick after pick for his teammates, but only gets the ball far too late, often only as a last resort, and early in the fourth quarter he is subbed out and sits on the bench, shaking his head. Somebody hands him his towel and his drinks, water and electrolytes. The photographers turn their lenses away from the game and toward him.

September 9, 2015. Today, Italy. In a European Championship tournament, every game is different, every day is a new day. The sport is not interested in history. The Italians are warming up: Andrea Bargnani, Marco Belinelli, and Danilo Gallinari. Looking around the arena, you see players' wives, players' children, players' parents in every corner. They are sitting up in the boxes and down on the sidelines. Grandmas and grandpas, friends and friends of friends. They have traveled to Berlin from all over the country; the German basketball world has taken a day off to see Nowitzki.

When the game starts, tensions run high. The whole arena is standing. A 42–42 tie at halftime, then a run for Germany, and suddenly they are up, 55–45. The Italians can't make a shot.

But then they do.

The Italian strategy is simple: they give up two points on defense because they know they can score three on offense. The Italians know they will eventually score again, because Belinelli and Gallinari and Bargnani have been scoring all their lives—in the Italian league, for the national team, in the NBA. They are experienced and patient enough to wait for their shots to fall.

The Italians give Schröder layup after layup, they almost seem to beg him to do it. Nowitzki does what he can, rebounding and pushing and banging down low, but today it becomes clear again that this German strategy does not work. Dirk is efficient when he touches the ball early in the attack. He's never been a role player.

The Italians play with four shooters; they stretch the court and shoot, shoot, shoot. It's a simple calculation. A Gallinari three forces overtime, and in the extra period, the Italians bait Schröder into rushing to the basket, just as he's done all game long. He scores once, then loses the ball twice—once, the referees miss a foul. Schröder stays down for a second too long, complaining, Belinelli brings the ball up, five Italians against four Germans, two quick passes, back, forth, *bam*, *bam*, then he takes another three: 89–82. That's it.

Dirk Nowitzki disappears through a side exit with his head down. It's just one game, I think, but we know that the next one could be his last.

September 10, 2015. We're all keeping quiet. Nobody's preparing a eulogy. If there's one thing we've learned in all those decades in the gym, it's that you don't talk about the future before important games. Today, Germany could be eliminated; today, we could witness Dirk Nowitzki's last international match. Everyone hopes there'll be another one, and if the Germans beat the Spanish today, and if the Italians or the Turks lose, it will. But that's unlikely. Everyone has expectations, of course, big emotions, standing ovations, tears. But we keep our mouths shut.

Today, Spain. The loser goes home. Today, I'll watch the game with legendary color commentator Andreas Witte at his workstation on the sidelines, up close and personal and live on millions of TV sets. Witte has the best seat in the house: midcourt, slightly elevated. We see everything.

Witte has been broadcasting basketball games since 1984, the national team since 1987, then the 1992 Olympics and the 1993 European Championships. He has seen it all, and now he walks into the arena just before the broadcast and doesn't say much, either. He is a quiet man with a historic voice.

We talk about the game against the Italians and the tactical intricacies, about nervousness and cigarettes and that he hasn't smoked for years. His phone rings. "Hold on," Witte says. Assistant coach Henrik Rödl is on the line—the two have known each other for ages. The conversation is short, the topics are clear: the starting five, the strategic plan, the follow-up to the previous day's game. And: What about Nowitzki?

Shortly before tip-off, we sit down in our superb seats. In front of us are two screens: one with the TV feed and the other displaying statistics. You can see even better than the coaches from up here. In front of us are the players' résumés, worked through and highlighted, interesting thoughts in pink and neon yellow. No notes about Nowitzki, Witte knows everything by heart. I ask him if he's happy to be able to work this big game. Is he prepared for a possible elimination?

Witte is prepared. I'm not.

The game is about to start. Nowitzki stands in line with his teammates and lowers his head. It may be the last time he hears the national anthem as a player, that's what everyone here thinks, so they all sing along a little too loudly. The Spaniards are greeted with respect—maybe it's fear, because it's rather bizarre that this team is struggling for survival here and now. No one would be surprised if the Spaniards won the title. Witte has his headset on and is talking to the basketball nation, but it is far too loud in the arena to understand anything he is saying. Every now and then, a snippet of TV voice filters through. "That's the big danger," I catch. "Nowitzki," he says, over and over, "Nowitzki."

When the game starts, it's so loud you can't think straight. I try to focus on Dirk. Memorize his every move. Every screen he sets, every pass he makes. Every three-pointer he hits. The arena is real today, 14,000 people, a home temple, a cauldron of expectations, a vicious circle.

Witte sits in front of the screen and wrings his hands, pounding the table and folding them. He runs his index finger across the screen as if analyzing a painting. When Nowitzki gets the ball in the low post, the first fans get on their feet. He dribbles three times, working his way forward inch by inch, and with each dribble, people stand up as if by remote control, because they might see the last flamingo fadeaway of this long national team career, or because they know he'll score, and when he does, the crowd erupts. It's 36–35.

Basketball is a peculiar game. The second half starts, and now, the Spaniards are more concrete and determined than the Germans. Sergio Llull and Sergio Rodríguez have seen such do-or-die situations hundreds of times. At 60–48 for Spain, the game seems over. Witte pleads with the screen; during timeouts, he turns up the courtside microphones to listen to what the coaches are now telling their teams.

Basketball is a terrific game: suddenly, things go well. The Germans suddenly forget their inexperience; suddenly, the young guard Maodo Lô takes shots he didn't take all tournament. A crossover like Tim Hardaway's. Witte: "This is the future. Remember this young man!"

Three-pointer by Schröder.

Three-pointer by Lô. "How important every shot now becomes!"

Dunk by Paul Zipser.

Three-pointer by Nowitzki.

Three-pointer by Lô. It's 73–72. Only one point to go. Time-out Spain.

Witte bangs his plastic bottle on the table. "The arena's right there," he roars. "It can't get louder than this! Incredible! My ears are about to

fall off!" The entire arena is on its feet, screaming, watching as the players head into the time-out: Schröder, Zipser, Robin Benzing, Lô. And
the great Nowitzki.

Dirk Nowitzki has played 153 games for the German national team;
he has scored 3,045 points. We remember all the great moments: Indianapolis 2002 again, Belgrade 2005 again, the shot over Jorge Garbajosa
again (he's sitting on the Spanish bench now, a man Nowitzki's age and
long retired). The 47 points against Angola in Hiroshima in 2006. We
remember Beijing 2008, the German flag and Dirk's sweaty suit. The
arena remembers it all. The last 18 years have been Dirk's years.

And now Dennis Schröder advances the ball, Germany down by
three points. Schröder sprints forward and is fouled on a running three-
pointer. Three free throws—he can tie the game. In the stands, the
crowd is pleading, praying, begging. Nowitzki is getting ready for the
rebound, Schröder is shooting. He makes the first free throw, he makes
the second. We can't watch the third. I stare at the notebook in front
of me.

And then the game is over. Germany is eliminated.

On any other day, the crowd would get up and head for the exits,
dejected, ranting, and complaining. But no one's leaving today.

Nowitzki stands on the baseline, giving a final interview for TV, a
kind of exit interview, inaudible to us, but everyone waits for him. Even
during the interview, they chant his name. Then Nowitzki steps onto
the empty floor and blows a kiss in the direction of his family. Everyone stands up; the crowd doesn't stop cheering. And Dirk stands down
below and looks around. He's soaking it all in. Then the deep breaths,
then the tears, or maybe it's just sweat. The raising of his arms, the lowering of his gaze, the solemn and precise bowing to his audience. The
journalists and I stand on our seats with our hands raised high, everyone earnest, everyone moved.

Again, Tilo Wiedensohler takes the perfect picture for this
Nowitzki moment: you see Dirk walking through the arena's corridor

alone. Neon lights, plastic floor, cable trays. He looks down at the floor, exhausted and tired. A couple of Spanish officials stand on the sidelines, staring at their cell phones. No one pays any heed. Dirk Nowitzki is completely at ease with himself and his sport. He has taken off his German national team jersey and is holding it in his right hand; you can read his name:

Nowitzki 14.

"I'll never forget that moment," he'll later say. "It was always an honor."

I Hate Basketball

SUMMER 2016

L OVE MAKES US DO reckless things sometimes. Take Jack Marquez, for example. We're in Oklahoma City, it's April 25, 2016, and my fellow journalist Matthias Bielek and I are standing at the counter of the only bar that's still open: Coyote Ugly. The drunks are reeling and rolling around us, all of them men and most of them wearing Oklahoma City Thunder jerseys. They're celebrating the Thunder's win over the Dallas Mavericks in the first round of this year's playoffs, 4–1. Scantily dressed waitresses are dancing on the counter and pouring drinks down the throats of the drunks. "Let's go, Thunder!" they're yelling, and their voices hit little caprioles of joy.

But Jack isn't interested in any of that; not in the women on the bar, not in the celebration of the others. Jack wants to talk with us about Dirk Nowitzki. Jack loves Dirk. He's wearing his number 41 jersey, Nowitzki's signature scribbled over his heart, he still knows the exact words Dirk used when he signed the jersey. Jack calls Dirk by his first name, as everyone does here. Jack's been watching Dirk play basketball since he was five years old.

A couple of hours ago, Dirk disappeared into the catacombs of the Chesapeake Energy Arena, his head hanging low. The Mavericks had given everything they had—the series was closer than 4–1 and 118–104 would suggest—but it wasn't enough to win. Dirk had been five years younger when he beat Oklahoma City the last time, in 2011, and the Mavericks championship team was more cunning, more talented, and better assembled. Kevin Durant and Russell Westbrook were kids back then; now they are superstars. The Mavs were the sixth seed in the West this year, with a record of 42–40, and secretly, everyone seemed to expect an early playoff exit. At least that's how it felt when you looked at the way the squad had been assembled and watched the players work. Dallas had invested a lot of hope in the forward Chandler Parsons, but he had turned out to be a disappointment—injured too often, not serious enough. He didn't even get on the court during the playoffs. The older players were past their primes, the younger ones weren't experienced enough. Dirk Nowitzki is 37 years old, but he was by far the best player on the Mavericks this season. That alone should suffice to explain their defeat.

In the end, OKC was too athletic and their bench too deep for the Mavericks. At least for a whole playoff series. Dirk Nowitzki scored 25 points tonight; he demanded everything from his body. And when that wasn't enough, he sneaked into the locker room with a blank expression. Everyone on the Mavericks staff stood in the long corridor and watched him go by. The feeling was one of sadness, the irrational hunch that an era had come to an end.

This will be Dirk Nowitzki's last playoff series.

When he comes out of the shower, the reporters turn like sunflowers toward the sun, a tangle of cameras and microphones. The questions are focused on the game; Nowitzki answers warmly and professionally like usual, but an immense fatigue is visible in his face. The disappointment. Dirk has sacrificed another year for his Mavericks and given everything he had. And once again, it hasn't been enough. "That could have been it," one of the beat writers says when Dirk hobbles out of the locker room. They've been saying that for years. His bones carry 1,485 games in the best league in the world, over 18 years; he has seen nearly 200 teammates come and go; countless writers and TV people and photographers; dozens of arenas, locker rooms, airplanes, and hotels—but Dirk doesn't leave without saying goodbye: fist bumps for the reporters, pats on the shoulder for the locker room attendants. On his way to the team bus, Nowitzki even goes back into the empty arena to wish the Thunder's security people good luck for the rest of the playoffs.

It's last call at Coyote Ugly, and Jack Marquez is telling us again why Dirk is his hero. His jump shot! His morals! His commitment to the vulnerable and poor! The championship, man! That unique, amazing, and beautiful championship! We know it, his friends know it, but now Jack is explaining it to two guys at the bar. One is wearing a Kevin Durant jersey, the other a checkered shirt.

"The championship!" Jack says. "Have you guys ever been champions?"

The guys are drinking tequila from water glasses. "Bullshit," one of them says to Jack. "Shut the fuck up," the other says. The anger and liquor muffle their voices. Jack is so excited about Dirk that he doesn't realize why he might want to hide his enthusiasm; he talks and cheers, on and on and on, the sheer intoxication of love making him misread the signs: the mood has taken a turn for the worse. When we leave the place, Jersey Guy and Checkered Shirt Guy are waiting for us outside. It gets loud before we know it. Jersey Guy spits out unprintable insults at Jack, but Jack doesn't back down from his love. He doesn't even think about it.

"Dirk is the greatest," he says. "You can say whatever you want."

All this love is making Checkered Shirt Guy nervous; something suddenly shifts within him, something breaks, and he rips his shirt off of his body. He doesn't simply take it off—no, he rips it apart in the front. It looks a little awkward because he has to pull at it a few more times. Then he's standing half-naked in Oklahoma City's pedestrian zone, wiry and tattooed, his shirt buttons bouncing into the distance on the sidewalk. The hooligan grabs Jack by the throat, screams and lifts him into the air, then throws him against the wall. A couple of punches are thrown but don't land; the half-naked man slams Jack's head against a flower box, and then Bielek and I, some other guests, and the bouncers are there—they seem like they've been waiting for this moment. Checkered Shirt Guy is led away, his friend carrying his buttonless bib behind him. Jack and his friends and Bielek and I are trembling in the night, but Jack smiles at us.

"Guys," he says. "Tell Dirk he's still the greatest."

★   ★   ★

A couple of weeks later, Dallas is an oven. The Cleveland Cavaliers and Golden State Warriors are currently battling for the title, it's an exciting series, but Dirk Nowitzki has only watched the rest of the playoffs sporadically. Oklahoma City survived the next round against the Spurs, and then led 3–1 against the Warriors in the Western Conference finals before letting the series slip through their fingers. Dirk brought the kids to kindergarten and sometimes played tennis; he also started getting back to his training after two weeks. It's slowly getting too hot in the city, sometimes above 100 degrees, and the Nowitzki family are ready to take off for Sweden and Germany. There's just one more appointment: Dirk's Heroes Celebrity Baseball Game, his annual charity baseball game.

Dirk's invitation always means two or three days together: athletes and celebrities, Texan oil tycoons and dignitaries. Everyone eats and dances with one another, everyone exchanges business cards and project ideas, everyone makes donations and collections—and in the end, they all play a very bad—and, at the same time really great—game of baseball in front of a sold-out crowd in the stifling summer heat. Welcome to the philantropics.

Last year, everyone sat in the tower room of the Joule Hotel in downtown Dallas while a tornado swept through the streets. Everyone

Yao Ming and Dirk Nowitzki, Shanghai, 2018

Yangtse River

Ritz-Carlton Hotel, Shanghai, 2018

Jade Buddha Temple, Jing'an district, Shanghai

Pearl Tower, Pudong

Exit ramp, Mercedes-Benz Arena, Shanghai

China Games, Shanghai, 2018

Airport shuttle

American Airlines Center, 2019

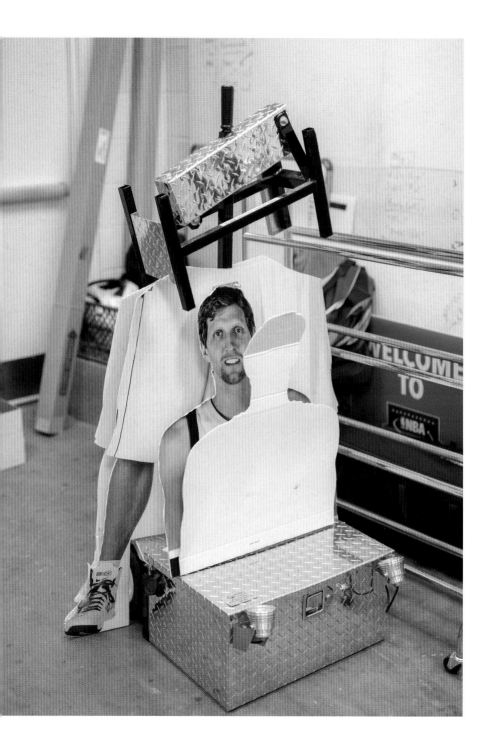

Jessica Nowitzki

Left: 41.21.1

Interstate 35 South

Pre-game, San Antonio

The house that Dirk built

AT&T Center, San Antonio, April 10, 2019

"I will miss the heck out of it."

was locked inside and happy that they were. This June, Dirk Nowitzki enters a warehouse in West Dallas on the evening before the game. The building has been converted into a club just for this evening: Klub 41. Graffiti artists have sprayed the walls with lavish praise: *Superstar* and *Legend* and *Wunderkind*. The club is a shrine to Dirk's career, a sort of church holding a congregation of three or four hundred people—dignitaries, superfans, the Mavericks, the Rangers, the Cowboys, the heroes of Dallas. Nowitzki is their mayor for these days, and when he enters the premises, he's greeted by fervid love, he's toasted and danced up. It's common knowledge: everyone here watches Dirk's games and perfectly understands what he's accomplished. It's a familial affection: they've watched him grow up. Dallas Cowboys quarterback Tony Romo takes photos with Nowitzki, two legends in soaking-wet shirts. They know each other well, two important athletes in the same city, and that connects them. Romo is two years younger than Nowitzki but has been struggling with injuries for some years now.

When Nowitzki is being driven north on the highway to Frisco the next afternoon, he's tired but happy. On big nights like this, his security people always drive. This makes it easy to chat on the way, so I'm also sitting in Dwayne Bishop's van. We drink double and triple espressos. It was a long night and today is the actual event. The Frisco RoughRiders' stadium has been sold out for some time; 12,000 spectators will be there. Dirk moans and groans at the thought of playing baseball beneath the scorching sun. He'd rather be preparing for the coming season in the air-conditioned training facility. "How hot is it going to be, Bishop?" he asks his security boss and driver. "Ninety-five degrees," Dwayne answers.

On the highway, we talk about the demands an NBA season makes on his body. "The months after are the months before," Dirk says, knowing the particular risks that tall people are exposed to. If you don't train properly, it's the heart that gives out first, Dirk says. An old teammate from Würzburg, James Gatewood, died of a heart attack only a couple of days ago. Dirk's been trying to get in touch with his widow all day so that he can express his condolences. Sean Rooks, who played with him in his first year in Dallas, also died recently, and last summer, death seized his national teammate Christian Welp. "Tall people," Dirk says, "have to watch out." He's prepared for this, he's talked about all these things with Casey Smith, his health and performance guru, and trainer Jeremy Holsopple. He knows that he can't just stop from one day to the next. He has prepared himself, even though the recently completed season won't be his last. His life as a player carries on. When we get off the highway in Frisco, there's an IKEA to the right of us. Dirk drops the philosophizing and the talk about the future, and instead tells us about his wife, who always drives to Frisco to buy her Swedish meatballs for Christmas, "and this fish goop in a tube"—köttbullar and caviar paste. Bishop and Dirk laugh their heads off, and then we arrive at the stadium. The game starts in three hours, but Dirk signs the first 50 autographs of the day right at the back entrance.

Later this afternoon, Dirk is standing on the grass of the Dr. Pepper Ballpark in a brand new baseball uniform, his hand on his blue and white heart. Everyone is there: Michael Finley; Dirk's favorite teammate, Brian Cardinal; his center from the championship team, Tyson Chandler; golfer Jordan Spieth; Cowboys wide receiver Dez Bryant, singers, actors, comedians. The scent of hot dogs and popcorn wafts above the wooden bleachers; there are Victorian-style columns and porches; there's the hissing of beer cans. Three propeller planes rattle above the stadium in formation, clouds of colored smoke behind them. The sold-out crowd stands up and sings "The Star-Spangled Banner" as well as "Take Me Out to the Ballgame," their hats in their hands, their gaze toward the red, white, and blue sky.

When the pathos and smoke subside, Nowitzki grabs a microphone. He's the host, and the reason most of the people are here. He greets everyone, then offers a big thank you and a few words about the work with children from lower-income families. And then it starts. The afternoon is slow and lazy, an All-American occasion. Nowitzki sits in the dugout the way you're supposed to: hat pushed back on his head, chewing sunflower seeds. A couple of the older guys have chewing tobacco in their cheeks and are spitting the soup into empty Gatorade cups.

Nowitzki grabs a glove every once in a while to cover first base. And every time he steps on the field, an irrational cheer bubbles up— even when he only stumbles across the baseball diamond awkwardly.

I've seen a lot of Dallas over the past years and have tried to get to the bottom of this city's love for him: I've had coffee with Shane Shelley in the hotel entrance countless times and talked about basketball with him; eventually, we started going to games together and I know he's in the stadium this afternoon. I've met people from the art world, like Brandon Kennedy, the director of the Dallas Art Fair, sitting in the third row behind home plate; and the bookseller and publisher Will Evans, on the first-base side in the evening sun. I've spent an afternoon with the firemen from Fire Station 41 in Preston Hollow and talked shop about Dirk with them (in order to extinguish a potential fire quickly, they know every material his house is built with: wood shavings, fiberglass, beams, veneered materials, and asbestos sheets). Dirk was someone that everyone there could agree about. In the bleachers are people of all ages, from all over—Latinos and Republicans, painters and construction workers, Nobel Prize winners and bartenders. There are fans of every color and shape, the widely traveled, the tattooed, the dapper and ecstatic. Even a few Germans.

While I walk slowly through the stadium during the game, it becomes clear to me that Dirk is seen in a fundamentally different way in Dallas than he is in the rest of America and the world: Texan love is rock solid. Everyone in the ballpark has their stats at hand: NBA champion in 2011, MVP in 2007, 13 selections to the All-Star team. They know Dirk's field goal percentages and rebound stats; they have memories of countless game-winning shots. They're even willing to come and watch him play terrible baseball—watch him act like a dilettante and make a fool of himself. He's become one of them. "If you're loyal to us," says broadcaster Jeff "Skin" Wade, who has accompanied Dirk ever since he arrived in Texas, "we're loyal to you." Such phrases sound like good PR, but the remarkable thing on afternoons like this one in Frisco, Texas, is that they are actually true.

There's this scene that unfortunately didn't make it into the final cut of the documentary *Der perfekte Wurf* that perfectly sums up the relationship between Dirk and Dallas. After I saw the rough cut of the film, it always remained a mystery to me why the director decided against it. Dirk is driving to a Dallas Cowboys game in Arlington and stops at the entrance to a parking lot. He lowers the window and asks where he can park. The parking attendant, an elderly Black man in a green uniform, recognizes Dirk and smiles. There's fatherly pride in his eyes. "In this city," the man says to Dirk, "you can park anywhere, son."

In the last inning, the sun goes down and then fireworks are set off. Dirk, Brian, Cardinal, and I are sitting next to one another on the bench, drinking beers in the midst of the booms and the lights. Amidst the *oohs* and *aahs*, Nowitzki grows quiet. He fixes his gaze on the night sky, like everyone else. No one is paying attention to him for a couple of minutes. "Check that out," he says, watching and smiling like a child. "I always loved fireworks."

After the game, the celebrities and the semi-famous disappear into the locker room; only Nowitzki stays on the field for a good hour in the pale blue floodlights and signs everything the fans can get through security—tickets, jerseys, framed pictures, balls, and toy cars. He signs his way around the entire stadium, a couple thousand autographs, and I will be witness to this unbelievable endurance more often this summer. One fan named Jason Quindao drove five hours to see Dirk today, and when Nowitzki actually stops next to him on his victory lap, tears of joy come streaming down Quindao's face. Nowitzki is suddenly overcome by the happiness as well, and he hugs the young man. In the background, a janitor is blowing the remains of the fireworks off the field. The pizza is already cold when we arrive in the locker room, but Nowitzki allows himself a single slice. He would never touch pizza during the season. The TV is still showing the fourth game of the NBA Finals, Cavaliers versus Warriors.

On the drive back, there's a moment of quiet after all the chaos. Scott Tomlin is sitting in the van's front seat, Brian Cardinal and Dirk are in the back, Bishop is driving. We're silent for a few minutes.

"I just wanted to say thank you," Dirk suddenly says to Scott as the van gets on the highway. "None of this could have happened without you."

"No, thank you, Dirty," Scott says and looks out the window. "You make our job easy."

Cardinal starts laughing.

"No, seriously," Dirk says. "I mean, this is my personal thing and you guys—"

"People are here because of you," Scott says. "I want you to . . . Thanks, bro."

Bishop turns the music up. "La la la la," he sings.

"No. worries," Dirk says, "but without you, no one would even know—"

"Stop it!" Cardinal says, grabbing Dirk by the neck, "before this ends in a wedding proposal."

*   *   *

We're at Hillstone for dinner, there's the famous barbecue ribs with coleslaw to celebrate the occasion. We sit at a table in the back corner of the restaurant, hidden behind beams, sculptures, and a giant wooden model of the *Titanic*. Dirk has a select number of restaurants he is able to visit in Dallas without being disturbed. He has his favorite tables and waiters who know him, who know what he likes. The guests at such places are proud to discreetly nod at him; no one will talk his ear off here. But tonight, when the main course arrives—seven orders of piping-hot ribs—a middle-aged man bends around the corner and pushes his way through the waiters and speaks the sentence that everyone at the table is afraid of.

"I don't want to disturb you," he says, "but could I ask for a photo for my daughter?"

The man looks at our full plates, which haven't been touched, he looks at the drinks in the barkeeper's hands, he sees that Dirk is trapped at the very back of the table.

"Really, sir?" Scott asks. "Are you serious?"

"My daughter would be incredibly happy," the man says and raises his hand apologetically. "My baby daughter, she'd be so unbelievably proud."

There's an episode of the American hidden-camera TV show *Punk'd* where Dirk is eating dinner with Michael Finley and Al Whitley in a restaurant; the situation is almost identical. In the show, a boy asks for an autograph between bites; Dirk signs and then keeps eating in peace. But the boy comes back with jerseys and balls and asks for more autographs. Dirk signs again. Dirk's tablemates are in on the joke and are pretty convincing in their disbelief of the brazen boy. When the kid comes back one more time with bag after bag of junk (baseball bats, jerseys from other teams, etc.), they seem like they're about to explode. At some point, Nowitzki asks whether it's really necessary. Promptly, the restaurant manager appears and huffily asks Dirk to never come back to the restaurant. Punk'd!

The show aired in 2005, but the scene is typical for Dirk Nowitzki. He's already signed thousands of autographs today; he's taken hundreds of photos and given a sincerely friendly smile in all of them. Jason Quindao drove home happy, and all the other 2,999 people have a nice new story to tell—"The day I met Dirk Nowitzki."

The man standing in front of our table won't leave; the waiters exchange nervous glances because they have been unable to prevent the situation. Everyone looks at Dirk.

"Okay, buddy, let's do it."

He puts his napkin down and awkwardly peels himself out of the corner, which means that everyone has to stand up and awkwardly wait with their napkins in their hands. The waiters are still standing by with the plates and the bottles of wine. Florian Krenz takes a sip of Pellegrino, Ingo Sauer is pissed, Scott and Cardinal grin because they remember the *Punk'd* episode. When Dirk stands next to the man, the guy cracks a "How's the air up there?" joke, and then pulls his phone out of his pocket.

"Where's your daughter?" Dirk asks.

"Oh, right," the man says. He scurries around the corner and all the way across the restaurant. We wait until he comes back with his whole family in tow: wife, son, daughter—all of them wearing embarrassed smiles. The son is placed next to Dirk first and photographed, then the wife, then the man, and finally the daughter. The girl is maybe ten years old; she looks like she's terribly ashamed of something. She stares at the ground.

"What's your name?" Dirk asks.

"Hm," the girl says.

"I'm Dirk," Dirk says. He smiles and looks into the father's camera. The girl makes a face.

"I'm Allison," Allison says. *Click. Click.*

"Group photo," the father says, then arranges the family around Dirk like hunters around an elephant. He puts the camera in Sauer's hand. "Smile everybody!"

"Okay, Allison," Dirk says. "Who's your favorite player?"

"I hate basketball," the girl says.

★   ★   ★

This is the summer of final occasions. At least Dirk sometimes now mentions the end when he's asked about it. After the baseball game in Dallas, he hosts his German benefit soccer game, Champions for Charity, in the

Mainz Bundesliga stadium in August. Twenty thousand spectators. His victory lap with a Sharpie takes longer than the game itself.

Yesterday, he decided to extend his contract with the Mavericks for two more seasons. No one knows about it yet, but last night he and Holger Geschwindner finalized the negotiations. Two years, $5 million per season. It might be the last contract of this size. He's going to spend the next few weeks in Würzburg and Randersacker and Rattelsdorf again—he has three or four gyms he shuttles between so that he can train in peace. From now on, he counts down the days to the beginning of the season, weighs himself every morning and sticks to his diet. This year: interval fasting, sugar-free.

On his last day of training, the *Süddeutsche Zeitung* shows up in Würzburg to take photos of Dirk for its portrait interview series "Don't Say Anything." The interviewee can only answer with gestures and facial expressions. Dirk is surprised. Geschwindner has told the journalists to just show up at the gym. Dirk didn't know about it in advance. After they're done training, there's still a half-hour photo shoot.

"Knucklehead," Dirk says.

"Whenever he knows about stuff like this beforehand," Geschwindner says, "he doesn't do a very good job."

The journalists ask their questions and Dirk makes funny faces. Eventually, he starts having fun with it, and when the photographer finally asks what it feels like to have a mentor, Geschwindner steps onto the photo set without shoes and Dirk jumps on his friend's back. Holger carries him, and the two of them are laughing for the camera.

Holger and Dirk. Dirk and Holger.

*   *   *

At the beginning of September, Nowitzki is sweating like an animal in the university gym of Wyższa Szkoła Menedżerska in Warsaw. We're here because the new DiBa commercials are being filmed in Poland this time. A myth doesn't happen once—a myth is what always happens.

The golden autumn is raging outside the gym's window, the sun battering down on the corrugated iron, the smell of chlorine seeping in from the swimming stadium next door. Red plastic seats, wall bars, the air thick and damp. Nowitzki sweats through one T-shirt after another, and when all of them have been used up, he wrings them out and starts from the beginning. The hoop is too hard, the ball too soft, the leather too sticky. Nowitzki has to do what an NBA player at his age has to do. The chaperone in Warsaw is called Karol, and he's sent out to buy towels.

Outside the window are the prefabricated apartment blocks built in the 1960s, under Soviet rule, as well as old apartment buildings from the turn of the last century and very, very old cobblestones. The gym is new. The eras and regimes get mixed up, and Nowitzki is feeling nostalgic. On the scoreboard, it says *Gospodarze* and *Goscie*, the Polish words for "home" and "visitors," and Dirk is holding onto these words today. He says them over and over, screams them when he scores—"*Gospodarze!*" he makes one; "*Goscie!*" and another. At some point, the Polish language brings him back to the old days, the old stories, as if he were in a game against Marcin Gortat and the gym were enemy terrain, as if the game were really important. "*Nowitzki zdobywa trzy punkty!*" he calls out, and the ball swishes through the rickety basket. "Last game winner of the summer!" he screams, and then he stands on the sidelines, panting. "I actually am feeling nostalgic. That might be my last summer training. That's what carried me through the summer: the thought that this could be the last time I have to do this."

While Geschwindner realigns Dirk's vertebrae on the sidelines, as he always does, they remember an old article about the multicultural German national team of 2003, written by a Maik Grossekathöfer. The story is about Dirk with the Polish last name and the Afro-Germans with dark skin tones, all the players with different roots and origins on the "best German national team there has ever been."

"What was that title again, Holger?" Dirk asks.

"The Pole . . . ," Geschwindner says.

". . . and the Chocolates," Dirk suddenly remembers. He grimaces. "That was before the European Championships in Sweden. That's when I twisted my ankle really bad in the preparation game against France in Braunschweig and we were knocked out in the second round. Missed the qualifiers for Athens. I still remember driving in the bus past the hall where everyone was still playing—2003, right?"

"Thirteen years," Geschwindner says. " 'The Pole and the Chocolates.' "

"Terrible. That was 13 years ago?" Dirk shakes his head and looks out the window at the apartment blocks and the chestnuts and linden trees in disbelief. "I was 25 back then." He groans as he picks himself up from the floor and kicks the flat ball across the gym.

"God," Dirk Nowitzki says. "How I'd love to be 25 again."

★   ★   ★

When I meet Nowitzki again in October, you can clearly see how systematically he has been working since Warsaw. At least, that's what I imagine. He looks thinner, his shot seems to be a fraction of a second faster, a few millimeters more precise. The Mavericks' new training center off Interstate 35 has just been inaugurated—it smells like fresh paint—and their home arena is visible on the other side of the highway. The future has begun, and expectations are high, as they always are at the start of a new season.

Nowitzki speaks less and seems more focused than a couple of weeks ago. The team acquired the explosive forward Harrison Barnes and the experienced Australian center Andrew Bogut, but everything else stays the same for Nowitzki. In his 19th season, he's still the central figure of the organization.

The Mavericks play the first game of the season in Indianapolis. Two fans are in the audience wearing superhero costumes and Nowitzki jerseys. Dirk immediately gets an isolation play on the left low post, gets the ball, takes the first shot of the new season, and misses. The game goes into overtime. Dirk scores 22 points, but the Mavericks lose.

It's the start of another season that might be his last. The Mavericks play in Houston. The Mavericks play in Utah. They lose their first five games, and then there's an overtime win against Milwaukee. Dirk is a little sick and has problems with his right foot. Darrell Armstrong calls him "The Big Mummy," and everyone thinks it's funny. People scream his name even when he sits on the bench in a suit. Even at away games. Jack Marquez and Jason Quindao will proudly wear their jerseys with the number 41 on them, and they will defend him to the death in some bar or another in America. "Tell Dirk he's the greatest." Tony Romo will be replaced on the Cowboys by the younger and faster Dak Prescott. So it goes. Careers end, players change teams, season goals go unrealized, but the city's love of Dirk will never diminish. It will grow. Why is that? I ask Shane Shelley. Is it Dirk's character? Is it because he's remained loyal?

Shane doesn't hesitate for a second.

"Twenty eleven," he says. "It's 2011."

4

THE GOAL

"Then, in truth, I was satisfied that I had
seen enough of the mountain; I turned my
inward eye upon myself, and from that time
not a syllable fell from my lips until
we reached the bottom again."

—FRANCESCO PETRARCH

The Look in the
Mountain Climber's Eyes

EARLY SUMMER 2011

THERE'S THIS ONE PARTICULAR Nowitzki moment from the
2011 Finals series between the Dallas Mavericks and Miami Heat.
It's the second of June, the Mavericks have lost the first game, and
they're down 15 points with 7:14 on the clock in the final quarter of the
second game. The score is 88–73.

I must have watched these last seven minutes and fourteen seconds
dozens of times in the years since, and I still know where I was when
these minutes were happening live (in the living room of the great
Patrick Femerling). I remember being absolutely certain they would
lose this second game as well and that the Mavericks would fall into
a demoralizing hole that would be almost impossible to get out of. I
was sure that things would go the way they had in 2006, as happens so
often in sports when you hope for a victory but have to admit that your
favorite team is unlikely to fulfill that hope. When you fall behind but
still believe that everything is still possible because there's enough time
on the clock and because the deficit is only a couple of points—because
you can play better than you have until now. And then the probability
diminishes, the deficit increases, and time is running out. Now rational assessment and irrational hope keep getting farther away from

each other until what you desire simply cannot take place anymore. That's when you know you've lost, but you can't acknowledge this truth. You don't want to accept it. You keep hoping until time is up and the final horn blows. Then you sit there, staring at the score, feeling totally empty and stupid as you watch the other side celebrate. That's what this was going to be like. I thought.

The score is 88–73 and the Miami Heat superteam built around LeBron James, Dwyane Wade, and Chris Bosh is certain it will win. Wade has just scored three points and performed a little self-congratulatory celebration in front of the Mavericks bench. Everyone is certain that this three-pointer is the game breaker; the whole arena is dressed in white. There's still 7:14 left on the clock and there's no reason why the Heat won't keep playing like they have. They've been defending the Mavericks shooters perfectly, and the Mavericks have only scored 73 points in the preceding 40 minutes of game time. At this rate, the game will end 105–86 in Miami's favor.

But that's not what happens. The Mavericks call a time-out. Who says what in these seconds is something no one can recall anymore. Everyone has just seen Wade's showboating; everyone is upset about the show of disrespect. There must be some strategic instructions given, but what happens next exceeds any plan. What happens now is something that *can't* be planned. It's essentially unthinkable, and everyone who has ever played the game knows this.

The Mavericks come out of the time-out and Dirk Nowitzki passes the ball to Jason Terry, who hits a baseline jumper: 88–75. Then Miami misses a shot; Jason Kidd quickly rebounds the ball and passes to Jason Terry for an easy layup: 88–77. There's still 5:45 left to play, and Miami coach Erik Spoelstra takes a quick time-out to get his players together. A totally normal time-out. The kind every coach would take before his players got sloppy. To remind them to be calm.

The Mavericks are focused when they return from this time-out; Terry has just made two baskets, and now he cleverly lets himself be fouled. He calmly makes both of the free throws, and the score is 88–79. The Heat miss on the next possession and, less than ten seconds later, the ball is in the basket again, thanks to one of Shawn Marion's unorthodox shots (he always shoots faster than the defense expects).

It's 88–81.

With 3:59 left on the clock, Nowitzki receives the ball on the left wing, probes the situation, threatens a shot, then fakes a baseline drive, and as soon as a second defender comes over to help Udonis Haslem, he knows another Maverick has to be open. Kidd is only one passing station away, and Nowitzki rockets the ball out of the initiated double-team. Kidd is the floor general, he sees everything and understands every movement, and when the ball arrives, he knows that he has to shoot immediately, so he shoots immediately—and makes it.

It's 90–84 with 3:50 left to play. The situation is totally different from what it was just three minutes ago. In basketball, six points are nothing.

With 3:17 left on the clock, it's almost the same play: Bosh and Haslem double Nowitzki, he passes out to Kidd, but this time Kidd isn't open—his defender has learned from the last time—so Kidd passes the ball to Terry, who goes one-on-one against Mario Chalmers on the right wing, beats him, stops at full speed, and takes the pull-up mid-range jumper. Four points to go.

Time-out Miami—again. This time, it's a nervous Miami timeout, a scared Miami time-out, a bewildered Miami Heat time-out.

And then Nowitzki happens. When Miami comes out of the time-out, Chris Bosh immediately loses the ball and two, three passes and nine seconds later, Dirk Nowitzki takes a midrange shot right in front of the Heat bench, 90–88. "Puts it up, puts it in!"—the words of Mike Breen will later become shorthand for achievement.

The game sloshes back and forth for a full minute, with no buckets—a missed shot by Nowitzki, a turnover here, a turnover there, two missed threes by LeBron James, then a fantastic defensive sequence by the Mavericks that puts the moral fortitude of this team on display.

They clinch four or five 50-50 balls, and then the ball ends up in Terry's hands. The Mavericks are running a routine three-on-one fast break. Terry passes to Marion; Dirk is trailing somewhat behind, then receives the ball and lays it off the backboard and into the net with his left hand in spite of his injured and splinted middle finger: 90–90, tie game, time-out Miami.

A panicked time-out, a deer-in-the-headlights Miami Heat time-out.

Dirk walks slowly to the Mavericks bench, totally focused. He walks like someone who is certain he will win. He strides through the white and the crowd's dismay, his mouth slightly open, his fist raised. There's no sign of emotion in his face. It looks like a mask, empty. But that's not quite right: if you look at his eyes in these moments, you get the impression that Dirk simply knows what's going to happen. "The past of the future," Geschwindner calls this experience, when time is no longer chronological, when it simply is. It's as if Dirk doesn't have an inkling of doubt; there's not the slightest glimmer of skepticism. In these seconds, Dirk perceives nothing that can get in his way.

When the teams come out of the time-out, the crowd is screaming, but the shouting is of no concern to Dirk Nowitzki. The play the Heat drew up brings them nothing—a makeshift three by Dwyane Wade, and he misses it.

Dirk gets the rebound; Kidd pushes the ball up the court, then passes it to Terry on the left. Terry moves into the middle and Tyson Chandler sets a smart and hard screen on Dirk's defender, Chris Bosh. Chandler knows what he's doing; he's only taking a small risk by pinning Bosh in place. No ref is going to call a foul if he sets a clean pick. Bosh can't get through, and Dirk has an open three.

This shot may be the most important one in his career.

He makes it: 93–90. "This is beautiful basketball," Jeff van Gundy exhales. Coach Carlisle clenches his fist, even though he usually stands stoically and judiciously on the sidelines. Dirk keeps his hand up in the air, showing his middle, ring, and pinky fingers: THREE!

Miami has one short, shocked time-out remaining.

Dirk's expression doesn't change as his teammates slap him on the back of the head, on his chest, and as he stretches out his hands for high fives. Nor does it change during his brief discussion with Carlisle or when all the players prepare for the next defensive sequence. Dirk pulls at his jersey with his right hand, a sort of tic, getting himself straight and ready, and then LeBron James prepares to inbound the ball.

LeBron has five seconds to get the ball on the court, so he lets some time pass. Every defender knows what needs to be done in a moment like this: which pass has to be stopped, which cut should be prevented. The players know what play the opponent is likely to run. The Mavericks have prepared their response for days, they've learned the Heat's playbook inside and out, and they've watched hours of tape to see how the Heat have solved problems like this. It's the moment when everyone knows everything about everyone else. James waits and waits, the offense goes through the planned patterns, and just when James has to throw in the ball, Jason Terry falls asleep. He's trying to deny the pass to Dwyane Wade, who often gets the ball in these situations. As it happens, Wade doesn't get the ball, but Terry loses sight of the person he's supposed to be defending. James, however, doesn't lose sight of Mario Chalmers, who is wide open right in front of the Mavericks bench. James rockets the ball to the other side of the court and right into Chalmers's shooting hand. He's ready. He makes the three to tie the game, just like he did in the 2008 NCAA championship game. Mario and his Miracle!

Ninety-three to ninety-three.

Now Dallas takes a time-out. Terry fell asleep, but there's still nothing agitated or rattled in Nowitzki's face. What happened before: not important. What's happening now: tie game. What's coming: the last 24 and a half seconds, in which he will win the game. Twenty-four and a half seconds are one possession plus a half second. Miami still has a foul to give. It's like being back in Rattelsdorf-Feggrube-Randersacker with Holger:

"Tie game, one possession, one foul to give?"

"Wait some and then wait some more, but not too long, because they're going to foul before the shot and we still need enough time to get a good shot off after the foul."

"And if they don't foul?"

Kidd milks the clock for ten patient seconds, then Terry fakes a screen and Dirk gets the ball behind the three-point line, top of the key, with 14 seconds left on the clock. This time, his defender is right up on him.

"They put Bosh on Nowitzki," Van Gundy says.

This is what we all want to see: tie game, the best player isolated on his defender, final seconds, the moment of truth. Showdown on Main Street.

When Dirk receives the bounce pass, he plants his pivot foot inside the three-point line, gathers himself and puts Bosh right where he wants him, makes it clear that he won't back down, although it would be easier—against this defender, against probability—to fall back and take the three. Instead, he sees a straight line to the basket. He puts the ball over his head, adjusts his non-pivot foot—once, twice. He doesn't miss a thing; he perceives everything: the painted area in front of him, red and yellow, all the defenders on the wing, all eyes on him, he sees Terry, Kidd, and Marion, and Tyson Chandler in Udonis Haslem's shadow on the baseline. Going to the right would work; to the left would, as well; right, left, all the Heat defenders are waiting for his decision.

Dirk goes to the right. He takes one, two dribbles that pull in the defenders, but then he spins, a reverse, and briefly pauses—and it's this pause that throws Bosh off balance. In that split second, he's anticipating a shot from the free throw line, but Dirk dances him out of rhythm and throws him for a spin. The Heat could have fouled, but now the movement toward the basket has started, sooner than expected and later than hoped. Might this be a last gasp of Heat arrogance? That they don't foul or double him?

"Seven to shoot," Breen says. "Nowitzki."

Chandler is working his way under the basket behind the defenders' backs. Bosh is a hundredth of a second too late because of Dirk's stutter step, and he is a few inches too close when Dirk goes past him to the left. Bosh's hand gets caught on Dirk's shorts—it looks like he's trying to hold him—but Nowitzki is already halfway to the basket.

Chandler's defender, Haslem, moves to stop Dirk at the rim, to block his shot or at least make it more difficult. But since everyone is staring at Nowitzki—spectators, teams, and referees—Chandler is able to put his hand on Haslem's back without anyone noticing. He gives him a slight push, indiscernible, impalpable, unwhistleable, and Haslem jumps a couple of inches past Dirk when he lays the ball off the board and in the basket with his left hand.

Dallas 95, Miami 93.

The Heat have used all of their time-outs. They need to bring the ball across the entire court in 3.6 seconds for one final shot. LeBron passes to Wade, who shoots a one-legged runner over Nowitzki, and when he sees that his shot is off the mark, he grabs at his nose as if he's been fouled. But he hasn't: there's only a foul if the ref blows the whistle. The game is over.

There's a story about the poet Francesco Petrarch, in which he climbed Mount Ventoux in Provence with his brother in the spring of 1336. Sheep were grazing on the slopes of the "windy" mountain, with its pale top, flanked for miles by fields and vineyards, but no human had any business being up above the tree line. It is said that no one had ever climbed the bare summit before—or at least no one had ever come back down to report on what they had seen from up top. Mountain peaks were divine spaces that weren't accessible to humans, but Petrarch and his brother went right up to the top and had a look around. At the base of the mountain, Petrarch then noted what he had seen in a letter to Francesco Dionigi Da Borgo San Sepolcro: "Off to the right, the mountains of the region about Lyon, and to the left the bay of Marseilles and the waters that lash the shores of Aigues-Mortes, although all these places were so distant that it would require a journey of several days to reach them. Under our very eyes flowed the Rhône." Petrarch describes how he started to be able to focus on feeling at one with nature and the stars and the universe. For him, climbing the mountain was a religious—or at least, spiritual—experience. He then had to find words for something there had never been words for.

I think of Petrarch whenever I watch footage of Dirk Nowitzki after this game, after this insane moment no one had thought was possible. One after another, his teammates congratulate him with slaps on the back of his head, his chest, his hands. Terry, Kidd, Marion, Sarah Melton, Scott Tomlin, Rick Carlisle, Brian Cardinal, Peja Stojaković, they all jump around him and on top of him—chest bumps, fist bumps, messing up his hair—but the look in Dirk's eyes never changes.

Dirk was alone at the summit.

I have to think about the first time I met Holger Geschwindner, when he compared Nowitzki to Reinhold Messner, the great Himalayan alpinist, and to extreme mountain climbers scrambling at high altitudes, both physically and mentally, and returning to our world speechless after descending from the heights.

Years later, Geschwindner will be very excited when he tells me about the documentary *Free Solo*, which depicts Alex Honnold's ascent of El Capitan on the Free Rider route without ropes or harness. The film depicts his concentration, the demanding nature of the endeavor, the expectations and the way of dealing with risks. It depicts the singularity of this experience. Petrarch is considered the father of mountain climbing; Messner has been on top of all 14 of the 8,000-meter mountains; and Honnold survived El Cap. Their eyes see for miles, but words fail them when they return to the ground. Dirk Nowitzki has the look of a mountain climber in the seconds after the game.

Dirk only seems to return to himself when the journalist Doris Burke asks her questions after the game. Burke asks him how the

Mavericks were able to turn the game around. Dirk shudders, then bends over the microphone and delivers a perfect analysis of the last minutes—play by play, the tactical schemes, the improvisations. *Nothing escaped him.* The series is tied 1–1; only three more wins until the championship.

★   ★   ★

The Mavericks' most successful season had started just ten months before, with a new contract for Dirk Nowitzki, agreed on in Mark Cuban's living room: $80 million for four years. Nowitzki could have received more—$16 million more, to be exact—but it was more important to him to have a big man by his side who was athletic and physical. To have a good team. Players who would do the work he couldn't do by himself. Players who filled the gaps and whose strengths complemented his own. After the extension, the Mavericks brought in Brendan Haywood from Washington, bigger and stronger than Dirk, as well as Tyson Chandler from Charlotte, who was known as being injury-prone. These signings weren't spectacular, but they were well thought out: Chandler seemed to be the polar opposite of Dirk in every regard. He jumped up and down, screamed, and beat his chest after every successful defensive play. Chandler was loud while Dirk worked quietly and led by example. Chandler would be called the "heart and soul of the team." And although they seemed to be totally different, both shared the same sense of humor.

The rest of the team was composed of solid players who were all slightly older than the average NBA player—seven of them had more than ten years of experience, but none of them had ever been a champion. The all-knowing and all-seeing point guard Jason Kidd had played in Dallas for a couple of years before Dirk's era and had spent the majority of his career in New Jersey and Phoenix. Jason Terry, who had been with Dirk when they lost to the Heat in 2006, was a streaky shooter and mischievous joker: at a barbecue after a preseason game in Florida, he had the Larry O'Brien Trophy tattooed on his right bicep to show just how serious he was about his ambitions of winning the title. Or maybe it was just to do something crazy and make the other guys laugh.

At small forward was Shawn Marion, a kind of universal basketball genius who could deliver everything a team needed: rebounds, steals, points when needed, and energy, energy, energy. The tiny point guard J. J. Barea had also been with the Mavericks since 2006. Caron Butler was a solid small forward with real guts and rage, and DeShawn Stevenson took on the role of the enforcer, the tough guy who frightens the opponent. There was also the quick French player Rodrigue Beaubois and his giant compatriot Ian Mahinmi. In midseason the Mavericks acquired the spindly defensive specialist Corey Brewer from Minnesota and Peja Stojaković from Toronto, arguably the greatest European shooter ever to play in the NBA.

Dirk's favorite teammate was power forward Brian Cardinal, who could never shake the feeling of being overpaid and, as a consequence, always worked harder than anyone else. Cardinal was a hardworking jokester, a glue guy, who understood what his team needed—whether that be screaming, hard fouls, or the right joke at the right time. They called him "The Custodian" because he cleaned everything up, mopped up the messes, and kept the place in running order.

In short: the 2010–11 Mavericks were an experienced and hungry team, professional and smart enough to go far. But no one had any expectations of them—after all, Nowitzki, Kidd, Marion, and Terry had always been on the losing end whenever they went for a title. They had a deep bench and several players with special individual skills. They had the luxurious problem of having to get all these veterans in line.

What the city expected was an early exit from the playoffs—like always. They had scaled down their expectations so as to spare themselves from disappointment; or at least my parking attendant friend Shane Shelley remembers going into the season being purposefully pessimistic. He didn't count on the championship, either.

The regular season fits these expectations: the basketball was all right: more wins than losses, low-scoring games, changes in weather and moods and discord. Business as usual. After a 93–92 loss in New Orleans, Coach Carlisle called his team "soft" to pique their sense of pride. Butler ruptured his Achilles tendon and worked like crazy to come back for the playoffs. Nowitzki missed a couple of games due to knee problems. In a game against his old team, Chandler clocked the trash-talking Chris Paul to show Carlisle and everyone else: the Mavs weren't soft. Nowitzki and Kidd philosophized about their team's chances and set goals for the rest of the season. Carlisle, normally a coach who calls out plays on the sidelines, handed over more responsibility to Kidd in the middle of the season, since the 38-year-old always made the right decisions. When Terry chewed out J. J. Barea for a couple of bad passes, a team meeting was called. Nowitzki later called it the "turning point of the season." All in all, a very normal season in the NBA, but this year would have a different ending for the Mavericks. The team finished the regular season with 57 wins, good for the third seed in the Western Conference playoffs, and a first-round matchup with the Portland Trail Blazers.

★   ★   ★

Before the playoffs, most other teams saw the Mavericks as the preferred opponents, despite their good seeding. Their poor playoff record since the Miami series five years ago had established the team's reputation: Dallas was a team that crumbled under pressure. In contrast, the Trail Blazers were a team no one wanted to face: long, tough, athletic players—LaMarcus Aldridge, Gerald Wallace, Nicolas Batum, Brandon Roy, and the smart and crafty Andre Miller—and an extremely loud home arena. The Blazers were a nasty matchup for Dirk and the Mavericks, but then the Mavs won the first two games at home without really playing all that well. Nowitzki and Kidd were the only two who were consistently solid, the rest of the team wavered. But it had been good enough for two wins: 89–81 (Nowitzki with 28 points) and 101–89 (33 points for Nowitzki).

Things change, however, when the Mavericks arrive in Portland. What had seemed like a chance to win the first series with confidence and solid basketball becomes more difficult in front of the screaming Portland fans. They lose the third game—as is often the case when a team is ahead in the series, when a team feels overly secure and confident and then stands in an unfamiliar arena, getting screamed at by opposing fans. No amount of experience can prevent situations like these. The third game ends 97–91 in the Blazers' favor, Chandler loses the matchup with Aldridge, the experienced point guard Miller mercilessly attacks the physically inferior Barea, and Coach Carlisle doesn't adequately respond to this mismatch. Barea keeps playing, Portland wins, Dallas's lead is down to 2–1.

Coach Carlisle will later call Game 4 "disgusting," a "historically catastrophic collapse." As is often the case when you receive a reality check, the Mavericks start the game well; everything goes according to plan: Dirk scores, Terry makes his shots, Kidd has everything under control. They're ahead 67–44 at the end of the third quarter, a secure lead, but then everything goes down the drain.

"My bad," Carlisle is reported to have said at the team meeting after the game. Brandon Roy exploded after having three very bad games, scoring 16 points in the second half alone, and Carlisle's game plan was not ready for that. Aldridge won the battle inside with Chandler again, and Wesley Matthews was the perfect complementary piece: 24 points from outside. The Blazers converted more than 70 percent of their shots in the fourth quarter and never turned the ball over. But Dallas still could have won if Kidd and Terry hadn't missed their threes in the final seconds. "That's my fault," Carlisle says. He gives the players a day off; it's Easter. "You don't need to do too much," he says. "Just come to the arena the day after and be ready."

When the team gets together before Game 5, Dirk seems to be

more focused and precise than he was in Portland. Everyone knows the significance of tonight. The Mavericks still have a good chance of surviving this round; the series is tied, 2–2. Despite the demoralizing collapse, everything is still possible; and when Dirk comes into the arena for the morning shootaround on game day, everyone notices that his demeanor has changed, but they can't say exactly how.

Years later, Coach Carlisle will still be able to remember how the mood shifted when Dirk entered the locker room. Carlisle has played for the Boston Celtics for a few years when Larry Bird's team was at its peak, and he likes to compare Bird and Nowitzki. Not because of their size or skin or hair color, but because of what he calls their "fierce competitiveness," the unconditional desire to win. "Whenever players like Larry have that look, they never lose," Carlisle will say, "and Dirk had the same look as Bird." The importance of the game and its intensity were evident on Dirk's face, Carlisle will say, in every gesture and every sentence said. And everyone felt that intensity.

The game is immensely important. Lose, and they remain the team that always collapses under pressure, and each player remains one who can't win. "Same old Mavs," Tyson Chandler says. "Always the same." Or win, and they clear this hurdle and change the perception entirely. "They don't come into my house and win," Dirk reportedly told Kidd on the flight back from Portland. "We're going to go up 3–2 and then fly to Portland and close the bag."

When Game 5 begins, the whole team is as focused as Dirk. Chandler has talked to the coach about playing a less measured and passive style; he wants to chase rebounds more instinctively. Terry and Kidd are also hyped by Dirk's focus. He doesn't normally make motivational speeches, those evocations of "you can do it if you only try hard enough" are not his sort of thing. Usually, he's pessimistic.

But these are not the "same old Mavs." No one is laughing, everyone has their sights on the goal. Chandler grabs 20 rebounds and scores 14 points, all under the basket, all accompanied by deafening roars. The extraordinary intensity almost creates a crisis: J. J. Barea, who has been bruised by the physically stronger Andre Miller all series long, takes a bad shot on offense that's followed by a blatant mistake on defense. As the game moves to the other side of the court, Dirk runs past Coach Carlisle and yells so loud that all the players, coaches, and team officials can hear him: "He can't play in this game!" And again: "He can't play in this series."

Carlisle will later say that he had never seen Dirk so worked up, so heated. Dirk even starts complaining during the next time-out. Carlisle only fully realizes what's happening when he talks with Jason Kidd after the game: Dirk has never spoken about another teammate like that, but he wanted to make it clear to himself and everyone else that there was no way they were going to lose. That he wouldn't *let them* lose.

A team could fall apart in a situation like this. Barea could have been outraged, the team could have split into two camps. "He can't play in this game." The coach could have lost his sense of authority. But the team doesn't fall apart—and slowly, everyone realizes that the Mavericks actually have a chance this year. Carlisle correctly reads the situation: he consults with Kidd and talks to Barea. ("Barea is just going to keep doing what he does anyway," Carlisle says. "Barea is Barea.") Dirk is the only person he doesn't need to speak to.

When Carlisle tells me about this game years later in his office, he knows how the story ended, of course. He is speaking from the perspective of the winner when he talks about "adversity" and a "sense of urgency." It's easier to talk about obstacles and difficulties if you've overcome them. There's a picture behind Carlisle's desk from the championship celebration in the locker room in Miami, ice tubs full of champagne bottles in the foreground and the team celebrating around them. Standing next to one another are Barea and Nowitzki.

But we're not there yet. On April 25, 2011, the Mavericks win Game 5 against the Portland Trail Blazers, 91–82. Without Barea on the court, Miller can't find any real mismatch. Dirk scores 25 points, but he only takes a single three—he keeps driving hard to the basket, lets himself get fouled, and makes his free throws ("Don't let them discourage you," Geschwindner had said 13 years before). He and Chandler take control of the game; they turn the tenor of the series in their favor, then fly back to Portland and close the bag as promised. This time, they aren't intimidated by the surroundings in Portland: they win, 103–96. The Blazers' fans even applaud them and wish them good luck after the game. The series was tough but fair. Dirk scored at least 20 points in every game, he roused his teammates and carried them. But above all, he kept that look of Larry Bird in his glory days. "We became the Champions in Game 5 of this series," Carlisle says, "because Dirk set the tone."

★   ★   ★

The Los Angeles Lakers are the reigning world champions. Historically, the Lakers belong to Magic Johnson, Kareem Abdul-Jabbar, and Shaquille O'Neal. They're the Showtime Lakers, the Jack-Nicholson-in-the-first-row Lakers. There's a statue of Jerry West in front of the arena, and his silhouette is the basis for the NBA logo. The Lakers have been in the Finals for the last three years in a row and they've won the last two titles. They have Kobe Bryant, arguably the best player in the league, the paradigm of discipline, ambition, and power. Their frontcourt features the Spaniard Pau Gasol, the young big man Andrew Bynum, and Lamar Odom. Doing the dirty work are Steve Blake and the tough and unruly Ron Artest (who will officially change his name to Metta World Peace in the fall of 2011); they have the experienced baller Derek Fisher, and above all, they have Phil Jackson, the most successful coach in the history of the league. The Lakers are too big, too mean, and too smart to be beaten by the Mavericks. In the week between the playoff rounds, journalists turn the winners of the Portland series into cannon fodder for the next series: the Mavs are too old, too slow, too weak and unstable. The two teams have already clashed in the regular season—there was pushing and shoving, skirmishes, technical fouls and ejections. "That was just a taste," Jackson reportedly said. "There's more to come."

In the week between the two series, Holger and Dirk go through their program every single day, no matter what—first in the arena's practice facility in Dallas, then in Los Angeles. No one is watching; they train at hours when no one else does. It's the same routines, the same access routes, and the same movements every time. "The fine details are what matters," Geschwindner says. Dirk receives the first requests for tickets, friends wanting to come by and watch the Lakers series, but he stops picking up the phone.

In Game 1, everything goes as you'd expect. The Lakers' game plan is effective, they're up 53–44 at halftime and they start the second half on a 7–0 run putting them up by 16.

But then Carlisle puts Corey Brewer, who barely even played in the Portland series, into the game. There has to be something to help Carlisle avoid a demoralizing blowout. Brewer hasn't been in Dallas very long, and he won't stay very long, either, but the wiry defender steps on the floor and delivers unnerving, insane intensity—a couple of steals as well as an emotionally important three-point shot from the corner.

The Mavericks hold the Lakers to 15 points in the fourth quarter because Kidd and Stevenson keep Kobe relatively cold. Nowitzki makes his free throws, Kidd makes his free throws, and the Mavericks enter the final seconds with a two-point lead.

Carlisle will later remember that his video analyst had done an excellent job of scouting the Lakers' inbound plays. They know exactly what's going to happen, but Bryant receives the ball all the same, shoots the three, and misses. The Mavericks escape with a 96–94 win. "We played well and had the necessary luck."

"Now, that was something worth watching," Dirk says.

In the second game, it's Barea again. He was a weak link when Portland attacked him with Miller, but he becomes a strong point against the Lakers. The Mavericks hold a narrow lead when he checks into the game, and he makes a few mistakes at first that Dirk criticizes loudly. But now it's clear as to how his orders are to be taken: Barea stays on the court, Dirk stays on the court, and they go on a 10–0 run over less than two minutes. The Lakers' nerves are running thin, the Mavericks win, 93–81, and go back to Dallas with a 2–0 lead.

The Lakers' true demise begins in Game 3. Holger Geschwindner sits in his seat behind the Mavericks' bench and observes everything. He watches how Jason Kidd takes over the job of defending Kobe Bryant in the fourth quarter. "I can't defend these guys all the time," the 38-year-old had told Dirk a couple of weeks ago. "But it's OK for a couple of minutes."

Geschwindner will later tell me that this game, this last quarter, was perhaps the most intense basketball he has ever seen. Defending Bryant, Kidd gives everything his aging body has to give. He gives everything he's learned in 16 years in the league. All his thoughts and instincts. And Bryant responds. The two of them stand across from one another like the enemies in Geschwindner's favorite film from the 1960s, *Cat Ballou*, Kid Shelleen versus Tim Strawn—*ping, pang, pow.* "The refs even stopped blowing the whistle," Geschwindner remembers. "Everyone just watched in awe."

Kidd wins the battle with Bryant because he stops him from getting the ball; and when he does have it, he's so exhausted that his shots lack the necessary poise and precision. Kidd even blocks a three-point attempt, which is a marvellous feat against Kobe Bryant in 2011. The duel between them is at the game's center, but the Mavericks are in a better position to be able to deal with it. While the Lakers disintegrate into their individual parts, the Mavericks remain a team.

Game 4 is a sensation. An abnormality. Something that cannot happen, but does. Dallas is leading by just four points after the first quarter, and then it hits the Lakers. Better said: the Mavericks hit the Lakers. With his trophy tattoo on his bicep, Terry shoots 10 threes and makes nine of them, a percentage he might normally make in practice—without a defender. Stojaković sinks all six of the threes he attempts—this game alone makes his signing worth it. This game is what you would call "modern basketball" because the three-point shot is an integral strategic tool, a weapon to be reckoned with.

The Los Angeles Lakers, the reigning champions, the most expensive team in the league, the front-runners for the title, are no match for these Mavericks. Bynum and Odom blow a fuse in the final quarter. Bynum swats Barea, 15 inches shorter than him, in midair on a drive, while Odom dishes out an elbow on Nowitzki. Both are ejected. The Mavericks win, 122–86, and sweep the reigning champions out of the playoffs.

★   ,   ★   ★

The Lakers series is over after four games. The Mavericks have taken care of the Angelenos so quickly that they have to wait more than a week for their next opponent—nine days, to be exact. They haven't had such a long break since last summer. It's early May and it's starting to get hot in Dallas. Only the first three games have been played in the other series, Oklahoma City versus Memphis, which will last the full seven games. That means over a week off for an aging team that has to budget its energy. The Mavericks practice, get treatment, and get healthy; they wait and try to not let up. There isn't a lot of talk during this interval: for once, Mark Cuban doesn't talk to the press, Dirk is monosyllabic, and Coach Carlisle doesn't have to say much. Everyone knows what's at stake.

Dirk and Holger are often alone in the house in Preston Hollow. Dirk wants to have as few guests as possible; he remembers the chaos of 2006, when the anticipation of winning had weakened the focus on taking care of the task at hand. He wants to do things differently this year. He wants to do them right. Dirk and Holger work through their routines and do nothing but concentrate. Day in and day out. Being alone doesn't mean being lonely; it means being undisturbed. The important things are ones you have to deal with on your own. Just focus on your craft. Don't categorize things all the time, don't make predictions, don't draw conclusions. Don't chatter or gossip. Don't explain yourself. Don't verbalize what you're doing to no end. Make the small practical steps, over and over: sleep, eat, shoot, *tak tadamm*, play basketball. Win a championship.

Years later, Geschwindner will compare this situation to that of the climber Honnold in *Free Solo*. Honnold had to deal with matters on his own, had to pull through and ignore all the noise. In these few days, Dirk might be the best basketball player on the planet; he can see the peak more clearly now than ever before.

When the series starts on May 17 in Dallas, it's a battle between generations. The Oklahoma City Thunder are young, with incredible players—they have Kevin Durant, James Harden, and Russell Westbrook, all future superstars who will dominate the league in the coming years. A year from now, they'll be old enough and good enough to beat the Mavericks, but they aren't there yet. When they meet Dallas in the 2011 Western Conference finals, their hard-fought series against Memphis has also taken its toll.

The city of Dallas has made use of this long break between games to come to terms with itself and its love of Dirk Nowitzki: it's been unconditional for a long time, but it continues to grow with every victory. They have gone through so much together: the yearly exit from the playoffs, the tragic loss in the Finals against Miami five years ago. And their affection was only strengthened by the single time that Dirk was in the tabloids, the Crystal Taylor saga. Could have happened to anyone! Dirk is one of them. And now they watch how he prepares and concentrates. The city gets a whiff of its chance. Paeans to Dirk appear almost every day in the newspapers; some analyze his loyalty, others stick to the technical and factual aspects of basketball, and the *Dallas Morning News* verifies the relationship between the team and the city and the star: "Trust in Dirk," it says.

When the series begins, it's clear within a couple of seconds that the Dirk Nowitzki who is playing in this game and series is the best version of him that has ever been or will be. Peak Dirk, Dirk galore. If you watch the highlights of the first game, it becomes clear just how dominant Nowitzki used to be. How great and unusual. I make a note of my "unjournalistic excitement" while I watch footage from the first half again. Maybe this game against the Thunder is Dirk's best game ever.

You can tell from the tip-off that his pre-series focus has carried over to the court. He makes his first six shots and, within the first 12 minutes, unpacks his complete arsenal in front of the Thunder bench. He lets them pick their poison: the stare-down fallaway, the spin move to the baseline, the turnaround, the one-legged flamingo, the cut and layup. At first, it's Serge Ibaka who guards Nowitzki. He's an incredible athlete and an outstanding defender, but despite his good defense, Dirk gets him in isolation three times in a row, and three times he kills him. The remarkable thing is, the ball never touches the rim on any of Dirk's three shots—all of them are perfect. *Splash.*

Over the course of the game, the Thunder will put five different defenders on Nowitzki: Ibaka, Nick Collison, Kendrick Perkins, Durant, Thabo Sefolosha—and none of the five can prevent Nowitzki from doing what he wants. He misses only when he is fouled. They hold him, hack at him, rip at his arms, and put their hands in his face. Ibaka waves his hands right in front of Nowitzki's nose, but he patiently waits for the smallest gap in his opponent's waving, then jabs and makes the basket. He's fouled 18 times in total, which is enough to put the entire Thunder frontcourt in foul trouble. He gets to the line and makes all 24 free throws in front of 22,000 spectators in the arena and an audience of millions in front of their televisions: he doesn't miss a single free throw. In spite of all the expectations. He takes 39 shots in total and makes 36 of them—that's 92 percent.

"Puts it up, puts it in!" the commentators yell. "He is putting on a shooting clinic."

"Holy mackerel!"

"Serge Ibaka should name his son Dirk."

After the game, Peja Stojaković is reported as saying that he had never witnessed such a great outing from a teammate, "the best performance I have ever seen." And in his diary of the championship, *This Year Is Different*, Bob Sturm writes about a "new level of ruthless, merciless, cold-blooded postseason savvy."

The Mavericks win the first game and barely lose the second. Then the series moves to Oklahoma City and the Mavs win both games there. They lead, 3–1. Dirk delivers everything everyone hoped he would deliver. The level of play and focus are incredible, the Mavericks defend and play bravely and cleverly, and in every game there's another player who also steps up—it's Kidd, then it's Terry, then Marion or Chandler or Barea or Stojaković. Or . . . or . . . or.

With every win in this series, the public perception of the team changes. Their view of Nowitzki also changes. At first, the TV experts are cautious, but all of a sudden, they're fans. "Maybe we'll have to change our mindset," Magic Johnson says on TV. The Mavericks are not a superteam of expensive stars; they play team basketball instead of one-on-one, they don't talk a lot, they get to work. Their favorite play is called "flow," where they're all improvising under Kidd's direction. The Mavericks' game is charged with a peculiar form of nostalgia. Values like team spirit and efficiency and loyalty are brought to the fore.

Dirk and Holger normally work through their daily training behind closed doors, nobody watching, nobody distracting them. But this isn't always possible at away games because there aren't any extra hours available in the arena—the home team gets priority, the stands need to be assembled, the flooring needs to be laid. Since no other court is available, the two of them train on the arena's court while camera crews install their equipment. A cameraman "accidentally" tapes the entire mysterious training that many people have heard about but no one outside the arena has ever seen. When the TV broadcast compares scenes from Nowitzki's best game to the peculiar training scenes in a split-screen montage during its halftime analysis, you can see how Dirk pivots in practice, how he puts the ball down, *tak tadamm*, and how he makes the exact same movement in a game against two defenders at the highest NBA level. Surprise! Dirk Nowitzki has practiced his unconventional moves!

Dirk seems to be annoyed when the split-screen video is shown. He's uncomfortable with people seeing how he gets ready for a game. "Dirk's always had the tendency to train in secret," Geschwindner will tell me years later, "so he can perform 'miracles' in the game." Geschwindner has to appease him. "There's no reason to be secretive," he says. They've been working on it for years and they know it's less about the exercises than about the precision and confidence in the execution. "You also have to translate it to the court."

The Mavericks win the clinching game in front of their home crowd in Dallas, 100–96. Before the game, Coach Carlisle told the audience to not let up. To stay loud. On edge. And the crowd responds, the atmosphere is loud and focused. The arena wants to win. The Mavericks withstand the youthful energy and athleticism of the young Thunder team, they withstand a good game from Durant, Harden and Westbrook, who will own the future, but right now, in the present, the Mavericks are smarter and more precise and concentrated.

At the presentation ceremony after the game, the Mavericks receive the Western Conference championship trophy—their first title in years—there are hats and T-shirts, but Dirk Nowitzki can only enjoy it for a moment. He disappears into the locker room before Sarah Melton can lead him to the camera teams and microphones. Dirk was supposed to stand on the podium to answer Doris Burke's questions, but he's already in the locker room. He's already focused on the next game. Who are they playing against? Still undecided. Where will they play? Also unclear. Miami and Chicago are still battling for entry into the

Finals. The only thing that's clear is that the Mavericks are there. He can give an interview later.

The next evening, Dirk is sitting in front of the TV with friends at his house on Strait Lane. They're watching the Miami Heat's critical Game 5 against the Chicago Bulls. In attendance are Scott Tomlin and his wife, Abby, Dirk and his future wife, Jessica Olsson, as well as a couple of other friends. Scott will later tell me that the memory of having lost the 2006 Finals was hanging over the evening like a dark cloud. He remembers that there was pizza (the Nowitzki way of celebrating victories: pizza, a glass of red wine, drive-thru on the way home). Everyone is rooting for Chicago. Or at least he, Scott, kept thinking about how the Mavericks squandered the lead over Miami and how they then sat in the locker room until the early morning and mourned the loss. He never wants to experience that again. Ergo: Chicago.

Dirk mostly watches the game in silence. He barely eats, and when the Miami Heat win the game and the series against the Bulls, he stands up and grabs the remote control. "Miami," he says. There's not a shred of doubt in his face, no anger, no desire for revenge or for making amends. No fear or hesitation. He just looks like he has to leave for business in the morning. "Let's go," he says and turns off the TV.

★　　　★　　　★

The Mavericks have another six-day break before the start of the next series—a badly needed break. Every day without a heavy workload is a good day, especially for Kidd's old bones and Dirk's stressed body. Both are playing considerably more than during the regular season. Dirk runs and wrestles with the best and toughest defenders; no one makes anything easy for him, they all pursue the same goal: stop Dirk. He has to fight for position every time, he carries the game and the responsibility. This is why every day, every hour of sleep, every minute of inner peace matters after a long season.

The Miami Heat in 2011 are a different team than they were in

2006. Dwyane Wade is still there, but this year it's the Miami Heat's unpopularity that attracts attention. Before the season, LeBron James announced his decision to play for Miami in a spectacular TV program that was in spectacularly bad taste ("I'm going to take my talents to South Beach" is how "King James" put it, a bizarre formulation that has been burned into basketball's memory). For purists and sports romantics, *The Decision* was a symbol of everything that had gone wrong with basketball: the exploding salaries, the focus on individual players, the way that superteams played the game. The Heat were the first team seemingly built for an audience that watches highlight reels, for smartphones, for clips and close-ups instead of broadcasts of entire games. The Heat had even presented their team in a manner that was just as over the top as the telecast of James's decision: it featured confetti and streamers before the season even started.

At the beginning of the Finals, the aversion to the Heat and the sympathy for the Mavericks can be felt everywhere (even in Germany). It's a deeply subjective feeling that's not backed by facts, a mixture of envy and boredom with the repeatedly successful. It's as if two schools of thought are facing each other: team play versus individualism, old school versus new school, dirt roads versus pink plastic. Chris Bosh, LeBron James, and Dwyane Wade are superstars and they will win their titles (anyone who knows anything about basketball knows this). But we're all hoping that it won't be this year. We're holding on to something that will fade. In basketball as well.

In the first game of the series, the teams feel each other out, try to get a read. The Heat and their coach, Erik Spoelstra (who, as fate would have it, played for TuS Herten in the second German division decades ago), have seen through the Mavericks in Game 1. They have seen how Nowitzki and Terry run the pick-and-roll, and they know from the previous playoff series how the Mavericks approach the crucial minutes of their games. LeBron James is both a horse and a cat, he's long and fast, smart and strong. And, together with Udonis Haslem, James can defend both Jason Terry and Dirk Nowitzki, and in the first game of the series, all of Spoelstra's ideas work the way they are supposed to. The Heat win the game, 92–84. On to the next one, but what's truly disturbing is that Dirk tears a tendon in his left hand while defending Chris Bosh on a play. His left hand isn't his shooting hand, but it's a cause for concern that he has to wear a plastic splint for the remainder of the Finals. No one knows how serious the problem really is. Dirk doesn't seem to be worried about it, and if he is, he doesn't talk about it.

Nothing is over yet, but it's not a good start.

In Game 2, the Mavericks don't seem to be totally awake or present; they lack precision. Nevertheless, the game remains close for a surprisingly long time. The Heat then go on a 13–0 run at the start of the fourth quarter, and it's a run that would have obliterated any other opponent in any other situation. They pull away to 15 points in less than three minutes, and the Mavericks are making it too easy for them. The Heat dunk and convert simple layups in transition, and when Wade crowns the run with a three right in front of the Mavs bench, Coach Carlisle has to call a time-out.

The Mavericks are going to lose. And if they lose, they'll be down 2–0. And whoever is down 2–0 cannot win the series anymore—statistically, the chances stand at less than 10 percent. There is still 7:14 to play, and they watch Wade celebrate and they hear the white-clad crowd cheer, they come together. "Nobody likes a show-off!" Terry reportedly yelled.

And then, as I said, Nowitzki happens. The look in the mountain climber's eyes.

When Doris Burke eventually stands next to Dirk after the game, she puts a reassuring hand on his back as if she wants to gently guide him back to this world. While Dirk dictates his perfect analysis of the game into her microphone, she seems almost surprised by the complete concentration behind the seemingly empty stare. 95–93. Dirk has liberated the Mavericks from an utterly hopeless situation—now, everything's possible.

★   ★   ★

Game 3 is close as well. The teams are now deep in the series; they know each other inside and out. The Heat have obviously been watching all of the Mavericks' playoff games on repeat, and they have identified that Jason Terry, Jason Kidd, and Dirk Nowitzki are the ones who normally take the shots and make them in crunch time. They defend the outside shots in Game 3 much better than they did before. The lead keeps changing in the final quarter, and the Mavs even get the final shot (something Holger and Dirk have been calculating for years: How many seconds are left? How many possessions is that? How many points?), and even if Dirk's calculations are correct and the Mavericks make these calculations a reality, he still has to make this final shot. Dirk gets the ball after a time-out, with four seconds left; he gets Udonis Haslem in position, plays the mind game he usually wins—you flinch first, you lose; you flinch, you're lost—but Haslem remains calm and doesn't flinch and Dirk misses. Once again, Dallas is down, two games to one.

Two days later, Dirk Nowitzki wakes up in the middle of the night with a fever, chills, snot. He's bathed in sweat and can't believe it. Why is this happening now? Right before the crucial game in an important series? Why him, of all people? He texts Casey Smith, the person he always texts when it comes to his body. Smith is a kind of emergency hotline for physical problems; he takes care of Dirk the way a lead mechanic does a race car. The two spend a morning of desperation, first at the doctor's office, then in the training facility, all the while performing the exhausting everything-is-normal-when-the-media-are-watching act. Dirk is pumped full of cold medicine and will be able to catch up on some sleep in the afternoon, but playing sports is out of the question. Not to mention professional sports. He has a temperature of 102. Dirk is hanging on the ropes.

The team fears the worst when Dirk arrives at the morning practice coughing and doesn't say anything before leaving with Smith right away.

But everyone has to keep quiet about it; no one is allowed to talk about it. Dirk is sick, Haywood is injured, most of the Mavericks are banged up, and Coach Carlisle and his assistants are working hard to find a solution for Game 4. And yet, no one whines, everyone keeps quiet.

Before the game, Holger and Dirk warm up in the training facility as usual, and although their session is shorter and less intense than normally, no one suspects a thing. Not even the handful of fans dining in the Old No. 7 Club who have the privilege of watching Dirk's warm-up program from the best tables, behind glass. He gestures toward the fans before going into the locker room as usual. And when he enters the arena, he has to grit his teeth to even be able to get through his warm-ups. The audience assumes that his fixed gaze is one of concentration. "The most important task for Dirk was to not let anything show," Holger Geschwindner says. "He was a decoy, a straw man." The Mavericks actually succeed in keeping the Heat believing that all is well right up until the start of the game.

Carlisle puts J. J. Barea in the starting five so that he won't have to rely on his outside shooters. At times, Barea can be a defensive weak point against physically superior opponents, but on offense he pokes his way into the defense like a needle into a balloon, whirling around the longer and physically stronger defenders and thereby creating open shots that his shooters wouldn't get without him. This is the plan Carlisle and his assistants came up with.

Before the game starts, the discussions in the media are mostly focused on this coaching decision: someone or other had whispered to the press that Stevenson was out and Barea was in. Carlisle wasn't happy about it at first, but then he realizes that the news about Barea is actually making it easier to keep Dirk's condition a secret. The entire team knows that they need to step up for him today. When the game starts, he gasps and sniffles his way through the first quarter; he makes all three of his shots, but nothing else afterward. Then the others take over.

Toward the end of the game it's the adrenaline. Dirk scores ten points in the final quarter and it's almost as if he's remote-controlled. The Mavericks win a hard-fought game by three points, 86–83. After the game, Nowitzki coughs his way through the questions at the press conference and Tomlin breaks off the media round earlier than usual. That the Heat weren't able to beat Dirk and the Mavericks despite his fever and snot is something the Heat will have to think about. Most importantly, this victory brings the Mavericks back into the winning mentality that they had in the first three series, against Portland, Los Angeles, and Oklahoma City: resilience and a cool head, enthusiasm, trust and confidence.

★   ★   ★

Tensions grow between the teams. DeShawn Stevenson and LeBron James are at war, Terry talks trash as usual, and James and Dwyane Wade make fun of Dirk's illness and fever as they walk to shootaround on the day of the next game. Wade coughs and laughs, LeBron laughs and coughs, and since they're doing all of this in front of cameras on the morning of the game, the joke causes a stir.

Despite Wade playing at a very high level and even dealing with his own nagging injuries, Dirk is the only player being talked about after Game 4. The game is even compared to Michael Jordan's famous flu game from 1997 ("Michael had this look," his teammate Scottie Pippen says. "He was in his own world."), which is probably the highest honor in the basketball world. For a shooting guard like Wade, a player who seems to thrive on recognition from others, such a comparison would be of great significance. The comparison is about greatness, will and toughness.

Nowitzki doesn't seem to be worried about any of this. He's in better shape two days after the fever. After Game 5, the video of "Cough Gate" makes the rounds on social media, but Dirk only sees it on an iPad on the team plane to Miami. The Mavericks have just won the fifth game, 112–103, they're only one victory away from winning the championship. "I didn't like it, I wasn't happy about it," Dirk will remember, "but angry? I wouldn't say that. I wasn't angry. I mean, it's not like it gave me more motivation. We're in the NBA Finals. I'm at my absolute max. One more game, we're only one win away from my dream. I don't need any more motivation. I didn't think, 'From now on I'll just play twice as hard.'"

The incident makes good copy for the media; speculation runs wild on the off day before Game 6. It doesn't really bother Nowitzki. "I thought it was a little childish, a little ignorant," he says in an interview. "I've been in this league for 13 years. I've never faked an injury or illness."

"And that was it," he'll tell me years later. "Me and the team didn't want to make a big deal out of it. I said how I felt. End of story. We were so focused on getting this game and winning. Things like that aren't very important in times like those."

★   ★   ★

Basketball teams are always on the alert in the playoffs; they're always on guard. If they lose, they lie awake at night, thinking about how they can win the next game, and if they win, they can't sleep because of the pressure not to lose the upper hand and the emotional tailwind. They don't want to give their opponents any hope.

The Mavericks are dressed in black when they get on the bus to drive to the arena for Game 6. As if they are going to a funeral. They want to bring the series to a close, but then there's the arena, bathed in radiant white. The Heat want to seize their last chance, they want to go back to Dallas, they want to take the confidence and air to breathe out of Dirk and his guys, right here and right now. It's really their final chance.

I can remember very clearly how people stood in the middle of a Berlin summer night in front of the Magnet Bar to watch the game. Shane Shelley is sitting in front of the TV in Texas, drinking his light beer. Haile has parked his taxi and is watching the game in a 7-Eleven near Love Field. Dirk's father is watching the game at a clubhouse in Würzburg. Robert Garrett is probably watching at a beach bar in Fisch-land. Wolf Lepenies wakes up his wife so they can watch it together on his computer. Holger Geschwindner sits in the stands of the American Airlines Arena in Miami, behind the Mavericks bench, sending his signals to Dirk if he needs them. Every last seat in the American Airlines Center in Dallas is full, even though the game is taking place in Miami. The game means a lot to all of them.

We all watch a game where Dirk doesn't shoot as well as usual. "Maybe I tried too hard," he will later say. The pressure is colossal, as are his expectations and that of the others. "Maybe I tried to force the win with a sledgehammer." He starts the game by making only one of 12 shot attempts.

We watch a game that is exactly what basketball purists hope for in moments like this. We watch Dirk's teammates take over. We watch Barea zigzag through the paint and DeShawn Stevenson strut through the white of the arena with a puffed-out chest, his gestures and threes lingering in the minds of the Heat. We watch Marion, Chandler, Mahinmi, Stojaković, Brewer. We watch Jason Terry score 19 points in the first half and take the scoring load off of Dirk's shoulders. We watch how Brian Cardinal is put in the game and defends with the purpose and intensity he was brought in for. He makes no compromises, he fouls hard, gets in Wade's way, makes a totally clean three. He eggs on Dirk, his friend, when he needs him the most. He makes jokes on the biggest basketball stage in the world.

"I love it! I love it!" he is reported as saying to Dirk.

"What are you talking about?" Dirk asks.

"No baskets in the first half?" Cardinal says. "Great! Now you can empty your clip in the second half!"

"You're crazy," Dirk says, and he has to laugh. At least for a second.

In the second half, Dirk takes the critical shots. He doesn't think about what has been and what could be. He plays his game.

We watch how he makes a difficult fadeaway at 2:27 before the final buzzer to bring the score to 99–89.

How Terry makes a midrange shot with 1:55 to go, 101–89, and how Dirk is perfectly aware that this lead cannot be overcome with just under five possessions. How Terry and Dirk hug each other for but a brief second; they're moved and they're not pretending. They know that they've achieved something major together.

How, with 29 seconds left, Dirk lays another ball in, soft off the board, with his left hand.

How he runs his fingers through his hair and over his face and suddenly *does* think about a before and an after, how he makes comparisons and tries to make sense of everything, how it suddenly seems to become clear to him where he is and what is taking place. How Dirk Nowitzki then jumps over the scorer's table shortly before the game is over and runs into the tunnel toward the locker room.

That night, we actually watch Dirk flee into the locker room, arms over his head, jersey pulled out of his shorts—a camera in the hallway will capture all of this for us—but we don't see how Scott Tomlin runs after his friend. Scott will later say that the two of them sat in the locker room together, Dirk hidden under a towel, Scott in a suit and tie. I just need 30 minutes, Dirk says, and Tomlin replies that he might be able to give him two—three tops. The presentation ceremony is about to start, and he *needs* Dirk to be there for it. He has *earned* it. Dirk doesn't move; he stares into the space in front of him. This is the moment when the pressure falls off his shoulders—all those years, all those hours, all those shots. "You're going to regret it someday if you're not there when they get the trophy," Scott tells Dirk. "You want to be out there, Dirty."

The masters of ceremonies are standing in the doorway, tapping on their wristwatches, their faces panicked because of the time constraints. The seconds are ticking. Ticking. Ticking. And then, without saying a word, Dirk finally stands up, and the two of them walk back into the arena, Dirty and Scooter, Scooter and Dirty.

There's a video taken from the opposite side of the stands, slightly blurry and from a handheld device. In this clip, you can sense what it must have meant to Dirk to win this championship. What it had cost him. You can see Dirk coming out of the tunnel and into the arena. He has thinned down in the past few weeks, and if you know Scott's story, then you notice that Dirk's eyes are slightly reddened. The camera zooms in on him as he slowly enters the arena. He had been alone with himself and his experiences, the mountain climber at the summit, and now he's slowly climbing down to this world.

His teammates greet him as though he never left. Someone hands him a championship hat, and he puts on the championship T-shirt. Dirk high-fives his way through his teammates, passive at first, but then slowly, of his own volition, one after another, they throw their arms around him, grab his neck, pound his chest, and with every rough, heartfelt touch, Dirk Nowitzki shakes off some of his burden.

His face becomes clearer, the look of the mountain climber gives way to a tired smile, then he laughs, and when he reaches the center of the stage, he has a big grin on his face. He stands there with his guys—his "brothers," he will later say. He watches the Larry O'Brien trophy be handed to Don Carter, the first owner of the Mavericks, in his white cowboy hat, and then he watches as it comes toward him, and when it finally reaches him, after all these years, the thousands of hours of training, the hardships and defeats, he grabs it and lifts it up in the air.

*   *   *

The next weeks are a whirlwind, a flood of images, a giant and happy blur: the iconic moment of Dirk receiving the Finals MVP trophy from the great Bill Russell. The tears of emotion from Holger Geschwindner. The hours after the win, the noise in the LIV Nightclub at Fontainebleau. Dirk wears Ian Mahinmi's horn-rimmed glasses and drinks champagne from an insanely expensive magnum bottle. The flight back to Dallas—Stojaković and Dirk with the trophy between them on the airplane carpet. Dirk and Cuban walking across the runway with their trophies. Later, there's the parade through the city, hundreds of thousands on the streets, and then, on the balcony of the American Airlines Center, Dirk sings "We Are the Champions" in a rather ragged voice. It will be a long summer. At the ESPY Awards in Los Angeles, Dirk is voted Athlete of the Year; he delivers an extremely engaging performance. Dirk flies to Germany and is celebrated by tens of thousands. President Obama invites the Mavericks to the White House. For weeks, Dirk Nowitzki's name will be on everyone's lips; everyone is happy for him and will keep these summer days in their memories. He will be called the "most marketable man in basketball," but he will go on vacation with his family.

★   ★   ★

When I talk to Scott Tomlin about this wild summer in 2011 and ask him about his memories, he lays down a scrapbook on the table between us. His wife, Abby, has collected all the accreditations from the playoff weeks when Scott came home totally exhausted at night. She took photos and gathered memorabilia.

Scott opens the book and tells me about a scene that seems unlikely, but actually took place in all the hustle and bustle around the championship. After the win and the flight back, the parade and all the ceremonies and official appointments, the team got together again. The location is The Loon, the windowless bar where Dirty, Filthy, and Nasty used to hang out in the early years.

Mark Cuban has brought the trophy and set it on the counter. Dirk and Scott are leaning on the bar when the TV above their heads suddenly starts showing a rerun of Game 6. Just like that, totally unplanned. The entire Game 6.

It's an absurd situation. Scott and Dirk stare at the screen. They were there, the PR guy and his protagonist, right there in the thick of things, and although the trophy is standing over there on the corner of the bar, and although they know they won, their heads still think it's possible that they just made everything up. They never found time in all the hustle and bustle to analyze the game and comprehend it—and now they're standing in front of the TV, stunned. Dirk and Scott stare at the screen and still have very peculiar worries about losing the game.

On one page of Scott's scrapbook, there are five pictures from this evening in The Loon. Scott and Dirk have taken their uniforms off—suit and jersey—and they're wearing normal T-shirts. Dirk has pushed his sunglasses up on his forehead, the left middle finger still in a splint. He's tan; he's been outside a lot in recent days. In one image, Scott grabs his head in bewilderment, genuine concern in his look. In another, Dirk is pointing at the screen as if he has discovered something he has never seen before. In the photo on the bottom right, they're laughing and clapping.

The goal has been reached.

5

IT'S A CIRCUS

"Here it is! The iconic shot for the iconic moment! He's done it, 30,000 points!"

—MARK FOLLOWILL

Sigma 40

O NE GOOD MOMENT IN all these years of research comes when
Dirk and I meet in the Mavericks' training facility on a Mon-
day morning. We leave the building through the back door; his car is
standing next to some battered dumpsters, and the Reunion Tower
can be seen in the distance. It smells like hops and yeast; Community
Brewing is next door. Repairmen are hammering, banging and nailing
some two-by-fours. Nothing would make you think that a professional
basketball team is practicing on the other side of the wall. No sign, no
fence, no security check. No one pays any attention to us. The American journalists stick to the rules and always use the front door; it's only
the Germans who are sometimes found lurking around back here.

It's flu season, and Nowitzki is beat. The kids didn't sleep well,
Malaika has the sniffles, Max is coughing, and Dirk's throat is scratchy,
too. It's a hopeless situation. All the same, he finished the first shift of
the day: a team practice to start, then an hour of working on his shot
with Holger, followed by stretching and physio and all the things he
has to do to be physically capable of keeping up with the others. To
jump with them. To have a chance of having his body be where his head
wants it to be. Approximately.

We take Dirk's new Tesla. A Model X. The car is perfect for Dirk, as he only drives in Dallas's city traffic, freeway speed limit 75 miles an hour. He flies everywhere else. Dirk steps on the gas—the acceleration excites him like a child, from zero to 60 in no time. We listen to '90s hip-hop. The Tesla remembers his taste. A Tribe Called Quest, the Beastie Boys, stuff like that.

Dirk had caught a lot of flak for his first car, a rented Toyota hatchback. Then he drove a Mercedes-AMG for ten years, a car from another era. Duffel bag in the back, and then off you went, roaring down the highway, 480 horsepower, a symbol of the young man he once was. A car from an era when stereos still had CD players; when his teammates were the same age as him and it mattered what car he drove. From a time when he didn't have children or Achilles problems or a world championship.

An NBA team's parking garage is a gallery of self-affirmation. In a culture where it's totally normal and acceptable to wear your success on your sleeve, cars have their own particular symbolism for the players. Dirk's car is an understatement. A Rothko. A Tadao Andō. No one would turn their head when they see a Tesla, but if you know what it is, then you nod your head in approval. The car looks like a standard midsize sedan on the outside, but on the inside, there's space for Dirk's legs where the engine block normally is. No frills, no bling, no golden rims or camouflage paint job. A totally normal license plate.

Not CH4MP2K11.

Not B1GD1RK.

Not SWISH41.

My ears pop as we drive off. The car produces a slight pressure so that germs and toxins cannot enter the interior. We stop amidst the roar of pickups and trucks, but then the traffic light changes, the car shoots off discreetly, and brakes again just as discreetly at the next intersection. The car always knows where it is. How much power is left. What really matters. At first, you don't notice how smart this car is.

Dirk Nowitzki often has to go to the doctor, and sometimes he takes this opportunity to chat. Time is scarce. For him, it's like taking his body to a garage. The time spent waiting passes more quickly if you talk. This morning, he has an appointment at Texas Sports Hyperbarics, a private practice at the end of a mini-mall near his house. The scratch in his throat could turn into a cold, and a cold would cost him ten days of not playing at the highest level. A couple of nights of sleeping poorly, a couple days of being in a bad mood, and the result would be some bad games that neither he nor his team needs at the moment, so he tries to do something to combat it. And I'm sitting next to him.

In the waiting room, I chat with a talkative retiree with diabetes who talks about Dirk without being starstruck. Hanging on the walls are pictures of the athletes who are treated here, and lines are drawn on the floor like in the gym in Randersacker. The old man says he comes here twice a week. He's 80 and has had two amputations, the right forefoot and some toes on the left one. All told, he's in good spirits. The retiree explains the principles of the treatment: the therapy improves tissue repair and regeneration; it enriches the blood with oxygen. The patient is given pure oxygen under high pressure for an hour, and this immensely improves tissue repair. Without this therapy, the retiree says, he would probably have died long ago.

"How do you know all this?" I ask.

"I used to be a veterinarian," he says.

A number of athletes also use hyperbaric therapy to be more prepared for competition and to regenerate more efficiently after the extreme stress on their bodies. Shaquille O'Neal, for instance. Michael Phelps. "It's actually something for the sick and old," the retiree says when Dirk comes out of the dressing room and shakes his hand. "Not for young people like you."

"Thank you, sir."

The bodies of competitive athletes are like cars. They need constant maintenance and care as well as occasional repairs. At the beginning of his career, Dirk drank soft drinks by the liter and ate anything that was put in front of him. Today, he sticks to water and his cutting-edge nutritional guidelines. He spends several hours a day on his fitness; he lies on his physiotherapist's table and lets the damaged limbs be stretched and massaged. As he gets older, his body is becoming more maintenance-intensive, which means it requires more time and effort and knowledge to keep him performing at the same level.

The metaphor of cars explains the fundamental difference between Dirk and an amateur athlete like myself: Dirk seems to view his body as a machine, something apart from himself. He owns it and drives it, like his Tesla. He regularly takes it in for maintenance and he observes from an optimistic distance while the vehicle is being repaired. As for me, I have the impression that I am my '98 VW Passat Kombi with 200,000 miles—tornado red and wrecked. I'm not very confident when I take it to the garage, I tremble during the inspection and think about it (and me) getting closer and closer to the junkyard. (I have an almost hypochondriacal relationship to this car). In short, I lack the distance that professional athletes seem to have to their bodies.

The best NBA teams might play 120 games in a season, and their schedules include flights and changing time zones and locations all the time. Some players can deal with these strains better than others. To perform all the time, the players need a lot of discipline as well as good technicians and mechanics. The technology of the body has developed radically in recent decades. Blood tests for stress checks have become standard; nutritionists and highly specialized doctors are on hand to help the athletes get in shape. The athletes know everything about their bodies, their analgesic tolerances and heart rates, and what mixtures of vitamins and proteins they have to take. Their body is their tool, their instrument. It's sometimes hard to fathom just how explosive some of the players can be, even at the end of a long season.

The NBA is a league of physical freaks. If you look at some of the players, their insanely defined biceps, their chests, and legs as long as trees, it's very hard for the average human to believe that there's not something suspicious going on. Innovation and illegality are often not very far from one another. Methods change, limits are adjusted. Kobe Bryant flew to Germany to accelerate the healing process in his knee with platelet-rich plasma injections; on the other hand, autohemotherapy is forbidden. The limit of what is possible constantly shifts, and sometimes it comes up against arbitrarily drawn lines that determine what's permitted.

But since the NBA is a self-contained enterprise, the league has developed its own laws and rules. Controls have been way more intense and stringent since the 2012 lockout. Doping and drug offenses are only made public after repeated abnormalities, but if you listen to journalists and insiders, you will occasionally hear rumors about who is taking steroids, who is smoking too much weed, and who had their best performances on speed.

Further regulations apply to the players on national teams. There are even more unannounced checks and a more rigorous list of penalties. Dirk has spent almost his entire life on the roster of the German national team, and he's been called out of bed an infinite number of times to pee in a cup under supervision. His game never depended on strength and explosiveness; nowadays, he plays without any real quickness. Everything about his game is finesse and focus, reading and understanding the game—and yet, he too makes use of science and medicine. There's no way around it at his age; he probably wouldn't be able to play anymore without his infrastructure and the scientific community's collective knowledge. He's a pragmatist with a penchant for yoga, osteopathy, and anthroposophical medicine. He prefers to think in the long term, and that also includes his body after his career.

In interviews, Dirk repeatedly notes that his extraordinary statistics are also due to the fact that he has been spared from severe injuries. The average NBA player only stays in the league for three seasons; significant injuries and physical problems have ended many careers. It's remarkable to play more than ten years, and Dirk's long career is an absolute exception. "I've just been playing basketball for a very long time, it's inevitable for some points and rebounds to add up," he says. For someone who has been "spared" from injuries, the list of maladies is impressive. An excerpt:

Ankles (right and left): 1994, 1996, 1997, 1998, 2000, 2002, 2003, 2004, 2005, 2007–10, 2012, 2017, 2019.

Pushed back incisors: 1997 (from Burkhard Steinbach's unintentional elbow in practice).

Two lost front teeth: 2001 (from Terry Porter's elbow).

Bridge knocked out: 2004 (collision with teammate Jason Terry).

Bit through tongue: 2008. ("In 2008, we played against the tough Brazilian team in the Olympic qualifications quarter-finals in Athens," he says. "At the time, they had a few physical boulders under the basket—Tiago Splitter, a really good player. I was on defense and my tongue comes out a little when I concentrate. And he fucking shoves my chin up and I bite through my tongue. Right in the middle of the tournament. A full-on hole, right in the middle of my tongue. I couldn't eat anything for days. I had to take aspirin before every meal because I couldn't get anything down otherwise. The most important games of my career, and I have a giant hole in my tongue. The doc looked at it and said, 'Nah, we're not sewing that up, we'll let it grow back together.' The mouth's mucous membranes regenerate incredibly fast, but it hurt. I can still feel the bump. Right here.")

Elbow laceration. ("That was against Houston. Carl Landry was my defender. I wanted to go by him to the right and then lay the ball in with my left. But when I went past him, my arm hits his teeth and he rips a giant hole in my elbow. You see, the problem was that Landry didn't have normal teeth. He already had porcelain teeth and they were jagged. I had porcelain shards in my bursa. That was the most pain I've ever experienced. Afterward, the doc had to dig around for half an hour in my bursa, sometimes just with his finger. He went this far into my elbow and dug these porcelain bits out of my elbow. That was intense. I'll never forget it.")

Extensor tendon tear, left middle finger: 2011, Miami.

Knee: 2012 (punctured and anthroscoped several times, 27 missed games).

Inflamed Achilles tendon: 2012–13.

Bone spurs and arthrosis in left ankle: 2015.

And so on.

In the middle of the room is a huge tube of inch-thick glass, the painted metal housing slightly yellowing at the edges. The Sigma 40. Dirk enters the room in hospital slippers and a light blue surgical gown, open in the back. He's told all other fabrics would rapidly incinerate in the tube. He can't bring a phone with him, no tablet or book. No watch. Nothing. Just Dirk and pressure and oxygen.

The Bulgarian medical assistant who used to be a doctor in Sofia welcomes us with a smile. The two are already acquainted. Dirk lies down on the steel rail, the doctor hooks him up to the cables that will monitor his pulse, and then she slowly guides him into the giant tube— the machine is just big enough for a giant like Dirk. She closes the lid and screws the tube shut, then slowly lets the gas flow in. It hisses; the pressure increases. It's as if the patient is 65 feet under the surface of a sea of pure oxygen, the Bulgarian says. "Unfortunately, I can't leave," she explains. "Some people have panic attacks when it's cramped and there's pressure. That can be really dangerous. You can't just break off the treatment. If the pressure drops too quickly, bubbles can form in your blood. And that can be fatal." But nothing of the sort is to be expected in Dirk's case, she laughs. He's good with pressure.

The glass is way too thick for there to be any form of direct communication. Dirk and I have to talk via an ancient intercom system. I ask my questions through a Bakelite phone, and Dirk's answers wheeze into the room through a crackling speaker. Later, when I listen to the recording of our conversation, I can hardly understand a word. I ask about his body, which is almost 40 and has to be checked on by physiotherapists all the time. I also ask about the great moment in the history of basketball that is waiting for him later today. He shakes his head as if he doesn't know what I'm talking about.

We talk about various TV series and hip-hop and music in general. Mumford and Sons. About how the singer from the Counting Crows sang his hit "Mr. Jones" at a concert in the American Airlines Center a couple of weeks ago and it sounded so different that you could barely recognize it. Just so that he could escape the monotony of constantly repeating himself. I ask about handing over the reins to the young and I ask about his body and I ask about aging.

It's a warped and bizarre conversation. Dirk talks about the origins of his nickname, the one his friends and teammates still use, crackling and fading in and out, and about the early years of his Mavericks, 1999 to 2005, about Filthy Finn, Nasty Nash, and Dirty Dirk. The others are long retired. Dirty is the only one remaining from these years.

Dirty.

At some point, the Bulgarian doctor asks us to be quiet. She needs to make an urgent call. No questions or answers for a couple of seconds. Dirk lies still and can't say or do anything. There are no screaming kids, no telephone, no coach's whiteboard. I'm sitting in front of the tube and waiting. I switch back and forth between looking at my notebook and the wall. The Bulgarian is talking in the background. Dirk is still smiling at first, but after a few minutes, his eyes close. The Bulgarian and I nod. We don't say a word, even though he wouldn't be able to hear us. I carefully hang the phone up in its holder and make a note of the metal's medical cream/white color, the quiet humming of the ventilation, and the Bulgarian's whispering. Dirk is dozing behind the glass like an extremely rare animal in formaldehyde, a curious and unique museum specimen. "Like an artwork by Damien Hirst," I write in my notebook. *The Physical Impossibility of Death in the Mind of Someone Living.* It feels like we've been looking at him like this for years.

Sharpies

HAVE AN APPOINTMENT WITH Jessica Nowitzki on the afternoon
of the big game, but Dirk opens the door when I show up at the house
in Preston Hollow.

"You again?" he says. "Come on in, man, take your shoes off."

Jessica is running late. She's still out with the younger kids. Kindergarten, errands, something or other, and Dirk and his daughter,
Malaika, are home alone. "Just a second," he says. Then I stand around
in the giant kitchen-cum-living-room in my socks. I take a look around
without moving an inch; I don't want to seem like I'm prying. For the
most part, everything looks like it does in the homes of regular people
with kids: ear drops and birthday cards on the kitchen table, high chairs
and balloons, felt-tip pens and crayons—nothing would suggest that a
world-famous basketball player lives here. Maybe everything is slightly
bigger, maybe there's a better assortment of art books that are more
nicely displayed. Dirk rumbles around in the next room; he's cleaning something or other up and something or other falls on the floor.
"Aargh," he yells, but he grins when he comes back into the kitchen.
He's holding two bottles of water and puts them in the fridge.

"It's nice here," I say.

"You've never been in the house?" Dirk asks.

"Only in the backyard."

"I'll show you around," he says and pours some water into a kid's cup before closing the fridge. "Jess is still out."

We step into the living room. "The living room," Dirk says in a tour guide's voice and then goes straight to a display case on the wall. Inside is an autographed boxing glove that Muhammad Ali sent to him after the 2011 championship, plus a certificate of authenticity written by his assistant since Ali couldn't write legibly anymore. You are the greatest. In the middle of the room is the piano Coach Carlisle gave him after the championship ("and sometimes he came over to play"). In a room that's part office, part closet, there's a signed and framed Larry Bird jersey hanging on the wall. The great Boston Celtics forward has always served as a reference point for Dirk, because he could shoot threes as a tall player and was mentally tough and insanely competitive—and because Dirk was always compared to Bird. Even when he was a kid in Würzburg. On the stairwell to the second floor is a signed guitar by the Rolling Stones guitarist Keith Richards.

There's a picture hanging in the dim light at the end of the hallway that depicts three oblong and otherwise indefinable shapes—they're amoeba-like, pink and luminous. "That's art," Dirk explains, grinning mischievously. Jessica chose the picture. "I could have done that," he says. "Or Malaika." He laughs because he knows it isn't true.

We enter the trophy room, a kind of man cave with a pool table and all of the collector's items from a long career. It's Dirk Nowitzki's personal Hall of Fame. On the shelves are the slightly deflated game balls from his big games; on each, a leather panel has been removed and replaced by one with embossed inscriptions—5,000 points, 10,000 points, 25,000 points. The 2011 Finals MVP trophy is standing on a slightly dusty wooden box. The 2011 ESPY Award for Best Athlete. The Magic Johnson Award for dignity in dealing with the media. The Twyman-Stokes Teammate of the Year Award. Trophies are stacked on top of trophies. There's the cup for winning the three-point contest in 2006 and a couple of custom-made Nikes. The only thing missing is the 2007 MVP trophy, which was given to him after the historic first-round defeat in Oakland in 2007—it's at his parents' house in Würzburg (he doesn't have any good memories from that year).

We pause in front of a collage of pictures that features original signatures from all the great NBA stars, Michael Jordan next to Charles Barkley, Hakeem Olajuwon, Scottie Pippen, and Steve Nash. The league had this picture made at some point; all players signed it and now everyone in the picture has a similar collage hanging in their house—the greatest players of all time, with themselves in the center. An ironing board is leaning in the corner. Dirk's trophy room is a place that would probably be the centerpiece of the house for many other players, but it's almost like a storage room for Nowitzki. "You're right, all that stuff always finds its way up here," Dirk says indignantly, but then he laughs. His life no longer takes place among the balls and trophies, the memories of his own greatness. He doesn't seem to think that this is remarkable.

Leaving the trophy room, we bend under the sloping roof and arrive in a kind of movie theater with ten leather chairs, the dream of every young basketball player who wants to be a rich and famous athlete. It's a room that could be on *MTV Cribs*, an emblem of luxury. Your own movie theater, your own home gym like Michael Jordan, a walk-in shoe closet! But cardboard boxes are stacked between the rows of seats at the Nowitzkis', there are boxes of T-shirts and programs and Dirk Nowitzki bobbleheads. Nowitzki apologizes for the mess. "We hardly ever use this room," he says. "Whenever we want to watch something, we do it downstairs in the living room."

The childhood dream of absolute luxury has become the pragmatic reality of a three-time father. The movie theater is only a junk room on the way to the playroom. A door is open next to the screen, and soft music is pouring out—a jingling, a rattling, a chirping.

"Malaika," Dirk calls and ducks through the narrow door to his daughter's playroom. "Your water."

★   ★   ★

Same house, different perspective: when Jessica Nowitzki comes home, she sets down two cans of Italian soda on the living room table between us. She sits down and puts her hands flat on the table. She has just been at the hairdresser, but now she's here. "Aranciata Rossa," she says, cracks a can open, and takes a sip.

"How can I help?" she asks.

One thing that immediately strikes you when you sit across from Jessica Nowitzki is her clear friendliness, her engaging assertiveness. She looks you directly in the eyes, she listens, she asks questions. Her schedule is tight—but when she's there, she's there. She talks about Dirk as her husband and not about Dirk the superstar. She talks about their life, their family, their goals. She knows who they are.

Jessica is responsible for the house and its style. Whereas Dirk had walked through the house to get to his jerseys and memorabilia, she has put a lot of thought into the design of the spaces and the hanging of the pictures. "Of course," she says when I ask her about it. "I moved in six, seven years ago. Dirk never really got into design," she says, "he only ever needed a sofa, a bed, and maybe a TV. He doesn't have a lot of time, and he had someone else help him take care of these things. But then I took over. I wanted to design spaces that we would both feel comfortable in." She worked in a gallery for years, she says, "and this house has really great walls."

Who she is: the daughter of a Kenyan mother and a Swedish father, he an engineer and an architecture enthusiast; she the creative head of the family. Two brothers, twins, both professional soccer players in England. Jessica talks about having an open house full of colors and sculptures and robes when she talks about her mother, and about the clear lines that her Scandinavian father favors. She and her brothers

grew up in this interplay between cultures. She laughs. "In this chaos," she says.

Jessica stands up and walks through the giant living room so that she can explain the sculptures. "These two in the display case," she says, "are a wedding present from my mother. Ebony. Two Maasai warriors, a man and woman, they're adorned with Maasai jewelry and Maasai robes. She also gave us the carvings up there on the wall." She and Dirk were married in Kenya in 2012, and there were so many presents they had to prepare a special shipment home.

I ask how she came to art. "Indirectly," Jessica Nowitzki says. "I wanted to work in travel after school. The short version is that I studied economics with a minor in travel management, then worked as a flight attendant for Ryanair for a year in Frankfurt-Hahn before packing my things and finishing my studies in Hawaii: bachelor of business administration. I didn't want to go straight back to Europe when I finished, I still had a visa, so I started looking for a job."

"And that brought you to Dallas?"

"I didn't know anything about the city, only that my mother always watched the TV show." Jessica laughs because she knows the same is true for many Europeans. The Nowitzkis also watched. Dallas—that was the Cowboys, cacti, and the Ewings. "I had relatives in Plano," she says, "so I came here. In my second week, I went to a temp agency to see what direction to go in. What jobs were available, which fields. And then the woman at the agency said, 'Wait a second, I have a job here that's not even in the system yet. It's in an art gallery. It just came in—the gallery's not even open yet. Would that be something for you?' 'Great,' I said. I was in the right place at the right time. She called the gallery, and I went straight to the interview in my normal clothes. The gallery was going to be working with international artists, the focus was on contemporary British art, and they had big plans and big ideas. I had a normal job in the office at first, but then my role expanded."

Jessica sometimes switches languages when she talks—German out of politeness, Swedish out of habit from speaking with the children—a reflection of the linguistic life at the Nowitzkis. She speaks her mother language with the children who bear Kenyan names and who speak German with their father and English with the nannies. "Coffee or tea?" she asks like the flight attendant she was ages ago.

Jessica moved up from the office job to gallery manager and remained there when it turned into a foundation in 2010. She supported young artists and searched for talent as well as managing the Goss-Michael Foundation's collection. She traveled around the world to visit art fairs and museums and meet artists and gallerists, but stopped when Malaika was born.

I ask about her relationship to art today. She no longer goes to a museum like a tourist, she says; instead, she goes to see artists she has been following for years. "I don't go to a museum just to go to a museum." She wants to discover artists, she says, in galleries and small museums. She observes the art world, and her job isn't really all that different from scouts who sit around in small gyms, watching young players, far from the big arenas in the big cities. "Lately, I've been really interested in painting," she says. "Depictions of Black femininity have become more important to me since my mother died, like Mickalene Thomas, for instance. She paints these half-naked Black women from the 1970s—very liberal, very beautiful, very three-dimensional. And she paints them with a very individual twist."

She and Dirk met at a charity auction that Jessica had organized for NBA Africa. She had heard of Dirk before—of course—and Steve Nash had also been a customer at the gallery. But they first met at the auction, where Dirk also purchased a picture.

I ask about their two worlds—her art world and Dirk's basketball world—and how they, in the most literal sense, hang next to each other: Ali's glove and the Maasai warriors; there's the Nowitzki Gallery on the second floor and the tapestry works and paintings on the ground floor. "The art will always be there," Jessica Nowitzki says and stands up. "With basketball, to me, it's very now."

"Follow me," she says. "I want to show you something."

She understands why Dirk loves basketball so much, she says. She's also an athlete—she and Dirk even played tennis on one of their first dates. She gets why he loves going to the gym, how happy it makes him. Dirk is a creature of habit, she says; he needs order. He's found his calling, she says. "But, of course, there are aspects of his work that I don't know a lot about. It's kind of a black box. There are some things that only he understands, and I'm not totally sure that he could explain them to me. Even if he wanted."

"Dirk is more of a pessimistic person," she says. And when she watches him play, she can clearly sense what state he is in. How he feels. She sees his dissatisfaction with his teammates, his chagrin with turnovers, she notices when his mood reaches a tipping point. "I watch him while he does his thing and I can almost read his thoughts," she says. "But I'd never step in. It's his job and he does it incredibly well. I watch him, but I'd never scream. I wouldn't want him to butt in with my work, either."

Jessica says that she would never sit in front of the TV to watch

ESPN alone. "Basketball is very now," she had said. She only ever watches with Dirk, and sometimes she has the impression that he isn't always aware of the influence he has had on the game. "It only happens occasionally," she says and shows me the direction. "Sometimes, when we're sitting in front of the TV and watching basketball together and Kevin Durant does Dirk's fadeaway, then there's a smile on his face." Jessica turns on the light to the second floor. "That's like a little epiphany for him. 'Oh, wow! That's something I thought up and now KD has that shot in his repertoire.' Dirk never says anything, but he knows it. And I know it. And we don't have to say it."

We stop in front of the picture that Dirk had joked about earlier. "Here," Jessica says. "Katherine Bernhardt, a painter from New York. She paints portraits as well as consumer goods and artefacts from pop culture. There's a graffiti element to the picture, an element of pop art. Neon and spray paints. Dirk didn't really like it at first, but a couple of days ago he asked me why it's hanging up here and not downstairs anymore." Jessica stares at the picture with its three amoeba-like shapes that aren't amoebas or phalli or condoms or whatever else that Dirk could make jokes about. She takes a good look at the picture.

"This picture," Jessica Nowitzki says, "illustrates our lives. It's colorful and vibrant, and it depicts three Sharpie pens. They're all over the place in this house because Dirk has to constantly sign autographs. 'This is actually about us,' I thought. It's funny, it has a sense of humor. I've followed the artist for a long time, but she's only now starting to become more famous." Jessica turns off the light and the moment is over just as fast as it began. The Nowitzkis seem to be a modern family, I think, two people with two professions, their spheres overlapping and complementing each other, and both are specialists in their field. "She's exhibiting in the Fort Worth Modern in spring," Jessica Nowitzki says. "Have you ever been? No? You have to go."

When we get back to the kitchen, Dirk has put the food for the kids on the table and is admonishing them. "Not just the crispbread," he says to Max, "the fish, too!" Jessica picks up the cans of soda from the table and throws them in the recycling bin. Dirk gets up. "Can you take over?" he asks, because he has to leave. His bag is already packed, today is game day, and the Lakers are waiting. A milestone. It will be a spectacle. "It's showtime!" Dirk says. "See you there."

It's a Circus

I︎T HAS TO HAPPEN today. On the morning of the day that Dirk Nowitzki might score his 30,000th career point, a dozen employees of the American Airlines Center are ripping open giant cardboard boxes full of T-shirts from China. The arena is empty, the air conditioning is humming, a radio is playing somewhere in the distance. The employees mechanically and silently place the gray T-shirts over the seats, the same movement over and over, and we observe how they unfold and spread them out, how they meticulously straighten them. The gray of the shirts seems strangely unfitting to me. The jumbotron is dark and silent above the court. The shirt brigade slowly works its way up the stands, level by level, until they reach the top, where the 2011 championship banner is hanging with the retired jersey numbers of Rolando Blackman and Brad Davis. The Mavericks will miss the playoffs this year, but today might be a rare opportunity to experience a big moment—a great feat for Dirk and T-shirts for the entire arena.

I've extended my stay for a week so that I can be here. There was no way of foretelling the precise moment with any certainty. Dirk keeps working like usual, but the journalists have been talking about practically nothing else for three days now. Dirk's season average is 12 points a game, and he has 29,980 in his career—there are 20 more to go. And yet, everyone is counting on the unexpected. The team is playing second-rate basketball and the writers are thankful for any material that deviates from the daily routine. The questions for Dirk's teammates no longer have anything to do with the game itself. Everything is focused on this historic milestone.

When Dirk sees the gray "30K" T-shirts draped over all the seats at shootaround, he wants them to be disposed of immediately—it's too much. He jokes. It's too much attention, too much individualist hoo-ha, too many layers of meaning poured over the normal game he's going to play tonight. This morning, he makes his little jokes and works through his rituals, but tonight he's supposed to write history. Or at least, everyone is counting on it.

There's no turning back: the T-shirts have today's date on them— "Mavs vs. Lakers Special Edition, 3.7.17." Scott tries to calm Dirk down: it's just that this is Dirk Week—there are Dirk Burgers, the Dirkwurst, a 30K bobblehead on Friday, and on Sunday, the rookie Dirk bobblehead with the boy band part in his hair and the '90s suit and the earring. "That's if it doesn't happen today," Scott grins, since he knows that if it doesn't happen today, he'll have to endure a few more days of Dirk's rantings and the press's obsessiveness about the topic.

"Dirkwurst? What a bunch of nonsense! What a circus!"

"No pressure," Scott says. "If it doesn't happen today, then it will on Friday. Or Sunday."

During the game, Scott and Sarah Melton are sitting at their desk, located behind the bench. Al Whitley is sitting on the ground next to his equipment, Bobby Karalla is hidden halfway behind his computer. Dwain Price from the *Fort Worth Star-Telegram* and Tim MacMahon from ESPN are there. The coaches are now wearing their suits, Jamahl Mosley, beige with a slim cut; Darrell Armstrong, bluish-black and

baggy American. Kaleb Canales, Mike Procopio, Mike Weinar. The entire arena is wearing gray. No one knows what's going to happen. Or how.

TV anchor Mark Followill and radioman Chuck Cooperstein are sitting in the commentators' seats right behind the scorer's table. Cooperstein can't rely on pictures; he has to conjure up the events, movements, and plays with his words. Followill pauses to let the images speak for themselves. But both have prepared in the way that anyone would prepare for a great moment: they've set out their tools, their statistics and words, but they don't yet know what they'll say when Dirk reaches his milestone, and they don't know exactly when they will say it.

I'm sitting next to Geschwindner in his usual seat, a couple of rows above the Mavericks' bench: section 117, row J, seat 17, right on the aisle. The standard ritual: a paper cup of Bud Light and a bag of hot, salted peanuts before the game. The American Airlines Center feels different than it did in the days and weeks before; you can feel the sense of expectation, the arena buzzing and whirring and bursting. I never imagined I'd be sitting here, but Jessica's seat next to Holger is empty—

she's right next to Mark Cuban, less than 15 feet from the bench. We sit and drink and crack peanuts in silence, and I think about how Holger sat above the bench in Miami in 2011, right where Dirk could always see him whenever there was a time-out, always in a direct line of sight. The cameras tracked down Holger Geschwindner at the ceremony afterward, the smart, scraggly man crying from emotion.

And then everything happens fast. "The Star-Spangled Banner," the team introductions—". . . from Würzburg, Germany . . ."—the murmuring and cheering that are noticeably more intense than usual, his face on the jumbotron, the tearing off of the tracksuit, the mouth guard in the right sock, the high fives and handshakes and pats on the back of the head. Geschwindner and I are silently sitting among the peanut shells. Words escape me, but Geschwindner is calm. No need to talk.

The game plan is clear: the ball goes to Dirk, he shoots without hesitation. He makes a midrange jumper right away, sinking his first three. He lets the second one fly, too early and tactically unwise, a heat check—none of this has anything to do with a regular game plan. Dirk wants to get the job done quickly. He wants to get the whole thing over with, and the arena wants to witness Dirk getting it over with.

Coach Carlisle draws up the next plays, Yogi Ferrell and Devin Harris deliver the ball to Dirk, Dirk shoots, and the Lakers seem like they're frozen. It's almost as though they know tonight's story cannot be told in any other way. Dirk makes two midrange shots over Tarik Black and Larry Nance Jr. He converts his free throws when he's fouled, and the number of points to go is constantly shown on the jumbotron above our heads. Five of five. A quick trademark fadeaway over Larry Nance Jr. Six for six.

When Dirk only has five more points to go, the crowd slowly gets up. Another three, 29,998, two more points, a roar of anticipation; and on the next possession the moment is finally there. Devin Harris brings the ball up the court and finds Dirk on the right wing. He's isolated again against the young power forward Larry Nance Jr., and

Nance obviously doesn't want to be the one whose picture will be seen in all the news flashes and tweets and newspapers and highlight reels tomorrow—as the futile defender, the extra starring in the big moment. So, he defends—and he defends well.

Now the whole arena is standing, even in front of Geschwindner and me—so we stand up, too. Geschwindner would never stand up otherwise. The majority of people are now holding their phones out in the air—they want to experience this moment and also brag about it later; they want proof of their presence in this moment. Donnie Nelson, who discovered Dirk and Holger decades ago, limps up the aisle, a jovial, heavyset man in a suit with genuine anticipation and emotion in his face. He doesn't say a word, but he nods at Holger. He wants to be next to Geschwindner in the seconds that will follow. Peanut shells crack under his feet.

Dirk holds the ball with his back to his defender for a few tenths of a second, his eyes dart over his shoulder, he briefly probes the situation the way he has probed this situation countless times before. He doesn't need more than this tenth of a second; he sees all the other nine players in their predetermined positions—he knows that he only needs to take care of Larry Nance Jr., so he gets Nance into position. One, two, three tiny steps of adjustment, then he has him where he wants him. It's the moment when everything is possible: a drive to the basket, a pass, a direct shot. Dirk has 100 possibilities; he's played through them 100,000 times—alone with Holger, alone with Brad Davis, alone by himself, in front of 500 spectators in Athens, in front of 22,000 in Belgrade, in front of tens of millions in front of their televisions and computer screens.

His defender knows all of this. Every possible move, every look that can turn into a pass, every twitch into a shot. The most likely is the most likely, and Nance knows that something will come. He senses that it's going to be a midrange jumper, but he doesn't *know*. It could be something else. And Dirk knows that Larry knows that Dirk

knows that Junior can only make a guess. The seven stages of con-
sciousness. And because Larry Nance Jr. can only guess, he's standing
maybe an inch too far away when Dirk decides to make his move.

All of this happens in front of the Mavericks bench. Later, when
we look at the video footage of these seconds, we will notice that Dirk's
teammates are already about to fall onto the court out of excitement—
Hold me back! Hold me back!—and that Mark Cuban was already
cheering in the back of his mind. You can see his smile and the open
mouths of the people in the rows behind him. We see Dirk's slight backward tilt, halfway letting himself fall; we see the ball, lifted with the left
hand into the right above the body at the same time, just beyond the
defender's reach, the motion that Dirk and Holger call "loading," and
how he then pulls the trigger and the ball is outside of the defender's
range for a fraction of a second. In the days to come, Holger and Dirk
will make jokes about this basket being pure luck since the shot was too
long and too flat, since Dirk's eyes followed the ball instead of looking
at the hoop. Et cetera. But the shot is made, the arena erupts. Explodes.
Goes absolutely crazy.

"Isolation, right baseline, jab step, up, fake, hits! The greatest international scorer in the history of basketball has become the sixth to
score 30,000 points in his career," Chuck Cooperstein celebrates on the
radio and Mark Followill yells on TV, "Here it is! The iconic shot for the
iconic moment! He's done it, 30,000 points!"

But because the referees can't simply halt the game after an
important shot, the game keeps going back and forth; the cheering
swells, and on the next offensive possession, the Mavericks get the ball
to Dirk almost by accident, in transition, top of the key, and because
nothing can really go wrong anymore and what needed to be done has
already been done, Dirk lets a three fly after faking out three defenders
and makes another perfect field goal in a perfect arc at 47 degrees, no
lateral flaw. The sound system in the arena amplifies the swish into a
plop—but because of the collective euphoria, no one is listening, the

moment overshadows its own staging. Dirk only needed 20 points to be inducted into the club of giants, and he already has 23 early in the second quarter, with 9:54 to play. Underpromise, overdeliver.

Then there's the time-out and the pack forming around him as he comes to the bench. From our seats, you can't see how Cuban clings to Dirk as he screams with excitement or how Dirk almost falls to the ground from all the hugging. He pulls himself up after a second, waves to the crowd, and looks over to Jessica and up at Holger. And when the general jumping around slowly subsides, a video is shown on the giant cube above our heads that coldly aims straight for the heart of the arena. All the great moments of this immortal career. The first make. The buzzer beaters. The endless slew of midrange shots. The dunks from the early years. The threes. Thirty thousand points are a lot of points.

Steve Nash, a kindred spirit even more than a friend, appears toward the end of the film. As Dirk's old buddy delivers a few moving and humorous words about the big moment, the camera focuses on Holger Geschwindner, who is standing between paper cups and peanut shells and memories and love and pride and wipes away a tear again, just as he did in 2011 in Miami. History turns a pirouette—time is a loop. The images make their way around the basketball world and if you look closely, you can see me standing directly to the left of Geschwindner in a blue zip-up hoodie and a light blue shirt with a slightly embarrassed grin and a sense of irrational pride in being there for this moment.

At the press conference after the game, Coach Carlisle notes that more members of the press are present than during the playoffs. "It's a circus." Then he delivers a wild homage to Dirk. Carlisle tries to make sense of what we all just witnessed, its historical meaning for sports culture. "Thirty thousand points are a lot of a lot of points," he says. He calls Dirk a "generational player" and an "extraordinary person." Carlisle mentions Larry Bird because he always mentions Larry Bird whenever he has to explain what makes Dirk unique. What he means to his teammates, the team, the city. To the game itself. Kareem Abdul-Jabbar, Karl Malone, Kobe Bryant, Michael Jordan, and Wilt Chamberlain.

And now, Dirk Nowitzki, from Würzburg-Heidingsfeld.

When Dirk steps onto the podium, the pack of journalists also take out their phones. Dirk makes some banter about just having had a Bud Light in the locker room to celebrate this special occasion—and, at the next game, a truck full of 30,000 Bud Lights will be standing in front of the arena.

"It's a zoo."

After the game, I sit with the German sportswriter André Voigt in one of the overcrowded bars nearby—last calls have been called off today. "Wow," Voigt says. He's usually someone who is able to explain everything, who never lacks an articulate opinion or insight. He orders another round. "Wow," he says and raises his glass.

"To Dirk!"

The next afternoon, Dirk goes through a light training to purge last night's celebration. "Sweat a little," he says. Family, friends, teammates, coaches, journalists, fans, and followers have been congratulating him. Hundreds. Thousands. Twitter. Instagram. Telephone. WhatsApp. Text messages. Emails.

"It's a circus."

The next evening, there's a team event for season ticket holders at Lone Star Park, on the outskirts of the city: Cirque du Soleil's show *Kurios: Cabinet of Curiosities*. The floodlights rise above the giant parking lots, the Texan Lone Star flag is everywhere. Republican season ticket holders have not been happy with team owner Mark Cuban's criticism of Donald Trump over the past few months, and right now, the team needs to take care of its fan base. Evenings like this are also part of the life of a professional athlete, and someone like Dirk is able to reconcile both sides in Dallas.

Dirk and the team walk down a rickety rope bridge into the circus tent's standing ovation. The show begins and people are flying all over the place—steampunks, contortionists, cyborgs, freaks, strongmen, clowns and heroes. The air smells of popcorn and fire-breathing petroleum, and the smallest woman in the world walks back and forth in front of Dirk. Jessica and Dirk were actually scheduled to leave before intermission, but they both sit in their seats at the edge of the ring, watching the whole circus. They're glowing.

On the third day after scoring his 30,000th point, Jessica has organized a banquet to honor Dirk at the Mirador in downtown Dallas with a small but illustrious group of guests. There's Veuve Clicquot and cabernet sauvignon from the Napa Valley, deviled eggs and wagyu beef. Coach Carlisle moderates the evening, there are toasts from Devin Harris and Mark Cuban ("I've learned more from you than from anyone else," he says. "How to stay grounded when things get crazy, despite the noise, despite the circus"). In attendance is also Tony Romo, the Dallas Cowboys quarterback, who describes Dirk as the "greatest athlete Dallas has ever had." Dirk's athletic trainer, Casey Smith, says Dirk makes everyone in the room feel like they're something special, like they're "the prettiest girl in the room."

Eventually Lisa Tyner stands up in between the main course and dessert. She's almost at a loss for words when everyone's eyes fall on her, but she slowly starts talking about Dirk's first years, about all the things they have been through since 1998, the things they have survived together. She is speaking like the mother of a son who grew up long ago, full of pride and candor, and she brings the whole room to tears although her intent was to be funny. "Not once, my boy," Lisa Tyner says and lifts her water glass, "not once have I ever been ashamed of you."

6

OLD MAN GAME

"No one who is young is
ever going to be old."

—JOHN STEINBECK, *EAST OF EDEN*

That's Game

N THE LATE SUMMER of 2017, Dirk Nowitzki is standing in the Sonnenstuhl sports center in Randersacker, a village near Würzburg, and is wringing out his soaking-wet T-shirt. The linoleum floor of the multipurpose gym is blue-gray, like the rainy sky outside, and it's 59 degrees, the complete opposite of a Texan summer. Dirk is leaving for America tomorrow, back for the start of his 20th season with the Dallas Mavericks. Having just turned 39, everyone expects this to be Nowitzki's final year as a professional athlete, and he probably even expects it himself. He fishes a new shirt out of his bag. During these summer workouts, he always works his way through three or four shirts and drinks a couple of liters of water. His next shirt, dark green, reads "That's Game." Quitting time. Game over. Time to go home.

That's game.

His 30,000th point is a distant memory. An eternity has passed since, an entire long summer. The Mavericks missed the playoffs; Dirk's season ended in April. Only sporadically did he follow the postseason and the Finals on TV, when Malaika and Max were in bed. The day the Golden State Warriors became champions, Dirk had already been back in the gym for a few weeks, grinding.

This morning, he's already been at it for two hours. Strength training, sprints, explosive drills. His old buddy Simon Wagner sprints with him, keeps Dirk's time, hounds him through the plastic cones, pushes him. One more, one more, come on! Simon is short and in shape; he's also a baller. The two of them play tennis together, both on TG Würzburg's squad, and Dirk was Simon's best man. They've known each other for an eternity.

Geschwindner enters the gym. We nod. It's the next shift; now comes the ball. Wagner and I stand on the sidelines and watch Dirk and Holger begin their work. Dirk's muscles are surely warmed up by now, but he stumbles across the court as though he's been retired for ages. Wagner watches and smiles. "He's three kilo overweight," he says. "Every kilo is killing his knees." For a few weeks now, Dirk has started eating like a hunter-gatherer again. The Paleo diet is his new thing to try to get back into playing shape. No processed foods, no cultivated cereals, no flour, just nuts and white meat. Wagner says that Dirk's mom, Helgus, is even baking nut bread for him. Dirk and Wagner used to go out for beers; now they chase each other through the gym instead.

Holger and Dirk slowly go through their rituals. Wagner has already left and I'm sitting on the linoleum, taking notes. An audience of one. For years now, I've watched the same events in the same sequence: shots close to the basket, from midrange, from behind the three-point line on the right side and on the left, pirouettes, sidesteps from the free-throw line, shots in motion, shots out of deep knee bends, squats and rolls, free throws with the left hand, then the right. The mood is different today—silly but also melancholic—perhaps because he's leaving for Dallas tomorrow. Jessica and the kids are already back. Dirk moans and groans, gasps and curses. Geschwindner cracks up about Dirk's moaning and groaning. "Check this out," Nowitzki says to me. "You've never seen this before." And then they do what they've always done—at least that's how it seems.

At the start of things, they talk. Dirk tells Holger about England, about the stop he and Jessica made in London on their way to Würzburg, to see her brothers. These days, Martin is in the Premier League with Swansea and Marcus plays left back for Derby County—and they hadn't seen one another in a while. In England, Dirk isn't recognized as quickly as he is in the basketball nations of the world. The English don't ask for autographs, he says. He could go to a soccer match and walk out of the stadium with the rest of the crowd on Anfield Road in Liverpool. No one stopped him. He was just a "tall bloke," that's all.

Jessica and Dirk used this opportunity to visit the British artist Damien Hirst with their kids. She had been in touch with him for years. "You know him?" Dirk shouts across the gym. "Hirst? The guy with the shark in aspic?"

"Formaldehyde," Geschwindner says.

"Comes from the bible or something," Dirk says.

"The Golden Calf."

"I never learned Latin."

Hirst's house was wild, Dirk says as he catches the ball, puts it on the floor, *tak tadamm*, bends his knees, goes up, shoots and hits it. The entrance was bizarre and he only realized after a couple of seconds that Hirst must have purchased an entire graveyard. *Tak tadamm.* The whole floor consisted of marble and granite and quartz gravestones lying on the ground. They must have been standing on hundreds of names and thousands of dates from previous centuries; on countless inscriptions in Latin and family mottos polished up neatly.

"Freak," Dirk says, hitting another three.

While there, Malaika wanted to hold one of Hirst's famous diamond skulls in her hands. The thing was insanely expensive, the most expensive artwork in the world. Afterward, Malaika made a couple of paintings with Hirst, spin paintings, by splattering red and blue and yellow and green on rotating canvases. *Tak tadamm.* One more three-pointer, then three free throws with the right hand, three with the left, then everything once more from the top. "Hirst," Dirk says between shots. "Looks like I have to talk myself up today."

A few days ago, Dirk saw another photo of his 30,000th point. He's constantly being asked about it, and now he wants to analyze the whole situation again. Geschwindner says Dirk had looked up way too early, as if he were an astronomer. He'd followed the ball, its trajectory.

"It was a terrible shot," Dirk says.

Tak tadamm.

Swish.

"True," Geschwindner says. "You went up too early and it was too flat and too long."

Tak tadamm.

Bonk.

"Still went in."

Swish.

"We're not doing this just for fun, you know."

Tak tadamm.

Swish.

"You might be inclined to think, 'He scored 30,000 points; by now, it's all just routine,'" Dirk says. "But you have to fight for it each and every day."

Over the last few years, I've watched every part of their workout dozens of times. I've watched them in summer and winter, in Dallas and Rattelsdorf, Ljubljana and wherever. It's always the same pattern: their initial talk is followed by pure action. The two of them trail off—sentences become words, words give way to gestures, and gestures to numbers and shots.

"Watch out now," Dirk says. "Twenty in a row."

"Twenty-five," Geschwindner says.

They break down Dirk's shot into its individual parts, then twist and turn each and every one of them. I'm not able to recognize the differences, but Dirk and Holger are speaking in nuances and intricacies. "I can only concentrate on one thing at a time," Dirk says, and Holger laughs louder than expected.

Nowitzki counts the makes, Geschwindner the misses, makes and misses, but they never sort the shots into groups of ten. They do this so that the Western way of thinking in decimals—the mental categorization in increments of ten, in percentage points and odds, in victory and failure, in either-or—is already banished from their thinking during practice. They do this so that Dirk never starts calculating during game situations, so that it never turns into a mental weakness. "The number of times the 11th shot is a miss is disproportionately high," Geschwindner has explained to me. "Because you're either pleased or displeased with what you've achieved instead of focusing on the mechanics."

The quantification and evaluation that spectators and journalists passionately engage in so as to better understand the sport should not play a role in Dirk's game. Especially when it matters. Those who do not quantify failure do not fail, and those who do not fail can keep playing. Dirk and Holger have maintained this unusual way of thinking since 1994. The goal of this training is to take the next shot as if it were the only one that mattered. What happened before and what could come later are irrelevant. "You want to make the next shot," Geschwindner says. "Only the next one."

I find this choreography moving every time. Watching someone completely absorbed in what they are doing has a meditative effect. Someone who really masters one thing, who moves in strict patterns and, at the same time, is completely free. Someone who is present in the moment.

On this summer day in August 2017, at 11:41 of all things, that is, at exactly 41 minutes past 11, Dirk Nowitzki shoots a one-legged off-balance three. The ball sails through the air in an almost perfect arc, bounces off the front of the rim, then over the backboard. It thumps three or four times in the backboard's frame and remains stuck above our heads. We stare at the ball. Nowitzki, Geschwindner, me. Panting, Dirk comes over to the baseline and opens his water bottle.

"That's it," he says between sips. "That might have been the last session."

Excuse me? I briefly freeze. Ever since I've known him, Dirk Nowitzki has cracked jokes about his age, his creaky bones, his fading mobility, diminishing speed and flexibility. For years, he has groaned and moaned as I've watched him work out in the summer. He always says this is his last workout before he keeps going. But could it be true this time? Is this, in fact, the last workout of the summer? The last one with Holger Geschwindner, the last one in the gym where they've spent so many summers, the gym where so many ideas were born? The flight back to America is booked and Dirk's T-shirt says "That's Game."

Dirk Nowitzki could have retired a long time ago, but every season that was supposedly his last was followed by the next last one. He has always refused to fulfill the typical expectations of an athlete's biography, never heeded the well-meaning advice, the "he must be in a lot of pain" reflex, the imperative folk wisdom to quit while you're ahead. Six years have passed since the Mavericks won the championship. That team was broken up long ago, and since then, the Mavs have never made it past the first round of the playoffs. Basketball has evolved; it's faster, the emphasis is more on offense. Dirk is slower now, but he keeps playing. If this were the moment he decided to stop, it would be sensational.

"The last workout?" I ask. "Seriously? The last one?"

Dirk spits on the floor, then wipes it away with his sneaker. The soles of his shoes squeak on the linoleum and we watch Geschwindner poke the ball out of the frame. Dirk has a grin on his face. Kitsch isn't his thing. "Just kidding," he says, chucking the water bottle into the corner. Geschwindner throws the ball toward us and Dirk carries on like he never said a word.

Now they let the ball do the work. Dirk puts it on the ground, his body gathers under it, and the momentum of the ball interlinks with the power of the body—*tak tadamm*. When body and ball spring upward together—just like we've seen thousands of times in Hagen and Dallas, Rattelsdorf and New York, Beijing and Los Angeles—they call it "slipping under" and "loading." *Tak tadamm.*

Then, some details: Dirk should "feel his last two fingers on the ball," the fingertips; he should spread the index and middle finger more; he should keep his eyes open, look up, do the *tak*, do the *tadamm*, eyes on front of the basket and not on the ball and its clean and clear and flawlessly calculated curve of more than 47 degrees inciding angle, a perfect arc, with no errors. His eyes should remain on the goal—and not on the stars up above. *Swish.* He doesn't make 25 out of 25. I keep a tally sheet (I'm just a spectator): once, it's 23; three times, it's 22. And seven times, it's 21 out of 25.

Countless coaches, players, and teammates have watched Dirk and Holger work out over the past two decades, and many have ventured that the secret must lie in the exercises themselves. If you were to copy Dirk's exercises, the idea goes, you could be like him. "But it's not about the repetition of the exercises," Geschwindner has explained to me. "It's about the tiniest variations in the repetition." The two of them call them "revision routines," which are less concerned with the shot than with rhythm, intonation, and intuition. These routines focus on the minute details in execution, and these details can only be perceived after you have repeated these fadeaways and free throws and three-pointers thousands of times, if not millions. The soft touch, the finest nuances of a keystroke, the run of a drummer, the saxophone's solo.

"B-ball is jazz."

Holger Geschwindner often talks about art and music when he articulates his ideas about basketball. But if you talk to Dirk about these nuances, he shakes his head and grins. He thinks it's "a bit much," even if he understands the approach. It seems as if this mental aspect isn't important enough for him to talk about. He calls Geschwindner "knucklehead" now. "Knucklehead." That's how the two of them talk. It's how you talk when you know each other really well, when everything has already been said.

When they're done shooting, the men do push-ups on their fingertips, then Geschwindner stands up. The ball rolls into the far corner of the gym. Dirk lets himself be bent and flexed on the sidelines, Geschwindner works the giant body like a lumberjack, heaving the long legs toward Dirk's head, again and again. Nowitzki lies on his back and groans. Then, rolled over, with his face down on the dusty ground, Geschwindner cracks Dirk's back again, vertebra after vertebra, from the lower back to the top and then back down again, until everything is in its right place.

"When you're as old as me, you can stretch all you want," Dirk groans. "But tomorrow, you'll have to start all over again."

"And if you don't," Geschwindner says, "the whole circus is over in no time."

By the time Nowitzki gradually picks himself up from the floor, Geschwindner has disappeared into the showers. Nowitzki is incredibly flexible for someone our age. He can put his hands flat on the ground while standing, and his head reaches his knees without difficulty. A half pigeon? The Adho Mukha Shvanasana? Easy. Even if he is three kilos overweight. And even if he's nearly 40. He slowly picks up his shirts from the floor, retrieves the ball, then surveys the empty gym. That's game. He's been here for more than four hours, and he's been coming here for more than 20 years. The sky clears outside. Dirk eyes the hoops, the wooden backboards, and the spots of sunlight on the linoleum a little longer than necessary. Dirk Nowitzki, I'll note, looks tired.

"Man," he says as he looks around. He seems to be saying goodbye. It looks as though he has decided this very second that he will never come back here again.

Take Two

SUMMER 2014

WHEN I MEET ERNIE BUTLER for the second time, the sun is shining on Bavaria. Everything is light blue and bright green. We have an appointment in Straßlach, south of Munich, up the river Isar, where Butler has been living for decades. I want to hear the rest of Ernie and Holger's story, the later years. As we walk into the local inn, Zum Wildpark, we are immediately seated at a table by the window. It's a warm welcome; someone places two beers in front of us on the checkered table without asking. The food also arrives without us having ordered. Butler takes a sip and wipes the sweat from his brow, thinks for a moment, and picks up where the music had interrupted us.

"All right," he says. "Holger."

In their first year together in the Bundesliga's first division, MTV Giessen wins the first German championship. It's 1965, in a high school gymnasium in Heidelberg. Holger passes to Ernie, who makes the deciding shot from 40 feet, 69–68. Young Geschwindner scores 16 points. "A catapult launch," writes *BasketballMagazin* in a portrait years later.

In the following years, Giessen and Geschwindner are the measure of all things in German basketball. They have the national team players

Klaus Jungnickel and Bernd Röder, and coach Laszlo Lakfalvi; they're constantly in the finals, win two more championships and a German Cup, play international club games against Simmenthal Milan and its part-time superstar and Oxford student Bill Bradley, later a legendary New York Knick. They play Tel Aviv. They play Real Madrid, and Geschwindner scores 26 points in the first game and 27 in the second. He studies mathematics and physics in Giessen (but never graduates), wins basketball games (more often than he loses), and walks through the city, a man about town with a talent for logic and absurdity. After the games, the team holds wild parties in Geschwindner's parents' basement. The opponents are also invited; everyone knows each other. The basketball world is tiny.

In 1968, the prospective squads are announced for the European Championships and the 1972 Olympic Games. Geschwindner changes teams and moves to Munich in 1971, where the games will take place. It's pragmatic and calculated. He wants to be on site.

Ernie Butler is 36 years old already, ancient for basketball at the time, but he still keeps playing—also in Munich. Their team plays at a fast pace, concentrating on offense, just the way that Geschwindner and Butler like it. "This team ran and ran and ran," Butler remembers, "but you need the ball to get out and run, so we defended like madmen." Geschwindner jumps, almost flies; he defends, rebounds, and shoots and shoots and shoots.

If you talk today about Geschwindner's playing days with his old teammates and coaches, they will relate anecdotes of audacity, unconventional play, and bravado. Of the freedom and joy in taking risks. How Holger stops in the middle of an uncontested fast break in a national team game and yells at the coach that it was too easy. Instead of the easy layup, he takes a long jumper and makes it. They talk about the courage to fail. How he thoroughly resists mediocrity and routine. Of his perpetual search for athletic and intellectual challenges. That Holger Geschwindner was never rattled and played better the more important the game was. In Europe. Against world-class talent. At away games. "Uncoachable," some say. "Insane," say others. But they all grin, full of nostalgia. They talk about his self-confidence and talent, his craft and improvisation. How high Geschwindner could jump! His ball handling! His calculations! How deeply he comprehended the game, both strategically and intellectually, how early he formulated his own philosophy.

In 1971, Butler stops playing and becomes a coach. But he remains faithful to his understanding of the sport: he does his work at practice, and when the game starts, he just lets the players play. "A coach shouldn't interfere all the time; otherwise, the players feel confined," he says. "The team has to be able to do what's necessary. Basketball is free—like jazz. You can't plan a solo, you have to play it."

There are thousands of stories to relate from this time, and Butler knows every single one of them. Like the flooding in Bloomington and Holger's lower back pain. How the children had to stomp around on his back, how the vertebrae cracked. Their games on the outdoor courts in Indiana. The stories from Ye Olde Regulator, the thing with the pole dance. Ernie Butler orders another beer. Straßlach is tiny and it's not far from his house. The bliss of the second beer, the flow of stories!

The 1972 Olympic Games are taking place on their doorstep—it's a real dream, a major goal. The two of them get to know a number of jazz musicians in Munich in the '70s, Ernie plays and Geschwindner talks to them about their music. He travels the world and encounters different styles wherever he goes: bebop in Chicago, cool jazz in New York. He travels to Bloomington with Butler; Ernie and his guys play on the porch. Jazz follows them through the years and the decades.

Their paths go in different directions. Ernie Butler gets married, works a day job as a teacher, and starts playing music more often at night. In 1977, Geschwindner moves on and the Butlers remain in Munich until someone pours motor oil in their stroller—black oil for the Black neighbors. Someone keeps calling child protective services on them. At first, they move to the southern part of the city before leaving for Straßlach. Naima is born around the same time as Dirk Nowitzki. The contact with Geschwindner becomes increasingly scarce, but it never breaks off. Whenever the two of them meet, everything is as it was. Everything remains new.

Geschwindner gets around. He studies mathematics and physics, attends lectures in philosophy and literary studies. He is fascinated by the tension between reason and art. He plays basketball all over Germany, in small towns and big cities. He travels. He listens to music to get in the right mood before the games. He's the only one doing this at the time—or at least he doesn't know anyone else who does. He loves long drives through Germany while blasting the radio. He loves Modest Mussorgsky's *Pictures at an Exhibition* and the third piano concerto by Sergei Rachmaninoff. He laughs his head off about German Schlager and sings along. He knows most concert halls between Munich and Hamburg, and the dives and bars between Heidelberg and Charlottenburg. Over the years, the jazz he listens to becomes more and more complex and free. He listens to Billie Holiday on the day of his last game in the Bundesliga. "(In My) Solitude." Or Aretha Franklin. Coltrane. Bix Beiderbecke. Chet Baker. Bob Marley. Thelonious Monk. He doesn't remember the details; there are too many.

"Holger Geschwindner," Ernie Butler says, "is not an easy guy." His life philosophy is too complex not to rub some the wrong way. Basketball is only part of his overflowing life. He loves discussions and hates lazy compromises. He doesn't want to make things easy for himself. "Cheating doesn't count," he says. The path of least resistance leads nowhere. When the basketball season is over, Geschwindner packs his things and hits the road. The Trans-Siberian Railway. In a UPS truck through America. Australia. Alaska. The Carpathians, China, Tierra del Fuego, and Afghanistan. The stories he brings back from his travels sound like novels. His friends call him "Geschwindl"—from *schwindeln*, to fib. He travels with light luggage, often only with his two red leather cases.

His travel reports often have numerous variations. Georg Kendl claims that Geschwindner only survived the fall into the gorge in Afghanistan by luck. "Whenever he falls," he says, "he falls like a cat. He always lands on his feet." Others say Geschwindner turned around and climbed back and had to nurse his skinned palms for weeks. Or: Geschwindner only thought about climbing the rope to the other side, but then decided against it. After all, he doesn't have a death wish. Or: the gorge wasn't really a gorge; it was more like a ford. Or: they were at the Hari River in 1974, not in 1978. When I ask him about this, he looks it up in his diaries: it states that on June 19, 1978, Dirk's birthday, he was living near Bamberg in a wooden hut without heating and his housemate was a pig named Bruno.

★   ★   ★

How things are connected: In 1964, Ernest Butler (29) meets Holger Geschwindner (18) in Giessen and they uncover the parallels between basketball and jazz. They develop their unique idea of basketball. Thirty years later, Geschwindner (48) meets Dirk Nowitzki (15) in a gym in Schweinfurt and they turn this idea into a concrete method. In 1997, Ernie Butler plays the saxophone at their first training camp at Lake Starnberg, Till Brönner joins in, and Geschwindner's training group dances and dribbles to the beat.

Sports and music are everywhere and always present. Geschwindner can clearly see the parallels. But it's only when he starts working with Nowitzki that he truly comes to understand everything he had thought and lived for all those years. "Explanatory constructions always come later," Geschwindner says, "when you are obliged to justify and explicate your knowledge."

Geschwindner is not a traditionally trained coach. What he knows comes from his own experience. His methods are based on his affinity for music, his numbers and calculations, his travels and readings, locker room sermons, and playing close games. He drops whatever doesn't work. And Ernie Butler's "b-ball is jazz" dictum is the core of this thinking.

In 2005, Geschwindner gets his hands on a treatise in his favorite bookstore in Bamberg, right across from Café Müller: *Intelligent Music Teaching*, the standard educational text by the educator and musicologist Robert A. Duke. In this book, Geschwindner finds what he had thought and then put into practice for all these years. He gives the book to the guys in his training camp: "Here, read this!" Nowitzki has been a world-class player for a long time, and his friends Marvin Willoughby, Demond Greene, and Robert Garrett are all experienced national team players. They read the book and witness the conceptual world of Holger and Ernie in print.

In 2018, I'm sitting in a lecture hall at the University of Music and Performing Arts Munich, taking notes. I'm at a symposium called Art in Motion, a conference about excellence in artistic education that is aimed at musicians and actors. The announcement text talks about "practice strategies," "continuous learning," and "facilitating creativity and flexibility." "Efficiency and effectiveness are not enough," it says.

Geschwindner picked me up at the airport this morning. The talk that he and Ernie Butler are going to give today isn't a big deal, he says, but you can clearly sense his excitement that their thinking and work is recognized. He is announced as "Holger Geschwindner, Institute of Applied Nonsense" in the program; the talk is called "B-ball Is Jazz: Learning from Interdisciplinary Experimentation." Nonsense in the university! Geschwindner loves it. He parks his car in a no-parking zone, but today, a ticket is no big deal. "Who cares," Geschwindner says. It's another hot summer day in Munich, but he's wearing the dark suit that he only takes out of his small suitcase for special occasions.

In the audience are students and educators, professors, and two or three cultural journalists, but mostly high-performance musicians from every kind of musical form and instrument. They're all wearing name tags on their summer shirts. Basketball players are nowhere to be seen; only Georg Kendl drove up from Starnberg this morning. The three older men stand to one side, drinking coffee from paper cups.

The symposium's first speaker is Robert A. Duke. Geschwindner and Butler sit in the first row and listen. Duke clearly illustrates his idea of an effective and intelligent musical education, of a pedagogy of linguistic and technical accuracy that goes together with artistic freedom—something that can easily be applied to sports.

For Duke, Yo-Yo Ma's versions of Bach's cello suites, Picasso's *Guernica*, and Michael Jordan's game are all the same, they're all art and not just craft (the same goes for his mechanic's ability to repair his Volvo). All of them require the acquisition of highly complex information that has to be evaluated, classified, and then combined with countless potential solutions that are highly specialized in order to implement one of these possibilities with precision. I'm paraphrasing.

According to Duke, becoming a musician is an active process. To learn the piano, there's one thing you need to do: play the piano. A teacher should never prevent students from having fun, should never force them through preparatory exercises and repetitions so that the students will be able to play "the good stuff" one day. Students need to have access to the good stuff right from the beginning, otherwise they might give up, disillusioned, before even reaching that stage. "If we want the students to learn to become historians, mathematicians, and pianists, we need to let them do the things that historians, mathematicians, and pianists do right from the beginning."

That's Geschwindner 101. Don't talk about the game, play the game. "Don't cluck, lay eggs" is written on the wall of his training gym in Bamberg.

Many believe that such a teaching plan is too complex and too dependent on the individual relationship between student and teacher.

In reality, its primary concern is with practicalities. With doing. The first requirement is to understand the object and its system perfectly. Teachers need to know what they're teaching. And what should be taught. Then comes breaking everything down into units that the students can understand and practice efficiently. "Everyone who has ever trained with Holger raves about his attention to detail," the former German international Johannes Herber writes in his text about "Geschwindner's Boys." They rave "about his ability to dissect each and every basketball move and to then make the necessary corrections."

It's about breaking down the movements into small units. About rituals and visualizing situations. About the progression of learning and the flow from one movement to the other. It's about normalizing and recoding pressure into moments of success. It's about moments of happiness. About not being afraid and having the courage to make mistakes. About finding the right words for all these things, the right vibration. It's about the love of the game.

It's also about the language Geschwindner and Nowitzki speak. There needs to be a unique vocabulary, since a good teacher should use their words in the service of teaching and real deeds—teachers shouldn't just give lectures and instructions. If the relationship goes well, the student and teacher will agree on common words that perfectly fit what they mean. A clarity that belongs to them alone. With words that leave no space for misunderstanding because what is said perfectly coincides with what is meant. Together, they invent signifiers and what's signified. At the foundation of Geschwindner's work are images and analogies; the ball is "loaded" and the body "slips under" (*drunnerschluppe*—sometimes he slips into the Hessian dialect), the ball is "wrapped" and guided on "rails." The elbow is the "aiming device," a made basket is a "goal" (after all, Geschwindner and Nowitzki come from a soccer nation). *Tor!*

During Duke's lecture, Butler and Geschwindner are nodding in their seats. Sometimes, they put their heads together and whisper.

The two of them have been thinking and working on these ideas for 50 years. This lecture today seems like validation of their work. When Duke finishes, Ernie and Holger walk, slightly bent over, onto the stage, two old friends and eternal boys who talk enthusiastically about their lives and what makes them excited: basketball, playing the saxophone, teaching, and learning, learning, learning.

After the lecture, Geschwindner talks with some students and Ernie Butler has a chair set out for him in the university's lobby. He looks satisfied, almost happy. The birds are chirping outside the window, the students are buzzing around us, and somewhere there's a drummer practicing.

I've met Ernie a number of times over the last few years—at the inn in Straßlach, on the shores of Lake Starnberg, sometimes here, sometimes there. We've talked about music and Naima, about basketball and Dirk, and about Holger and his stories. For all these years, Ernie has remained a permanent fixture in this system; he's been there since the beginning. His pedagogy is an open, benevolent form of teaching; it sings and it swings, it's playful and flowing. It's not only work.

Now he's sitting in the sun. An old man, his pace slowed down a long time ago, his voice rough and beautiful, his eyes shining. We talk about today's lecture and what it meant to Holger; we compare music and the game. We talk about the rare joy of the ball moving around, when the passes reach their targets, when the shots fall, when you breathe and run and run and breathe, when the rhythm takes you, the beat, the melody, when you . . .

When you, man, when you.

As I listen to Ernie Butler, I understand that Nowitzki's game is more than a profession or a business. It's rhythm and melody, culture and friendship, freedom and flow.

Ernie Butler smiles and talks about the immense joy he experienced when he used to run south along the banks of the Isar on summer days like today, past the Hellabrunn zoo, the smell of the place behind him, his footsteps on the white gravel and dry grass, when the air whirred and the clear water rushed by and the big birds flew down to a landing. "And you run along the river and you see a couple of swans," Ernie Butler says, and his eyes are shining, perhaps from the glare of the light in the lobby. "And you *are* the river and you *are* the swans and you *are*."

Old Man Game

A N NBA SEASON EXTENDS from autumn to early summer. It's a long succession of 82 games, played every two or three days, and good playoff teams may even top 100. Half of these games are played away from home; the teams are constantly on the road. An NBA player's world consists of 29 arenas, 29 hotels, 27 airports, one bed at home, and a summer residence between seasons. But even when a player is in his own bed at home, his suitcases are always packed—a team never stays in one place for more than a week. NBA players are nomads, but they are nomads who see very little of the world they travel through.

All these places are similar. Players look down at the cities, the street grids and river bends, while the plane is landing, then ride on access roads with the city skylines on the other side of the bus window. They eat in one banquet hall after another and sleep in a hotel that often belongs to the same chain as the one before. They forget their room numbers, wander around the hotel corridors, and stand in elevators, staring into space. They sign jerseys in the lobby, drive to the arena, and come back again. The names of the places begin to blur together: George Bush International, Staples Center, American Airlines Arena (Miami), American Airlines Center (Dallas). Sometimes, the players go out for a bite to eat in the backrooms and hidden niches of restaurants. And sometimes, the players go out to clubs and drink Hennessy and Coke behind velvet ropes. In their single rooms, the players gaze out the windows and watch the sun set—or rise. They call home and they sleep—until room service rings. Nowitzki has been doing this for 20 years; he is familiar with this tristesse, the feeling of being cut off from the rest of the world.

The sun rises in Sacramento. I've arrived too early. The Mavericks don't land until this afternoon and I have the whole day. The distance from the hotel to the river and then on to Discovery Park doesn't seem all that far. I put on my running shoes and get moving. On the day of away games, I usually run in a large arc toward the arena in which the game is played. I want to get an impression of the city I've just arrived in, to get some sense of where I am. In Houston, I run toward the Toyota Center and around Minute Maid Park, where the Astros play, then along the Buffalo Bayou and through Sabine Park. I run into the residential areas of Piedmont Park in Atlanta and all the way down to Philips Arena, over highway bridges and through dangerous neighborhoods. I run for miles across enormous parking lots surrounding the football stadium and Bankers Life Fieldhouse in Indianapolis. I run past the shacks and garages behind the Chesapeake Energy Arena in Oklahoma City and through the crowded streets around Madison Square Garden in Midtown Manhattan and the drifting snow at Barclays Center in Brooklyn. I run along riverbanks, access roads, between gas stations and warehouses, through parking lots, past all the loading ramps.

And so, today it's Sacramento. Sitting on the banks of the Sacramento and American rivers, the more or less large and more or less charming capital of California was once home to the writer Joan Didion as well as to the filmmaker Greta Gerwig. Home to the middle class as well as to the uprooted, it is also the home of the Sacramento Kings, the city's only major professional sports team. With no football or baseball teams, basketball is very important here. I run past two outdoor courts, but no one is playing this early in the morning. I run past the mirrored government buildings; giant palm trees stick out like cutouts against the sky, raucous ravens on the roofs. There are homeless people on every corner. During the crisis of American psychiatry in the 1970s, countless clinics closed and individual practices were supposed to take on the patients. But ever since the system collapsed, many people in need have been forced to live on the streets.

It is warm in California, and the laws are leniently enforced. I pass one tent after another along the banks of the American River, as well as shopping carts and bicycle carcasses. Plastic bags flutter in the trees less than a mile from the gold-painted bridge straight out of Gerwig's film *Lady Bird* and the Old Sacramento that Didion depicted in *Slouching Towards Bethlehem*. Everyone knows that America is a land of contradictions, and the contrast becomes more pronounced in the West. The spic-and-span Golden 1 Center, home of the Kings, sits in the middle of this divide.

I return to downtown Sacramento and run around the arena. When the Mavericks fly in from Dallas at around noon, they will look down at the rivers and fields and forest and farmland. Then they will land and sleep and eat before walking to the shootaround through the tunnel connecting the hotel and the arena. After that, we'll meet. Nowitzki is now in the middle of the season that many believe will be his last. After returning to Dallas in the fall, he was in excellent physical and mental condition from his work in Randersacker, but the Mavs won only one of their first seven games, and now they've only tallied 16 wins to 36 losses. The season is a flop, but the arenas are full, and Nowitzki is met with respect in the places where bitter rivalry once dominated. Despite all the losses and the difficulty of potentially reaching the playoffs, the spirits on the team are high and I want to accompany Dirk on this annual West Coast road trip.

★   ★   ★

The evening before the game against the Kings, Dirk Nowitzki is walking through downtown Sacramento with his hood pulled over his face. Although we have texted on and off, we haven't seen each other since the workout in Randersacker half a year ago, and Dirk looks thinner now, more tired. He smiles, but you can tell immediately that his mood could be better. Derek Earls and Dwayne Bishop, Dirk's longtime security staff, walk in front of and behind him while Geschwindner saunters at his side.

As we walk to Morton's Steakhouse, downtown Sacramento is mostly deserted, but Dirk is recognized after only a couple of feet. Someone screams "Nowitzki!" from the other side of the street and we act as if nothing has happened. Nevertheless, Earls and Bishop pick up the tempo—if we proceed at our leisurely pace, we might never reach the restaurant. We lower our heads; the crowd is approaching. "Let's go," Earls says. There are suddenly five people in Dallas Mavericks jerseys on the next corner and ten on the one after that. "Dirk!" they scream. "I love you, man!" When we reach Morton's Steakhouse, a horde of fans is already waiting with their felt-tip pens, their photos and jerseys and scrapbooks. Dirk nods, scribbles his name, smiles. You cannot hide seven feet, and hoopers recognize their idols even when they're hidden under hoodies.

For dinner, Dirk orders his usual: salad, grilled chicken with capers, and steamed vegetables. Water, please. Sauce on the side. Thank you. Nearly every warm meal Dirk eats during the season looks like this. Red meat and carbohydrates are avoided, and alcohol and processed foods are forbidden. His 20 years of experience as a professional athlete equal 20 years of experience with his body; Dirk started the season with 12 percent body fat, and toward the end it will be only ten. His awareness of his body is such that he can feel a glass of lemonade in his joints the next day.

Bishop selects the wine this evening, a California pinot noir. The sommelier comes to open the bottle. "Excellent choice," he says, and he has the best glasses brought to our table, but Dirk raises his hand. No wine for me, thank you.

When the food is served, Bishop leans his telephone against the water bottles on the table. Two of the Mavericks' next three opponents are playing on the screen in front of us: the Sacramento Kings and the Golden State Warriors. The next bottle of wine arrives and we raise our glasses in honor of Vince Carter, the oldest player in the league, a former Maverick, who now plays for the Kings. We then raise our glasses in honor of Peja Stojaković, always fresh, always dressed so smartly, who won a title with the Mavericks and is now managing the Kings.

The guys joke around and tell their stories. We're huddled around the phone as if it were a campfire, four men who have the entire menu and wine list of Morton's Steakhouse memorized, and me. While Geschwindner and Dirk's security staff wheel out their old stories, Dirk grows more and more quiet. He's watching the game with increased concentration, and in the middle of the fourth quarter, he turns on the sound. The score's 89–86, it's close. Suddenly, the only thing being talked about is basketball, which is what all of this is really about, it's why we're here at this table. When the game shifts and the Warriors start getting the upper hand, coffee is ordered at Morton's. Tomorrow is game day, tip-off is at eight. For Dirk, this means going to bed early. We disappear through the kitchen into the night; the cooks are standing in a row along the stoves, saluting us with their spoons and knives.

★   ★   ★

The Kings' arena is supposed to be sold out, but a lot of seats remain empty. Not even season ticket holders attend every single game, and the meeting between these two teams is meaningless to the outcome of the season. The show the Kings put on is professional: the oversized Sacramento cowbell is rung, and a couple of fans have even brought their traditional bells—ding, dong—but everything feels staged, somewhat plastinated. The playoffs are virtually unreachable for both teams, and tonight's game is pure entertainment—at best, a treat for connoisseurs and those nostalgic for Dirk's career.

The American writer Thomas Beller once wrote about the beauty of the "Old Man Game" for *The New Yorker*. Contrary to what the term implies, Beller's interest is not in aging men, but in the way some special players think and play, a remarkable skill set that doesn't immediately strike the observer because the players are not physically spectacular. Such players do not jump higher and sprint faster than the competition; they use disguise and deception to create an imbalance on the court, which only they can see through, for fractions of a second. Such players can throw their opponents for mental and physical loops. They can read the game and they are always standing exactly where the game needs them to be. This style of play correlates with the age of players only because it requires experience, tranquility, and composure—or, as the case may be, extraordinary talent.

In his article, Beller raves about Andre Miller's intelligence and Kyrie Irving's horizontal dribbling, about Tim Duncan's inconspicuous dominance and the subversive game of the Argentine Manu Ginobili—players who know what's going to happen. Those who do not jump, but wait for their opponent to land. Who know that then it will be too late to stop them.

A game like the one in Sacramento today is a feast for people like Beller and me. Two of the most important progenitors of the Old Man Game are playing each other: Vince Carter and Dirk Nowitzki. Carter is now 41; he has morphed from the high-flying, "half man, half amazing" into a player with laser-like vision. He spent a few years in Dallas with Dirk, and their families hung out together. Tonight, they are happy like little kids to be out on the court together again.

Also playing for Sacramento is Zach Randolph, who has had an Old Man Game since his college days. Built like an armoire from the previous century, Randolph has hands like Goliath and feet as nimble as David. He looks like a bear, but dances like Travolta—his footwork is among the best in the league.

What is noticeable about these three old men is that, even though they are no longer the quickest or the strongest, they still have more than enough speed and strength to play in the best league in the world.

When people like Beller and me sit courtside to watch these players, we recognize ourselves in them. We can't jump anymore, either. We're also getting slower, but we maintain that our *understanding* of the game is our strength—to be honest, it's the only advantage we have left. "Old Man Game is fascinating," Beller writes, "in part, because it reflects the NBA's version of the American anxiety about aging and death." Dirk was able to live off his special physical capabilities, his athletic talent, for many years, but now he is one of those players who have adapted their game to their changing bodies. Who are able to push back the inevitable by a few years.

Speaking of time passing, there's an image from 2011. The Mavericks have just become champions and Dirk is sitting in the first row of the team plane, next to Peja Stojaković. Dirk is wearing Ian Mahinmi's black horn-rimmed glasses and he looks relieved. But if you look closely, you can see the traces of hardship on his face and the splint on the middle finger of his left hand. In this image, Stojaković is looking at the camera in disbelief. It's almost like he still can't compute what had happened. Two of the greatest European shooters in NBA history are grinning like a couple of adolescent shoplifters. The trophy's sitting between them on the airplane floor.

Dallas acquired Stojaković from the Toronto Raptors during the championship season. He had been struggling with back problems, but was able to get into shape just in time to finish off the Los Angeles Lakers in the fourth game of the second round of the playoffs, where he shot a perfect percentage from behind the arc. Six of six, for three.

I've wanted to talk to Stojaković ever since I started writing about

Dirk. They're from the same basketball generation, have experienced very similar periods of losing and winning, and Dirk and the Mavericks would have probably never won the championship without Stojaković. I want to talk to him because Dirk knows this and often repeats it. Because they share the greatest moment of their careers, two of the greatest Europeans in NBA history.

The assistant general manager of the Sacramento Kings is impeccably dressed when we meet, just as the guys described him last night at the steak house. Confidently stylish and meticulous, he's achieved mastery of all the tie knots and business maneuvers, the half Windsor and the double budget. There's a hint of respectable cologne in his game day office in the arena, and on the wall behind him hangs the famous *Sports Illustrated* cover of the 2002 Kings: Chris Webber, Doug Christie, Vlade Divac, Jason Williams, and Peja Stojaković. The caption reads, "Sacramento Kings: Basketball the Way It Oughta Be." We don't have a lot of time. The music is already booming in the arena below us. Stojaković pushes a chair in my direction, sits behind the table, and looks me right in the eyes.

A year older than Dirk, Stojaković played in his first game in the NBA on the same day as Nowitzki, February 5, 1999. Both were overwhelmed, both scored only two points in their first game. Stojaković arrived at the NBA with considerable professional experience at Red Star Belgrade and PAOK Thessaloniki, while Dirk had only played 18 games in the German Bundesliga. During his playing days, Stojaković was perhaps the greatest non-American shooter in the world. With the national team of the Federal Republic of Yugoslavia, Stojaković won the European Cup and the World Cup—something Dirk was never able to achieve because of his origins. He just couldn't do it; Germany just does not win the World Cup. The Kings retired Stojaković's number 16 jersey; it's hanging in the rafters here in Sacramento. Dirk won the three-point competition at the All-Star Weekend once, Stojaković did it twice, and he still makes jokes about it when the conversation turns to Dirk. Over the span of their careers, they played countless times against each other, on the international stage and later in the NBA. Six or seven times a season, Stojaković guesses. That would be more than 100 games—and 100 games is a ton.

Over the years, the two of them have been compared over and over. Who's the better shooter? Who's softer? And later: Who was the greatest European to ever play in the NBA? Arvydas Sabonis came into the league too late, Dražen Petrović died too early. Did Vlade Divac smoke too much? Is it Tony Parker, with his four championships? Pau Gasol? Toni Kukoč? Peja or Dirk?

These constant comparisons, along with their age and their origins, have inextricably intertwined their careers. And although they always respected each other as opponents, they were only able to play together in Peja's last year as a pro, the year they became champions. Back problems have ended his career. Stojaković is an old man by NBA standards, and he's sitting across from me in a tailor-made suit. Dirk is still wearing his jersey.

We talk about PAOK Thessaloniki's insanely hot home court as well as about the Ischeland gym in my hometown of Hagen, where he also played. The clock reads 20 minutes to game time and I have to explain that I didn't come here to talk about his career, I'm interested in his first memory of Dirk, his impression of him. At the start of these conversations, I am always a little worried that I will annoy the person sitting across from me by asking about Dirk and not about their own legacy. But almost always, the opposite is true: like many other important athletes, Stojaković seems relieved that he does not have to spend another half-hour interview with his own legend, detailing his official biography. As he starts to talk about Dirk, his posture and the look in his eyes change. He leans back, crosses his legs, and starts his Dirk story.

The first time he really took notice of Dirk was in 1999, the year they both came to the league after the lockout. As two Europeans who were facing similar difficulties in adjusting to America and the perplexing inner workings of the NBA, they spoke often in their early years. These conversations frequently revolved around playing time and adjustments, and it was only much later that he realized what was special about Dirk. "His approach to life is very different from us Balkans," he says, laughing—aware of the stereotypical comparison: German reliability and clockwork precision versus Serbian summers filled with grilled fish, Slivovitz, and unfiltered cigarettes on the Adriatic coast. "Dirk always had enough discipline to control himself off the court. Eating right, doing yoga. Dirk's a good example of how to be a real professional."

There's an interruption. Jason Williams enters the office without knocking. Completely ignoring me, the former point guard exchanges a couple of jabs with his small forward. They joke about who looks like what and who weighs how much now, and they both laugh their heads off. Like Dirk, Williams was selected in the 1998 draft, and like him, Williams is an NBA champion—he won in 2006 with Miami, against Dirk. Williams disappears as fast as he entered. Ballers are ballers for life. As he watches Williams head toward the arena, Stojaković says, "White Chocolate." All those no-look passes, those ankle breakers and floaters—then Peja turns back to my recorder.

Even though the words sound rehearsed, I realize that there is real warmth in his voice. He says that the Americans often repeated a bunch of tired phrases like "be patient" and "work hard" back then, and that neither he nor Dirk wanted to hear them while they were fighting for minutes and respect. Their paths were similar; the tasks and difficulties they faced, too. But both of them were able to come to terms with their new roles and their new country after the first year. Stojaković then outlines the big games they played against each other. His eyes shine; the greatness of these games lingers on. They often guarded each other. "Dirk is a very special player," he says. "After Larry Bird, there was no one at this position that could shoot so well. But now everyone's trying it—because of Dirk."

But that's not all.

Dirk kept to himself at first, then he was mostly silent on the court but friendly and approachable off it; and for the longest time, Stojaković didn't really understand how he could do so well for so many years. "Being an athlete is very tiring. Your mind gets tired because you do the same things over and over." After almost two decades of playing basketball at the highest possible level, of enduring the monotony and fatigue, Stojaković knows what he's talking about. "You always need to reposition and recharge yourself."

He only realized that Holger Geschwindner was the one who kept Dirk on the right track when he came to Dallas. And yet, "the right track" is not a straight line. There is no clearly defined and restricted path. It's full of loops and detours and alternatives. "As a young person, it's easy to forget that there's more to life than sports," Stojaković says. "Things that make your life fuller. And Holger never let Dirk forget these things. He gave him books, music, whatever."

The clock is ticking, the game is getting closer, and Stojaković is talking about the year they won the championship. He is talking about the unbelievable shooters the Mavericks had at the time: Jet, Kidd, Barea, Dirk, himself. He portrays the image of Dirk that's burned in his brain: Dirk holding three fingers up in the air after making a three while the arena goes to pieces, cheering—thumb, index, and middle fingers. "That's how you can tell someone is European," Stojaković says. Americans indicate a three with different fingers. He stretches his arm into the office air and tells story after story—the one on the plane, the one with the championship parade, the story of Dirk's European Championship finals in Belgrade in 2005. The Kings' general manager, Vlade Divac, another pioneer of American basketball's internationalization, walks by and bangs on the office window. "Game's starting!" he roars. "Let's go!"

Stojaković grabs his suit jacket off the chair and shouts something at Divac in Serbian, something that can't be quoted. Peja laughs because he knows that every European baller knows these phrases from the playgrounds and gyms of the Old World. He smooths his tie, nods, and holds the door open.

"Here we go."

We take the elevator down, the door opens, the crowd divides. Stojaković nods to the right and greets to the left. We enter the arena at the exact moment the visiting team is being announced. Below us, Dirk Nowitzki is walking onto the court of Sacramento's brand new Golden 1 Center for his 1,447th regular-season game in the best league in the world.

When Stojaković starts up again, it becomes clear that he sincerely wants to find the right words for Nowitzki, formerly his adversary and now his friend. "Dirk Nowitzki is the greatest European to ever play in the NBA," says Predrag "Peja" Stojaković. He shakes my hand the way only a baller from the Balkans can: a declaration both of love and of war. He turns to go, pauses, grins. "But to this day," he says, as the applause for Dirk and his long career gets louder in the background, "I still think I was the better shooter."

Dirk Nowitzki scores the first five points for the Mavericks—a two, a three. Randolph lets his opponents dance and fly by him, and Carter plays calm and collected. Dirk doesn't shoot often, but when he does, his success rate is high. The Mavericks make a spirited run at the beginning of the fourth quarter and Nowitzki tops it off with an enthusiastic three. Fifteen points, seven rebounds. Everything is clicking when Dirk is on the court, but Coach Carlisle pulls him with 1:27 left in regulation. The substitution seems weird to me. Normally, Dirk is only standing on the sidelines at the end of the game if the Mavericks are leading by a huge margin. Nevertheless, Carlisle breaks with his usual pattern, even though the game is close. The Mavericks still win without Dirk, 106–99.

The World According to Nash

DIRK HOBBLES THROUGH THE lobby of the Ritz-Carlton to col-
lect his old friend Steve Nash. All empty phrases are skipped, and
they quickly get into how their wives, children, bodies, and jobs are
really faring. They don't need to explain a thing; each knows what the
other is up to. The elevator arrives, we squeeze in, and I realize I'm riding with two of the most important basketball players ever to play the
game, two Hall of Famers. Nash is dressed in post-career civilian attire,
Dirk is still in a Nike T-shirt and Mavericks fatigues. Tomorrow, one of
them will run out on the court of the Staples Center, and the other will
sit down to dinner with his wife and children, occasionally sneaking a
peek at the TV in the corner to check the score. There are many things
that connect them, but what separates them is the finish line.

In the years after his controversial departure from Dallas in the summer of 2004, Nash became the conductor of the Phoenix Suns' fast-paced
game. He was the brains of coach Mike D'Antoni's legendary "seven seconds or less" teams that featured players like Amar'e Stoudemire and
Shawn Marion. The Suns played the fastest and most spectacular basketball, pioneering a new approach that has since come to dominate the
league. Like Dirk Nowitzki, Steve Nash revolutionized basketball.

The Suns reinvented the game in those years by spreading the floor, shooting threes faster and better than anyone else, playing an endless array of pick-and-rolls, and passing the ball faster and with more creativity. Their offensive attacks lasted seven seconds or less; they scored before the opponents had gathered themselves on defense. As Bill Simmons wrote on the sports and culture website *Grantland*, "Phoenix built a high-powered Formula One racing car" around Nash. The Suns scored more points than their opponents because they shot the ball more often, and they shot the ball more often because Nash was able to think faster than anyone else.

For nine years, Nash was the mastermind of the game's best offense. He had by far the most 50–40–90 seasons in league history—years where players make better than 50 percent of all their field goals, 40 percent of their threes, and 90 percent of their free throws. Although his shot was an accurate weapon, he was, at heart, a playmaker, and, as Bruce Arthur wrote in the *Toronto Star*, "he made teammates sing."

Nash's game was the foundation for a creative revolution in the NBA. Instead of grinding their opponents to pieces, today's players fillet. The point guards who dominate the league today have Nash to thank for their playmaking adaptability. Damian Lillard and Chris Paul, for instance, are both small, agile point guards who think, direct, and dominate the game, Nash-style, and it is no surprise that Nash occasionally worked with Steph Curry, who modeled his game after Nash's. Nash has made the unexpected, the unbelievable, the radical, and the surprising the new standard in basketball, and he was voted the MVP of the league twice in a row in Phoenix—not bad for a skinny, undersized point guard from the West Coast of Canada.

As Lee Jenkins wrote in *Sports Illustrated* about the legacy of Nash's career, "when the Heat's Goran Dragić deploys the up-and-under, that's Steve Nash. When the Spurs' Tony Parker runs three pick-and-rolls on the same possession, when the Trail Blazers' Damian Lillard lets it fly because a foolish defender sneaks under a screen, when the Mavericks'

Rajon Rondo drives inside, circles back, and patiently finds a cutter, that's also Steve Nash. . . . All these young point guards enjoy freedoms Nash made possible."

After seven years in Phoenix, Steve Nash went to Los Angeles in the summer of 2012, hoping to make one last run with a new team. His old coach Mike D'Antoni had become the head coach of the Lakers, and Nash signed a contract for more than $30 million. But in his first game with his new team, he broke his leg. He fought his way back onto the court, but his hereditary back problems kept getting worse from the strain and overload. "I can play quality basketball once a week," he told Bill Simmons in 2012, "but in the NBA, you need to do that three or four times a week."

Although the nerve problems in his lower back caused cramps and constant pain in his leg muscles, he came back. But the size of his contract killed the mood—for the fans, at least. In their eyes, Nash was not necessary, and he was greedy—even if they were able to recognize that, as a real, living person, you don't simply throw away $9.7 million a year.

Steve Nash fought long and hard against his impending retirement, and he documented this revolt in a highly personal manner. Produced together with his cousin and business partner Ezra Holland, Nash's documentary series *The Finish Line* is an impressive attempt to narrate the frailty of his body and the fatigue of his mind, showing all of the doubts, injections, and concerns about life without basketball.

There's a scene in the first episode in which Nash is walking to the beach with his dog. He then sits on a wall at the Manhattan Beach promenade in a green hoodie. Nash reflects on the effects that this phase of a career has on an athlete's psyche. "Every athlete, when they lose their skill, they lose a big part of themselves," he says. "The part that they built their life around. That has always been a huge part of their purpose, self-esteem, identity. So, when the skill goes, it's like there's been a death." In the Bruce Arthur interview for the *Toronto Star*, Nash said he was convinced that an athlete has to die twice: first at the end of his career, and then at the end of his life. At some point, Nash's body made the decision for him: his back simply couldn't withstand the grueling demands of professional sports anymore.

The last of the four episodes in Nash's documentary series is called "Dinner with Dirk," and it features the two of them sitting down for dinner with equipment manager Al Whitley. Somewhat timidly, Nash and Nowitzki are musing in front of the cameras about what they could have achieved together. About their years together in Dallas, the years after as opponents, about the end. After a while, Nash asks Dirk for his honest opinion: "What would you do if you were me?" Dirk hesitates because the camera is focused on his face. "That's a tough question," he says, smiling hesitantly. But then he decides to ignore the camera and answer Steve's question sincerely. You can see that this question affects him. "I'm not sure, bro," he says. "If I'm honest?"

"Yeah," Nash says.

"You know what you go through," Dirk says, "all the treatments, in and out, I don't know if I could do it. All the rehab, knowing it doesn't really get better and then play one more game and it's worse again. I don't know if could do it."

It's been three years since then, and Steve Nash is still looking for ways to talk about sports. The World According to Nash. The parallels between today and that episode of Nash's documentary series are undeniable—they even filmed it in this Ritz-Carlton. The moments that can be related always take place on the days off. Since then, Nash has survived the death of the athlete and has made the leap into the hereafter, producing films, developing training apps, and commentating on soccer games for television. Nash and his family live by the Pacific; his fourth child has just been born. He no longer has back pain; he skateboards, plays soccer, and commutes every week to San Francisco to work with Kevin Durant on his ball handling. A couple of months ago, in 2017, he received his first championship ring, as a player development coach for the Golden State Warriors. He likes coaching; he likes the game again. Now it is Dirk who is struggling.

And now, the two friends are sitting across from each other in Dirk's hotel room, flip flops and sneakers, the drawn curtains decorated in the charming North Korean palette of green, gray, olive, and currant. While Nash's cousin Ezra calibrates the equipment and mics, Nash and Nowitzki chat about Premier League soccer—about this one insane push through the middle field and that one sublime shot into the upper left corner.

When the microphones are in place, the banter ceases. Dirk listens to what the series is about: excellence. Both Dirk and Nash are professionals in this setting—short briefing, autopilot on, go.

"I was always interested in the people who are really good at what they do," Nash explains. "Is there anything similar about them, are their lives similar, are there repetitive patterns?"

"Just in sports?" Dirk asks. "Or in other fields, too?"

"Let's start with sports," Nash says. "You're our first guest."

"What an honor!" Dirk says.

They start their conversation with simple biographical data—parents and childhood, beginnings and inspirations. At first, Dirk speaks in the familiar recurring phrases, his usual sentences and stories: "listen to the body" . . . "sitting down with Holger and my family." He speaks more to the podcast listener than to his buddy. Nash asks about the source of Dirk's competitive spirit as well as about his parents and sister. They talk about tennis and handball and his childhood spent on TG Würzburg's grounds, down on the banks of the river Main. Nash keeps trying to get Dirk to talk about his extraordinary talent and his recipes for success; he is trying to coax him into giving plausible reasons for such an extraordinary career, but Dirk is hesitant. He is often asked about the secrets to his success, but he never knows what to answer. He isn't even sure if there is a secret.

When they talk about Dirk's first encounter with Holger, they abandon the standard interview tone. They talk about intuition, fingertip push-ups, the voluntary nature of Holger's training, the extreme degree of individuality in the collaboration between Dirk and Holger. Nash has watched the two of them train many times; he's practiced with Dirk for years. They both really know what they are talking about.

The podcast turns into a serious conversation about their love of the game. It is difficult for athletes of this caliber to find the words for the almost metaphysical experience of playing the game at the highest level—Geschwindner explained this paradox to me in the Starbucks on Mockingbird Lane years ago—and both Nash and Nowitzki are struggling to find the appropriate words and images.

I'm sitting on the bed, grinning like a child. This would be a crazy experience for just about any basketball fan: two of the greatest players of all time in the same room, trying to explain their joy of the game. Two people who are incredibly good at what they do. Federer and Nadal. Aretha Franklin and Beyoncé. Pacino and DeNiro. Ezra and his sound engineers stare at the control levels on their devices; the only noise in the room is the clicking of my photographer Tobias Zielony's camera. Dirk and Nash talk about the rare flashes when they have complete control over what is happening. When nothing can stop them. When they are totally present. When they know what will happen (the past of the future).

Nash describes the feeling of having a different perception of time in these in-game situations; it's as if all the other players are bogged down and only he can move and think quickly. It's as if he's invulnerable.

Dirk talks about those moments of absolute self-confidence, those moments when you are totally free of doubt. "I know what I need to do," he says, "and I know that I'm going to do it. No one can do anything about it. Those are the moments when I decide." Or something inside of him. Something irrational, Geschwindner would later explain to me. Some *it*.

Nash: "It took a couple of months for me to get used to not playing. It wasn't easy." Dirk grins. He doesn't want to talk about the end yet. At least not for the record.

"How long's the podcast now, Nashy?" he asks. Nash laughs. He knows Dirk's tone of voice when he wants to be polite while also making it clear that it's time to call it quits.

"An hour and a half," Ezra says.

"It's too long, Nashy! No one's going to want to listen to this!"

That's a wrap. Nash takes off Nowitzki's mic, they high five and pull the curtains back. Down below, there's Los Angeles, acting as if nothing had happened. There's the Staples Center, a couple of major construction sites, and an intimation of the Pacific on the horizon. It's the afternoon now, and the recording is in fact too long: one hour, thirty-eight minutes, seven seconds. But nobody cares. This wasn't about fitting a format, it was about finding words for their passion, about seeking closure.

"That was a little embarrassing."

"It was fine. Nice work, Steve-O."

"It was only the first one. I still have to find my voice."

"You should do some more."

The two hug like the old friends they are. Nash next to Nowitzki: wiry, smart, in control of his body, which has increasingly less pain. Nash is free, he can do as he pleases: work one day with Kevin Durant on his shooting, then ride his skateboard on the boardwalk the next. He gets to be a dad every day. And if he wants, he can drink a beer in the afternoon. But he doesn't play anymore, and there's no way to go back to the arenas and to the crucial moments of big games. Cheers, mate. A mixture of melancholy and optimism hangs in the room.

After Nash and his sound engineers say goodbye, we stay in the room a little longer. Zielony gathers his cameras. Dirk stands at the window; the buildings sprawl to the horizon and the arena is below his feet. He's had a number of big games down there, and he'll be playing here again tomorrow. Like Nash, he has a family: three children, all in preschool. The happy days after his career are waiting for him. It almost looks as though Dirk is staring at his own future.

Thomas Mann House

PACIFIC PALISADES
FEBRUARY 2018

HEADING TOWARD THE PACIFIC in the afternoon: Zielony, Geschwindner, and me. The city is spread out like the backdrop in an apocalyptic movie. Tobias honks and drives like a lunatic while quoting from Mike Davis's *Ecology of Fear*. When the world collapses, the end will begin in this city. Geschwindner laughs; he seems to be enjoying this. He's always happy to hear thoughts that are different from those heard in the world of sports. We crawl through the Fashion District and along Skid Row, then head onto the Santa Monica Freeway. There's a pillar of smoke on the horizon, and the hotel staff had advised us that under no circumstances should we touch the homeless downtown—tuberculosis and scabies are making the rounds, and even the hip dachshunds of the hotel guests are wearing small, apocalyptic rubber booties when they walk along West Eighth Street.

Tobias isn't a sports photographer, he's an artist who mostly takes pictures of outsiders and gangsters, architecture and plants ("undergrowth," he says). But he's very interested in sports and will take the photos for this book. In Los Angeles, he wants to have a look at Dirk Nowitzki and his world.

Today is Super Bowl Sunday; every Angeleno is sitting on their porch or in a sports bar, but we're driving out to Pacific Palisades with Holger Geschwindner. The Mavs are off, too. We're leaving the world of sports behind us. Sunset Boulevard is totally deserted. We sneak along the water. A thick haze hangs on the coast. The famous German exiles Thomas Mann and Lion Feuchtwanger lived in the hills above the ocean, and Mann wrote *Doctor Faustus* here in the 1940s.

Geschwindner got the idea to visit Thomas Mann's villa on San Remo Drive. He loves places where artists and thinkers used to work, places where ideas were born. Thoughts, arrangements, theories. We roll slowly past the villas and palm trees, the hortensias and bougain-villeas, knock on the door of the Villa Aurora without announcement, then sneak into Feuchtwanger's library and leaf through his first edi-tions. The birds are chirping, lawn mowers are singing, the smell of grilled meat is wafting in from somewhere. Dirk and his team are going to watch the football game at the hotel.

We've driven out here so that Zielony could take some pictures of Holger. We would really like to photograph him outside of the standard gym settings, ideally by the ocean. Holger is often described as a "men-tor" in Germany, but in America he's the "shooting coach," and Nash has referred to him as the "master coach." There is no single identifiable role ascribed to him; he's a sort of all-weather jacket for Dirk. He pro-tects Dirk from storms, frost, and heat. After all these years, he still is the janitor, psychologist, manager, driver, astrologist, PR consultant, clairvoyant, and friend. Dirk's daughter, Malaika, calls him "Granny." It doesn't matter to him who people think he is. He's a free man.

Holger Geschwindner doesn't like having his picture taken, and he horses around whenever Tobias takes out his camera. He makes a funny face, turns away, or sticks his tongue out like Albert Einstein. It's a game, and we laugh. But whenever the camera is in the bag, we talk about culture and politics, about the Feuchtwangers and Manns, and about transatlantic relationships. Trump and Texas. We talk about Dirk's career and about what will come after. Geschwindner sees much more in Dirk than simply a basketball player. For him, Dirk's the per-fect international ambassador: with one foot in Germany and the other in America, a shared game and idea. It was never only about basketball; it was always about the bigger picture.

The current athletic situation frustrates Geschwindner—the close game in Sacramento, and he isn't all that optimistic about tomorrow's game against the Los Angeles Clippers. He doesn't want to talk about basketball at all, the tactics and the omnipresent mood of farewell, but he does observe that the young people are thinking about the end a lot right now. He, by contrast, is trying to imagine the future.

When we turn onto San Remo Drive, a pickup is blocking the driveway to the Thomas Mann House. There are sacks of cement and stacks of wood everywhere, cordoning tape flaps in the wind, and con-struction workers in helmets are screaming orders in Spanish. Michael Douglas and Catherine Zeta-Jones reportedly live next door; Matt Damon and Adam Sandler live nearby. A few months ago, Geschwind-ner had read in the *Süddeutsche Zeitung* that the Manns' former villa was up for sale and he had pulled out all stops to prevent it from being demolished. He made calls and worked behind the scenes—we even wrote a letter to Mann's famous grandson Frido, but never received a reply. Geschwindner mobilized his contacts with ambassadors and the German ministry of foreign affairs. Had it been necessary, he would even have bought the house himself, he laughs. Tobias looks up the price of the house: $15 million.

Geschwindner imagines what you could do in a house like this, what ideas could be cooked up, what matters could be put into motion. "Thomas Mann sat up here," he says, "and told everlasting stories." How does that have anything to do with Dirk Nowitzki retiring from basketball? Geschwindner seems to be thinking about Dirk's future more and more often. About what comes after. "You write your book," he says. "And then the next one. But it isn't that easy for the other guy." The other guy. That's how he sometimes refers to Dirk these days; it's as though his nature has changed, as though the boy has turned into a man. He has spoken about freedom so very often, and for months now, Dirk seems to be laying claim to this freedom. Just as Geschwindner had always imagined. But it's not easy for him.

Artists and intellectuals petitioned, and a couple of weeks ago, the house was bought by the German federal government and saved from demolition. The German president will inaugurate the house in a couple of weeks, and afterward the first fellows will start to work on Thomas Mann's porch. But right now, the pool is still empty, the paint is cracked, and there are mixing machines under palm trees. We sneak around the house but are sent away because we're not wearing helmets: "No hard hat, no access." Geschwindner messes around with Thomas Mann's mailbox, and Zielony takes a picture. Geschwindner pretends to leave a message for Germany's greatest writer and Nobel laureate: *Greetings from Dirk Nowitzki, the other big German in America.*

Nowitkzi

THE GAME AGAINST THE Los Angeles Clippers the next evening takes an entirely unexpected course. The whole arena is clad in red, the atmosphere is heated, and the Clippers' main objective is to make it to the playoffs. "Giving up doesn't count," Geschwindner said this morning at shootaround. He seemed to be in good spirits, almost optimistic. But then again, he often says such things when he would prefer to say nothing at all.

Dirk will play his 50,000th minute in the NBA today. He's a legend, and everyone knows his name, but when he takes off his warm-up shirt and the game begins, the hand-sewn letters on his back are jumbled: N O W I T K Z I.

It isn't a good omen.

The Mavericks aren't playing all that bad, and are actually leading, 96–87, after a gorgeous layup from Dennis Smith Jr. Then it's 101–91 with 4:42 to go. Coach Carlisle takes his veterans out during the next time-out. Dirk sits on the bench and becomes a witness to his team's collapse.

This might be the moment the end begins.

Los Angeles edges closer and closer, the lead shrinking and melting, the guys fighting back frantically and in vain. The Mavericks' young bucks can't get anything going; it's a tug-of-war, a back-and-forth, but the experienced Clippers win, ending the game on a 13–0 run. A couple of careless turnovers by Smith, a steal by Maxi Kleber followed by a rushed layup. The Clippers take the lead with 24 seconds left and they don't give it up. The Mavs gave the win away.

Dirk sits stoically at the end of the bench, warm-ups on and a towel over his shoulders. The older players have to just watch the collapse of the team. Matthews and Harris stare at the proceedings in silence. Normally, they wouldn't let a game like this slip through their fingers. Normally, they would be on the court. But today, they aren't allowed to intervene.

After the game, Dirk gets dressed in the locker room without saying a word. He is slower than the others, often getting treatment from the physiotherapist before showering. The mood is awful and no one dares to speak to him. Everyone just circles slowly around the huge pile of laundry in the middle of the room, a mountain that a couple of journalists sneak photos of. There are codes of conduct here. You don't speak to a naked loser. Harsh reality has replaced the euphoria of the conversation with Nash. Everyone could see that the reserves were overwhelmed, but that didn't change anything. Yesterday, Dirk had told Nash about the big moments of his career, but today is reduced to the routine of defeat. The journalists are sheepishly milling about. Dirk finally nods. They hold their recorders in his face. The first question is about the mixed-up letters on his jersey: N O W I T K Z I.

Everyone expects some comic relief, but Dirk doesn't do us the favor. "I just saw it," he says coolly. "That sums up our season pretty well. The young guys need to learn. They need to experience these situations to get better." "Dirk, was that your last game in Los Angeles?" "We'll have to wait and see." These questions about the end will never stop.

As the Mavericks' Boeing 767-277 lifts off toward San Francisco, we journalists are still sitting in the belly of the arena, sorting out what happened. There are a few Germans—Jürgen Schmieder from the *Süddeutsche Zeitung,* Dean Walle, Zielony—a couple of Texans, and me. There are still a few Bud Light cans in the press room fridge. We won't be following the team until the next morning, when we take early flights on the cheaper airlines, Virgin and Alaska. In the NBA, games are played with the bags already packed. When the final buzzer sounds, it's off to the next one. In less than nine hours, Dirk and the team will be in a rented gymnasium, preparing for the matchup against the Golden State Warriors.

The defeat feels like it didn't have to happen. It could have been avoided; of that, we are certain. The game was lost in such a clumsy manner, very unlike Coach Carlisle's Mavericks. The coach had seen that his reserves were overwhelmed, and yet did nothing to stop it. Something about the situation has rubbed Dirk the wrong way; there's no other explanation for his frigid mood. He usually is able to accept a defeat, it's part of the game, and being a good basketball player also means being able to deal with losing. But not like this.

It is sometimes difficult for Europeans to understand the structure and mentality of American professional leagues. The National Basketball Association is a huge enterprise; the individual teams are franchises, and the players are employees not of the individual teams, but of the league itself. Unlike in Europe, the worst teams in the league are not relegated to a lower division—instead, the worst teams receive the right to select the best young players in the draft prior to the next season. This is supposed to keep the league balanced and strong. Every game should be as interesting as any other.

But since there is no relegation, there's no fear of being demoted to a lower league if you lose. What's at stake are only a team's image and finances. One absurdity of American professional sports is that if a team has no chance of reaching the playoffs, and hence a championship, then the rest of the season is meaningless. Some teams even begin to welcome losses two-thirds of the way into a season. The closer a team lands to the bottom of the standings, the better their chances of being able to pick the best young players in the draft. Thus, losing becomes a short-term goal in aid of building a better team in the long run, an approach called "tanking." In principle, it's a loophole that can be used by anyone who is pragmatic and future-oriented.

This strategy feels wrong to Europeans, who maintain a romantic notion of sports' purity. Their professional clubs have plenty of serious problems, but no incentive to intentionally lose games. In American basketball, however, management and long-term strategies are more clearly regimented and visible. External thought processes that have nothing to do with the game or its rules can sometimes determine how the game is played and who wins, who loses. Which player plays, which player is rested. To the subjective viewer, tanking can feel like economics trumping the spirit of competition—or, at least, what fans believe is the spirit of competition. But because the league wants to sell tickets to all games, TV contracts need to be fulfilled, and beer needs to be sold, talk of this strategy is strictly forbidden. If players, coaches, or team officials talk about tanking, they face financial penalties. After all, who wants to pay $100 to see a game where both teams are playing to lose? Or the best players are sitting on the bench in crunch time?

For athletes who deliver their physical and mental peak performance every day, the idea of deliberately losing is absurd. These athletes only became NBA players because they have continually competed amongst the best and proven themselves since childhood. They invest in their bodies every day so that they are in a position to win. Their lives have been focused on succeeding. They have conditioned their thinking, developed high-performance bodies and created highly specialized conceptual worlds in order to be better than the millions and millions of other basketball players around the world. Players want to play "meaningful basketball." Soon, Dirk's teammate Wesley Matthews will say that it is physically impossible for him to play basketball without trying to win.

The journalists in the arena's catacombs speculate: since Dirk

arrived, Dallas has played winning basketball; a losing strategy is foreign to them. ("Maybe he profited from a certain kind of youth movement in his first year," a Texan interjects.) The American writers are
hesitant to say it, but tonight's game could have been the first game
of this kind in Dirk's era. "We'd have to make ten mistakes in a row
to lose this game," one of the journalists grumbles, "and we made 11."
Schmieder empties his beer, chucks the can across the room, and sinks
it in the trash can.

"That looked intentional," he says.

San Francisco

W HEN WE LAND IN San Francisco the next day, the sun is shining down on the bay. Nowitzki cancels our meeting at the St. Regis because he wants to get in an extra workout and then go to physio. Suddenly, we have a couple of free hours, a familiar situation at away games when you are constantly waiting for the next bus, the next practice, the next meal.

Scott Tomlin and I spend the afternoon in a dive bar called Tequila Mockingbird around the corner from the hotel. Some of the guys from the media entourage are also here, sitting at the far end of the counter. The beers have names like Mirror Pond and Elysian Space Dust. The city outside is like a film noir set; outside are panhandlers and their dogs, beginnings and endings, heaven and hell.

Scott has seen it all. He's been steering the Mavericks' stories for nearly 15 years now; his department is the eye of the needle that every journalist needs to pass through if they want to get to Dirk. If you plan to write about Dirk, you'd better not mess things up with Scott. He and Sarah Melton sometimes play good cop, bad cop with us. Scott takes care of the coordination, the introductions, and looks after you. He makes things happen. He can remember an infinite number of first names and knows all the faces they belong to. He has read every single story that has ever been written about Dirk—and he has overseen most of them himself.

Scott is also a guardian, a gatekeeper, a bearer of secrets. He knows what makes a good story and whether or not that story should be told. Scott is the one who sat with Dirk in the locker room for the entire night after the Miami series in 2006, drinking beer with him. He's heard every curse, and he helped Dirk get through the Crystal Taylor saga. He also brought Dirk back onto the court when Dirk collapsed in the locker room after winning the title in 2011. Scott has been there for the ups and the downs. He is discreet. He can immediately sense when the circus becomes too much for Dirk. He finds gracious words to end the litany of questions from us press people. No matter what happens, Scott remains friendly. He almost never talks about himself, but today he orders another beer and taps his forefinger on the counter.

The sportswriters at the other end of the bar get up to leave. They chat with us for a second. Like me, they follow the team on commercial flights, and like me, they also have half a day off. Times have changed. In the past, a lot of the reporters traveled on the team plane—there was a whole press section on board. Now every NBA team has its own crew, its own documentary filmmaker, photographer, and blogger. These days, only one or two of the beat writers are allowed to travel with the team. The Mavericks sell the remaining seats as all-access tickets to wealthy fans with limitless budgets. The writers pat Scott on the back and ask their questions about the future. He tells them they'll have to wait until tomorrow, during the official availability. They want to buy him a beer, but he turns it down and laughs. Two of the sportswriters return to the hotel to write their preliminary reports; the others go to their favorite restaurant at the wharf. "We're getting seafood," one says. "Like we do every year in SF."

Speaking of the future. After the sportswriters are gone, Scott tells me about a very attractive offer he received from another NBA team—

lucrative, at the highest level, good people, a successful organization—but says he will stay with the Mavericks. He still has a job to finish in Dallas. He says he's curious as to what stories will develop here. He says his job isn't a dream right now, but it's no catastrophe, either. I would guess he knows what we all suspect: that winning games isn't a priority at the moment, but he doesn't utter the word *tanking*. He still has command over the authorized vocabulary after the first or second beer. He's always on message.

Scott knows the business; he's an optimist. "Just wait," he says when I come at him with my European systemic skepticism, my romanticism, the spirit of competition and "the soul of the game." With pessimism, kitsch, and my ideas about how the game should be played. "Just wait," he says cryptically. He smiles. "Next year will be better."

Scott knows that Dirk's image floats above the team's current afflictions. Right now, the team is playing unfortunate ball, nerves are shot, and negative speculation is mounting. But that won't hurt the perception of Dirk and his aura, Scott says. Earlier, the journalists were complaining, but they would never say a bad word about Dirk.

Scott thinks Dirk could easily take 20 shots a game, and he's been badgering him with this idea for days now. "Shoot, Dirty!" he says. People would love to see Dirk play for longer stretches and shoot more often, but Dirk isn't sure. He doesn't play basketball for himself; he wants his team to win. He doesn't want relaxed competition—no bonuses for legends—he doesn't want a farewell tour. No special treatment. Last year, Kobe Bryant played his last season and even scored 60 points in his final game. But to get that many, he had to shoot the ball 50 times. Such a farewell tour inevitably stretches the fabric of a team. Dirk sat in front of the TV spellbound and watched the game. I resolve to ask Dirk whether he has a mental image of the end of his own career. After all, everyone else is imagining what it will be like. They're asking whether the end is imminent. Is today's game his last one in Oracle Arena? These are questions we journalists have, questions we receive no answers to. Then Scott polishes off the pint of Elysian Space Dust IPA, carefully places it on the counter, and declares for the first time that Dirk will definitely play next season. Dirk's last game will be in April 2019, he says. He laughs. It will all be over in April 2019.

★   ★   ★

The general mood on the team isn't great. Speaking on a podcast hosted by Julius "Dr. J" Erving, Marc Cuban will later imply that losing "might be the best option" for the team. But there are certain linguistic restrictions in the NBA, designed to prevent the games from seeming meaningless and to keep people coming to the arenas. One might speak about "giving the young players the chance to prove themselves," but Cuban crosses the line. Later, he will make an apology and receive a substantial penalty, more than half a million dollars, for his unvarnished honesty.

During Dirk's career, it had never been an option to aim for the bottom. When he came to Dallas 20 years ago, the team played terribly but quickly got better. This was in large part due to Dirk's mentality, as well as that of Steve Nash and Michael Finley: it was worth giving the young players a chance to prove themselves in their early years, because they were good. And because none of them were familiar with losing strategically, it was out of the question. "That's not who I am," Dirk will later say when asked about Cuban's fine. "You need to play the best you can in this league. Always." When a slack attitude sets in, it changes the spirit of the team and the organization. It kills the focus. "You need a winning culture," Dirk says. "And if you accept that giving half your energy and losing are somehow OK, then you'll never get that out of your head."

★   ★   ★

Another dinner at Bob's Steakhouse with Dirk and his friends. Earls and Bishop, Geschwindner and Nowitzki, Scott and me. We're talking about the Mavericks' current situation. And, like every evening before a game, Dirk orders his usual: salad, steamed vegetables, and the catch of the day—sauce on the side, water, please. But then he hesitates and thinks it over and calls the waiter back. "Whatever," he suddenly says. "I'll have the creamed corn. And onion rings for everybody. And the jumbo shrimp cocktail. And a glass of red wine."

Everyone at the table looks awkwardly into their glasses. We don't say a word because we know how Dirk must be feeling right now, what's on his mind: he doesn't want to end his career with this kind of basketball. This isn't his world; he doesn't work this way. Dirk hands the menu back to the waiter. We watch as the sommelier puts a glass down. He starts filling Dirk's glass, slowly, carefully. Bishop had made the selection today: pinot noir again. Dirk raises his hand. "Thanks," he says when the glass is half full. "Thank you."

"Cheers!" Earl says.

"To excess!" says Bishop.

"Screw it!" Dirk says and raises his glass. He grins, but it's a defiant grin. This was the season that could have been his last. We raise our glasses. "Screw it!!"

When I enter his suite the next afternoon, Dirk is sitting between orchids, hotel room art, and fruit plates. He's reading. It is one of those long afternoons before an away game, where he has nothing to do and can do nothing. It's an afternoon for room service and for talking on the phone. So, he's sitting up here, reading *East of Eden* by John Steinbeck for the book club he has with Harrison Barnes, Maxi Kleber, and Dwight Powell. "Our book club," he says. They are going to read Ibram X. Kendi's *Stamped from the Beginning* next, a history of racism in the US. They each propose a book, one by one. They all read it, then meet on afternoons like this to discuss the book. "Better than watching TV," he says—even though there's a basketball game playing in the background on mute.

It's unusual for NBA players to have a book club. Most of them are in their early to mid 20s and prefer to spend their free time with Play-Station, Fortnite, Twitter, and Instagram. Dirk thinks he's too old for all of that, and you have to do something worthwhile with the downtime. Right now, their club consists of four people: one American, one Canadian, and two Germans. They read novels (Steinbeck was Dirk's idea), Barnes brings in the political nonfiction, and Kleber is next.

Dirk asked me to bring a large latte from the Peet's Coffee around the corner. He couldn't go down to the coffee shop himself, even though we're on the road on a normal business day. Beneath the window of room 2818 are the parks and large museums of the city, but visiting them would be too time-consuming. Bishop and Earls are busy today, and he can't go into the museum without security. With all the scribbling of autographs, there would be no time for Jackson Pollock, too many selfies for Nan Goldin. So, he's lying on the sofa and reading the last pages of Steinbeck's novel. "There could be some more fireworks at the end," Dirk says, and he sounds as though he's talking about the end of his own career. I suddenly remember the afternoon a couple of years ago when Dirk sat in the dugout during the baseball game and watched the rockets fly into the air. "There's so much going on, but it's rather slow at the end. It's missing something. For my taste."

Despite the recent upheavals, Dirk seemed to be focused. And besides the half glass of wine, onion rings and creamed corn in Bob's Steakhouse, he has kept working like always. He let go for a second, but only a little, and this keep-on-keeping-on is the reason why he's here to begin with. Right now, he's drinking water; a protein drink bottle is on the table. He mixes it himself according to the instructions of a nutrition scientist. "Antioxidants, algae, and other junk," he says. "It's supposed to help with recovery."

We chat about this and that for a couple of minutes. About California, the game in Los Angeles again, and about Geschwindner, who wants to drink an Irish coffee near Fisherman's Wharf out of nostalgia. Then we get to work. I've brought a couple of Tobias Zielony's books with me, *Story/No Story* and *Jenny Jenny*. Dirk slowly thumbs through them, the photos of prostitutes, gangsters, and lost children, the pages of Naples' housing blocks at night, the reservations in Manitoba, the pale sun of Trona. He thumbs through all these lives that are completely different from his own and through all these places where he will never set foot.

At some point, we come to my book and its potential title. "*The Great Nowitzki?*" he asks. "Seriously?" There's a stack of paper sitting between us on the table. I read a few pages aloud. Dirk sits and listens about him scoring his 30,000th point. He listens to Holger's story about Afghanistan, says "never ever," laughs, and then asks when the book is going to be published. "After your final game," I say.

Dirk looks at me. He grins. "That could be awhile," he says. He gets up and walks across the suite as if he's been sitting still for too long. He puts a couple of magazines in order, arranges the orchids, and chucks a pair of socks into a sports bag across the room. Then he sits down again.

"How do you imagine your end?" I ask, but too abruptly, too directly. This question has been circling in my head for a while now, but while I am asking it, I realize it sounds harsher and more impolite than it is meant to be. As if I didn't care. But Dirk doesn't miss a beat.

"Just play, and when the season is over, say, 'Thank you. That's it. It was a blast. I'm done. My body is done. I've given everything I had.' All Tim Duncan did was send the Spurs an email—'By the way, Tim Duncan is retiring.' Sure, we could do a little more. Maybe a press conference. But I don't want people to make a big production. 'Hey, this is your last game in this arena, this is your last game in that arena' for the entire year. That'd probably get annoying. I just want to say, 'That's it. Career's over.'"

That's game.

"Do you have a clear image of your last day?"

"I know it's getting closer. But I don't want to think about it too much. Otherwise, the end would always be on your mind and you wouldn't be able to enjoy the present. I still want to keep the end open. I just hope I can play again next year. If I can, and next year goes like this one, it's pretty clear that everything will be over at the beginning of April 2019."

"Who will be there for your last game?"

"For years, my dad has been trying to find out whether the coming year will be my last year. He wants to fly in his buddies from Würzburg. He should do it if that's what he wants. But I don't need anybody in particular. The people who are close to me have seen enough games. The last game . . . they don't need to see me hobble up and down the court one more time."

The doorbell to his suite rings. Tobias has brought more coffee. He puts the cups on the table and unpacks his camera. "Keep talking," he says, then starts taking pictures.

"Kobe's farewell game was awesome," Dirk says. "But you can't plan something like that. He scored 60 points in his final game. On national TV, everyone saw it. The Lakers were down in the fourth quarter. They gave him the ball every time. Kobe was so exhausted, he could hardly stand up after the time-out. But then he powered through it and scored 60 in the end. And, to top it all off, the Lakers won. And he scores the deciding basket. You can't make something like that up. What a career, what an ending. Nuts. I had goose bumps while I watched the game," Dirk says. "That's not something you can plan."

To me, his answers still sound unpolished; the exact wording hasn't yet been set in stone. But in the coming weeks and months, they will become part of his standard repertoire after every game and at every appearance and press conference. Everything will circle around the end, but thinly veiled as questions about the season, his teammates, his body. Sometimes, the question will be asked directly. Sometimes, the questions will be about him, but mostly they will be about the end of something bigger, something that has accompanied all of us for all these years. More than anything: about our own slow disappearance. Maybe that thought is going too far, I think. Dirk has always tried to remain a normal person, and not become a symbol, a surrogate. And yet, that's exactly what he has become. It's as if we want to know what our end is going to be like from Dirk Nowitzki.

"A lot of people imagine how they . . ." I say, and Dirk grins because he guesses where I'm going with this. "It doesn't matter how you imagine the end," he says and gets up. He's talked about these things enough for now. "It probably will be different."

Darkness slowly settles over San Francisco, the city lights blink and flicker. We still need to take some pictures. Tobias's camera circles around us until it is totally dark and the only lights in the room are Tobias's flash and Dirk's telephone. He looks tired in the twilight; time is pressing. There's a dinner scheduled tonight, downstairs in the dining room. One more picture, Tobias says, one more, and Dirk looks past the camera and back into the twilight. Maybe the next team meeting is on his mind, maybe a treatment with the physio. Or the insolent questions about his present and future, his unspoken answers, all the plans and expectations he's keeping to himself for the time being. "OK," he says. "One more." Tobias presses the shutter. Dirk's T-shirt says, "Only in Dallas."

★   ★   ★

The next evening, the Dallas Mavericks are playing against the best team in the world, the Golden State Warriors. Tobias and I take the BART train to the other side of the bay, the heavy ships and docks in the evening sun, the elevated train tracks and one tent city after another below. Oakland is the tough sister of San Francisco. We drift over the bridges and gigantic parking lots with the crowd. The arena is sitting in front of us like an old, tired animal.

Oracle Arena is the oldest arena in the whole league, a relic from another era. Ice hockey and basketball have been played here since 1966, and the Warriors have been playing in Oakland since 1971. The Grateful Dead have played almost 70 concerts in this arena and Berkeley is not far away. Nothing about this building has been made for the present. The infrastructure is battered, the train station is too small for all the modern, carless people, the improvised security controls take forever. People drink and shout in the waiting lines, smoke billows from the parking lots. There's barbecue. The giant red lettering on the facade seems out of place: Oracle is a software giant, but the arena was built before the invention of the home computer. But the air is buzzing; there's an old-style energy here that is rarely found in the modern NBA arenas. Maybe in Indianapolis. Or New York. Or Oklahoma City. The Warriors will only play here for one more year, then they will move to San Francisco, where the tech money is, the big bucks.

As we enter the arena, optimism hovers tangibly in the air. Oracle Arena may be battered and cramped, but it has history, it has seen big games. The Warriors are the reigning NBA champions, and the lack of space creates a frenetic basketball atmosphere. Everything is yellow and blue, and you can feel the heat of the fire fountains. The Warriors flags wave. The game day stagecraft seems more real than it does in other arenas. Everything has an optimistic patina, a jumble of history and anticipation.

Dirk has had a number of magnificent and devastating moments in this arena. On February 7, 1999, he scored his first field goal here; it was his second game in the league. And in 2007, he experienced the lowest of lows when the Mavericks entered the playoffs as the top seed after playing their best season ever, 67 wins and only 15 losses. Dirk was at the height of his powers and the expectations were tremendous. But his old coach Don Nelson, now with the Warriors, knew exactly how the Mavericks and Dirk could be disrupted. Nelson played with an extremely small lineup; the Warriors swarmed around Dirk like mosquitoes. The Warriors' playoff-slogan that year was "We Believe";

the arena was louder and yellower than ever. Dallas was eliminated in the sixth game of the series—Dirk only made 2 of 13 shots in 39 minutes of action, and the final score was 111–86. "Sometimes the pressure wins," he says. He had thought that 2007 would be his year. Everything had been prepared for another run at a championship, and suddenly they were standing there, empty-handed. Everything had been in vain: the summer in Germany, the away games at Minnesota in the winter, the flights, the empty gyms and hotel corridors.

On his way to the visitors' locker room—and this is one of the iconic moments of his career—Dirk randomly grabbed a huge black trash can and heaved it at the wall with all his power and wild rage. He can no longer remember whether it was a trash can or a chair—that's what he says, at least—but the hole 12 feet above our heads is still there. The Warriors have covered it with a pane of plexiglass and, years after the incident, Dirk climbed a ladder to sign it. The security staff in front of the locker room point to the dented trash can still standing below the hole.

With their four superstars, Stephen Curry, Kevin Durant, Klay Thompson, and Draymond Green, the Warriors are the ne plus ultra of the modern game. This is the future. The Warriors play basketball the way Holger Geschwindner must have once imagined it: a good coach, a holistic philosophy, and outstanding individual talent. Coach Steve Kerr is eloquent, politically engaged, with insight into human nature. He has ideas and he has players who can implement them. His team plays fast, creatively, with flow and tact. It also helps that they have three of the best shooters in the game.

I observe Kevin Durant during warm-ups. It's almost like he is dancing. He wraps the ball around his body like Dirk, a number of his movements look very similar to Geschwindner's training exercises, and Durant's one-legged fadeaway is a perfect copy of Dirk's shot. Durant has never made it a secret that he is fascinated by Dirk's game, and now Steve Nash is his personal trainer. This is the legacy of Dirk Nowitzki: other superstars are copying his signature moves.

The story of the game can be told quickly. The arena is loud and friendly to Dirk. For three quarters, the Mavericks keep pace with the Warriors and there's no sign of giving up. Everyone is making an effort to play meaningful basketball, the real game. But the Warriors take over in the fourth quarter and clearly win in the end. The difference this year is striking. The Mavericks will miss the playoffs and the Warriors will march right into the Finals and become champions. Nowitzki looks focused, almost angry about everything; he tallies a double-double—16 points, 11 rebounds. He is the Mavericks' best player again.

The rest of the team hits the showers, but there's a moment full of melancholy as Dirk shuffles off the court and through the south tunnel. Maybe this has been his last game in this arena. He walks slowly past a giant playoff banner, the bare ventilation pipes, the cable lines, the outstretched hands and the "Oakland Hole." He walks past the history and the memories he has made in this arena and doesn't even look up.

The room is just as it always is after a loss: silent, heavy, smelly, salty. Socks and clothes fly through the room and Dirk quietly disappears into a back room. Through the doorframe, you can see his feet dangling over the edge of a massage table while the physiotherapist works on his battered groin. His toes twitch, his pain is visible. We can feel his discontent. The journalists look in the other direction. Tobias wants to take photos but is reprimanded: no photos in the locker room. There are strict rules here.

Just outside, Holger Geschwindner is leaning against a concrete pillar, jotting down his thoughts and figures into a small notebook. "The pressure is gone," he says. He looks grim, pissed. "Everything that is said from now on will be meaningless." He keeps writing silently. We watch as the luggage is loaded on the bus. The Mavericks are heading back to Dallas. The first bus, the second bus, the airport's runway, Utah's Great Salt Lake at night, the lights on the edge of the Grand Canyon.

The road trip is over.

Why Another Year?

APRIL 12, 2018

THE MAVERICKS' 2017–18 SEASON basically ended on the West Coast. The team stuck out the remaining two months, but Dirk had to cut the season short. He did not play the last four games, because he was already thinking about next year. Nobody knew why Dirk was out, but after the last home game, he announced he had had surgery to repair his left foot. He did not want to waste time with meaningless games; rather, he would start rehab right away.

"This year wasn't a good year," he summarized at the press conference after the season finale, a blowout loss to the Phoenix Suns. The 24–58 record, the team's strategy, his ankle, his own play. A sexual assault scandal that shattered the team's front office. Significant changes would have to be made to completely alter the structure and culture of the business. Players needed to be drafted, a winning culture needed to be reestablished. There had been talk about a guard named Trae Young, and a wunderkind from Slovenia called Luka Dončić. "I want to help lead this organization out of these bad times," Dirk said. He wished all of us a good summer and hobbled out of the room on crutches. "Meaningful basketball games," he said. "I want to play real basketball."

...

The next afternoon, Dirk is sitting on the terrace in Preston Hollow. The birds are chirping, his foot is up on a garden table. The children are shrieking in the yard; his wife is out with the youngest. Dirk pulls his phone out of his pocket and we look at the X-rays of his ankle. He's sent them to Doc Neundorfer, and they talked about everything down to the last detail. Bone spurs have made his ankles so immobile that he could barely make moves specific to basketball, he says.

"What does that mean?" I ask. " 'Moves specific to basketball'?"

"That means I couldn't really turn in the last few years," he says, zooming in on his ankle. "Whenever I tried to change directions, my foot kept going straight." He holds the phone up in front of me. "Here. And here. And here." Moves specific to basketball also include abrupt stops, sudden starts, and constant jumping and landing.

Despite his age and battered ankle, Dirk Nowitzki still averaged 12 points per game and almost six rebounds in the season that just ended. These are good numbers—for someone in their twenties. They're highly unusual for someone who is almost 40—there are only a few examples that are comparable in the history of the league: Karl Malone, Kareem Abdul-Jabbar, Michael Jordan. Every team needs someone to put up those kinds of numbers. "What's remarkable," Doc had said on the phone while making his jokes, "is that you can still play at all."

Dirk sits on his terrace and knows that the end is near. His children come running out of the backyard and jump all over their father, a glass of water here, a rice cake there. Malaika is shy and inhibited as she stands there, not entirely sure which language she should use with the guest—her father keeps switching between English and German—and Max squeals and shouts. Dirk sets him down and hobbles into the kitchen to take care of them. "More coffee?" he asks. He looks wounded.

As I watch him go, I ask myself what keeps Dirk Nowitzki going. The tough questions from the journalists are still echoing in my head, as are the voices at the bar. Is he just another athlete sacrificing himself on the altar of professional sports? Why does he take such risks with his body? Is he even taking risks? Why does he keep going when he could easily stop? When he simply could live the good life that's been whirling around him for some time. The sun is shining, the birds are chirping, the children are arguing about something or other, but then they make up. He could drink wine instead of water if he wanted. He could read and play tennis and go to parent-teacher conferences. He could, he would, he should.

"It's like dying," Steve Nash said in Los Angeles a few weeks ago. "An athlete dies twice."

When Dirk comes back to the table, he's forgotten the coffee, but he doesn't want to get up again. It's too late for caffeine anyway. The kids dart back to their toy cars and balls. Dirk carefully frees his leg from the bulky protective boot; it needs some sun. The stitching is still taped, but the threads will be taken out soon and then the rehabilitation can commence. He didn't make the decision lightly, but he chose to not play in the final games of the season so that he would get a head start and be back, healthy, in time.

I look at his foot and want to ask why he keeps playing, but Dirk already knows. For a few seconds, he looks at me as if it was the one question he had been waiting for—the question everyone's been asking him lately. With that specific expression he always has when he already knows the answer to the question, his mouth slightly open, a joke in his eyes, a quip forming on his lips.

"Why?" he asks. "Why another year?"

The answer is simple: because we would all keep playing if we could. Because we all keep running even though we get slower. Because we don't want to stop and because giving up isn't the answer. Because we all keep going to the gyms, to the outdoor courts, even though we can't dunk anymore. We remember that specific feeling, *tam-tam-tak*, we want to feel these steps and this power before it leaves us forever. This speed, that flying around of the ball and its sound. We all want to keep playing as long as we can. And Dirk's still got enough in him for the best league in the world, and he knows there's no way to go back there once he leaves. The thought of another season with a healthy ankle seems to make him downright euphoric.

"I'll be able to move laterally again," he says and laughs. "And I'll still be able to shoot the ball at 50."

China Loves You

OCTOBER 2018

S HANGHAI IN OCTOBER 2018, another Ritz. Hundreds of fans are standing by the hotel's driveway, waiting for Dirk, day and night. Neatly penned in behind barriers, everyone, literally everyone, is wearing his jersey, number 41. In the lobby, his younger teammates are shocked when Nowitzki walks the few feet from the hotel entrance to the bus and a deafening squeal breaks out in the crowd as if the Mavericks were the Beatles and this was 1966. "What a circus!" he shouts as he signs autographs and the fans climb over each other to somehow get closer to him. Zielony and I try to stay out of the way. The barricades sway with love when the team bus finally leaves, honking. "What a circus!" Dirk says in the back of the bus, but you can tell he appreciates the affection despite all the stress. He smiles.

He turned 40 a few months ago. But he decided to play another year and not be concerned with the end the entire time. At the draft this summer, the Mavs made a move no one expected and landed the player they had wanted: the 19-year-old Luka Dončić. Dončić is by far the most mature player in this year's draft class, and Donnie Nelson and the Mavericks capitalized on American prejudices and resentment against European players—just like they did with Nowitzki 21 years ago. Dončić is too slow and not athletic enough, the skeptics say; he never played college basketball and has too much baby fat. And yet, the Slovenian is everything you could ask for in a modern guard: he reads the court like a veteran, he has Old Man Game, he has a strong body, good size, excellent body control, and Balkan core strength. He already has two years of service as the starting point guard for Real Madrid under his belt and has won everything there is to win in Europe. He's smart, charming, marketable. He's someone you can build a successful team around. He'll replace Dirk Nowitzki one day, and Dirk knows it. "Luka can play!" he says.

He has watched Dončić practice and when he talks about Luka's game, he laughs, pounds the table, and raises his index finger. "His game is that of a 25-, 26-, 27-year old. For being 19, he makes unbelievable passes. The way he reads the floor, how he sees things develop!" Dirk seems honestly excited. I'm surprised. I wonder if there isn't a tinge of envy for the person who still has his whole career in front of him. But Nowitzki doesn't mention it. He radiates enthusiasm instead of melancholy. Dirk honestly seems to be looking forward to playing with Dončić. And to what awaits the young man afterward. He has experienced it himself.

The ankle surgery was half a year ago, and ever since, Dirk has worked to get into shape. He looks lean, more chiseled and angular than usual. He adheres to his strict rules regarding nutrition, even more so than usual. In 21 years, he's never weighed as little as he does now. The last time he was this skinny was his first year in the league. Back then, he was a 19-year-old beanpole with a ludicrous metabolism. Not a single ounce was on his ribs, and he didn't have a clue as to how to cook pasta.

It's somewhat different with Dončić. Luka's maybe carrying a few pounds too many. The coaches want to let him learn the hard way: they will play him until he realizes he can withstand the rigors of a long season more easily with a lighter body. Dirk doesn't want to get involved.

"Everyone needs to experience things for themselves," he said. "How you feel at your best. That you can better survive 48 minutes on the court if you weigh a few pounds less." Dirk only understood how to work with his body after the Miami series in 2006. "I wish I would have known this earlier. I was already 28 when I made a radical change. After we lost to Miami, I realized I had to change something. I pressed the reset button and did a proper detox, no more alcohol, no more dessert, no more soft drinks."

After the operation, everything went according to plan at first. "I felt great," he says. "In great shape. The thing with my foot is only a small setback." After the bone spur was removed, the peroneal tendon became inflamed; the unfamiliar range of movement was too much. Dirk had an MRI because he was afraid it might be a stress fracture. It wasn't. It was an inflammation—arduous, painful, incalculable. Basketball is out of the question. He won't play in Shanghai; the only thing he can do is wait to get healthy. He's here anyway. He pulls open the curtains on the bus and waves to the crowd outside. He doesn't seem unhappy.

The Mavericks have been sent to China for two preseason games against the Philadelphia 76ers, in Shanghai and Shenzhen, to make the American professional league more popular in its most important international market. Not that it's necessary—the Chinese love basketball, and there's a strictly organized obsession that surrounds it, an orchestrated fervor you won't even find in the homeland of basketball. It's a peculiar mixture of structured rigor and deregulated commerce. Merchandise and streaming subscriptions sell better in China than anywhere else in the world. The Mavericks arrived with three planes, several containers full of equipment, the team and its owner, coaches and media, cheerleaders and sponsors—more than 200 people in all. The Texas state circus is in town and Dirk is the main attraction. The Great Nowitzki.

In the late afternoon, he's going through his fitness program on the 53rd floor of the Ritz, overlooking the Yangtze River, dripping and

panting on a stepper. After a few bright, blue days, a dense haze has settled over the city. Below us, the river flows, the lights of the tour boats
glimmer. The gym has been closed off for half an hour, but a few fans
in Nowitzki jerseys are finagling their way in, making it all the way to
the door. Most of them have rented a room in the hotel because of him:
3,500 yuan a night to catch a glimpse of Dirk. He's had 30 minutes to
focus on his cardio program, but then word gets around that he's up
here, and he has to leave.

From Dirk's hotel room, you can see the river, the buildings flash-
ing, and behind them, one residential tower after another as far as the
eye can see. The ocean is somewhere beyond the horizon. A total of 1.3
billion people live in China, and 300 million of them follow basketball.
Dirk Nowitzki has just showered, his suit for the evening is hanging in
the wardrobe, the air in the room is steamy after ironing. His toes are
stuck in two sickly-green plastic clamps that are supposed to improve
the mobility of his foot. We're sitting at the table. Zielony circles around
us, the camera barely audible.

I ask whether he'll ever get used to the Chinese enthusiasm for
him. "It's different from anywhere else," he says. He'll be recognized
elsewhere, sure, but the attention here is multiplied a hundredfold. "Of
course it's strange," he says. "But I've been playing for 20 years and the
first time I was here was in 2008. The championship helped, for sure.
My MVP year, then the Finals MVP. When I get out of the bus, they
always scream, 'MVP!'" He laughs. He would never call himself that,
but now he's repeating the acronym, turning it round and round. "That
people almost crush themselves on the barriers in front of the hotel for
an autograph is a unique experience. It's cool that they respect what I've
achieved." MVP, indeed. All those jerseys, all those tickets. The most
valuable player.

There's a gala tonight at the Shangri-La Hotel, and then a players-
only dinner at an authentic dumpling restaurant in the mall below,
where Dirk will order water before going back to the hotel to try and

somehow sleep off the jet lag. He's been doing this for years, he's familiar with time changes and long-distance flights, and he has flown around the world an estimated 55 times. All those road trips, all those international games. He says he has strange sleeping habits. He never shuts his eyes on the plane because if he did, he wouldn't be able to sleep in the hotel room later. He fights through the tiredness and stays awake until they arrive.

★　　　★　　　★

Dirk has his mind set on a temple. He's been harboring the wish ever since the Beijing Olympics, a decade ago. There was no time back then, but yesterday, on the way from the airport, he saw a brightly lit temple and remembered this old wish that had been shelved. He texts us the next morning to come over immediately. We sneak out of the hotel to see at least a tiny bit of China outside of our packed schedule. We ride through the city in a minibus; only two or three friends are with us today, Finley and Tomlin, as well as security and the translator. We drive through the din of morning rush hour, along the river and across squares, ringing bicycles and rattling mopeds. Suddenly, a gate opens and we enter a courtyard, surrounded by bird song and cedars. Welcome to Jade Buddha! Two monks greet Dirk, customarily hospitable, presents are exchanged—a prayer chain for a Mavericks jersey—and then we are led through the empty temple.

Dirk stands in front of a shrine with ancient writings, observes the people wafting incense in the courtyard, asks about the calligraphy workshop, listens to the gongs and the chanting, passes over the wood of the pews with his hand. The monks explain that they sometimes roll out basketball hoops at night and play three-on-three in the courtyard. Dirk can hardly believe it. No one is pushing, no one is screaming his name; an unexpected calm washes over the tour group. The monk has a good command of English; he explains the significance of various Buddha statues—one for a long life, one for peace, and so on. As we stand in front of a huge gong, Nowitzki is told to hit it as hard as he can. He should make a wish. Whatever he wants.

He swings backward and lets the wood crash against the gong. He laughs, a little boy allowed to make noise where noise is forbidden. He swings again and again, and with the last blow, he suddenly looks like he is truly making a wish.

At the tea ceremony toward the end of the tour, photographers are present once again and they take pictures of the visibly nervous master of ceremonies. They photograph her warming and rinsing her cups and pots, washing the tea with trembling fingers, Dirk trying to calm her, and the two of them then calmly drinking the tea from minuscule cups. "Best tea I've ever had!" Dirk will later say. The rest of us squeeze between thin paper screens and watch. When we leave, he is given a year's worth of green tea. Outside the temple, he has to sign a few autographs. We leave as quickly as we came.

As the bus stops at a traffic light, in the honking and shouting of Pudong in the morning, one of the security staff asks Dirk what he wished for. A long life? Happiness? Money? Laughter breaks out in the bus.

"A healthy left foot," Dirk says.

★   ★   ★

During the days in Shanghai, Dirk Nowitzki represents the league and the Mavericks, America and Germany. He leads workshops with Chinese children, gives a few interviews, and sits on a couple of panels. He meets Yao Ming, the greatest Chinese basketball player, who is half a head taller than him, as well as the African legend Dikembe Mutombo, and he rides an elevator up with Julius "Dr. J" Erving. Dirk holds his own with these legends, but there's nothing relic-like about him. He isn't here to be rewarded for what he has achieved.

On the last night in Shanghai, Dirk packs his suits, books, and sneakers, then takes the second bus to the arena. He looks at the city passing on the other side of the window, all those lights, all those people, and the glowing arena on the river.

"What a circus!" he says.

Before the game, he sets up two folding chairs in the corridor in front of the locker room and we sit between mops and cleaning buckets. The preparation for the upcoming spectacle is raging all around us. On their way to the locker room, his teammates pass by, offering fist bumps and high fives, a few loud insults and jokes. Some of these guys are half his age or just a little older. Harrison Barnes. Luka Dončić. Dwight Powell. Maxi Kleber. There's progress, Dirk says; the foot is making progress. It will still take a while, but what matters is the upcoming next season.

This world is what matters.

Although he won't play tonight, there's an eruption when Dirk Nowitzki enters the arena. Someday, he'll be admitted into the sport's hall of fame. Everyone knows it. As he walks slowly to center court to welcome the audience, Shanghai, the world, the Chinese orchestra sings his song. "M-V-P!" they scream. "Most Valuable Player."

The game is rough; we're at the beginning of a long season. But the Mavericks' bad years seem to be over. Dirk is sitting on the bench with the players and trainers, focusing on how the game swings back and forth and into the future. Barnes, Kleber, Powell, Dončić—Nowitzki is part of this movement. Sometimes, his face is shown on the giant screens above our heads—"China loves you!"—and he laughs. He doesn't want any farewell presents, but in the third quarter, his old neighbor Wang Zhizhi presents him with a guitar—*strum, strum, strum*—in memory of their years together on Cole Avenue, back in 2001.

When the game is over, the circus packs up its boxes and suitcases. The buses slowly roll down the loading ramp in the yellow light. They're heading toward the airport, toward Shenzhen, toward America. Dirk hides his face under his hood.

*   *   *

His record season begins two months later. Dirk Nowitzki's 21st year with the Dallas Mavericks—no player in league history has played for one franchise this long. The Mavericks are winning, the problems of the past few years seeming to be a vague memory. At times, the team plays enthusiastic basketball, and in early December, they're on pace to make the playoffs. Nowitzki sits in the first row and applauds. He cheers on the youngsters and pushes them. Behind the scenes, he keeps working. Working and working. But the inflammation won't go away. At the end of November, he finishes his first real practice in seven months and 26 days with the team. They were long months; love is hard work.

On December 13, 2018, after 254 days, Dirk Nowitzki plays six minutes in an away game in Phoenix. His first shot is a fadeaway bank shot, and he makes it. Three days later, he is subbed in shortly before the end of the first quarter in a home game against the Sacramento Kings. Everyone in the arena stands up and cheers. Nowitzki plucks at his jersey the way he always does when he tries to gather himself. He steps on the court, and before his first inbound pass, he touches the ball, once, twice, as if he's making sure that he's really on the court and playing basketball again. On the first offensive play, he receives the ball far behind the three-point line. We've seen this move a thousand times before. He fakes, checks the situation, sees everything and knows everything, bends his knees, shifts his center of gravity, lets the demons of the last months fly by him. He could shoot, but he passes to a team- mate in a better position. There is nothing left to prove; he does it all for the team. High fives with Luka Dončić, father and son, both smiling. Dirk Nowitzki is back. Once again, he's playing.

The Finish Line

ON THE AFTERNOON BEFORE his final home game in the American Airlines Center in Dallas, Texas, Dirk can't sleep. It's April 9, 2019. The spring sun is beating down on the porch behind the house on Strait Lane. He's sitting to the side, not talking much, pretending everything is normal. The Texan grackles are scrambling in the trees. Behind him, the house is full of people—his children, their nanny, his father is visiting, his sister is in the city, his father-in-law from Sweden. His mother had to stay in Würzburg; her health didn't cooperate, so she'll be watching everything on TV. They'll talk on the phone. A couple of old friends are also here: Holger Geschwindner, Ingo Sauer, Simon Wagner. The doors are closed to everyone else.

Normally, Dirk takes a two-hour nap before every game. From two to four, for 21 seasons. That's 1,667 naps, give or take, but sleep today is out of the question. He's tried to lie down, but had to get up immediately. Too nervous. "Butterflies in my stomach," he says, because no other image occurs to him. He's not used to this feeling; usually, he is focused and unemotional when he drives to the games—he usually knows exactly what has to be done.

Today, his phone is lying next to him on the garden table; he put it on silent and turned it over, but it keeps buzzing and vibrating. People want to mark this momentous occasion, they're trying to find words for it, and some just want a ticket to the game. Way too many people have his number, he thinks. The interest is deafening; you can't hear your own thoughts.

Dirk Nowitzki is sitting in the shade behind his house, drinking his last sip of espresso. He's barefoot and in a T-shirt. Somewhere, a lawn mower is making a racket and one of the gardeners is barking his orders in Spanish behind the tennis court. The laughter of children. Dirk is quieter than usual.

In recent weeks, he had been mulling over what he should do. His ankle doesn't work right anymore. *It just doesn't work*, he thought, *it's not any fun anymore*. And then, yesterday, he made a decision. "It's not fun anymore." He shakes his head in disbelief. He alternates between staring at the Texas sky and his backyard's spring green for a few seconds, then he goes into the house and puts the coffee cup in the dishwasher. Today is the day.

Dirk Nowitzki stands in front of his closet. He always picks out a suit before the game. In the early years of his career, he drove to games in jeans and a hoodie, but then the new NBA dress code arrived. He felt like he was wearing a costume for a couple of years, but he feels all right in a suit now. He's 40 years old and knows how to knot a tie. Nowitzki is not a man with a penchant for symbolism, but as he looks at his row of suits, he decides on the light blue one, a kind of dove blue, the color that is closest to the blue of his Mavericks. This color means something to him. It means something to him to walk into the arena in this color tonight. The tie is also a shiny blue.

And then he falters as he stands in front of the bathroom mirror. First, it's a vague idea, a thought that has been lingering in the back of his head for weeks—months, even, maybe even years. He's been asked about it a thousand times and he always places the same words between himself and this question: *I have to listen to my body . . . we'll sit down and think about it calmly at the end of the season . . . as long as it's still fun . . .* But now, alone in front of the bathroom mirror in his house in Preston Hollow, he realizes that the time has come. It's not fun anymore. Dirk looks himself in the eye; the suit is hanging over there, waiting for him. And Dirk Nowitzki—seven feet tall, 245 pounds, one of the greatest basketball players of all time—thinks, *This is the last time I'm getting dressed for a game.*

He stuffs the white shirt into the light blue trousers, slowly fastens the buttons, takes his tie in his hands, and before he can start tying it, he senses *tears welling up*, as he later describes it. He senses he is folding, he feels how this vague idea, which had been elusively encircling him in the last weeks and months, is suddenly becoming very real.

Then, all of a sudden, his wife, Jessica, is standing next to him. What is said in front of the bathroom mirror is something he will keep to himself; to divulge that would be going too far.

Dirk needs a couple of minutes to pull himself together. Standing in front of the sink, he's distraught. He wrestles with this mournful relief and the clarity of parting—*It hit me like a flash*—and when he finally recovers from the most emotional moment of the day, as he will later call these minutes, he throws some cold water on his face, brushes his teeth, and ties the knot of his tie.

He eats his pre-game pasta at the large table in the kitchen, the way he would on any other game day. Jokes are cracked during the meal; it's almost as though it's someone's birthday—a normal birthday, not a big one. A celebration with the inner circle only. When he is finished, he takes a bottle of water from the fridge, the one with green glass and red and white lettering, Mountain Valley Spring Water, as he always does before he leaves the house, but then he has to stay for a bit to sort out a few more ticket questions. Who is going to sit in the four family seats? Who is going to be upstairs in the box? Who is going to sit behind the bench? They've made a list, and Jessica is going through it with him. There are quite a few tickets that need to be handed out today;

the seating arrangements are more complicated than they thought. Dirk scribbles names on envelopes and goes over the list. Scott Tomlin calls to remind him of the schedule. The pragmatics of saying goodbye: everyone wants to be there, and Dirk needs to give them tickets. When they're done, he takes his suit jacket off the chair and hugs everyone in the room. He looks at his phone: 3:59 p.m., he's still on time.

Dirk is driving today. There's the blue suit and the white shirt. The handkerchief, the freshly shined shoes. "Let's go," he says and throws his travel bag in the car. He's already packed for San Antonio. Not much—just his toothbrush, his chargers, his iPad. The book he's currently reading. Everything else has already been loaded and shipped. It's four now. Dirk and Holger take the Range Rover today; the two Teslas are being used by the visitors.

Holger Geschwindner sits in the passenger seat even though he's a terrible passenger. Checkered shirt and a leather jacket, like always and anywhere in the world. Usually, Holger is behind the wheel, except for home games, when Dirk drives. That's one of those Holger-and-Dirk things: the two of them have their rituals, the journeys are similar. The gate to Dirk's property slowly slides open and the car carefully rolls out of the driveway and along the narrow street without a sidewalk. The lush green of the hedges, the brown water of Bachman Creek. The hum of the motor as the car turns onto Royal Lane. The ticking of the blinker.

The traffic is thick and heavy today, there's been an accident somewhere and they stand more often than they move. Dirk's phone rings; it's Scott again, he wants to know whether they're on their way. "We are, man!"

"They're waiting at the arena," he says. "The people are waiting, Dirty."

Dirk had planned to listen to a very specific song on the way to the arena. "It was one of my favorite songs back in the '90s," he later tells me. Holger and Dirk don't say much—only the bare necessities, although a lot could be said. Dirk will later tell me that they talk about the game only for a second, "how the game will feel," and when the traffic starts moving again, he turns on the music he has picked for today: "Good Riddance" by Green Day, a song to fire him up, a song to say goodbye, and just as the light turns green and they turn onto the toll road down to the arena, the song begins. It starts with a metaphor for life-changing moments, a turning point, a crossroads, but then the phone rings and interrupts the song. It's Scooter again, but Dirk doesn't pick up this time. He accelerates, weaves into the traffic and drives faster.

They head south, as they always do, and the song is the perfect soundtrack for this last drive because Dirk listened to it late that one night in 1997, when they were sitting by Don Nelson's pool and decided to come to America. It's perfect because this song is still being played at thousands of high school graduations and funerals and weddings, because this song ties Dirk's past and present together, because the times and the memories blend together, and because he has hummed these lines so many times on team buses and limousines, before important games and meaningless ones, in big and small moments. *It's something unpredictable, but in the end, it's right . . .* And when the car gets off the tollway and drives down Harry Hines Boulevard, Dirk returns Scooter's call—"Okay, we're there in two minutes!"—and then they are recognized at the traffic light at the corner of Olive Street, even though he never takes the Range Rover on game days. He hears the screaming and cheering when they see him—"Thank you, Dirk!"—but Dirk drives on through this jumble of emotions.

I hope you had the time of your life.

He drives the car slowly down the ramp. He turns off the engine. The bomb dog sniffs the car, the security guard smiles, and the friendly lady at the gate laughs. That's how it's always been, for all these years. "Thanks, my boy," she says. "Thank you for winning tonight!"

And then Dirk parks the car and gets out.

...

Dirk Nowitzki has a strange feeling as he enters the Mavericks' locker room shortly before five. At least that's what he'll tell me later. A peculiar feeling. *This is the last time that I'll go into this locker room*, he thinks. *That I'll change here. That I'll get ready for a game.*

He usually turns off his phone as soon as he enters the locker room and then leaves it in his locker as he lies on the physio tables to get stretched and kneaded and have his ankle taped, but today he still needs to settle a couple of questions about tickets, leave the envelope for Jessica, and text a couple of people.

While he's lying on the physio table, he receives a message from a friend in Phoenix who has heard that Charles Barkley is supposedly in Dallas. "What are you talking about?" Dirk texts back to his friend. "Either you're talking bullshit, or you've just given away a huge surprise." He laughs about it with the therapist and immediately forgets it. He turns his phone off.

Dirk Nowitzki's final season was different from all the others. It was a transitional season, a changing of the guard, a season of recognition. After they returned from China, Dirk worked pragmatically and precisely, the way he always had. He fought for his health. In November, he started practicing with the team. He was back on the court for the first time shortly before Christmas.

In January, J. J. Barea—the important compatriot from the 2011 championship, the opponent in the 2008 Olympic qualifier, and the friend Dirk has fought so many battles with—tears his Achilles tendon on an unfortunate move against the Minnesota Timberwolves. Dirk hopes he will be spared from such an injury. His own foot never gets healthy; sometimes he has to take painkillers and receive injections.

Dirk gets more playing time in February and is named to the All-

Star team, this time as an honorary member. The league starts bowing at his feet. In a game against Miami, Dirk trades jerseys with Dwyane Wade, for old times' sake.

It becomes clear that the Mavericks will once again miss the playoffs, but the mood is confident and focused on the future. In spring, the Mavericks acquire Dirk-reincarnate Kristaps Porziņģis in a trade with the New York Knicks. He's another potential superstar, a potential heir to the Empire of Dirk. The team seems to be in good hands and the young players closely observe Dirk at work: Dončić, Porziņģis, Powell, and Kleber are the future, and they have the chance to witness one last time how Dirk goes about his business. He's a kind of mentor, a living example. Dirk, in turn, watches the guys follow in his footsteps.

And then the audience starts applauding. Applause for Dirk becomes a thing across the entire league. He gets his first standing ovation in Boston. Then in Charlotte. In Los Angeles, Clippers head coach Doc Rivers takes a time-out with ten seconds left to play so that the fans can celebrate Nowitzki. And they do. At his final game in Oracle Arena in Oakland, everyone is talking about the story of the Oakland Hole. All the young power forwards in the league intimate that Dirk Nowitzki is their idol. Rivalry turns into respect. Dirk only reluctantly lets everyone celebrate him, so people clap all the more fervently.

Newspapers in every city print declarations of love disguised as game analyses. The internet is bursting with reverence. The authors write pieces about what Dirk means to them, as if they've been waiting for this opportunity. Some turn philosophical, others melancholic, and still others look at the big picture. "The end of an era," they write, and "Letting go of Dirk Nowitzki and remembering greatness." Everyone has their own personal story to tell.

Dirk and Holger warm up together one last time at the AAC. Two or three camera teams have crept in to film the ritual. Nothing is normal about today, and Dirk repeats the joke he made a couple of months ago in Randersacker—and two years ago in Warsaw and three years ago in Rattelsdorf. But the joke isn't a joke this time. "I'm never doing this routine again," he says to Holger, and Holger grins. Because they've been speaking to one another in their own language for ages, figuratively and sincerely, because they understand one another. "I'm sick and tired of this." *Tak tadamm. Swish.* "I've been doing this for 25 years, and I'm never going to do it again."

When their half hour is over, the body warm and the shot loaded, Dirk Nowitzki climbs the stairs to the locker room for one last time. He doesn't look back. Michael Finley stands at the top of the landing and holds the door open for him. He smiles.

At his locker, Nowitzki puts on his jersey one last time and a photographer takes pictures that will be shown on the jumbotron shortly thereafter—black and white, full of melancholy. Then there's the team meeting, the preparation for the opponent—no pathos, Dirk will later remember, no big speech, and then Dirk Nowitzki and his Dallas Mavericks huddle at the entrance to the players' tunnel, where no fan or journalist can see them.

"Let's end the season right," Devin Harris says, and the players put their hands together. One more time, before he runs into his arena for the last time.

"Play good defense," Dirk Nowitzki says to his team, and his words are swallowed by the raucous shouting of the guys, so he shouts as well. "And pass me the ball!"

And they do. Dirk gets the ball early and often—he scores almost at will. The game flies by, and when it's over, a mood settles in that I've never experienced in a sports arena and probably never will again. I look around, and I know that everyone feels the same way. It's a mixture of happiness at the fact of being here, pride in Dirk Nowitzki, the memories gathered over the past 21 years, getting lost in the images and music that fill the arena, a rare being here and now. Most people leave their phones in their pockets and simply stare at what's coming.

Dirk Nowitzki revolutionized his position. He was a four who could play all over the floor and who moved his giant body as though he was 12 inches shorter. He shot the ball better than anyone else his size. He changed his sport—basketball after Dirk Nowitzki is a different game than it was before him—more variable, smarter and more creative. The world championship he brought to Dallas is burned into the collective memory of the city; it changed its self-perception. Dallas is his city.

Dirk seems to have truly forgotten about the rumor that Barkley might be in attendance. When the legends stand in their spotlights and deliver their speeches, Dirk is genuinely excited; his eyes have an almost childlike sense of wonder. "That something like that was even possible," he will later say. "That, for me, such icons . . ."

And then he is given the microphone. If you look at footage from these minutes, it's easy to see that Dirk is struggling with himself and with this moment. He's standing there with the microphone in his hands, but his arena doesn't let him speak. Pippen and Barkley fire up the crowd—louder, louder, they wave, be louder!—and when the cheering has subsided, a heckler screams, "We love you, Dirk!" in the enveloping silence and everything starts over from the top. Dirk has to wait for more than a minute to get a word in, the right words for this occasion, but this love is eternal. He breathes in, breathes out, and then breaks the spell and says farewell.

*   *   *

The next days are a whirlwind. A contradiction. A tragedy, a celebration. At the press conference after his final game in his arena, Dirk explains that he was no longer having any fun. That his body wasn't playing along anymore. That he has actually suspected it for the entire season.

"I'll miss the heck out of it," he says. "But it's time."

The Mavericks fly to San Antonio that evening. When the team arrives deep in the night, there's a huge crowd gathered in front of the hotel with posters and jerseys, and Dirk signs as many autographs as he can. But when he finally gets to his room, he will later tell me, he can't sleep. He lay on his hotel bed and stared at his phone, he will say, at all the messages, tweets, and congratulations. He says that Iker Casillas, for instance, the legendary goalie from Real Madrid, sent him a message. He can't get his head around the fact that Casillas even knows who he is.

He's just had 30 points and ten rebounds. He's just made a moving speech in front of 22,000 people. He has just sat at a table with Pippen, Barkley, and Bird and listened to their stories. He has just looked down at Dallas from the airplane window—and now he's looking out at San Antonio at night from the hotel window. When he finally falls asleep, it's three or maybe four in the morning.

He gets up late and has breakfast with the team and coaches and physiotherapists; they sit there for a long time and exchange stories. He tries one more time to sleep, but there are too many messages and congratulations. "Too emotional," he says. "Way too emotional to sleep."

He gets ready around noon. "One last pre-game pasta," he will later say. "I had noodles before every game of my career. I don't think I'll eat pasta for a very, very long time. And I won't miss it." He puts on his suit, packs his things, checks out. He's feeling a little bit empty and drained, but still signs another hundred autographs before taking the bus to the final game of his career.

It ends where it began. The sun disappears behind San Antonio's AT&T Center as we walk across the parking lot to the arena. Hundreds of fans have made the trip from Dallas down to San Antonio; old enemies hug each other and take selfies. Earlier today, Holger Geschwindner and Donnie Nelson walked to the nearby Alamo Stadium Gymnasium, which is where Dirk's American story began on March 29, 1998. This is where Dirk laid the cornerstone for his career at the Hoop Summit—33 points and 14 rebounds—and this is where it will end. Twenty-one years and 12 days. Everything comes full circle.

Even in San Antonio, they play a moving video. It shows Dirk and Tim Duncan, Dirk and David Robinson, Dirk and Tony Parker. It shows the bitter playoff battles, the famous foul by Manu Ginobili—*and one*! It also shows that famous moment when Dirk lost his tooth and kept playing. It shows Dirk's bloody grin. Robert Horry, Bruce Bowen. Dirk and the great Gregg Popovich. The Spurs won most of the time—but not always.

We watch Dirk watch the video, a flood of images, a proliferation of big moments, and at some point, San Antonio stands up and Dallas stands up and Dirk yet again has to wipe a few tears from the corner of his eye. This is his real final game.

The whole arena watches in awe. Every play could be the last they will ever see of Nowitzki. Will Dirk come in for the last time with 7:35 left on the clock in the fourth quarter? Was that his last time-out? Did he corral his last rebound at 7:03? Did he make his last baseline jumper at 5:34? The last long two at 2:21? Does the last time-out of his career come at 1:27? Does Coach Carlisle draw up the last play for Dirk Nowitzki on his clipboard? When the huddle breaks, does Dirk step onto the court for the last time?

The whole arena is standing; it's enemy territory that has become friendly, "M-V-P!" they chant. "M-V-P!" The most valuable player in the league, they think. And then Dirk receives the ball above the free throw line, top of the key, and he gets his defender Drew Eubanks into position. He hesitates briefly, then takes the last shot of his eternal career.

Shot number 26,376.

He makes it.

Basket number 12,389.

★   ★   ★

My years with Dirk Nowitzki end where they began: at the Dallas Fort Worth Airport. I order fries and a milkshake, Geschwindner style. I look at the giant planes and small machines outside the window, I watch a couple of videos of Dirk from the previous days and read a few articles. I try to summarize what I've seen and heard and understood in the preceding years with Nowitzki. I've gotten to know an incredibly good basketball player and a genuinely sincere person. A sentence occurs to me that I had noted years ago in Rattelsdorf after practice.

"Dirk Nowitzki is like us," I wrote back then. "Only much, much better."

AUTHOR'S NOTE

THIS BOOK HAS NOT simply been translated from German into English—it has been edited with an American readership in mind. We cut here and added there. It's a "cultural translation"—and I am indebted to Shane Anderson, Tobias Schnettler, and Tom Mayer for their valuable help with this.

In order to understand the Nowitzki system, I had to become part of it. The work on this book would have never been possible without the help of editors, sponsors, and institutions—it was way too long and expensive to have done it on my own. I would like to thank all supporters and sponsors, especially ING, my longtime publishing house Kiepenheuer & Witsch, and the editors who commissioned the pieces.

Parts of this book have already appeared in different forms: "Eine andere Liga" in *ZEITmagazin* (2012), "Das System Dirk" in *DBmobil* (2014), "Das Grosse Kribbeln" in *Der Spiegel* (2015), "Das Buch Holger" in *50 Jahre Basketball Bundesliga* (2015), "Fadeaway" in *ZEITonline* (2015),"The Basketball Diaries" in *ZEITonline* (2015), "Sagt Dirk, er ist der Größte" in *Socrates* (2016), "It's a Circus" in *Fortyone* (2017), "Der Weitermacher" in *Die Welt* (2018), and "Irgendwann passiert alles zum letzten Mal" in *ZEITonline* (2019).

...

This book was published in the original German in late 2019, a few months after Dirk Nowitzki's last game. That was only two years ago, but many things have changed since: Kobe Bryant died in a tragic accident, the COVID-19 pandemic held the world in its grip, Steve Nash became the Brooklyn Nets' head coach, and Luka Dončić became an MVP candidate. Dirk Nowitzki did what he always said he would do—he spent more time with his wife and kids, traveled the world, and ate ice cream. He does not play basketball anymore, but he did not change one bit.

ACKNOWLEDGMENTS

WOULD LIKE TO THANK everyone who has provided me with information, advice, and insight into their world.

A very special thanks goes to Eric Asch, Matthias Bielek, Christoph Biermann, Bijan Dawallu, Gordon Debus, Daniela Dröscher, Erin Edmison, Will Evans, Kerstin Gleba, Henning Harnisch, Peter Harper, Johannes Herber, Markus Hoffmann, Hauke Hückstädt, David Hugendick, Matthias Kalle, Brandon Kennedy, Florian Krenz, EJ van Lanen, Helge Malchow, Bobby Karalla, Tong Mao, Timo Meisel, Sarah Melton, Uli Ott, Elisabeth and Winfried Pletzinger, Tilman Rammstedt, Torben Rosenbohm, Ingo Sauer, Shane Shelley, Sven Simon, Saša Stanišić, Tobias Tempel, Scott Tomlin, Lisa Tyner, André Voigt, Florian Werner, Wanda Wieczorek, and Tilo Wiedensohler.

I'd like to thank Olaf Petersenn for his ideas and enthusiasm about books like this. He brought this book on its way . . .

. . . and Jan Valk helped it reach the finish line with an incredible level of commitment. He took the rap for me and I am very grateful to him.

Tom Mayer, who patiently waited and then came off the bench to decide the game.

Shane Anderson, who translates like a baller and plays like a poet.

Tobias Schnettler was always there, from the playground to crunch time. He's the multi-position player every author needs.

I would like to thank Tobias Zielony for his vision, his observations, and his magnificent pictures.

Thanks to Holger Geschwindner for his openness, the challenges, and all the fall-off-the-bone-tender ribs.

I'd like to thank Dirk Nowitzki, who showed me how great and wonderful it can be to dedicate oneself to one thing. *Der große Nowitzki.*

Above all, I want to thank Bine Nordmeyer and Martha, Fritzi, and Anna. For everything. This book belongs to them.

BIBLIOGRAPHY

WOULD LIKE TO THANK all the writers who have documented, described, and analyzed Dirk Nowitzki's career over all these years. Without their work, this book would have never been possible. A number of precious stories, facts, and statistics have found their way into my text or were cause for me to ask people who were involved.

I would particularly like to highlight Joachim Mölter and Peter Sartorius's book *Nowitzki*—which was published in collaboration with Dirk in 2007. Holger Geschwindner's book *Nowitzki* is an important point of reference and an insight into his conceptual world. The chronology and the framework for facts and data from the early years is well documented in Dino Reisner's books. The 2011 championship year is depicted in detail in Bob Sturm's *This Year Is Different*. Ian Thomsen's *The Soul of Basketball* brilliantly contextualizes the importance of the championship. The work on the oral history *Angewandter Unfug* (Applied Nonsense), which was published in a limited edition of only 200 copies for Holger Geschwindner's 70th birthday, provided a number of opportunities to speak with companions and friends. These encounters are referred to in this book without any particular reference.

Dirk Nowitzki's career has been documented visually and statistically almost in its entirety. Historic photos and film footage have often been the basis for my descriptions. If I wasn't there, I've used them to supplement and check eyewitness accounts as well as textual sources. Almost every game is on nba.com, youtube.com, and countless other platforms on the internet. I've consulted basketball-reference.com and nba.com for statistics and numbers.

ABOUT DIRK NOWITZKI

Frerks, Ole. *Das Nowitzki-Phänomen. Dirk und die neue Generation (The Nowitzki Phenomenon: Dirk and the New Generation)*. Aachen: Meyer & Meyer, 2019.

Geschwindner, Holger. *Nowitzki. Die Geschichte (Nowitzki: The Story)*. Hamburg: Murmann, 2012.

Kalwa, Jürgen. *Dirk Nowitzki. So weit, so gut. Von Würzburg zum Weltstar—eine etwas andere Biographie (Dirk Nowitzki: So Far, So Good: From Würzburg to World Star—A Somewhat Different Biography)*. Hildesheim: Arete, 2019.

Reisner, Dino. *Dirk Nowitzki. Vom Wunderkind zum Weltstar (Dirk Nowitzki: The German Giant)*. Kempen and New York: TeNeues, 2017.

———. *Dirk. Die Dirk-Nowitzki-Story (The Dirk Nowitzki Story)*, 2nd exp. edition. Munich: copress, 2010.

Sartorius, Peter, and Joachim Mölter with Dirk Nowitzki. *Nowitzki*. Reinbek bei Hamburg: Rowohlt, 2008.

Sturm, Bob. *This Year Is Different: How the Mavs Won It All: The Official Story*. New York: Diversion Books, 2012.

Thomsen, Ian. *The Soul of Basketball. The Epic Showdown between LeBron, Kobe, Doc, and Dirk That Saved the NBA*. New York: Houghton Mifflin Harcourt, 2018.

REFERENCED

Bauer, Josef Martin. *As Far as My Feet Will Carry Me: The Extraordinary True Story of One Man's Escape from a Siberian Labor Camp and His Three-Year Trek to Freedom*. New York: Skyhorse Publishing 2008.

Bradley, Bill. *Life on the Run*. New York: Quadrangle, 1976.

Döblin, Alfred. *Berlin Alexanderplatz* (transl. by Michael Hoffmann). New York: New York Review of Books Classics, 2018.

Fitzgerald, F. Scott. *The Great Gatsby*. London: Penguin, 1994.

Härtling, Peter. *Hölderlin*. Munich: DTV, 2017.

Kendi, Ibram X.: *Stamped from the Beginning: The Definitive History of Racist Ideas in America*. London: Vintage, 2016.

Millman, Dan. *Way of the Peaceful Warrior*. Tiburon, CA: H. J. Kramer, 2006.

Nagel, Thomas. *What Is It Like to Be a Bat? / Wie ist es eine Fledermaus zu sein?* (ed. and transl. by Ulrich Diehl). Stuttgart: Reclam, 2016.

von Weizsäcker, Carl Friedrich. *The History of Nature* (translator unknown). Chicago: University of Chicago Press, 1976.

Zielony, Tobias. *Story/No Story*. Berlin: Hatje Cantz, 2010.

———. *Jenny Jenny*. Leipzig: Spector Books, 2013.

FURTHER READING

Adams, Tim. *On Being John McEnroe*. New York: Crown, 2005.

Basketball Bundesliga (ed.): *50 Jahre Basketball Bundesliga* (*50 Years Basketball Bundesliga*). Berlin: Verlag Die Werkstatt, 2015.

Didion, Joan. *We Tell Ourselves Stories in Order to Live: Collected Nonfiction*. New York: Knopf, 2006.

Herber, Johannes. *Almost Heaven. Mein Leben als Basketball-Profi* (*Almost Heaven. My life as a Professional Basketball Player*). Berlin: Berlin Verlag, 2015.

McCallum, Jack. *Seven Seconds or Less: My Season on the Bench with the Runnin' and Gunnin' Phoenix Suns*. New York: Simon & Schuster, 2007.

McPhee, John. *A Sense of Where You Are: A Profile of Bill Bradley at Princeton*. New York: Farrar, Straus, and Giroux, 1999.

Ribbat, Christoph. *Deutschland für eine Saison. Die wahre Geschichte des Wilbert Olinde jr.* (*Germany for a Season: The True Story of Wilbert Olinde Jr.*). Berlin: Suhrkamp, 2017.

———. *Basketball. Eine Kulturgeschichte* (*Basketball: A Cultural History*). Munich: Wilhelm Fink, 2013.

Simmons, Bill. *The NBA According to the Sports Guy*. New York: Ballantine/ESPN Books, 2009.

Voigt, André, and Jan Hieronimi: *Planet Basketball 2*. Hamburg: Basketballnerds, 2015.

Wallace, David Foster. *String Theory*. New York: Literary Classics of the United States, 2016.

INDEX

Abdul-Jabbar, Kareem, 192, 273, 321, 386
Afghanistan, 75–79, 378
Aguirre, Mark, 48
Aikman, Troy, 52
Aitmatov, Chinghiz, 91, 116
Alamo Stadium Gymnasium (San Antonio), 177, 406–7
Alba Berlin, 13, 39, 98, 184, 185
Aldridge, Marcus, 269, 270
Alemannia Aachen, 125
Aleš (commercial shoot chaperone), 107–8, 112, 113, 114, 117, 118, 119
Alexander the Great (Fox), 75
Ali, Muhammad, 306, 311
All-Star Games, 192, 350, 402–3
Amani Secondary School (Kabul), 75
AmCham Transatlantic Partnership Award, 98, 100
American Airlines Arena (Miami), 288, 343
American Airlines Center (Dallas), 3, 4–9, 29–30, 32, 34, 35–37, 46, 50, 52–53, 54, 74, 291, 304, 314–15, 316–18, 319–20, 343, 397, 401, 404–5
American River, 344, 345

Applied Nonsense (book), 168
Arigbabu, Stephen, 212
Armstrong, Darrell, 255, 315–16
Armstrong, Louis, 121
Artest, Ron (Metta World Peace), 273
Arthur, Bruce, 356, 357
Art in Motion symposium, 338–39, 340–41
AT&T Center (San Antonio), 406, 407, 408
Athens, Greece, 204, 206, 214, 224
Athletic, 71
Atlanta, Ga., 143, 206, 344
Atlanta Hawks, 233
Auburn University, 164
Austria, 107, 119
Avenue club (Berlin), 227–28

Backöfele restaurant (Würzburg), 182
Baeck, Stephan, 234
Baker, Chet, 336
Baker, Vin, 22
Baltic Sea, 153, 160
Bamberg, Germany, 23, 39, 89, 147, 185, 337, 338, 339

Barcelona, Spain, 204, 206, 212
Barea, J. J., 20, 268, 269, 270, 272, 274–75, 276, 279, 285, 288, 353, 402
Bargnani, Andrea, 235, 236
Barkley, Charles, 5, 8, 22, 48, 154, 163–64, 196, 204, 206, 307, 402, 405, 406
Barnes, Harrison, 254, 376, 377, 395
BasketballMagazin, 333
Batum, Nicolas, 269
Bauerfeind, 109
Bauermann, Dirk, 140, 180, 204
Bavaria, 85, 86, 107, 232, 333
Bayer Leverkusen, 18, 140
Bayless, Skip, 192
Baylor Tom Landry Center, 176
"B-Ball Is Jazz: Learning from Interdisciplinary Experimentation" (Geschwindner lecture), 338, 341
Beastie Boys, 298
Beatles, 131
Beaubois, Rodrigue, 268
Becker, Boris, 70, 71
Beiderbecke, Bix, 336
Beijing, China, 205, 214, 224, 234, 239
Belgrade, Serbia, 26, 29, 206, 210–11, 212, 224, 234, 239
Belinelli, Marco, 235, 236
Beller, Thomas, 348, 349
Benetton Treviso, 18
Benzing, Robin, 239
Berlin, Germany, 61–62, 98, 126, 165, 184, 223, 225–26, 227–28, 230, 288
Berlin Zoological Garden, 225–26, 227
Bernhardt, Katherine, 312
Beverly Hills Cop (film), 74
Bias, Len, 18
Bielek, Matthias, 241, 244
Bird, Larry, 5, 8, 72, 123, 180, 204, 206, 271, 273, 306, 320, 352, 406
Bishop, Dwayne, 218, 245, 246, 249, 346, 375, 376, 377
Black, Tarik, 317
Blackman, Rolando, 35, 48, 314

Blake, Steve, 273
Bloomington, Ind., 123, 125, 335
Bob's Steakhouse (San Francisco), 375–76, 377
Bodiroga, Dejan, 20
Bogut, Andrew, 254
Boll, Timo, 214
Bosh, Chris, 26, 260, 261, 262, 264, 265, 282, 283
Boston Celtics, 180, 271, 306
Bourdieu, Pierre, 63
Bowen, Bruce, 407
Bradley, Bill, 62, 334
Brandt Hagen, 18, 19–21, 22, 23–25
Breen, Mike, 261, 265
Breitengüssbach, Germany, 162
Brewer, Corey, 268, 274, 288
Brooks, Scott, 34
Bryant, Dez, 246
Bryant, Kobe, 6, 47, 64, 65, 109, 203, 273, 274, 275, 301, 321, 374, 379
Bundesliga, 17, 23, 25, 40, 78, 86, 90, 165, 173, 180, 184, 185, 333, 336, 350
Burke, Doris, 266–67, 280, 283
Buschmann, Frank, 22, 223
Butler, Caron, 268, 269
Butler, Ernest, 103, 121–28, 129–30, 131–34, 135, 138, 147, 333, 334, 337, 338, 339, 340–42
Butler, Naima, 121, 122, 128, 336, 341
Bynum, Andrew, 273, 276

Café Moscow (Berlin), 227
Canales, Kaleb, 316
Capel, Jason, 178
Cardinal, Brian, 34, 55, 81, 246, 248, 249, 251, 266, 268, 288–89
Carlisle, Rick, 8, 34, 99, 203, 226, 262, 263, 266, 269, 270, 271, 272, 273, 274, 276, 280, 283, 285, 306, 317, 320–21, 322, 354, 367, 369, 407
Carter, Don, 290
Carter, Vince, 34, 347, 348, 349, 354

Casanova Bar (Giessen), 124, 128, 130,
    135
Casillas, Iker, 406
Cat Ballou (film), 78, 275
Chalmers, Mario, 261, 263
Chamberlain, Wilt, 65, 321
Champions for Charity, 251–52
Champions League (soccer), 225, 228
"Champ Is Here, The" (song), 223
Chandler, Tyson, 246, 262, 264, 265, 267,
    269, 270, 271, 273, 279, 288
Chaplin, Charlie, 78
Charlottenburg, Berlin, 336
Chesapeake Energy Arena, 241, 344
Chicago Bulls, 18, 280–81
China, 26, 391, 392, 393, 394, 395, 402
Christie, Doug, 350
Cirque du Soleil, 321–22
Clausen, Karl, 126
Clausen, Theo, 126–27, 139
Cleveland Cavaliers, 244, 249
Clooney, George, 67
Collison, Nick, 37, 278
Coltrane, John, 130, 336
Connersville, Ind., 123
Conrad, Joseph, 91
Cooperstein, Chuck, 200, 316, 319
Counting Crows, 304
Coyote Ugly (Oklahoma City), 241, 243
Creme, Nick, 119
Crosby, Bing, 122
Csíkszentmihályi, Mihály, 132–33
Cuban, Mark, 8, 99, 123, 198–99, 201,
    202, 213, 217, 226, 267, 276, 291,
    292, 317, 319, 320, 321, 322, 375
Curry, Stephen, 356, 383
CVJM Würzburg, 72

Dallas, Tex., 2–3, 4, 6, 14, 29, 31–33, 52,
    57, 61, 66, 80, 160, 167, 174–75, 176,
    182–83, 184, 186, 187–90, 198, 199,
    244–45, 247, 249, 255, 268, 276, 277,
    297, 298, 309–10, 321, 405, 406

Dallas (TV show), 175, 309–10
Dallas Cowboys, 52, 174, 175, 245, 246,
    248, 255, 322
Dallas Mavericks:
    Cuban's purchase of, 198–99
    in Dirk's 30,000th-career-point game,
        316–21
    Dirk's final game ever with, 406–7
    Dirk's final home game with, 3, 6, 7, 8,
        402, 403–5
    Dirk's final season with (2018–2019), 3,
        389, 396, 402–3, 404, 406–7
    Dirk's first season with (1998–1999),
        48, 49, 186–87, 188, 194–95, 196–97,
        198, 350, 351–53, 381
    in drafting and pursuit of Dirk, 2, 23,
        47, 48, 49, 176, 179, 181–84, 193
    in exhibition game vs. Alba Berlin,
        98–99, 101
    Nash's departure from, 201–3, 210
    in promotional trip to China, 389, 391,
        392, 394, 395
    in 2001 NBA playoffs, 200
    in 2002 NBA playoffs, 200
    in 2006 NBA playoffs and Finals, 29,
        212–13, 267, 352
    in 2007 NBA playoffs, 213, 381, 383
    in 2009 NBA playoffs, 215, 216,
        217–18
    2010–2011 regular season of, 266–69,
        349, 353
    in 2011 NBA playoffs and Finals, 26, 33,
        46–47, 63, 242, 259–65, 266–67, 269–
        76, 277–79, 280, 281, 282–90, 349
    in 2012 NBA playoffs, 14, 15, 27, 30, 31,
        34, 35, 50, 51, 52–55, 56, 58–59
    2016–2017 season of, 254–55, 314
    in 2016 NBA playoffs, 241–42
    2017–2018 season of, 192, 325, 345,
        346, 347–48, 354, 355, 367–68, 369,
        370–71, 373, 374, 375–76, 380, 384,
        385
    see also specific players

Dallas Morning News, 22, 27, 34, 53, 57,
    194, 215, 216, 277
Dallas Stars, 35
Damon, Matt, 365
D'Antoni, Mike, 164, 355, 357
Davis, Brad, 35, 48, 314, 318
Davis, Mike, 363
Davis, Miles, 134
Decision, The (TV special), 282
Demirel, Mithat, 39, 211, 212, 224
Denver Nuggets, 217, 218
Der perfekte Wurf (*The Perfect Shot*) (doc-
    umentary), 6, 172, 248
DiBa, 81, 105, 109, 110, 111, 252
Didion, Joan, 344, 345
Dietrich, Wilfried, 206
Dionigi Da Borgo San Sepolcro,
    Francesco, 265
Divac, Vlade, 350, 351, 353
DJK Eggolsheim, 86, 87, 88
DJK Würzburg, 7, 22–25, 72, 85, 137–39,
    140, 143, 144, 156, 162, 164–66, 171,
    173, 174, 180, 184–85, 203
Doctor Faustus (Mann), 364
Dončić, Luka, 5, 8, 385, 389–91, 395, 396,
    403
Dopatka Arena, 18
Dortmund, Germany, 22, 163
Douglas, Michael, 365
Dragić, Goran, 356
Dr. Pepper Ballpark (Frisco, Tex.), 246
Duke, Robert A., 338, 339, 340–41
Duncan, Tim, 200, 213, 348, 378, 407
Durant, Kevin, 14, 34, 54, 242, 243, 277,
    278, 280, 312, 358, 361, 383

Earls, Derek, 218, 346, 375, 376, 377
East of Eden (Steinbeck), 323, 376
Eatzi's delicatessen (Dallas), 187
Ecology of Fear (Davis), 363
El Capitan, 266
Erving, Julius "Dr. J," 375, 394
ESPN, 57, 312, 315

ESPY Awards, 291–92, 306
Eubanks, Drew, 407
EuroBasket, 144
EuroLeague, 18, 165
European Championships, 198, 205–6,
    210–11, 223, 225, 226, 227, 230,
    233–40, 254, 334, 353
European Cup, 26, 29, 109, 232, 350
Evans, Will, 247

Falco (Austrian singer), 107
FC Barcelona, 144, 225, 227
FC Bologna, 144
Federer, Roger, 14, 26, 43, 214, 360
Femerling, Patrick, 204, 212, 224, 259
Ferrell, Yogi, 317
Feuchtwanger, Lion, 364
FIBA U18 European Championships, 140,
    141–42, 170
Fiedler, Adam, 18
Finish Line, The (documentary series),
    357, 358
Finley, Michael "Filthy," 48, 49, 179, 183,
    187, 195, 199, 200, 201, 210, 213,
    246, 250, 292, 304, 393, 404
Fisher, Derek, 273
Fitzgerald, F. Scott, 13, 98
Fleming, Chris, 223
Followill, Mark, 295, 316, 319
Fort Worth Modern, 312
Fort Worth Star-Telegram, 57, 315
Foster Wallace, David, 14, 26, 43
Fox, Lane, 75
France, 141, 170
Frankfurt, Germany, 223, 225
Franklin, Aretha, 336, 360
Frantz, Jochen, 70
Frazier, Walt, 62
Free Solo (documentary), 266
French Lick, Ind., 123
Fresno State University, 140
Frisco, Tex., 245, 246, 248
Frisco RoughRiders, 245

Gala, 16
Gallinari, Danilo, 235, 236
Gamba, Sandro, 175, 176, 177
Garbajosa, Jorge, 26
Garrett, Benjamin, 154–55, 157
Garrett, Robert "Robse," 7, 21, 144, 147,
  148, 150–51, 152, 153–55, 156, 157,
  158–59, 160–61, 162, 164, 165–66,
  171, 174, 180, 185, 224, 288, 338
Garrity, Pat, 182
Gasol, Paul, 273, 351
Gatewood, James, 24, 245–46
Gatlin, Keith, 18
Gaw, Frank, 142
Gaze, Andrew, 206
Geertz, Clifford, 62
Georgia Dome, 143, 206
German Basketball Federation, 137
German Cup, 334
Gerwig, Greta, 344, 345
Geschwindner, Holger:
  adventurous spirit and travel of, 42,
    75–79, 118, 335, 336–37
  at Art in Motion symposium, 338–39,
    340–41
  athleticism of, 78, 88, 125–26, 127, 128,
    155, 335
  author's first meetings with, 38–45
  as basketball player, 40, 78, 85, 86, 88,
    125–28, 129, 143, 148, 155, 333–35,
    336
  "B-ball is jazz" philosophy adopted by,
    134–35, 331, 337, 338
  in becoming Dirk's coach and mentor,
    88–89, 91
  books assigned to players by, 91, 116,
    140–41, 158, 338, 353
  business card of, 44, 156
  Butler in discovery of, 121, 125–28,
    337
  Butler as mentor and friend to, 128,
    129–30, 131–34, 336
  childhood of, 126

clothing of, 39, 77, 87, 170–71, 176,
  177, 183, 197, 320, 400
coaching concept and philosophy
  developed by, 40, 89, 90, 136, 335,
  336, 339–40
on college tours with Dirk, 180–81
in conflicts with coaches and officials,
  137–38, 141, 156, 170
criticisms and skepticism about, 155,
  171, 174, 180, 335
Dirk discovered by, 39, 40, 85, 86–88,
  89, 136, 337, 360
and Dirk's final home game, 2, 3, 4, 7,
  400–401, 403–4
Dirk's friendship with, 1, 91, 118, 180,
  332, 364
Dirk's greatness predicted by, 89,
  90–91
on Dirk's impending retirement,
  365–66
as Dirk's mentor, 1, 16, 40, 139, 170,
  364
Dirk's positioning tweaked by, 37, 89,
  90, 115, 136
Dirk's private training and practices
  with, 16, 34, 37, 50, 51, 62, 81, 88,
  91, 113–17, 141, 182, 229, 232–33,
  252–54, 274, 276–77, 279–80, 285,
  297, 326–32, 360, 403–4
Dirk's shared training vocabulary with,
  82, 331, 340, 404
Dirk's stretching and adjustments with,
  83, 253, 297, 332
Dirk's summer practice sessions with,
  61, 74, 80, 81–83, 136–37, 141, 182,
  198, 232–33, 252–54, 326–32, 345,
  346, 404
and Dirk's 30,000th point, 317, 318,
  319, 320, 328
disciplinary tactics eschewed by, 134,
  135, 148, 156
eccentric reputation of, 16, 40, 62, 157,
  335

Geschwindner, Holger (*continued*)
  education for players encouraged by,
    139, 141, 158
  family background of, 126, 129–30
  fictional scenarios drawn up in prac-
    tices by, 89–90, 91, 140, 209, 263–64,
    284, 340
  in first practice sessions with Dirk,
    89–90, 91
  flow emphasized by, 135, 140, 152, 340,
    341
  focus on details and nuances in coach-
    ing by, 37, 41, 89, 115, 136–37, 139,
    329, 331, 340
  gorge incident and, 76–77, 78–79, 337
  humor encouraged at practices by, 116,
    156
  improvisation emphasized by, 21, 90,
    135, 209
  individual training tailored to individ-
    ual players by, 155, 158, 339, 360
  intelligence and intellectual pursuits of,
    41, 43, 78, 119, 128, 139, 148, 158,
    334, 336, 338, 364
  jobs held by, 40, 78, 85–86
  Lake Starnberg training camp of,
    146–52, 337
  mathematics and physics in approach
    of, 21, 40, 42, 89, 90, 115, 136–37,
    331, 337
  and Mavericks' pursuit of Dirk, 176,
    179, 181, 182, 183–84
  mental and psychological elements in
    approach of, 21, 91, 116–17, 140–41,
    181, 197, 209, 329
  Middle East bus trip of, 75–79, 337, 378
  military service of, 118, 159
  mistakes downplayed in approach of,
    134–35, 164, 329
  at Munich Olympic Games, 78, 143,
    206, 214, 334, 335
  music appreciation of, 130–31, 135,
    331, 335, 336, 353

  nightlife of, 78, 129–30, 135, 334, 336
  Nike Hoop Summit and, 166, 171,
    173–76, 177, 179, 180
  peaks over averages stressed by, 62–63,
    329
  personal privacy maintained by, 39–40,
    41
  philosophy studied and employed by,
    42–43, 78, 97, 224, 336
  physical appearance of, 38, 77, 78, 87,
    125, 127, 197
  rituals and repetition in practices of,
    62, 82–83, 115, 274, 276, 326–28,
    329, 331, 340, 403
  schooling of, 126, 131, 139, 334
  sense of freedom for players stressed in
    approach of, 89, 150, 152, 156, 157–
    58, 159, 161, 162, 341, 360, 366
  $70,000–a-year-to-be-happy theory
    of, 110
  as shadow coach during games, 21, 41,
    138–39, 141, 162–63, 177, 275, 288
  small Würzburg crew trained by, 155–
    59, 160–61, 338
  speaking style and quirky turns of
    phrase by, 41, 42, 157, 162
  as supportive of players, 156–57
  tax evasion issue of, 26, 31, 40, 211
  traditional coaching methods rejected
    by, 89, 91, 148, 155–56, 157, 158,
    164, 337
  troublemaking and stubborn reputa-
    tion of, 40, 127, 156
  unconventional shooting game of,
    164
  unconventional training exercises and
    techniques of, 91, 136–37, 155, 195
  in visit to Mann's villa, 364–66
  as Würzburg assistant coach, 143, 144,
    156, 164–65
  Zielony's photos of, 364, 366
"Geschwindner's Boys" (Herber), 340
Giebelstadt Army Airfield, 105, 106

Giessen, Germany, 123, 124, 125, 127, 128, 130, 333–34, 337

Ginobili, Manu, 348, 407

Gnad, Hansi, 234

Golden 1 Center (Sacramento), 345, 347, 350, 354

Golden State Warriors, 164, 196, 213, 244, 249, 325, 347, 359, 369, 380, 381–84

Gomez, Mario, 227

"Good Riddance" (song), 401

Gordon, Jens-Uwe, 23

Gortat, Marcin, 253

Goss-Michael Foundation, 80, 310

Grabow, Bettina, 68

Grabow, Holger, 68, 72, 138

Graf, Stefanie "Steffi," 63, 71

Graf-Friedrich-Magnus-Alumnat boarding school, 126

Grand Canyon, 181

Grand Hotel Union (Ljubljana), 111

Grantland (website), 356

Grateful Dead, 381

Gray, Keith, 17

Greece, 29, 206, 211

Green, Draymond, 383

Green Day, 401

Greene, Demond, 21, 144, 147, 148, 149, 152, 155, 156, 157, 158–59, 162, 164, 174, 180, 185, 338

Gretzky, Wayne, 192

Grof, Martin, 17

Grossekathöfer, Maik, 253

Grothe, Matthias, 20–21, 22, 23–24, 25, 37

Guernica (Picasso), 339

Guido (author's schoolmate), 17

Gulf War (2003), 192

Gumbrecht, Hans Ulrich, 63–65

Hagen, Germany, 17, 18, 19, 20, 21, 23, 53, 351

Haile (Eritrean cabdriver), 28–30, 32, 38, 57, 186, 288

Hala Tivoli, 113, 115, 116, 118

Hamann, Steffen, 204

Hamburg, Germany, 21, 158, 336

Hamburg State Library, 200

Hardaway, Penny, 143

Hardaway, Tim, 238

Harden, James, 14, 34, 54, 57, 59, 277

Hari River Valley, 76, 337

Harnisch, Henning, 18, 20, 72, 140, 144, 209–10, 234

Harper, Derek, 48

Harrington, Al, 177, 179

Harris, Devin, 8, 317, 322, 368, 404

Haslem, Udonis, 261, 264, 265, 282, 284

Hasselhoff, David, 93, 107

Haywood, Brendan, 267, 285

Heart of Darkness (Conrad), 91

Heidelberg, Germany, 138, 162, 333, 336

Heidingsfeld, Germany, 138

Heinrich, Robert, 138

Hepburn, Audrey, 67

Herber, Johannes, 224, 340

Heroes Celebrity Baseball Game, 244, 245–49, 251

Herrmann, Senior Staff Sergeant, 163

Herten, TuS, 282

Hill, Grant, 143

Hillstone restaurant (Dallas), 228, 249–51

Hirst, Damien, 304, 327

History of Nature, The (Weizsäcker), 141

Holiday, Billie, 336

Holland, Ezra, 357, 359, 360

Holsopple, Jeremy, 230, 231, 246

Honnold, Alex, 266, 277

Hoosiers (film), 123

Horry, Robert, 407

Hotel Walfisch (Würzburg), 23

Houston, Tex., 344

Houston Rockets, 194, 196, 255, 302

Hyatt Regency (Dallas), 175, 176

Ibaka, Serge, 37, 53, 278, 279

"(I Can't Get No) Satisfaction" (song), 131

Iceland, 234

"I Have a Dream" (King speech), 163
"I'm an Old Cowhand" (song), 122
Indiana, 123, 125, 335
Indiana Pacers, 123, 254
Indianapolis, Ind., 26, 29, 205, 210, 224, 234, 239, 254, 344
Indiana University, 123
ING-DiBa, 81, 105, 109, 110, 111, 252
Institute for Advanced Study (INS; Berlin), 62
Institute for Advanced Study (Princeton), 62
Intelligent Music Teaching (Duke), 338
Interconti Hotel, 211
Irving, Kyrie, 348
Isar River, 341–42
Ischelandhalle, 17, 19, 21, 23
Island of Roses, 151
Italy, 22, 119, 165, 206, 235–36, 237

Jackel, Mike, 234
Jackson, Jim, 48
Jackson, Phil, 273, 274
Jadakiss, 223
Jade Buddha, 393–94
Jagla, Jan, 204
James, LeBron, 64, 65, 66, 109, 260, 261, 263, 265, 282–83, 286
Jamila (Aitmatov), 91, 116
Japan, 206, 213
"Jeannie" (song), 107
Jenkins, Lee, 356–57
Jenny Jenny (Zielony), 378
Johnson, Earvin "Magic," 72, 192, 273, 279
Joppich, Jens, 205, 206, 228, 229
Jordan, Michael, 65, 67, 68, 72, 143, 204, 206, 286, 307, 321, 339, 386
Joule Hotel (Dallas), 244–45
Jovaiša, Sergei, 17
Joyce, Michael, 43
Jungnickel, Klaus "Dschang," 127
Juventus Turin, 225
J. Wolf's painting company, 143

Kabul, Afghanistan, 75, 76
Kalkstein, Don, 231
Karalla, Bobby, 315
Karol (Warsaw chaperone), 253
Kemp, Shawn, 5, 8
Kendi, Ibram X., 376
Kendl, Georg, 42, 75, 76, 77, 78–79, 141, 145–46, 147, 149, 337, 339
Kennedy, Brandon, 247
Kennedy, John F., 175
Kentucky, University of, 179–80, 181
Kenya, 66, 81, 309
Kerr, Steve, 164, 383
Kidd, Jason, 22, 34, 48, 53, 55, 81, 260, 261, 262, 264, 266, 267, 268, 269, 270, 271, 272, 274, 275, 279, 281, 284, 353
Kincheon, Sly, 17
King, Martin Luther, Jr., 163
Kleber, Maxi, 368, 376, 377, 395, 403
Klepac, Branko, 147, 149
Klose, Miro, 227, 228
Knight, Phil, 142–43
Koch, Michael, 18, 140
Kranjska Gora, 119, 120
Krenz, Florian, 105–6, 107, 112, 114, 117, 118, 228, 251
Kruel, Bernd, 20–21, 22, 23–24, 25, 37
Krüsmann, Peter, 18
Kuisma, Martti, 140
Kukoč, Toni, 18, 20, 351
Kürbis (Pumpkin) bar (Giessen), 127
Kurios: Cabinet of Curiosities (Cirque du Soleil show), 321–22
Kurtinaitis, Rimas, 17, 48

Lady Bird (film), 345
Lake Starnberg, 145–47, 149–51, 337, 341
Lakfalvi, Laszlo, 334
Landry, Carl, 302
Larry O'Brien Trophy, 47, 51, 268, 290
Laubach, Germany, 126, 127, 128, 135
"League of His Own, A" (Pletzinger), 96

Lepenies, Wolf, 61–63, 66, 99, 100, 288
Leverkusen, Germany, 180, 184
Lewis, Rashard, 177, 179
Life on the Run (Bradley), 62
Lillard, Damian, 356
Lincoln Memorial (Washington, D.C.),
163
Liszt, Franz, 131
LIV Nightclub (Miami), 291
Ljubljana, Slovenia, 105, 107–8, 111,
112–13
Lloyd's of London, 224
Llull, Sergio, 238
Lô, Maodo, 238, 239
Lone Star Park, 321–22
"Looking for Freedom" (song), 93, 107
The Loon bar (Dallas), 187, 196, 292–93
Los Angeles, Calif., 214, 361, 362, 363–64,
365
Los Angeles Clippers, 192, 365, 367–68,
403
Los Angeles Lakers, 47, 192, 273–76, 313,
315, 317–19, 349, 357, 379
Louis, Joe, 63

MacMahon, Tim, 315
Madison Square Garden (New York), 62,
344
Magic Johnson Award, 306
Magnet Bar (Berlin), 288
Mahinmi, Ian, 34, 268, 288, 291, 349
Main Post, 174
Majorca, 81
Malone, Karl, 321, 386
Mann, Frido, 365
Mann, Thomas, 364, 365, 366
Marčiulionis, Šarūnas, 48
Marion, Shawn, 53, 261, 262, 264, 266,
268, 279, 288, 355
Marko (German point guard), 19
Marley, Bob, 336
Marquez, Jack, 241, 243–44, 255
Marta (author's first girlfriend), 18

Martin, Kenyon, 217
Mashburn, Jamal, 48
Matthews, Wesley, 270, 368, 370
Max Planck Institute, 78, 85
McCallum, Jack, 191
Melton, Sarah, 31, 217, 266, 280, 315, 372
Memphis Grizzlies, 212, 276, 277
Meng, Jürgen, 72
Mera Peak, 42
Messi, Lionel, 225
Messner, Reinhold, 43, 266
Metta World Peace (Ron Artest), 273
Miami Heat, 26, 33, 47, 57, 196, 213, 259,
260–65, 266, 267, 269, 277, 280–84,
285–89, 303, 317, 352, 356, 373, 391,
403
Michigan, University of, 181
Miller, Andre, 269, 270, 272, 274, 348
Miller, Reggie, 22
Miller Hall (Giessen), 123
Milwaukee Bucks, 181, 193, 255
Minnesota Timberwolves, 402
Mirador restaurant (Dallas), 322
Mister B's (Munich jazz bar), 121–22,
127, 128
Monk, Thelonius, 130, 336
Monroe, Earl, 62
Morton's Steakhouse (Sacramento),
346–47
Mosley, Jamahl, 315
Mosley, Walter, 133
Motley's Pub (Bloomington), 123
Mount Zion Church (Connersville), 123
MTV Giessen, 124–25, 127, 333–34
Mumford and Sons, 304
Munich, Germany, 78, 85, 121, 206, 234,
334, 335–36, 338
Munich Oktoberfest, 121
Munich RSV Bayern 1910 (rowing and
yacht club), 145–47, 151
Mussorgsky, Modest, 336
Mutombo, Dikembe, 394
Müürsepp, Martin, 182

Nadal, Rafael, 360
Nagel, Thomas, 43
Naima Butler Trio, 121–22
Naismith, James, 126
Nakić, Ivo, 165, 174
Nance, Larry, Jr., 317–19
Nash, Steve "Nasty," 6, 49, 164, 179, 182,
    183, 187, 189, 191–96, 197, 198, 199,
    200–203, 210, 213, 292, 304, 307,
    311, 320, 355–61, 362, 368, 383, 387
Nazis, 126, 131
NBA, 18–19, 22, 48, 49, 98, 99, 107, 109,
    110, 113, 149, 177, 179, 181–82, 183,
    184, 185, 194, 205, 216, 223, 233,
    236, 245, 249, 273, 298, 300, 301,
    307, 343–44, 350, 351, 352, 354, 356,
    357, 369–70, 373, 375, 381, 398
    see also specific teams and players
NBA Africa, 311
N'Dong, Boniface, 157
Nelson, Don, Sr. "Nellie," 6, 47, 48, 49,
    176, 179, 181–82, 183, 186–87, 194,
    196, 381, 401
Nelson, Donnie, 6, 47–52, 57, 175–76,
    179, 181, 182, 183, 184, 318, 389, 406
Nennstiel, Pit, 127
Neuhaus, Arnd, 18
Neundorfer, Thomas "Doc," 141, 147, 148,
    150, 160, 386
New Jersey Nets, 267
New Orleans Pelicans, 269
New Yorker, 16, 348
New York Knicks, 62, 334, 403
Nielsen, 109
Nietzsche, Friedrich, 43, 97
Nike, 16, 22, 47, 109, 142–43, 162–63,
    177, 225, 307
Nike Hoop Summit, 163, 166, 171, 175,
    176, 177–80, 181, 184, 189, 193, 407
Nowitzki, Dirk:
    ability to read and predict game on the
        court, 24, 25, 53, 86, 137, 178, 264,
        301, 318–19, 396
    aggressive play of, 178, 281

aggressive play of opponents against,
    53, 165, 196, 209, 210, 278, 281, 302
aging of, 59, 81, 82, 101, 228–29, 242–
    43, 254, 299, 300, 301, 304, 325, 330,
    332, 349, 386, 389, 398
alcohol mostly avoided by, 2, 59, 107,
    118, 138, 161, 231, 346, 347, 376, 391
AmCham gala in honor of, 98–101
ankle injuries of, 5, 51, 163, 254, 302,
    386, 387, 390, 391, 394, 395, 396,
    398, 402
athletic physique and fit condition of,
    81–82, 83, 150, 196, 198, 228, 229,
    231, 254, 297, 332, 345, 346, 390, 391
authenticity of, 66, 100, 216
author's first interview with, 58–59
author's first meeting of, 31
author's first story on, 93–94, 96–97
autographs and fan interactions of, 31,
    97, 99, 113, 117, 187, 188, 225, 241,
    246, 248, 250–51, 252, 312, 346, 377,
    389, 394, 406
as averse to following own media cov-
    erage, 96–97
awards of, 29, 47, 98, 100, 140, 210,
    211, 213–14, 291–92, 306–7, 392
on Bavarian select team, 137
at Beijing Olympics (2008), 16, 26,
    214–15, 227, 234, 239, 393
books read by, 91, 116, 140–41, 338,
    353, 376–77, 400
boyhood home of, 60, 68, 73–74, 172
Cardinal's friendship with, 81, 268,
    288
cardio and strength training of, 80, 225,
    230–31, 326, 391–92
cars driven by, 4, 80, 189, 298, 300, 400,
    401
Champions for Charity game held by,
    251–52
in championship celebrations, 32, 46,
    187, 272, 290, 291, 292–93, 349, 353
charitable work of, 7–8, 106, 188, 244,
    246, 251–52

childhood and early adolescence of, 8, 60, 68–73, 74, 107, 154, 155, 206, 226, 234, 306, 359

clothing and hair of, 23, 55, 57, 66, 70, 99, 183, 188, 193, 195, 315, 355, 398, 399, 400

college recruitment of, 164, 179–81

commercials and endorsements of, 16, 60, 81, 105, 106, 107–10, 111–13, 116, 118, 252

in comparisons to Bird, 271, 273, 306, 320, 352

competitive spirit of, 197, 199, 271, 306, 359, 374, 375, 376

as controlling every aspect of game, 25, 201, 273, 360

"Cough Gate" and, 286–87

criticisms and initial skepticism about, 21, 48, 49, 57, 165, 171, 174, 178, 179, 180, 185, 186, 194, 200, 215

Crystal Taylor scandal and, 26, 31, 203, 215–19, 277, 373

Dallas's love for, 3, 4, 7, 9, 28–29, 30, 32–33, 52–53, 57, 188, 189–90, 245, 247–48, 255, 277, 401, 405

in decision to finally retire, 398–99, 405

disciplined work ethic of, 5, 73, 144, 158–59, 182, 197, 198, 199, 201, 208, 210, 213, 219, 228–29, 230–32, 244, 252–53, 254, 325–26, 328, 352, 372, 377, 390

dissatisfaction aimed at teammates by, 272, 275, 311

DJK Würzburg advancement game missed by, 166, 171, 173, 174, 180

on DJK Würzburg team, 20, 21–25, 53, 72, 85, 137–39, 140, 143, 144, 162, 164–66, 171, 180, 185, 203, 350

on Dončić's game, 390

as down-to-earth and approachable, 7, 16, 31, 66, 94, 95, 97, 100, 110, 188, 190, 208, 243, 353, 393, 394, 408

early 2000s NBA seasons of, 50, 198–200, 304, 352–53, 375, 398

emotional displays of, 7, 8, 29, 204–5, 208, 289–90, 373, 383

in European Championships, 198, 205–6, 210–11, 223, 225, 226, 227, 230, 233–40, 254, 353

in European Cup, 26, 29, 109, 232

false stories and myths about, 93, 111

fame and popularity of, 2, 3–4, 6, 9, 15, 16, 25–26, 28–29, 30, 31, 32–33, 52–53, 57, 60, 66, 74, 92–93, 94, 97, 99, 100–101, 109, 110, 187, 211, 212, 214, 223, 224–25, 239, 241, 243, 244, 245, 247–48, 254, 255, 277, 327, 346, 377, 389, 391, 392, 395, 401, 403, 405, 406, 407

fans' initial dislike for, 186, 194

in FIBA U18 European Championships, 140, 141–42

final NBA game of, 379, 406–7

final NBA home game of, 2–9, 397–402, 403–5, 406

final NBA season of, 5, 389, 396, 402–3

first Dallas apartment of, 187

first NBA season of, 48, 49, 64, 186–87, 188, 194–95, 196–97, 198, 350, 351–53, 381, 390

first real international game of, 143–44

flexibility of, 23, 332

focus and concentration of, 10, 24, 31, 34, 37, 51, 74, 83, 86, 94, 95, 117, 158, 210, 213, 214, 232, 254, 262, 271, 276–77, 278, 279, 280, 283, 301, 375, 377, 384, 397

free-throw shooting of, 15, 54, 58, 178, 193, 273, 278, 317

on German national teams, 22, 26, 29, 39, 109, 140, 141–42, 143–44, 162–63, 198, 204–7, 208–12, 213, 214–15, 223, 224–25, 226, 227, 230, 231, 233–40, 253–54, 301, 302, 353

German vs. American appreciation for, 6, 15–16, 63–64, 65–66

Nowitzki, Dirk (*continued*)
Geschwindner and, *see* Geschwindner,
Holger
as greatest European to ever play basketball, 7, 15, 354
height of, 20, 22, 23, 25, 70–71, 73, 86,
137, 138, 149, 155, 159, 161, 176,
177–78, 179, 193, 195, 196, 197, 210,
245–46, 346, 399
Heroes Celebrity Baseball Game held
by, 244, 245–49, 251
hyperbolic therapy of, 299, 303–4
illnesses of, 200, 255, 284–85, 286–87,
297, 299
impending retirement and, 3, 5, 57,
325, 330, 345, 365–66, 368, 374–75,
376, 378–80, 386–88, 398–99
improvisation in play of, 21, 53, 90,
209, 267
injuries of, 5, 26, 47, 51, 57, 101, 113–
14, 163, 254, 269, 283, 302–3, 349,
385, 386, 387, 390, 391, 394, 395,
396, 398, 402, 407
as international ambassador for
Germany and basketball, 9, 16, 63,
98, 100, 365
joking and sense of humor of, 5, 93,
108, 116, 138, 148, 208, 233, 234,
246, 252, 267, 315, 319, 330, 399, 404
knee injury of, 101, 113–14, 269, 303
at Lake Starnberg training camp, 147,
148, 149, 150, 151, 152
lanky physique of, 9, 23, 25, 70, 71, 73,
83, 86, 178, 188, 194, 390
legacy of, 7, 9–10, 383, 405
life in Dallas during early NBA seasons
of, 186–87, 188, 195, 196, 198, 292
locker of, 51
love for the game of, 10, 360
marketability of, 16, 109–10, 111, 292
maturity and wisdom of, 94
Mavericks' pursuit and drafting of, 22,
23, 47, 48, 49, 176, 179, 181–84, 193

media relations and press conferences
of, 31, 55, 57, 59–60, 64, 66, 81, 179,
183, 193, 215, 217, 218, 223–26, 239,
242, 252, 266–67, 283, 286, 321, 368,
372, 373, 374–75, 379–80, 385, 405
memory of, 59, 141–42, 185, 205
as mentor to younger players, 5, 403
military service of, 160, 161–62, 163–
64, 171, 217
mural of, 188
music enjoyed by, 298, 304, 306, 400–401
Nash's documentary and podcast interviews with, 358, 359–61
Nash's friendship with, 187, 192–93,
194, 195, 199, 202, 203, 213, 320,
355, 359, 361
NBA contracts of, 49, 189, 252, 267
NBA record of 21 seasons with single
team held by, 3, 9, 396
nicknames of, 70, 194, 200, 203, 304
nightlife and dining out of, 118, 187,
195, 225–28, 245, 249–50, 291,
292–93, 346–47, 375–76, 377
in Nike exhibition game (Dortmund),
22, 163–64
Nike Hoop Summit and, 163, 166, 171,
173–75, 177–80, 181, 193, 407
Nike's interest in, 142–43, 162–63
as not very materialistic, 110–11, 308
observation as tool of, 59, 137, 138,
177, 264, 318, 396
Olympics as lifelong dream of, 143,
198, 204, 205, 206–7, 214
organized youth basketball played by,
22, 72–73, 85, 86–87, 88, 137, 154,
155, 226
on Peach Ball Classic team, 142, 143
physical and mental demands on, in
comparisons to mountain climbers,
42–43, 265–66, 277
physical toll on, 5, 59, 82, 101, 113,
245–46, 281, 299, 300, 304, 326, 330,
384, 386, 387, 398, 405

physiotherapy of, 5, 201, 231, 297, 300, 368, 372, 380, 384, 402, 406

prejudices and assumptions in perception of, 65

pressure as handled by, 47, 97, 112, 116, 117, 179, 196, 201, 204, 207–9, 210, 212, 214, 215, 219, 288, 290, 303, 383, 384

Preston Hollow home of, 1, 276, 281, 305–13, 386–87, 397–98, 399, 400

privacy guarded by, 2, 66, 97, 100, 110, 203, 217, 280

quickness of, 23, 25, 47, 64, 176

remarkably long career of, 301–2, 325, 344, 367, 386

in revolutionizing of the game, 7, 10, 15–16, 26, 63, 405

salaries and wealth of, 110

saxophone learned by, 140

schooling and poor grades of, 136, 139–40, 141, 144

security staff of, 218, 245, 346, 347, 377, 393, 394

self-confidence of, 97, 196, 197, 209, 215, 262, 281, 360

in Shanghai preseason trip, 389, 391–95

shy and self-conscious demeanor of, 70, 71, 73, 138, 179, 183, 193, 196, 353

signature flamingo fadeaway shot of, 15, 24, 47, 53, 238, 278, 289, 312, 383

Stojaković's career compared to, 350–51, 352

strange sleeping habits of, 393

strict diet of, 59, 107, 213, 229, 249, 299–300, 326, 346–47, 352, 376, 377, 390, 391

tennis and handball played by, 70, 71–72

30,000th career point milestone of, 1, 295, 314–22, 328, 378

three-point prowess of, 23, 24–25, 53–54, 262, 306, 307, 319, 350, 353, 354, 396

trash talk by, 72, 142, 148

in 2001 NBA playoffs, 200

in 2002 NBA playoffs, 200

in 2006 NBA playoffs and Finals, 26, 29, 93, 212–13, 276, 281, 352, 373, 391

in 2007 NBA playoffs, 213, 381–83

in 2009 NBA playoffs, 216, 217–18

in 2011 NBA playoffs and Finals, 9, 14, 26, 33, 46–47, 63, 242, 259, 260, 261, 262–65, 266–67, 269–73, 274, 275, 276, 277–79, 280, 282, 283–84, 285, 286, 288–90

2012–2013 NBA season of, 101

in 2012 NBA playoffs, 14, 15, 30, 34, 52–55, 58–59

2016–2017 NBA season of, 254–55

in 2016 NBA playoffs, 241–42

2017–2018 NBA season of, 345–46, 354, 367, 368, 369, 371, 374, 384, 385, 387

at Universal Studios, 119

University Park house of, 189–90

wedding of, 66, 80–81, 309

Wiedensohler's photos of, 204, 205, 207, 208, 219, 239–40

workouts, practices and training by, 5, 16, 34, 37, 50, 51, 61, 62, 73, 74, 80, 81–83, 89–90, 91, 113–17, 136–37, 140, 141, 144, 155, 159, 167, 182, 183, 186–87, 195, 198, 209, 211, 225, 230–33, 244, 252–54, 274, 276–77, 279–80, 285, 297, 311, 321, 325–32, 345, 346, 360, 372, 391–92, 403–4

in World Championships/World Cup, 26, 29, 109, 205, 206, 210, 213, 234

Nowitzki (Geschwindner), 134–35

Nowitzki, Helga "Helgus," 6, 60, 68–71, 88–89, 90–91, 93, 99, 107, 111, 139, 143, 167, 171–72, 173, 174, 176, 180, 187, 226, 227, 307, 326, 359, 397

Nowitzki, Jessica Olsson, 7, 9, 66, 80, 81, 99, 167, 226, 227, 246, 305, 306, 308–13, 316–17, 320, 322, 326, 327, 386, 399, 402

Nowitzki, Jörg-Werner "J-Dub," 6, 7, 9, 60, 68–71, 72, 88–89, 90–91, 99, 106, 107, 139, 140, 141, 143, 167, 168–71, 172, 173, 174, 176, 180, 182, 214, 226, 227, 288, 307, 359, 379, 397
Nowitzki, Malaika, 109, 167, 297, 305, 306, 308, 310, 325, 326, 327, 362, 364, 386, 387, 397, 398
Nowitzki, Max, 167, 297, 313, 325, 326, 327, 362, 386, 387, 397, 398
Nowitzki, Silke, 6, 7, 9, 68, 69, 70, 72, 99, 107, 167, 211, 226, 359, 397
Nürnberger, Kai, 234

OAKA Arena (Athens), 204
Oakland, Calif., 380, 381
Obama, Barack, 6, 292
Ochsenfurt, Germany, 154, 158, 160
Odom, Lamar, 273, 276
Oklahoma City, Okla., 2, 241, 344
Oklahoma City Thunder, 14, 15, 34, 41, 47, 50, 54, 57, 58, 241, 242, 243, 244, 276, 277–79, 280
Olajuwon, Hakeem, 307
"Old Man Game" (Beller), 348
Old No. 7 Club (Dallas), 285
Olimpia Ljubljana, 113
Olsson, Marcus, 327
Olsson, Martin, 327
Olympic Games, 16, 26, 72, 78, 126, 143, 198, 204, 205, 206–7, 214–15, 227, 234, 237, 239, 302, 334, 335, 393
Olympic Stadium (Berlin), 225
Olympic Village, 206, 214
O'Neal, Shaquille, 143, 192, 273, 299
Oracle Arena (Oakland), 374, 380–81, 383, 384, 403
Ott, Uli, 106, 150

Pacific Palisades, Calif., 364, 365
Paleo diet, 107, 229
PAOK Thessaloniki, 350, 351
Parker, Tony, 213, 233, 351, 356, 407

Parsons, Chandler, 242
Paul, Chris, 269, 356
Payton, Gary, 22
Peach Ball Classic, 142, 143
Perkins, Kendrick, 278
Perneker, Klaus, 21, 140, 141, 143, 164
Perot, Ross, Jr., 182, 198
Pešić, Marko, 212, 224
Pešić, Svetislav, 19, 180, 234
Pestalozzi School (Giessen), 125
Petrarch, Francesco, 257, 265–66
Petrović, Drazen, 212, 351
Phelps, Michael, 299
Philadelphia 76ers, 391
Phoenix Suns, 3, 47, 48, 164, 182, 189, 191, 193, 196, 201–2, 203, 210, 213, 267, 355–56, 357, 385, 396
Physical Impossibility of Death in the Mind of Someone Living, The (Hirst), 304
Picasso, Pablo, 339
Pictures at an Exhibition (Mussorgsky), 336
Pierce, Paul, 48
Pippen, Scottie, 5, 8, 18, 22, 68, 72, 143, 164, 204, 206, 286, 307, 405, 406
Piqué, Gerard, 227
Pirlo, Andrea, 225
Pitino, Rick, 144, 180
Poland, 252–54
Popovich, Gregg, 407
Porter, Terry, 200, 302
Portland Trail Blazers, 17, 46, 269–73, 274, 356
Porziņģis, Kristaps, 403
Powell, Dwight, 8, 195–96, 376, 395, 403
Premier League soccer, 327, 359
Price, Dwain, 315
Princeton Tigers, 62
Procopio, Mike, 316
Puerto Rico, 26, 204
Punk'd (TV show), 250, 251

Quindao, Jason, 248, 250, 255

Rachmaninoff, Sergei, 336
Randersacker, Germany, 167, 230, 231, 263, 299, 345, 346, 404
Randolph, Zach, 348–49, 354
Rattelsdorf, Germany, 74, 80, 81, 147, 155, 159, 160, 182, 263, 404
Raveling, George, 142–43, 162, 163, 177
Real Madrid, 334, 390, 406
Reder, Dieter, 42
Red Star Belgrade, 350
Reed, Willis, 62
Reunion Arena (Dallas), 48, 175, 186–87
Reunion Tower (Dallas), 3, 175, 188, 297
Richards, Keith, 306
Rilke, Rainer Maria, 227
Rinjani, Mount, 77
Ritz (Shanghai), 389, 391–92
Ritz-Carlton (Berlin), 98
Ritz-Carlton (Los Angeles), 192, 194, 355, 358
Rivers, Doc, 403
Robertson, Oscar, 123
Robinson, David, 200, 407
Röder, Bernd, 126–27, 334
Rödl, Henrik, 209, 210, 237
Rodríguez, Sergio, 238
Rolling Stones, 131, 306
Rollins, Sonny, 130, 132
Romo, Tony, 245, 255, 322
Rondo, Rajon, 357
Röntgen Gymnasium, 72
Rooks, Sean, 246
Rot-Weiss Koblenz, 62
Roy, Brandon, 269, 270
Ruhr Valley, 17
Rush, JaRon, 178
Russell, Bill, 47, 65, 291
Ryanair, 309

Sabonis, Arvydas, 17, 48, 351
Sacramento, Calif., 344–45, 346
Sacramento Kings, 344, 345, 346, 347–49, 350, 353, 365, 396

St. Regis hotel (San Francisco), 372
San Antonio Spurs, 57, 59, 93, 196, 200, 210, 212–13, 244, 356, 378, 407
Sandler, Adam, 365
San Francisco, Calif., 372, 373, 377, 378, 380, 381
Saturn (electronics chain), 85
Sauer, Ingo, 119, 251, 397
Schaffartzik, Heiko, 235
Schmeling, Max, 63
Schmieder, Jürgen, 368–69, 371
Schrempf, Detlef, 5, 8, 72, 185, 210
Schröder, Dennis, 233, 234, 236, 238, 239
Schultze, Sven, 204–5
Schwarzer, Christian, 214
Schweinfurt, Germany, 139, 337
Scola, Luis, 175
Second Baptist Church (Noblesville, Ind.), 123
Sefko, Eddie, 57
Sefolosha, Thabo, 278
Serbia, 143, 206, 234–35
Seven Seconds or Less (McCallum), 191
SG Randersacker, 230
Shakira, 228
Shanghai, China, 389, 391, 392, 393–95
Shangri-La Hotel (Shanghai), 392
Shelley, Shane, 32–33, 57, 247, 255, 268, 288
Shenzhen, China, 391, 395
Shins, the, 154
Sigma 40, 303
Simmenthal Milan, 334
Simmons, Bill, 356, 357
Slouching Towards Bethlehem (Didion), 345
Slovenia, 105, 113, 118–20
Smith, Casey, 246, 284, 322
Smith, Dennis, Jr., 367, 368
Songaila, Darius, 175
Sonnenstuhl sports center (Randersacker), 325, 332
Southern Methodist University (SMU), 38, 44, 189
Southwestern First League, 124

Southwestern Regional League, 40

Spain, 26, 165, 211, 236–37, 238, 239

Spajse restaurant (Ljubljana), 118

Spiegel, Der, 16, 216

Spieth, Jordan, 246

Splitter, Tiago, 302

Spoelstra, Erik, 260, 282, 283

Sports Illustrated, 49, 350, 356–57

Springfield, Mass., 126

SSV Hagen, 17

SSV Weissenfels, 174, 180

Stahl, Pit, 72, 85, 137–38, 139, 143

Stamped from the Beginning (Kendi), 376

Stanford University, 63

Staples Center (Los Angeles), 192, 343, 355, 362, 367

Star Klub (Giessen), 130

Starnberg, Germany, 145, 150, 151

Starnberg Gymnasium, 145

Stein, Marc, 22–23, 25, 57, 194

Steinbach, Burkhard, 23–24, 138, 147, 149, 157, 164, 185, 302

Steinbeck, John, 323, 376, 377

Stevenson, DeShawn, 268, 274, 285, 286, 288

Stojaković, Predrag "Peja," 266, 268, 276, 279, 288, 291, 347, 349–54

Story/No Story (Zielony), 378

Stoudemire, Amar'e, 164, 355

Straßlach, Germany, 333, 336, 341

Strasbourg, France, 233

Sturm, Bob, 279

Süddeutsche Zeitung, 365, 369

Super Bowl Sunday, 191, 193, 363–64

Sydney, Australia, 198, 206

Taylor, Crystal, 26, 203, 215–19, 277, 373

Tequila Mockingbird (San Francisco), 372, 373

Terry, Jason, 34, 53, 55, 81, 260–61, 262, 263, 264, 266, 267–68, 269, 270, 271, 275–76, 279, 282, 283, 284, 286, 288, 289, 302

Texas Rangers, 245

Texas Sports Hyperbarics, 299, 303–4

TG Würzburg, 326, 359

Thallmair, Tom, 146–47

This Year Is Different (Sturm), 279

Thomas, Mickalene, 311

Thomas Mann House (Los Angeles), 365–66

Thompson, Klay, 383

Tivoli Hall, 113, 115, 116, 118

Tomlin, Abby, 281, 292

Tomlin, Scott, 4, 6, 34, 58, 60, 179–80, 217, 249, 250, 251, 266, 281, 286, 289–90, 292–93, 315, 372–74, 375, 393, 400

Toronto Raptors, 349

Toronto Star, 356, 357

Traylor, Robert, 181

Trent, Gary, 198

Tribe Called Quest, A, 298

Triglav National Park, 119

TSV Hagen, 17

TUSEM Essen, 70

Tutschkin, Alexander, 70, 71

TV Eggolsheim, 40, 155

25hours hotel (Berlin), 225

Twyman-Stokes Teammate of the Year Award, 306

Tyner, Lisa, 183, 188–89, 322

Typhoon (Conrad), 91

UBC Münster, 19

Ukraine, 233

Under-22 European Cup, 22

Universal Studios, 119

University of Music and Performing Arts Munich, 338

University Park, Dallas, 189–90

Upper Panjshir Valley, Afghanistan, 75–79

USA Today, 14, 16

US Dream Team, 72, 143, 204, 206

Utah Jazz, 59, 200, 255

Van Gundy, Jeff, 262, 264
Ventoux, Mount, 265–66
Villa Aurora (Los Angeles), 364
Vincke school gym, 17
Voigt, André, 321
Volkach barracks, 160, 161, 162, 163–64, 171, 217

Wade, Dwayne, 33, 110, 260, 262, 263, 265, 282, 283, 286, 288, 403
Wade, Jeff "Skin," 6, 57, 110, 248
Wagner, Simon, 326, 397
Waldorf Astoria (Berlin), 225
Walker, Samaki, 183
Wallace, Gerald, 269
Walle, Dean, 369
Walter, Fritz, 63
Wang Zhizhi, 187, 395
Warsaw, Poland, 252–54
Webber, Chris, 350
Weinar, Mike, 316
Weissenfels, Germany, 180
Weizsäcker, Carl Friedrich von, 78, 141
Wells, Bubba, 182
Welp, Christian, 140, 234, 246
West, Jerry, 192, 273
Westbrook, Russell, 14, 34, 54, 242, 277, 280
White Men Can't Jump (film), 65
Whitley, Al, 200, 250, 315, 358
Wiedensohler, Tilo, 204, 205, 207, 208, 219, 239–40
Wilkins, Jimmy, 96

Williams, Jason, 350, 352
Williamson, Zion, 154
Willoughby, Marvin, 21, 74, 152, 156, 157, 158, 185, 224, 338
Wimbledon, 70, 81
Witte, Andreas, 237–39
World Championships/World Cup, 26, 29, 109, 119, 205, 210, 213, 234, 350
Wucherer, Nicolas, 138, 164
Würzburg, Germany, 8, 9, 16, 20, 22, 23, 48, 68, 69, 74, 89, 92, 93, 94, 106, 138, 142, 143, 154, 155, 159, 167, 168, 174, 180, 182, 227, 288, 306, 307, 325, 327, 379, 397
Würzburger Kickers, 169
Wysocki, Konrad, 204
Wyższa Szkoła Menedżerska, 252–54

Yangtze River, 391, 392, 393
Yao Ming, 6, 203, 394
Ye Olde Regulator, 335
Young, Trae, 385
Youth Training for Olympia, 72
Yo-Yo Ma, 339
Yugoslavia, Federal Republic of, 350

ZEITmagazin, 13
Zeta-Jones, Catherine, 365
Zielony, Tobias, 360, 361, 363, 364, 365, 366, 369, 378, 379, 380, 384, 389, 392
Zingst, Germany, 153–54, 160, 171
Zipser, Paul, 238, 239